FIFA OFFICIAL LICENSED PRODUCT

© 2005 FIFA

WORLD FOOTBALL RECORDS 2012

TIKI-TAKA | THIRD EDITION

This edition published in 2011

Copyright © Carlton Books Limited 2011

Carlton Books Limited
20 Mortimer Street
London W1T 3JW

All rights reserved. No part of this publication may be re-
produced, stored in a retrieval system, or transmitted in any
form or by any means, electronic, mechanical, photocopying,
recording or otherwise, without the prior permission of the
copyright owner and the publishers.

A CIP catalogue record for this book is available from the
British Library

10 9 8 7 6 5 4 3 2 1

ISBN: 978-1-84732-840-3

Editor: Martin Corteel
Designers: Paul Chattaway & Brian Flynn
Picture research: Paul Langan
Production: Rachel Burgess

Manufactured under licence by Carlton Books

© The FIFA Brand OLP Logo, the Historic Emblems, Mascots
and Posters of the FIFA World CupTM as well as the Jules
Rimet Cup are copyrights and/or trademarks of FIFA. All
rights reserved.

This publication is produced under a licence by FIFA but
the content of this publication has not been provided or
approved by FIFA. FIFA gives no warranty for the accuracy or
the completeness of the content or information contained
in this publication and disclaims all responsibility and all
liability to the fullest extent permissible under the applicable
law for any expenses, losses, damages and costs which
may be incurred by any person in relation to such
content or information.

Printed in Dubai

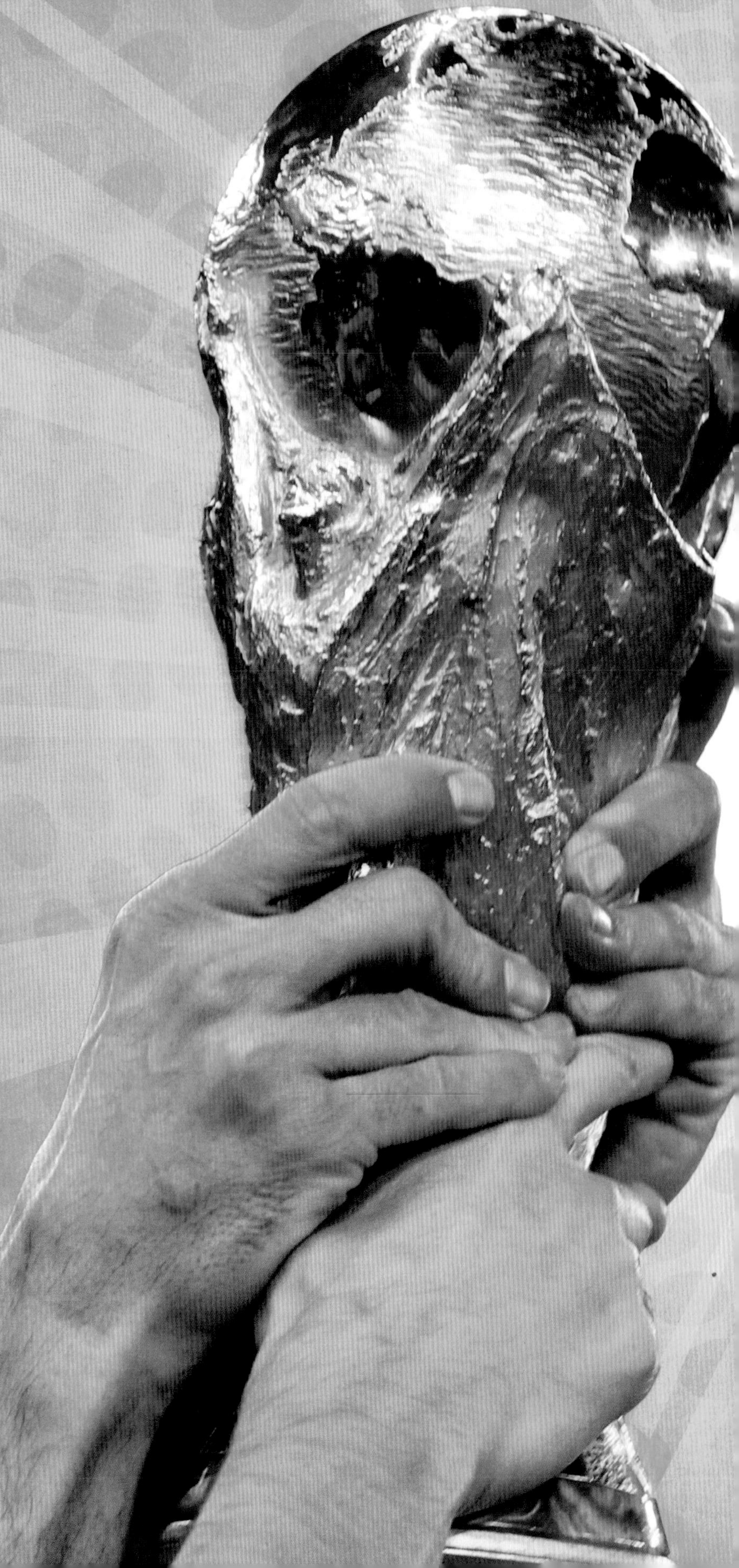

FIFA
OFFICIAL
LICENSED
PRODUCT
© 2005 FIFA

WORLD FOOTBALL RECORDS 2012

KEIR RADNEDGE

⚽ CONTENTS

ONE of the great attractions of association football is the non-stop momentum of the game and this latest edition of *FIFA World Football Records* seeks to reflect that.

Simultaneously, fans are still looking back to the memorable moments of the 2010 FIFA World Cup finals in South Africa while looking ahead with renewed optimism to the 2014 FIFA World Cup finals in Brazil.

Spain, one of the world game's most powerful nations, were long-overdue winners in 2010; Brazil, record five-times world champions, are rebuilding in the hope of becoming, next time around, the first host nation winners since France in 1998.

The 2014 FIFA World Cup is already well under way. It kicked off on 15 June 2011, at the Ato Boldon Stadium in Couva, Trinidad and Tobago. Belize beat Montserrat 5-2 in the first of a scheduled 824 qualifying ties. Deon McCauley of Belize wrote his name into football history with the first goal of the entire tournament in the 24th minute.

Here was solid evidence that the FIFA World Cup is not only about the giants. In spanning the height and breadth and depth of the football pyramid, so this book has evolved to match the ups and downs of FIFA's membership. This means the national teams but also the individual players and managers and the ever-changing records they continue to set.

Yet while the FIFA World Cup is the pinnacle of achievement it is not the only story. The international game is bubbling with other national team as well as club tournaments while domestic leagues and knockout cup competitions also have an unshakable grip on fans' thirst for information.

Within these pages readers can find the main events and the sideshows, the giants and the giant-killers, the greatest players and the eager debutants ... from Brazil to Belize.

Xavi Hernandez goes past Czech Republic captain Tomas Rosicky as 2010 FIFA World Cup winners Spain continued the defence of their UEFA European Championship crown in a March 2011 qualifier.

PART 1:
THE COUNTRIES

SOME call it soccer, others say futbol or calcio or futebol – but go to virtually any country on earth and someone will be speaking about this game by whatever label. Association football knows no boundaries of race or politics or religion.

The structure is simple, helping ensure the sport's international success. At the head of the world football pyramid is FIFA, the world federation. Supporting FIFA's work are the six regional geographical confederations representing Africa, Asia, Europe, Oceania, South America, plus the Caribbean, Central and North America. Backing up the regions in turn are the national associations of 208 countries – and thus FIFA can boast more member countries than even the United Nations or the Olympic movement.

The countries are pivotal. They field the national teams who have built sporting history through their many and varied achievements in world-focused competitions such as the FIFA World Cup. But they also oversee the growth of football in their nation – from professional leagues to the game at grass-roots level.

Representative teams from England and Scotland played out the first formal internationals in the late 19th century, thus laying the foundation for the four British home nations' unique independent status within a world football family otherwise comprised of nation states. The original British Home Championships was the first competition for national teams but its demise, as a result of a congested fixture list, has left the Copa America in South America as the oldest survivor – apart from the Olympic Games.

Keen interest in the Olympic Games in the 1920s led directly to the launch of the FIFA World Cup in 1930 – and subsequently the regional championships whose winners now compete every four years at the FIFA Confederations Cup. The next such event will be staged in Brazil in 2013 – one year ahead of the country's staging of the FIFA World Cup finals, the ultimate celebration of the world's favourite sport.

FIFA is the football world's governing body and their headquarters are in Zurich, Switzerland. Delegates from all 208 national federations attend the FIFA Congress (held every non World Cup year)

EUROPE

As soon as modern association football's rules were written in England the game's growth was rapid – enthusiasm spreading swiftly across Europe, the cradle of the game. Within only a few years the sport's laws were being carried even further, across the world's oceans, by students, engineers, sailors, soldiers and businessmen – igniting the passion now evident from fans on any given day in any given country ... as millions of 2010 FIFA World Cup-winning Spaniards will happily testify.

Thomas Muller turns away after scoring for Germany in their 4-1 defeat of England in the 2010 FIFA World Cup round of 16 tie. It was England's heaviest FIFA World Cup finals defeat.

ENGLAND

England is where football began; the country where the game was first developed, which saw the creation of the game's first Football Association and the first organized league, and which now plays host to the richest domestic league in the world. But England have not had it all their own way on the international scene. Far from it. One solitary FIFA World Cup™ win apart, as hosts in 1966, the Three Lions have found it hard to shake off the "underachievers" tag when it comes to major tournaments.

IF THE CAP FITS

England's players in the historic first game against Scotland all wore **cricket-style caps** while the Scots wore hoods. England's "fashion statement" prompted the use of the term "cap" to refer to any international appearance. The tradition of awarding a cap to British international footballers still survives today.

HAVE A BASH, ASH

Chelsea left-back **Ashley Cole** overtook former Arsenal player Kenny Sansom as England's most-capped full-back when he represented his country for the 87th time against Denmark in February 2011. The man voted his country's best international of 2010 by home fans also holds the record for most England appearances without a goal, having reached 88 without once hitting the net.

IN THE BEGINNING

The day it all began ... 30 November 1872, when England played their first official international match, against Scotland, at Hamilton Crescent, Partick. The result was a 0-0 draw in front of a then massive crowd of 4,000, who each paid an admission fee of one shilling (5p). In fact, teams representing England and Scotland had played five times before, but most of the Scottish players had been based in England and the matches are considered unofficial. England's team for the first official game was selected by Charles Alcock, the secretary of the Football Association. His one regret was that, because of injury, he could not pick himself to play. In contrast, the first rugby union international between England and Scotland had been played in 1871, but England's first Test cricket match was not played until March 1877, against Australia in Melbourne.

RUNAWAY SUCCESS

England have hit double figures five times: beating Ireland 13-0 and 13-2 in 1882 and 1899, thrashing Austria 11-1 in 1908, crushing Portugal 10-0 in Lisbon in 1947 and then the United States 10-0 in 1964 in New York. The ten goals were scored by Roger Hunt (four), Fred Pickering (three), Terry Paine (two) and **Bobby Charlton**.

FIRST DEFEAT

Hungary's 6-3 win at Wembley in 1953 was the first time England had lost at home to continental opposition. Their first home defeat by non-British opposition came against the Republic of Ireland, who beat them 2-0 at Goodison Park, Liverpool, in 1949.

NAUGHTY BOYS

Alan Mullery was the first of 12 England players sent off in senior internationals. Mullery was dismissed in the semi-final of the UEFA European Championship against Yugoslavia in Florence on 5 June 1968. David Beckham is the only one of the 12 to have been sent off twice for England.

ENGLAND'S BIGGEST WINS

1882	Ireland 0 England 13
1899	England 13 Ireland 2
1908	Austria 1 England 11
1964	United States 0 England 10
1947	Portugal 0 England 10
1982	England 9 Luxembourg 0
1960	Luxembourg 0 England 9
1895	England 9 Ireland 0
1927	Belgium 1 England 9
1896	Wales 1 England 9
1890	Ireland 1 England 9

ENGLAND'S BIGGEST DEFEATS

1954	Hungary 7 England 1
1878	Scotland 7 England 2
1881	England 1 Scotland 6
1958	Yugoslavia 5 England 0
1964	Brazil 5 England 1
1928	England 1 Scotland 5
1882	Scotland 5 England 1
1953	England 3 Hungary 6
1963	France 5 England 2
1931	France 5 England 2

SENIOR MOMENT

Goalkeeper **David James** became the oldest player to make his FIFA World Cup debut, aged 39 years and 321 days when he first appeared for England at the 2010 competition in South Africa. He kept a clean sheet in a goalless Group C draw against Algeria after coming into the side to replace Robert Green, who had made an embarrassing error in England's opening game against the USA.

FAITH IN EXPERIENCE

England's 2010 FIFA World Cup squad was the oldest they have ever taken to the tournament, with an average age of 28.7. The record was previously held by the country's 1954 squad, with an average age of 28.4. Both selections featured a 39-year-old – goalkeeper David James in 2010, winger Stanley Matthews in 1954. The 2010 selection also went into the tournament with a total tally of 900 international appearances between them, an average of 39.1 apiece – beating the earlier record of England's 1990 squad with its average of 32.2 caps per player.

HEAD FOR GOAL

Robust and commanding centre-backs had the honour of scoring both the last England goal at the old Wembley stadium, closed down in 2000, and the first in the new version, which was finally opened in 2007. Tony Adams scored England's second in a 2-0 win over Ukraine in May 2000 – Germany's Dietmar Hamann hit the only goal of the final international at the old Wembley, four months later – and captain **John Terry** headed his side ahead in the new stadium's showpiece June 2007 friendly against Brazil, which would end 1-1.

BLANKS OF ENGLAND

A goalless draw against Algeria, in Cape Town in June 2010, made England the first country to finish 10 different FIFA World Cup matches 0-0. Their first was against Brazil in 1958, while the tally also includes both second-round group games in 1982 against eventual runners-up West Germany and hosts Spain.

BEST GERMANY

England suffered their heaviest-ever FIFA World Cup finals defeat when losing 4-1 to Germany in Bloemfontein, South Africa, in the second round of the 2010 tournament. Before then, their largest loss had been 4-2 against Uruguay, in a 1954 quarter-final. Germany managed more goals in one match than England scored in the entire 2010 tournament – defender Matthew Upson scored England's consolation goal in Bloemfontein, after only **Steven Gerrard** and Jermain Defoe had scored in three first-round matches. Back in September 2001, England enjoyed a 5-1 away win over Germany, in a FIFA World Cup qualifier in Munich, thanks to Michael Owen's hat-trick and goals by Steven Gerrard and Emile Heskey. Germany still progressed further at the following year's FIFA World Cup in South Korea and Japan, though, losing to Brazil in the same final after England were knocked out by the same opponents in the quarter-finals.

THE LONG AND THE SHORT OF IT

At 6ft 7in, centre-forward **Peter Crouch** is the tallest player ever to stretch above opposing defences for England – while **Fanny Walden**, the Tottenham winger who won two caps in 1914 and 1922, was the shortest at 5ft 2in. Sheffield United goalkeeper Billy "Fatty" Foulke was the heaviest England player at 18st when he played against Wales on 29 March 1897.

TEENAGE PROMISE

Theo Walcott became England's youngest full international when he played against Hungary at Old Trafford on 30 May 2006 at the age of 17 years 75 days. On 10 September 2008, he became England's youngest scorer of a hat-trick in a 4-1 win away to Croatia in Zagreb, aged 19 years 178 days. The previous youngest international was Wayne Rooney, who was 17 years 111 days old when he played against Australia in February 2003.

WAITING FOR THE CALL

Four England internationals played at the 1966 FIFA World Cup yet missed out on the triumphant final against West Germany – **Ian Callaghan,** John Connelly, Jimmy Greaves and Terry Paine. Liverpool winger Callaghan would then endure the longest wait between England appearances, when he went 11 years and 49 days between his showing in a 2-0 win over France at that 1966 tournament and his return to international action in a goalless draw with Switzerland in September 1977. The game against the Swiss was his third – and penultimate – outing for England.

BECKHAM'S RECORD

David Beckham played for England for the 109th time when he appeared as a second-half substitute in the 4-0 win over Slovakia in a friendly international on 28 March 2009. That overtook the record number of England games for an outfield player, which had been set by Bobby Moore, England's 1966 FIFA World Cup-winning captain. Beckham, born on 2 May 1975, in Leytonstone, London, made his first appearance for his country on 1 September 1996, in a FIFA World Cup qualifying match against Moldova. He was appointed full-time England captain in 2001 by the then new manager Sven-Goran Eriksson – stepping down after England's quarter-final defeat by Portugal in the 2006 FIFA World Cup.

MEET THE NEW BOSS

Striker Andy Cole had a different England manager for each of his first four international appearances: Terry Venables for his debut against Uruguay in 1995, Glenn Hoddle against Italy in 1997, caretaker boss Howard Wilkinson against France and permanent replacement Kevin Keegan against Poland, both in 1999. Cole would win only 11 more caps, under both Keegan and Sven-Goran Eriksson.

ALEXANDER THE LATE

The oldest player to make his debut for England remains Alexander Morten, who was 41 years and 114 days old when facing Scotland on 8 March 1873 in England's first home game, at The Oval in Kennington, London. He was also captain that day, and is still the country's oldest-ever skipper.

HEROES AND VILLAINS

Fabio Capello picked four current and four former Aston Villa players in his England squad for April 2011 games against Wales and Ghana. The West Midlands club have provided more England internationals than any other side, **Gareth Southgate** being the "Villan" with the most caps of all – 42 of his 57 were won while playing for Villa, including the 1996 UEFA European Championship semi-final against Germany when he fatefully missed his penalty in a shoot-out. Tottenham Hotspur have provided more England goals than any other club – Peter Crouch's against France in November 2010 was the North London club's 190th.

GRAND OLD MAN

Stanley Matthews became England's oldest-ever player when he lined up at outside-right against Denmark on 15 May 1957 at the age of 42 years 104 days. That was 22 years and 229 days after his first appearance. Matthews was also England's oldest marksman. He was 41 years eight months old when he scored against Northern Ireland on 10 October 1956.

TOP SCORERS

1	Bobby Charlton	49
2	Gary Lineker	48
3	Jimmy Greaves	44
4	Michael Owen	40
5	Tom Finney	30
=	Nat Lofthouse	30
=	Alan Shearer	30
8	Viv Woodward	29
9	Steve Bloomer	28
10	David Platt	27

CAPTAIN SOLO

Claude Ashton, the Corinthians centre-forward, set a record when he captained England on his only international appearance. This was a 0-0 draw against Northern Ireland in Belfast on 24 October 1925.

TOP CAPS

1	Peter Shilton	125
2	David Beckham	115
3	Bobby Moore	108
4	Bobby Charlton	106
5	Billy Wright	105
6	Bryan Robson	90
7	Steven Gerrard	89
=	Michael Owen	89
9	Ashley Cole	88
10	Kenny Sansom	86

CAPTAINS COURAGEOUS

The international careers of Billy Wright and **Bobby Moore**, who both captained England a record 90 times, very nearly overlapped. Wright, from Wolves, played for England between 1946 and 1959 and Moore, from West Ham, between 1962 and 1973, including England's FIFA World Cup win in 1966.

SHARED RESPONSIBILITY

Substitutions meant the captain's armband passed between four different players during England's 2-1 friendly win over Serbia and Montenegro on 3 June 2003. Regular captain David Beckham was missing so Michael Owen led the team out, but was substituted at half-time. England's second-half skippers were Owen's then-Liverpool team-mates Emile Heskey and Jamie Carragher and Manchester United's Philip Neville. The first time three different players have captained England in one FIFA World Cup finals match was against Morocco in 1986, when first-choice skipper Bryan Robson went off injured, his vice-captain Ray Wilkins was then sent off and goalkeeper Peter Shilton took over leadership duties.

CAMEO ROLE

Tottenham Hotspur striker **Jermain Defoe** has come on as a substitute for England more often than any other player, 29 times since his debut in March 2004 – and his initial 17 starting appearances all ended in him being replaced before the end of 90 minutes.

THE REAL HOME OF FOOTBALL

Contrary to popular belief, myth and most football record books, the original home of the England football team is The Oval. It was The Oval in Kennington, London – more famous for cricket (and the venue for the first Test match in England in 1880) – which hosted the first "unofficial" international games (five in all) between representative teams from England and Scotland between 1870 and 1872. The Oval went on to host England's first "official" home international (their second game), which turned out to be England's first international victory (4-2 over Scotland), as well as wins against Wales and Ireland in the fledgling British Home Championship.

WHO'S THE GREATEST?

Fabio Capello is the most statistically successful England manager, with a win ratio of 68 per cent, followed by **Sir Alf Ramsey (below)** and **Glenn Hoddle** tied on 61 per cent. Sir Alf's 1966 FIFA World Cup victory, however, puts him head and shoulders above all the rest. Technically, caretaker manager Peter Taylor has the worst record – a 100 per cent record of defeat. But then, he was in charge for only one game – a 1-0 defeat to Italy in Turin, a game that saw David Beckham making his first appearance as England captain. Don Revie, in the 1970s, and Steve McClaren, in the 2000s, are the only full-time managers to have failed to qualify for any international tournament. Terry Venables was spared the need to qualify for his only tournament, Euro 1996, since England were hosts. McClaren's 16-month tenure (during which Venables served as his assistant) is also the shortest full-time reign as national team manager.

COMING OVER HERE

Argentina were the first non-UK side to play at Wembley – England won 2-1 on 9 May 1951 – while Ferenc Puskas and the "Magical Magyars" of Hungary were the first "foreign", or "continental", side to beat England at home, with their famous 6-3 victory at Wembley in 1953. This humiliation marked Alf Ramsey's last game as an England player. England first tasted defeat to a "foreign" side when they lost 4-3 to Spain in Madrid on 15 May 1929. Two years later England gained their revenge with a 7-1 win at Highbury.

WRONG WAY!

Though the goal is sometimes credited to Scottish striker John Smith, it is believed that Edgar Field was the first England player to score an "own goal", which was his fate as Scotland crushed England 6-1 at The Oval on 12 March 1881. By the time Field put the ball in his own net, Scotland were already 4-1 up. The full-back, who was an FA Cup winner and loser with Clapham Rovers, is in good company. Manchester United's Gary Neville has scored two own goals "against" England.

ROLL UP, ROLL UP

The highest attendance for an England game came at Hampden Park on 17 April 1937, when 149,547 spectators crushed in to see Scotland's 3-1 victory in the British Home Championships. Only 2,378 turned up in Bologna, Italy, to see San Marino stun England after nine seconds in Graham Taylor's side's 7-1 victory that was not enough to secure qualification to the 1994 FIFA World Cup.

FIRST AND FOREMOST

England's first official international was a 0-0 draw against Scotland in Glasgow on 30 November 1872, though England and Scotland had already played a number of unofficial representative matches against each other prior to that. Given that England's only opponents for four decades were the home nations – and only Scotland for the first seven years, it is not surprising that England's first draw, win and defeat were all against their northern neighbours. After the goalless first game, the second fixture – played at The Oval on 8 March 1873 – proved a more exciting affair: England won 4-2 in a six-goal thriller. In their third game, back in Glasgow almost exactly a year later, Scotland evened things up with a 2-1 win. These fixtures completed the trio of first wins, defeats and draws for the oldest participants in international football.

THE ITALIAN JOB

Italian **Fabio Capello** became England's second foreign coach when he took over from Steve McClaren in January 2008 and led the country to the 2010 FIFA World Cup in South Africa. Capello already had happy memories of national stadium Wembley from his playing days – he scored the only goal for Italy on 14 November 1973, giving them their first-ever away win against England. Capello has said he plans to step down as England coach after the 2012 UEFA European Championship.

YOUR COUNTRY NEEDS YOU

The first England teams were selected from open trials of Englishmen who responded to the FA's adverts for players. It was only when these proved too popular and unwieldy that, in 1887, the FA decided that it would be better to manage the process through an International Selection Committee, which continued to pick the team until Sir Alf Ramsey's appointment in 1962.

MANAGERIAL ROLL OF HONOUR

Name		P	W	D	L	F	A
Walter Winterbottom	(1946–62)	138	77	33	28	380	195
Sir Alf Ramsey	(1962–74)	113	69	27	17	224	98
Joe Mercer	(1974)	7	3	3	1	9	7
Don Revie	(1974–77)	29	14	7	8	49	25
Ron Greenwood	(1977–82)	55	33	12	10	93	40
Bobby Robson	(1982–90)	95	47	30	18	154	60
Graham Taylor	(1990–93)	38	18	13	7	62	32
Terry Venables	(1994–96)	24	11	11	2	35	14
Glenn Hoddle	(1996–98)	28	17	6	5	42	13
Howard Wilkinson	(1999–2000)	2	0	1	1	0	2
Kevin Keegan	(1999–2000)	18	7	7	4	26	15
Peter Taylor	(November 2000)	1	0	0	1	0	1
Sven-Goran Eriksson	(2001–06)	67	40	17	10	127	60
Steve McClaren	(2006–07)	18	9	4	5	32	12
Fabio Capello	(2008–)	35	24	5	6	79	31

RED MIST

Careless-tackling Paul Scholes is not only the sole England player to be sent off at the old Wembley Stadium, against Sweden in June 1999. His red card while playing for Manchester United against Manchester City, in an April 2011 FA Cup semi-final, made him the first player to be sent off at both the former stadium and the rebuilt version. More happily, Scholes was the last player to score a hat-trick on the old Wembley turf, against Poland in March 1999. The first at the replacement stadium was Italy Under-21 striker Giampaolo Pazzini, in a 3-3 draw with England Under-21s in March 2007.

WONDERFUL WALTER

Walter Winterbottom was the England national team's first full-time manager – and remains both the longest-serving (with 138 games in charge) and the youngest-ever England manager, aged just 33 when he took the job in 1946 (initially as a coach and then, from 1947, as manager). The former teacher and Manchester United player led England to four FIFA World Cups.

FRANCE

France – nicknamed "Les Bleus" – are one of the most successful teams in the history of international football. They are one of only three countries to be World and European champions at the same time. They won the FIFA World Cup™ in 1998 as tournament hosts, routing Brazil 3-0 in the final. Two years later, they staged a sensational, last-gasp recovery to overhaul Italy in the Euro 2000 final. The French equalized in the fifth minute of stoppage time, then went on to win 2-1 on a golden goal. France had previously won the UEFA European Championship in 1984, beating Spain 2-0 in the final in Paris. They reached the 2006 FIFA World Cup™ final too, but lost to Italy in a penalty shoot-out. France also won the 2001 and 2003 FIFA Confederations Cup and took the Olympic football gold medal in 1984.

KOPA – FRANCE'S FIRST SUPERSTAR

Raymond Kopa (born on 13 October 1931) was France's first international superstar. Born into a family of Polish immigrants (the family name was Kopaszewski), he was instrumental in Reims's championship successes of the mid-1950s. He later joined Real Madrid and became the first French player to win a European Cup winner's medal. He was the playmaker of the France team that finished third in the 1958 FIFA World Cup finals. His performances for his country that year earned him the European Footballer of the Year award.

PLATINI'S GLITTERING CAREER

Michel Platini (born in Joeuf on 21 June 1955) has enjoyed a glittering career, rising from a youngster at Nancy to become one of France's greatest-ever players, a hero in Italy, and now the president of UEFA. He was also joint organizing president (along with Fernand Sastre) of the 1998 FIFA World Cup finals in France. Platini was the grandson of an Italian immigrant who ran a café in Joeuf, Lorraine. He began with the local club, Nancy, before starring for Saint-Etienne, Juventus and France. He was instrumental in France's progress to the 1982 FIFA World Cup semi-finals and was the undisputed star of the UEFA European Championship two years later, when France won the tournament on home soil.

MICHEL PLATINI (league and national career)

Duration	Team	Appearances	Goals
1972–79	Nancy	181	98
1979–82	Saint-Etienne	104	58
1982–87	Juventus	147	68
1976–87	France	72	41

SIT DOWN PROTEST

Even before France's 2010 FIFA World Cup campaign collapsed into anarchy and industrial action, there were tensions between rival members of the squad. Playmaker Yoann Gourcuff was reported by the French media to have been frozen out by other members of the squad, while senior centre-back William Gallas did not see eye-to-eye with young midfielder **Samir Nasri**, formerly his team-mate at Arsenal. After Gallas moved across north London to Tottenham Hotspur in summer 2010, Nasri refused to shake his hand before the clubs' two English Premier League meetings the following season.

UP FOUR THE CUP

Reaching the 2010 FIFA World Cup might have been a struggle – and a controversial one at that – but it did mean France had qualified for four FIFA World Cups in a row for the first time ever. Include the 2008 UEFA European Championship and that made Raymond Domenech the first France coach to lead his country at three consecutive major finals tournaments.

CROSSING THE BARRIERS

France's teams have usually included a high proportion of players from immigrant backgrounds or ethnic minorities. Three of France's greatest players – Raymond Kopa, Michel Platini and Zinedine Zidane – were the sons or grandsons of immigrants. In 2006, 17 of France's 23-man FIFA World Cup squad had links to the country's former colonies.

FRANCE AND FIFA

France were one of FIFA's founding members in 1904. Frenchman Robert Guerin became the first president of the governing body. Another Frenchman, Jules Rimet, was president from 1921 to 1954. He was the driving force behind the creation of the FIFA World Cup and the first version of football's most coveted trophy was named in his honour.

IT'S A SHAME ABOUT RAY

France's failure to win a match at the 2010 FIFA World Cup meant coach **Raymond Domenech** equalled but failed to exceed Michel Hidalgo's record of 41 victories in charge of the national side. Domenech did at least end his six-year reign having surpassed Euro 84-winning Hidalgo's tally of matches in the job. Domenech's final game, against South Africa, was his 79th as coach, four more than Hidalgo achieved. Domenech, a tough-tackling defender who was picked for France by Hidalgo, proved an eccentric as national coach. He admitted partly judging players by their star signs and responded to being knocked out of the 2008 UEFA European Championship by proposing to his girlfriend on live television.

KISSING COLLEAGUES

Marseille colleagues centre-back **Laurent Blanc** and goalkeeper **Fabien Barthez** had a special ritual during France's run to the 1998 FIFA World Cup crown. Before the game, Blanc would always kiss Barthez's shaven head, even when the veteran defender was suspended for the final.

WRONG KIND OF STRIKERS

During France's disastrous 2010 FIFA World Cup campaign, the players went on strike, refusing to train two days before their final Group A match, in protest at striker Nicolas Anelka being sent home early for insulting coach Raymond Domenech. France finished bottom of the group after a goalless draw with Uruguay and defeats to Mexico and hosts South Africa. The country's president Nicolas Sarkozy ordered an investigation into all that had gone wrong, while former French international defender Lilian Thuram called for captain **Patrice Evra** to be banned from playing for the team ever again. New coach Laurent Blanc refused to consider any members of the 23 in the 2010 FIFA World Cup squad for France's first match after the finals, a friendly in Norway, and they lost 2-1.

TOP CAPS

1	Lilian Thuram	142
2	Thierry Henry	123
3	Marcel Desailly	116
4	Zinedine Zidane	108
5	Patrick Vieira	107
6	Didier Deschamps	103
7	Laurent Blanc	97
=	Bixente Lizarazu	97
9	Sylvain Wiltord	92
10	Fabien Barthez	87

HAND OF GAUL

France qualified controversially for the 2010 FIFA World Cup finals. All-time leading scorer Thierry Henry was cast as the villain of their play-off against the Republic of Ireland in November 2009, when he clearly controlled the ball with his hand before setting up William Gallas's extra-time winner. Henry later apologized for what was dubbed "The Hand of Gaul" or "Le Main de Dieu". FIFA turned down the Irish FA's pleas for a replay or an unprecedented 33rd place in the following year's finals.

TOP SCORERS

1	Thierry Henry	51
2	Michel Platini	41
3	David Trezeguet	34
4	Zinedine Zidane	31
5	Just Fontaine	30
=	Jean-Pierre Papin	30
7	Youri Djorkaeff	28
8	Sylvain Wiltord	26
9	Jean Vincent	22
10	Jean Nicolas	21

HENRY BENCHED

France's record scorer Thierry Henry missed out on an appearance in the 1998 FIFA World Cup final because of Marcel Desailly's red card. Henry was France's leading scorer in the competition with three goals in the group games. Coach Aime Jacquet planned to use him as a substitute in the final, but Desailly's sending-off forced a re-think. Jacquet decided to reinforce the midfield – Arsenal team-mate Patrick Vieira going on instead – so Henry spent the full 90 minutes of the final on the bench. But Henry does have the distinction of being the only Frenchman to play at four different FIFA World Cups, in 1998, 2002, 2006 and 2010. He passed Michel Platini's all-time goal-scoring record for France with a late brace against Lithuania in October 2007.

DESCHAMPS THE LEADER

Didier Deschamps was the most successful captain in France's history, leading them to victory in the 1998 FIFA World Cup and at Euro 2000. He won 103 caps and skippered the team a record 55 times between 1996 and his international retirement in July 2000. He first wore the captain's armband in a 1-0 win over Germany on 1 June 1996 and led the team that lost on penalties to the Czech Republic in the Euro 96 semi-finals.

UNITED FOR ABIDAL

Defender **Eric Abidal**, a key member of the French teams at the 2006 and 2010 FIFA World Cups, was enjoying his best form for Spanish club Barcelona when diagnosed with liver cancer in March 2011 – but managed to recover in time for a surprise return to action by the season's end. Club rivalries were put aside when players from rivals Real Madrid wore T-shirts bearing the supportive message "Animo Abidal" after their UEFA Champions League tie against Abidal's former club Olympique Lyonnais a few days later. Barcelona fans then clapped throughout the 22nd minute of their La Liga game against Getafe, in recognition of Abidal's shirt number. Remarkably he was fit enough to return to action, as a substitute, in Barcelona's UEFA Champions League semi-final victory over Madrid in May 2011. Abidal started in the final and, although not the captain, was given the armband to lift lift the cup after their 3-1 win over Manchester United.

BITTERSWEET FOR TREZEGUET

Striker **David Trezeguet** has bittersweet memories of France's clashes with Italy in major finals. He scored the "golden goal" that beat the Italians in extra-time in the Euro 2000 final, but six years later, he was the man who missed as France lost the FIFA World Cup final on penalties. Trezeguet's shot bounced off the bar and failed to cross the line.

LILIAN IN THE PINK

Defender **Lilian Thuram** made his 142nd and final appearance for France in their defeat by Italy at Euro 2008. His international career had spanned nearly 14 years, since his debut against the Czech Republic on 17 August 1994. Thuram was born in Pointe a Pitre, Guadeloupe on 1 January 1972. He played club football for Monaco, Parma, Juventus and Barcelona before retiring in the summer of 2008 because of a heart problem. He was one of the stars of France's 1998 FIFA World Cup-winning side and scored both goals in the semi-final victory over Croatia – the only international goals of his career. He gained another winner's medal at Euro 2000. He first retired from international football after France's elimination at Euro 2004, but was persuaded by coach Raymond Domenech to return for the 2006 FIFA World Cup campaign and made his second appearance in a FIFA World Cup final. He broke Marcel Desailly's record of 116 caps in the group game against Togo.

PRESIDENTIAL PARDON

Imperious centre-back Laurent Blanc was known as "Le President" during his playing days – now he is the national coach, succeeding Raymond Domenech after the 2010 FIFA World Cup. Blanc was unlucky to miss the 1998 FIFA World Cup final after being sent off in the semi-final for pushing Slaven Bilic in the face, though replays showed the Croatian defender to have over-reacted. Blanc did enjoy some redemption by being part of the French team that won the UEFA European Championship two years later. He took the French manager's job 12 months after leading Bordeaux to the 2008–09 domestic championship, ending Olympique Lyonnais's run of seven league titles in a row.

FRENCH EXODUS

France's 23-man squad for the 2010 FIFA World Cup was reduced to 22, just three days after their opening game, when third-choice goalkeeper Cedric Carrasso suffered a thigh injury. Uncapped Monaco goalkeeper Stephane Ruffier cut short a holiday and flew to South Africa, but was barred from replacing Carrasso because the tournament had already started. The French squad was then reduced to 21 before what would be their last match, against South Africa, when disgruntled striker Nicolas Anelka was expelled for disciplinary reasons.

THE FULL SET

Four France stars have a full set of top international medals – FIFA World Cup, UEFA European Championship and European Cup winners. Marcel Desailly, Bixente Lizarazu, Didier Deschamps and Zinedine Zidane all played in France's winning teams of 1998 and 2000. In addition, Desailly won the European Cup with Marseille in 1993 and Milan the following year. Deschamps won with Marseille in 1993 and Juventus in 1996; Lizarazu with Bayern Munich in 2001; and Zidane with Real Madrid in 2002.

ALBERT THE FIRST

Albert Batteux (1919–2003) was France's first national manager. Before his appointment in 1955, a selection committee had picked the team. Batteux was also the most successful coach in the history of French football. He combined managing France with his club job at Reims. His biggest achievement was guiding the national team to third place in the 1958 FIFA World Cup finals. The team's two big stars, Raymond Kopa and Just Fontaine, had both played under his charge at Reims.

HIDALGO REIGNS LONGEST

The longest-serving France manager was Michel Hidalgo, another who played under Albert Batteux at Reims. He was appointed on 27 March 1976 and stayed for more than eight years. Hidalgo was also the first France coach to win a major trophy – the UEFA European Championship in 1984. He retired straight after France's victory on 27 June. He had also steered France to the FIFA World Cup semi-finals in 1982, when they lost to West Germany in highly controversial circumstances.

JACQUET'S TRIUMPH

Aime Jacquet, who guided France to FIFA World Cup victory in 1998, was one of their most controversial national coaches. He had been attacked for alleged defensive tactics despite France's run to the semi-finals of Euro 96 and a record of only three defeats in four years. A month before the 1998 finals, the sports daily *L'Equipe* claimed he was not capable of building a successful team!

NO TIME FOR FONTAINE

Former striker **Just Fontaine** spent the shortest-ever spell in charge of the France team. He took over on 22 March 1967 and left on 3 June after two defeats in friendlies.

OVAL BALL

The father of France's most capped goalkeeper Fabien Barthez was also a French international. Alain Barthez was a fine rugby union player who won one cap for France.

FRANCE MANAGERS

Albert Batteux	1955–62
Henri Guerin	1962–66
Jose Arribas/Jean Snella	1966
Just Fontaine	1967
Louis Dugauguez	1967–68
Georges Boulogne	1969–73
Stefan Kovacs	1973–75
Michel Hidalgo	1976–84
Henri Michel	1984–88
Michel Platini	1988–92
Gerard Houllier	1992–93
Aime Jacquet	1993–98
Roger Lemerre	1998–2002
Jacques Santini	2002–04
Raymond Domenech	2004–10
Laurent Blanc	2010–

BLINK AND YOU'LL MISS HIM

Unfortunate defender Franck Jurietti's international debut proved bittersweet – it lasted just five seconds and he never had another chance. The Bordeaux full-back came on just before the final whistle of France's match against Cyprus in October 2005, amounting to an international career even shorter than fellow defender Bernard Boissier's two minutes against Portugal in April 1975.

WINNING WITH YOUTH

In the early 1990s, France became the first European country to institute a national youth development programme. The best young players were picked to attend the national youth academy at Clairefontaine. Then they went on to the top clubs' academies throughout the nation. The scheme has produced a rich harvest of stars. FIFA World Cup winners Didier Deschamps, Marcel Desailly and Christian Karembeu started at Nantes. Lilian Thuram, Thierry Henry, Manu Petit and David Trezeguet began with Monaco and **Zinedine Zidane** and Patrick Vieira were graduates from Cannes.

PACKING THEM IN

A record home crowd of 80,051 people were inside the Stade de France, in Saint-Denis, to see France take a major step towards qualifying for the 2008 UEFA European Championship with a 2-0 defeat of Ukraine in June 2007. The goals were scored by Franck Ribery and **Nicolas Anelka**.

EARNING THEIR STRIPES

France are the only country to play at a FIFA World Cup wearing another team's kit. In the 1978 tournament in Argentina, for a first-round match at Mar del Plata, *Les Bleus* were forced to wear the green and white stripes of a local club side, Atletico Kimberley, when they met Hungary. France brought their second, white, kit instead of their normal blue, while Hungary turned up in their second strip, white, too. The quick-change did not seem to affect France, who won the match 3-1.

ROUX SETS THE PACE

Former Auxerre coach Guy Roux holds the record for the most Ligue 1 games in charge. Roux (born on 18 October 1938) guided his team through 890 matches during a 44-year spell. He took over as player/coach in 1961 and only retired as coach in 2005. He led Auxerre from the old third division to becoming French champions in 1996. They also won the French Cup four times, in 1994, 1996, 2003 and 2005. Roux knew that an unfashionable provincial club like Auxerre could not compete financially with the big clubs, so he developed a youth policy that produced a succession of stars, such as Eric Cantona and Basile Boli. Roux's success was one of the catalysts for the now highly successful French Federation's national youth development programme.

JACQUES HAMMERED

Jacques Santini is statistically France's most successful manager, despite being in charge when they failed to retain their UEFA European Championship crown in 2004. He won 22 of his 28 games in charge, between 2002 and 2004, a success rate of 79 per cent – ahead of closest challengers Aime Jacquet and Roger Lemerre, both on 64 per cent. Former Lyon coach Santini lost just two games for France – though the last of these was their Euro 2004 quarter-final against eventual champions Greece. He had already upset supporters back home by announcing a post-tournament move to English club Tottenham Hotspur.

GERMANY

Politics may have divided the country in two for over 40 years, but few countries can match Germany's record in international football. Three-time winners of the FIFA World Cup™ (1954, 1974 and 1990) and three-time UEFA European Championship winners (1972, 1980 and 1996), in 1974 they became the first country in history to hold the World and European titles at the same time – and have remained a fearsome opponent in top-level football matches ever since.

SHOOT–OUT SURE–SHOTS

German teams have always put in hours of preparation for penalty shoot-outs. Their last two major successes – the 1990 FIFA World Cup and Euro 96 successes – both came after shoot-out victories in the semi-finals. England were the Germans' victims on both occasions.

BELITTLE ITALY

Germany have never managed to beat Italy in an international tournament, suffering high-profile defeats such as the 1970 FIFA World Cup semi-final which ended 4–3 after extra-time. The last time Germany beat Italy in a friendly was back in 1995 – but despite a 1-1 draw in a **February 2011 friendly,** Germany can celebrate one recent success against their European rivals. From the 2011–12 season onwards, Germany's Bungesliga will have four clubs eligible for the UEFA Champions League, gaining an extra space at the expense of Italy's Serie A, based on clubs' European competition performances in recent seasons.

FOR CLUB AND COUNTRY

Italy's first-round departure from the 2010 FIFA World Cup, after Internazionale were crowned European club champions, means West Germany remains the only country to have won the FIFA World Cup in the same year that one of its clubs has clinched the European Cup or UEFA Champions League. Captain Franz Beckenbauer lifted both trophies in 1974, one for West Germany and the other for **Bayern Munich.**

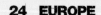

BOTH SIDES NOW

Eight players appeared for both the old East Germany and then Germany after reunification in October 1990.

Player	East Germany	Germany
Ulf Kirsten	49	51
Matthias Sammer	23	51
Andreas Thom	51	10
Thomas Doll	29	18
Dariusz Wosz	7	17
Olaf Marschall	4	13
Heiko Scholz	7	1
Dirk Schuster	4	3

EAST GERMANY –
TOP APPEARANCES AND GOALS

Appearances

1	Joachim Streich	98
2	**Hans-Jurgen Dorner**	96
3	Jurgen Croy	86
4	Konrad Weise	78
5	Eberhard Vogel	69

Goals

1	Joachim Streich	53
2	Eberhard Vogel	24
3	Hans-Jurgen Kreische	22
4	Rainer Ernst	20
5	Henning Frenzel	19

PARTY LIKE IT'S MATCHDAY 99

Germany (and West Germany) have now played more FIFA World Cup finals matches than any other country. Their 2010 semi-final defeat to Spain was their 98th in the competition, one ahead of losing quarter-finalists Brazil. **Germany's third-place play-off win** took their overall tally to 99 matches – comprising 60 wins, 19 draws and 20 losses, with 203 goals scored and 115 conceded.

GERMANY JOIN THE 200 CLUB

Thomas Muller's third-minute goal for Germany against Argentina in their 2010 FIFA World Cup quarter-final, setting his side on the way to a 4-0 victory, also made Germany the second country to complete a double century of World Cup goals. Joachim Low's side ended the 2010 competition on 203 overall, just seven behind Brazil. Germany's first finals goal was scored by Stanislaus Kobierski in a 5-2 victory over Belgium in 1934. Germany's 2010 team became the first since Brazil in 1970 to enjoy three separate four-goal sprees at one FIFA World Cup, by trouncing Australia 4-0, England 4-1 and Argentina 4-0.

DIAMOND STUDS

The Germans have always been in the forefront of technical innovation – as they showed in the 1954 FIFA World Cup final. The pitch in Bern was wet and rain was falling. West Germany were one of the first teams to wear removable studs, so were able to change them at half-time. Their Hungarian opponents wore traditional fixed-studded boots – and Hungary's goalkeeper, Gyula Grosics, slipped on the wet turf as Helmut Rahn scored West Germany's winning goal.

HISTORY MAN

East and West Germany met only once at senior national team level. That was on 22 June 1974, in the FIFA World Cup finals for which the West played hosts. Drawn in the same group, East Germany produced a shock 1-0 win in Hamburg. Both teams progressed to the second round.

GOLDEN WONDER

Germany became the first team to win a major title thanks to the now-discarded golden goal system when they beat the Czech Republic in the Euro 96 final at Wembley. **Oliver Bierhoff**'s equalizer forced extra-time after Patrik Berger scored a penalty for the Czechs. Bierhoff grabbed Germany's winner five minutes into extra-time to end the game and the championship.

THE 1954 "MIRACLE OF BERN"

West Germany's FIFA World Cup victory in 1954 was considered crucial to the country's unity and future economic success. Winning coach Sepp Herberger's biographer wrote: "That was the real founding day of the West German state." The victory was portrayed again by the movie-maker Sonke Wortmann more than 50 years later in a film called *Das Wunder von Bern* ("The Miracle of Bern").

MULLER TIME

Twenty-year-old **Thomas Muller** was one of the undoubted stars of the 2010 FIFA World Cup, despite only having made his international debut in March that year, in a 1-0 defeat to Argentina. At a post-match press conference, he was mistaken for a ballboy by Argentina coach Diego Maradona, but had his revenge with the opening goal in Germany's convincing 4-0 win over the same opposition in the 2010 quarter-finals. Muller made both his Bayern Munich club debut and his first appearance for the German under-21s at the start of the 2009–10 season, but his impressive form in midfield and attack convinced Germany coach Joachim Low to fast-track him to full international status. Muller had played just twice for his country by the time the tournament started, but scored five goals in six games in South Africa. He missed the semi-final defeat to Spain as he was serving a suspension after receiving a yellow card – his second of the tournament – for handball in the Argentina match. Like his (unrelated) namesake Gerd at the 1970 and 1974 FIFA World Cups, Muller's exploits in South Africa came while wearing the number 13 shirt.

"DER BOMBER"

Gerd Muller was the most prolific scorer of the modern era. Neither tall nor graceful, he was quick, strong and had a predator's eye for the net. He also had the temperament to score decisive goals in big games, including the winner in the 1974 FIFA World Cup final, the winner in the semi-final against Poland and two goals in West Germany's 1972 UEFA European Championship final victory over the USSR. He netted 68 goals in 62 appearances for West Germany and remains the leading scorer in the Bundesliga and all-time record scorer for his club, Bayern Munich.

EURO GLORIES

Five German players have been voted European Player of the Year. Gerd Muller was the first West German winner in 1970. He was followed by Franz Beckenbauer in 1972 and 1976, Karl-Heinz Rummenigge in 1980 and 1981 and Lothar Matthaus in 1990. Matthias Sammer, who began his career in East Germany, was the first winner from the reunified Germany, picking up the award in 1996.

A LAHM CALL

Versatile full-back **Philipp Lahm,** who can play on either flank, is the youngest man to captain Germany at a FIFA World Cup. He was 26 when he stood in for the injured Michael Ballack at the 2010 tournament in South Africa, though unable to repeat his spectacular long-range strike against Costa Rica at the 2006 FIFA World Cup on home turf – the opening goal of the competition. Lahm played every minute of every Germany match at the 2006 FIFA World Cup and in qualifiers for the 2010 event, but was finally given a rest for the third-place play-off against Uruguay in South Africa.

DER KAISER

Franz Beckenbauer is widely regarded as the greatest player in German football history. He has also made a huge mark as a FIFA World Cup-winning coach, administrator and organizer. Beckenbauer (born on 11 September 1945) was a 20-year-old attacking wing-half when West Germany reached the 1966 FIFA World Cup final. He later defined the role of attacking sweeper, first in the 1970 FIFA World Cup finals, and then as West Germany won the 1972 UEFA European Championship and the 1974 FIFA World Cup. When West Germany needed a coach in the mid-1980s, they turned to Beckenbauer, despite his lack of experience. He delivered a FIFA World Cup final appearance in 1986, a Euro 88 semi-final and 1990 FIFA World Cup triumph in his final game in charge. He later became president of Bayern Munich, the club he captained to three consecutive European Cup victories between 1974 and 1976. He also led Germany's successful bid for the 2006 FIFA World Cup finals and headed the organizing committee. No wonder he is known as "Der Kaiser" ("the Emperor") for his enormous influence on German football.

MAGICAL MATTHAUS

Lothar Matthaus is Germany's most-capped player. He appeared in five FIFA World Cup finals – 1982, 1986, 1990, 1994 and 1998 – a record for an outfield player. Versatile Matthaus could operate as a defensive midfielder, an attacking midfielder, or as a sweeper. He was a FIFA World Cup winner in 1990, a finalist in 1982 and 1986 and a UEFA European Championship winner in 1980. His record 150 appearances – spread over a 20-year international career – were split 87 for West Germany and 63 for Germany. He also scored 23 goals and was voted top player at the 1990 FIFA World Cup.

TOP CAPS
(West Germany & Germany)

1	Lothar Matthaus	150
2	Miroslav Klose	109
3	Jurgen Klinsmann	108
4	Jurgen Kohler	105
5	Franz Beckenbauer	103
6	Thomas Hassler	101
7	Michael Ballack	98
8	Berti Vogts	96
9	Sepp Maier	95
=	Karl-Heinz Rummenigge	95

TOP SCORERS
(West Germany & Germany)

1	Gerd Muller	68
2	Miroslav Klose	61
3	Jurgen Klinsmann	47
=	Rudi Voller	47
5	Karl-Heinz Rummenigge	45
6	Uwe Seeler	43
7	Michael Ballack	42
=	Lukas Podolski	42
9	Oliver Bierhoff	37
10	Fritz Walter	33

KLOSE ENCOUNTERS

Miroslav Klose drew level with Gerd Muller as the country's most prolific FIFA World Cup scorer when he took his tournament tally to 14 in South Africa in 2010. He had opened his overall account with a hat-trick against Saudi Arabia in 2002, scoring five goals that summer, before winning the Golden Boot with five strikes in his homeland four years later. His four goals at the 2010 FIFA World Cup included the opener against England in the second round and two in the quarter-final against Argentina. Polish-born Klose managed more goals for Germany at the 2010 FIFA World Cup than his meagre three during a disappointing 2009–10 domestic season for Bayern Munich. Klose also holds a rather more unenviable FIFA World Cup record, having been substituted an unlucky 13 times – more than any other player.

SUPER SEELER

All-action centre-forward Uwe Seeler was the top West German player of the late 1950s and '60s. He scored 43 goals in 72 appearances and played, and scored, in four FIFA World Cup finals tournaments (1958, 1962, 1966 and 1970). He also skippered the Germans to the 1966 FIFA World Cup final and the semi-final in 1970. He scored more than 400 league goals in a 19-year career with his home club, Hamburg.

GOLDEN GLOVES

Sepp Maier was at the heart of West Germany's triumphs of the early 1970s, including the 1972 UEFA European Championship and the 1974 FIFA World Cup. He remains West Germany's most-capped goalkeeper, winning 95 caps in an international career lasting from 1965 to 1979. He played his whole club career for Bayern Munich and helped them win the European Cup three times. A car crash in 1979, in which he received life-threatening injuries, ended his playing days, but he went on to become a goalkeeping coach for both Germany and his old club.

STRENGTH IN DIVERSITY

Germany is increasingly cosmopolitan, not only as a country but also as a national football team – as shown by the fact 11 of their 23 squad players at the 2010 FIFA World Cup could have qualified to play for at least one other country instead. These included Polish-born forwards Lukas Podolski and Miroslav Klose, Turkish-descended playmaker **Mesut Ozil**, half-Tunisian midfielder Sami Khedira, Brazilian-born striker Cacau, and full-back Dennis Aogo, son of a Nigerian father.

KEEPING A LOW PROFILE

Until **Joachim Low**, Germany had followed a recent trend of being led into FIFA World Cup finals by former playing legends who had already starred in the competition on the field rather than on the touchline: 1974 FIFA World Cup winners Franz Beckenbauer (coach in 1986 and 1990) and Berti Vogts (1994 and 1998), and 1990 FIFA World Cup winners Rudi Voller (coach in 2002) and Jurgen Klinsmann (2006). Low, Klinsmann's assistant in 2006, then became the first man to coach Germany at a FIFA World Cup without having been to any finals as a player since Jupp Derwall in 1982. Derwall had at least won two international caps during his player career, both in 1954 – but missed out on a call-up for that year's FIFA World Cup, which West Germany won.

OTTO THE FIRST

Germany's first international manager was Otto Nerz, a qualified doctor who played for Mannheim and Tennis Borussia Berlin as an amateur. A strict disciplinarian and an admirer of English football, he led Germany to third place in the 1934 FIFA World Cup finals. They lost 3-1 to Czechoslovakia in the semi-finals, but beat Austria 3-2 in the third-place play-off. The Nazi government sacked Nerz in 1936 after Germany's shock defeat by Norway in the football tournament at the Nazi showcase Berlin Olympics.

GERMANY'S MANAGERS

Otto Nerz	1928–36
Sepp Herberger	1936–64
Helmut Schoen	1964–78
Jupp Derwall	1978–84
Franz Beckenbauer	1984–90
Berti Vogts	1990–98
Erich Ribbeck	1998–2000
Rudi Voller	2000–04
Jurgen Klinsmann	2004–06
Joachim Low	2006–

BONUS BATTLE

Helmut Schon's 1974 FIFA World Cup winners came close to walking out before the finals started. Schon was prepared to send his squad home in a row over bonuses. A last-minute deal was brokered between Franz Beckenbauer and federation vice-president Hermann Neuberger. The vote among the squad went 11-11, but Beckenbauer persuaded the players to accept the DFB's offer. It was a great decision: they beat Holland 2-1 in the final.

GOAL RUSH

Germany's biggest win was 16-0 against Russia in the 1912 Olympic Games in Stockholm. Gottfried Fuchs of Karlsruhe scored ten of the goals, which remains a national team record to this day.

SCHON IN SAARLAND

Helmut Schon is remembered as one of Germany's most successful managers. He started his international coaching career with Saarland, now part of Germany, but which had been made a separate state (with a population of 970,000) after the country's post-war division. Saarland's greatest moment came in the 1954 FIFA World Cup qualifiers, when they beat Norway 3-2 in Oslo to top their qualifying group. They were eventually eliminated by Sepp Herberger's West Germany.

NEW BOYS REUNION

Borussia Dortmund midfielder **Mario Gotze** and Mainz striker Andre Schurrle jointly became the first German football internationals who had been born after the reunification of East and West Germany in 1990, when they appeared as 79th-minute substitutes in a November 2010 friendly against Sweden.

QUICK START

Defender **Arne Friedrich** had made only two Bundesliga appearances when he was selected for his Germany senior debut in a 2-2 draw against Bulgaria in 2002. After switching from full-back to centre-back, he finally scored his first international goal in his 77th appearance for Germany – against Argentina, in a 2010 FIFA World Cup quarter-final. When not playing football, Friedrich is a keen cook and has even published his own book of recipes.

GERMANY'S BRONZE AGES

The 2010 FIFA World Cup third-place play-off between Germany and Uruguay was a rematch of the same tie at the 1970 tournament, when West Germany won 1-0. The German side again took third place 40 years later, thanks to a dramatic 3-2 victory in Port Elizabeth's Nelson Mandela Bay stadium. The result, secured by Sami Khedira's late goal, meant Germany had a record four third-place finishes at FIFA World Cups, having also come third in 1934 and 2006.

SEPP'S SURPRISE

Sepp Herberger (1897–1977) was one of the most influential figures in Germany's football history. He was their longest-serving coach (28 years at the helm) and his legendary status was assured after West Germany surprised odds-on favourites Hungary to win the 1954 FIFA World Cup final – a result credited with dragging the country out of a post-war slump. Herberger took charge in 1936 and led the team into the 1938 FIFA World Cup finals. During the war years he used his influence to try to keep his best players away from the heavy fighting. When organized football resumed in 1949, the federation decided to advertise for a national coach, but Herberger persuaded DFB chief Peco Bauwens to give him back his old job. He had a clause in his contract guaranteeing him a totally free hand in organization and selection policy. Among Herberger's favourite sayings was: "The ball is round and the match lasts 90 minutes. Everything else is just theory."

ITALY

Only Brazil (with five victories) can claim to have won the FIFA World Cup™ more times than Italy. The Azzurri became the first nation to retain the trophy (through back-to-back successes in 1934 and 1938), snatched a surprise win in Spain in 1982, and collected football's most coveted trophy for a fourth time in 2006 following a dramatic penalty shoot-out win over France. Add the 1968 UEFA European Championship success to the mix and few nations can boast a better record. The success story does not end there. Italian clubs have won the European Cup on 11 occasions and the country's domestic league, Serie A, is considered among the strongest in the game. Italy are a true powerhouse of world football.

SECOND TIME LUCKY

The only time a major international tournament has been settled by a replay was Italy's win over Yugoslavia in the 1968 UEFA European Championship. To the delight of their fans, hosts Italy won the second game 2-0, two days after a 1-1 draw in the same Stadio Olimpico in Rome.

OFF THE SPOT

Only England have lost as many FIFA World Cup penalty shoot-outs as Italy – three apiece. **Roberto Baggio**, nicknamed "The Divine Ponytail", was involved in all three of Italy's spot-kick defeats, in 1990, 1994 and 1998. Left-back Antonio Cabrini is the only man to have missed a penalty during normal time in a FIFA World Cup final – the score was 0-0 at the time but, fortunately for him, Italy still beat West Germany 3-1 in 1982.

BLUE BOYS

Internazionale full-back **Davide Santon** became Italy's second-youngest international of the post-war era when he played against Northern Ireland in a June 2009 friendly, aged just 18 years and 155 days and following just 20 first-team appearances for his club. Another Internazionale defender, the richly moustachioed Giuseppe Bergomi, was 42 days younger on making his debut against East Germany in April 1982, just three months before helping Italy win the FIFA World Cup. Even more junior were Casale midfielder Luigi Barbesino, 18 years and 61 days old against Sweden in July 1912, and record-holder Renzo De Vecchi, an AC Milan defender who was aged 16 years and 112 days when lining up against Hungary in May 1910.

RECORD RUN

In two spells as Italy coach, 2004–06 and 2008–10, Marcello Lippi achieved a run of 31 consecutive matches unbeaten – equalling the world record held by Javier Clemente of Spain and Alfio Basile with Argentina.

ROTTEN RETURN

Italy's players were pelted with tomatoes by angry fans when they returned home after crashing out of the 1966 FIFA World Cup at the group stages. After a nervy and unconvincing 2-0 opening victory over Chile, they slumped to a 1-0 defeat to the Soviet Union – and then crashed to a humiliating reverse against North Korea, by the same scoreline.

IN SAFE KEEPING

During World War Two, the Jules Rimet Trophy, the FIFA World Cup – won by Italy in 1938 – was hidden in a shoebox under the bed of football official Ottorino Barassi. He preferred to keep it there, rather than its previous home – a bank in Rome. The trophy was handed back to FIFA, safe and untouched, only when the FIFA World Cup resumed in 1950.

TRIED AND TRUSTED

Marcello Lippi's reliance on his 2006 FIFA World Cup-winning stars for the 2010 campaign meant nine players featured in both squads, including captain Fabio Cannavaro and full-back **Gianluca Zambrotta** who both played most in qualifiers – 810 minutes, or nine out of 10 matches – and then all 270 minutes in South Africa.

TOP DRAW

No team has finished more FIFA World Cup matches level than Italy, who took their tally to 21 with 1-1 draws against both Paraguay and New Zealand in Group F, at the 2010 competition in South Africa. Their first draw had also been 1-1, against Spain in a 1934 quarter-final tie. Italy's Giuseppe Meazza scored the only goal of a replay the following day, and Italy went on to lift the trophy for the first time that year.

TOURNAMENT SPECIALISTS

FIFA WORLD CUP™: 17 appearances – winners 1934, 1938, 1982, 2006
UEFA EUROPEAN CHAMPIONSHIP: 7 appearances – winners 1968
FIRST INTERNATIONAL: Italy 6 France 2 (Milan, 15 May 1910)
BIGGEST WIN: Italy 9 USA 0 (Brentford, London, 17 August 1948 – Olympic Games)
BIGGEST DEFEAT: Hungary 7 Italy 1 (Budapest, 6 April 1924)

FLYING HIGH

Vittorio Pozzo is the only man to have won the FIFA World Cup twice as manager – both times with Italy, in 1934 and 1938 (only two players, Giuseppe Meazza and Giovanni Ferrari, were selected in both finals). Pozzo also led Italy to the 1936 Olympics title. Born in Turin on 2 March 1886, Pozzo learned to love football as a student in England, watching Manchester United. He returned home reluctantly when his family bought him a return ticket for his sister's wedding – and then refused to let him leave Italy again. Pozzo fired up his Italian team ahead of their 1938 semi-final against Brazil by revealing their opponents had already booked their plane to Paris for the final – Italy won 2-1.

CHAMPS TO CHUMPS

Italy's dismal 2010 FIFA World Cup campaign was the worst in their history, despite going into the tournament as defending world champions. Their two draws, and 3-2 defeat to Slovakia, meant they ended a FIFA World Cup without a win for the first time ever. Finishing bottom of their first-round group was also unprecedented. The poor showing must have left 2006 World Cup-winning coach **Marcello Lippi** regretting his decision to resume control in 2008. Immediately after the Slovakia match, which ended the defending champions' run, Lippi insisted the players should not be faulted and he should take all blame. He had already announced his intention to resign after the finals.

ITALY'S NATIONAL COACHES

Vittorio Pozzo	1912, 1924
Augusto Rangone	1925–28
Carlo Carcano	1928–29
Vittorio Pozzo	1929–48
Ferruccio Novo	1949–50
Carlino Beretta	1952–53
Giuseppe Viani	1960
Giovanni Ferrari	1960–61
Giovanni Ferrari/Paolo Mazza	1962
Edmondo Fabbri	1962–66
Helenio Herrera/Ferruccio Valcareggi	1966–67
Ferruccio Valcareggi	1967–74
Fulvio Bernardini	1974–75
Enzo Bearzot	1975–86
Azeglio Vicini	1986–91
Arrigo Sacchi	1991–96
Cesare Maldini	1997–98
Dino Zoff	1998–2000
Giovanni Trapattoni	2000–04
Marcello Lippi	2004–06
Roberto Donadoni	2006–08
Marcello Lippi	2008–10
Cesare Prandelli	2010–

COMEBACK KID

Paolo Rossi was the unlikely hero of Italy's 1982 FIFA World Cup triumph, winning the Golden Boot with six goals – including a memorable hat-trick against Brazil in the second round, and the first of Italy's three goals in their final win over West Germany. But he only just made it to the tournament at all, having completed a two-year ban for his alleged involvement in a betting scandal only six weeks before the start of the tournament.

HELPING HANDS

Goalkeeper Angelo Peruzzi was a 14-year-old ballboy at the 1984 European Cup final between Roma and Liverpool. He made 16 appearances for Roma before playing for Juventus, Internazionale and Lazio as well as 31 times for Italy between 1995 and 2006.

JUVE GOT A FRIEND

Although their performances turned out disappointingly in the end, former Italy under-21s captain **Giorgio Chiellini** might have felt happy just to be lining up alongside legendary Juventus team-mate Fabio Cannavaro in central defence for the 2010 FIFA World Cup. Despite winning his first cap in 2004, Chiellini was left out of the 2006 FIFA World Cup squad and then was inadvertently responsible for Cannavaro missing the 2008 UEFA European Championship with an ankle injury caused by Chiellini's training-ground tackle.

HOME GROWN

More than 80 years separated the first and latest foreign-born players to wear the blue Azzurri shirt. Argentina-born Julio Libonatti made the first of his 17 appearances in a 3-1 defeat by Czechoslovakia in Prague on 28 October 1926. The latest is Sao Paulo-born defensive midfielder Thiago Motta, who even played twice for Brazil's U-23 side at the 2003 CONCACAF Gold Cup. But he was later eligible to switch to Italy due to his Italian grandparents on both his mother's and father's sides. The Internazionale player made his Italy debut in February 2011 and scored his first international goal in his second Italy appearance, against Slovenia the following month.

TOP CAPS

1	Fabio Cannavaro	136
2	Paolo Maldini	126
3	Dino Zoff	112
4	Gianluigi Buffon	104
5	Gianluca Zambrotta	98
6	Giacinto Facchetti	94
7	Alessandro Del Piero	91
8	Franco Baresi	81
=	Giuseppe Bergomi	81
=	Marco Tardelli	81

TOP SCORERS

1	Luigi Riva	35
2	Giuseppe Meazza	33
3	Silvio Piola	30
4	Roberto Baggio	27
=	Alessandro Del Piero	27
6	Alessandro Altobelli	25
=	Adolfo Baloncieri	25
=	Filippo Inzaghi	25
9	Francesco Graziani	23
=	Christian Vieri	23

ZOFF THE SCALE

Goalkeeper **Dino Zoff** set an international record by going 1,142 minutes without conceding a goal between September 1972 and June 1974. Zoff was Italy's captain when they won the 1982 FIFA World Cup – emulating the feat of another Juventus goalkeeper, Gianpiero Combi, who had been the victorious skipper in 1934. Zoff coached Italy to the final of the 2000 UEFA European Championship, which they lost 2-1 to France thanks to an extra-time "golden goal" – then quit a few days later, unhappy following the criticism levelled at him by Italy's prime minister, Silvio Berlusconi.

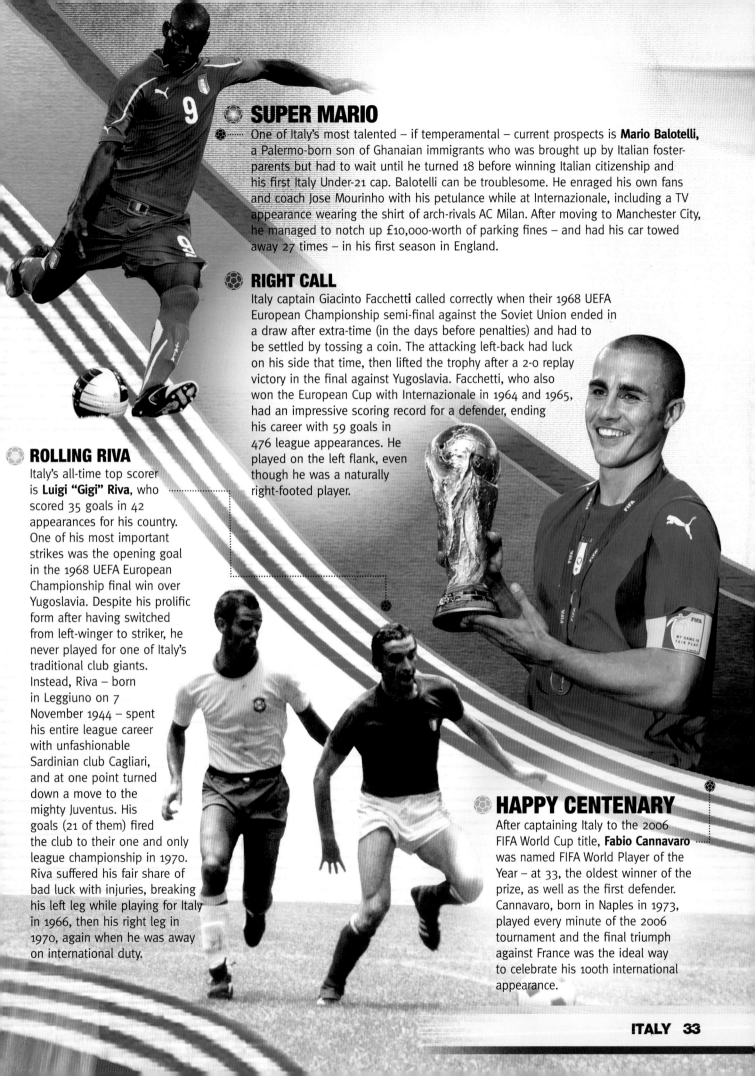

SUPER MARIO

One of Italy's most talented – if temperamental – current prospects is **Mario Balotelli,** a Palermo-born son of Ghanaian immigrants who was brought up by Italian foster-parents but had to wait until he turned 18 before winning Italian citizenship and his first Italy Under-21 cap. Balotelli can be troublesome. He enraged his own fans and coach Jose Mourinho with his petulance while at Internazionale, including a TV appearance wearing the shirt of arch-rivals AC Milan. After moving to Manchester City, he managed to notch up £10,000-worth of parking fines – and had his car towed away 27 times – in his first season in England.

RIGHT CALL

Italy captain Giacinto Facchetti called correctly when their 1968 UEFA European Championship semi-final against the Soviet Union ended in a draw after extra-time (in the days before penalties) and had to be settled by tossing a coin. The attacking left-back had luck on his side that time, then lifted the trophy after a 2-0 replay victory in the final against Yugoslavia. Facchetti, who also won the European Cup with Internazionale in 1964 and 1965, had an impressive scoring record for a defender, ending his career with 59 goals in 476 league appearances. He played on the left flank, even though he was a naturally right-footed player.

ROLLING RIVA

Italy's all-time top scorer is **Luigi "Gigi" Riva**, who scored 35 goals in 42 appearances for his country. One of his most important strikes was the opening goal in the 1968 UEFA European Championship final win over Yugoslavia. Despite his prolific form after having switched from left-winger to striker, he never played for one of Italy's traditional club giants. Instead, Riva – born in Leggiuno on 7 November 1944 – spent his entire league career with unfashionable Sardinian club Cagliari, and at one point turned down a move to the mighty Juventus. His goals (21 of them) fired the club to their one and only league championship in 1970. Riva suffered his fair share of bad luck with injuries, breaking his left leg while playing for Italy in 1966, then his right leg in 1970, again when he was away on international duty.

HAPPY CENTENARY

After captaining Italy to the 2006 FIFA World Cup title, **Fabio Cannavaro** was named FIFA World Player of the Year – at 33, the oldest winner of the prize, as well as the first defender. Cannavaro, born in Naples in 1973, played every minute of the 2006 tournament and the final triumph against France was the ideal way to celebrate his 100th international appearance.

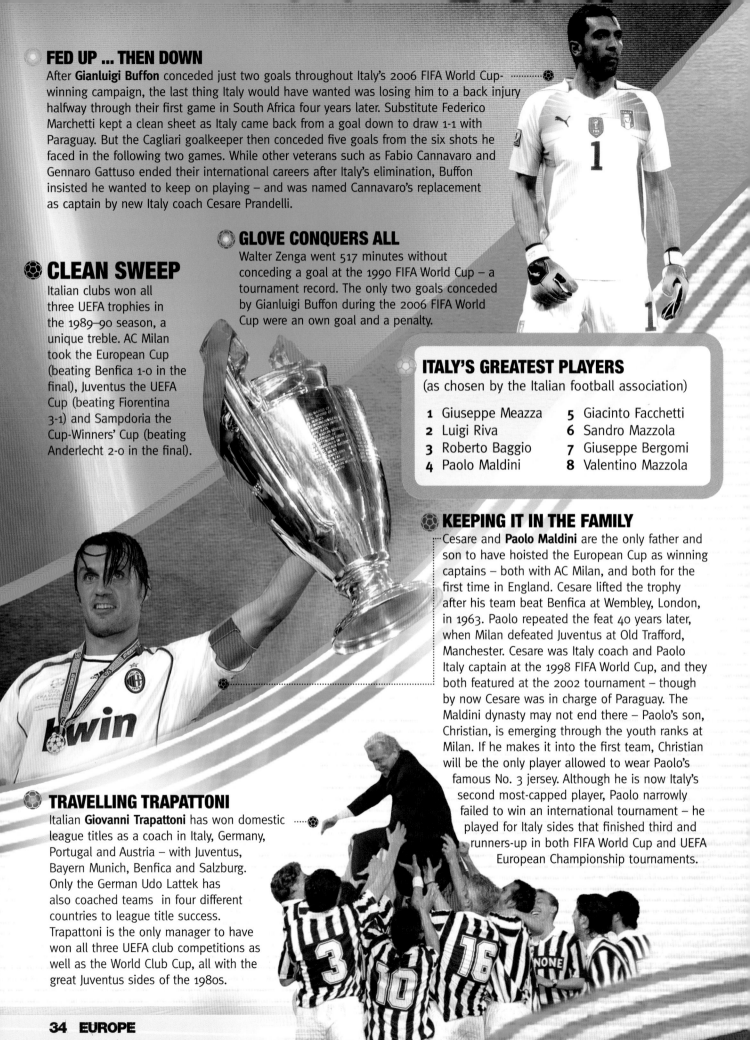

FED UP ... THEN DOWN

After **Gianluigi Buffon** conceded just two goals throughout Italy's 2006 FIFA World Cup-winning campaign, the last thing Italy would have wanted was losing him to a back injury halfway through their first game in South Africa four years later. Substitute Federico Marchetti kept a clean sheet as Italy came back from a goal down to draw 1-1 with Paraguay. But the Cagliari goalkeeper then conceded five goals from the six shots he faced in the following two games. While other veterans such as Fabio Cannavaro and Gennaro Gattuso ended their international careers after Italy's elimination, Buffon insisted he wanted to keep on playing – and was named Cannavaro's replacement as captain by new Italy coach Cesare Prandelli.

GLOVE CONQUERS ALL

Walter Zenga went 517 minutes without conceding a goal at the 1990 FIFA World Cup – a tournament record. The only two goals conceded by Gianluigi Buffon during the 2006 FIFA World Cup were an own goal and a penalty.

CLEAN SWEEP

Italian clubs won all three UEFA trophies in the 1989–90 season, a unique treble. AC Milan took the European Cup (beating Benfica 1-0 in the final), Juventus the UEFA Cup (beating Fiorentina 3-1) and Sampdoria the Cup-Winners' Cup (beating Anderlecht 2-0 in the final).

ITALY'S GREATEST PLAYERS

(as chosen by the Italian football association)

1	Giuseppe Meazza	5	Giacinto Facchetti
2	Luigi Riva	6	Sandro Mazzola
3	Roberto Baggio	7	Giuseppe Bergomi
4	Paolo Maldini	8	Valentino Mazzola

KEEPING IT IN THE FAMILY

Cesare and **Paolo Maldini** are the only father and son to have hoisted the European Cup as winning captains – both with AC Milan, and both for the first time in England. Cesare lifted the trophy after his team beat Benfica at Wembley, London, in 1963. Paolo repeated the feat 40 years later, when Milan defeated Juventus at Old Trafford, Manchester. Cesare was Italy coach and Paolo Italy captain at the 1998 FIFA World Cup, and they both featured at the 2002 tournament – though by now Cesare was in charge of Paraguay. The Maldini dynasty may not end there – Paolo's son, Christian, is emerging through the youth ranks at Milan. If he makes it into the first team, Christian will be the only player allowed to wear Paolo's famous No. 3 jersey. Although he is now Italy's second most-capped player, Paolo narrowly failed to win an international tournament – he played for Italy sides that finished third and runners-up in both FIFA World Cup and UEFA European Championship tournaments.

TRAVELLING TRAPATTONI

Italian **Giovanni Trapattoni** has won domestic league titles as a coach in Italy, Germany, Portugal and Austria – with Juventus, Bayern Munich, Benfica and Salzburg. Only the German Udo Lattek has also coached teams in four different countries to league title success. Trapattoni is the only manager to have won all three UEFA club competitions as well as the World Club Cup, all with the great Juventus sides of the 1980s.

PRANDELLI'S PLEDGE

After agreeing to take over from Marcello Lippi as Italy coach after the 2010 FIFA World Cup, ex-Fiorentina boss **Cesare Prandelli** did travel to Africa during the tournament – but watching the football was not his only aim. He watched Italy play New Zealand on television in Zanzibar, Tanzania, where he and his daughter were opening a school in memory of Prandelli's wife Manuela, who died of cancer three years earlier. Prandelli's first competitive home match in charge of Italy, in September 2010, was in the familiar surroundings of Florence, where he had just spent five popular years as Fiorentina coach. His new team celebrated in style, beating the Faroe Islands 5-0. Alongside Prandelli's appointment, the Italian federation had handed technical roles to former playing greats Roberto Baggio and Gianni Rivera and ex-Italy and AC Milan manager Arrigo Sacchi.

MEDAL COLLECTORS

Giovanni Ferrari not only enjoys the status of having won both the 1934 and 1938 FIFA World Cups with Italy, he also shares the record for most Serie A titles, with eight triumphs. Five were with Juventus, two with Internazionale and one with Bologna. He shares the record of eight league championship medals with Virginio Rosetta, twice with Pro Vercelli and six times with Juventus, and Giuseppe Furino, all with Juventus.

ITALIAN LEAGUE TITLES

Juventus	27	Lazio	2
Internazionale	18	Napoli	2
AC Milan	18	Cagliari	1
Genoa	9	Casale	1
Bologna	7	Hellas Verona	1
Pro Vercelli	7	Novese	1
Torino	7	Sampdoria	1
Roma	3	Spezia	1
Fiorentina	2		

GRAND OLD TEAM TO PLAY FOR

Every Italian FIFA World Cup squad has featured at least one Juventus player. The Turin team, known as the "Grand Old Lady" of Italian club football, were relegated a division in 2006 after being found guilty of match-fixing – and, as a result, were forced to endure their first season outside the top division since the club's foundation in 1897. Their 51 trophies are an Italian club record – and, in 1985, they became the first team to have won the European, UEFA and Cup-Winners' Cups.

BEEFING UP

The stadium shared by AC Milan and Internazionale is popularly known as San Siro, after the district in which it is located. Its official title, however, is Stadio **Giuseppe Meazza**, named after the star inside-forward on the pitch and dance enthusiast off it who played for both clubs as well as Italy's 1934 and 1938 FIFA World Cup-winning sides. Meazza, born in Milan on 23 August 1910, was first spotted by an Inter scout while playing keepy-uppy in the street with a ball made of rags – but was so thin he had to be fattened up with plenty of steaks. His last goal for Italy was a penalty in the 1938 World Cup semi-final against Brazil – taken while trying to pull up his shorts, whose elastic had broken.

DOUBLE AGENTS

Former Brazil international Leonardo's appointment as Internazionale coach in December 2010 made him the fifth man to have managed both major Milan clubs – all of them taking the helm at AC first. He followed in the footsteps of Italians Giuseppe Bigogno (at Milan from 1946 to 1949, then at Inter in 1958), Ilario Castagner (Milan 1982–84, Inter 1984–85), Giovanni Trapattoni (Milan 1975–76, Inter 1986–91) and Alberto Zaccheroni (Milan 1998–2001, Inter 2003–04).

TRAGIC TORINO

Torino were Italy's most successful club side when their first-team squad was wiped out in an air crash at Superga, above Turin, on 4 May 1949. The club has only won the Serie A title once since then, in the 1976–77 season. Among the victims was star forward Valentino Mazzola, who had gone along on the trip despite being ill. His son **Sandro Mazzola**, only six at the time of the disaster, went on to star in the Italy teams that won the 1968 UEFA European Championship and finished as FIFA World Cup runners-up two years later.

NETHERLANDS

The walled banks of orange-shirted Netherlands fans may have become a regular feature at the world's major football tournaments, but that has not always been the case. It wasn't until the 1970s, with Johan Cruyff and his team's spectacular brand of Total Football, that the country possessed a side worthy of the modern legend. They won the UEFA European Championship in 1988 and have regularly challenged for the game's major honours.

NETHERLANDS MANAGERS (SINCE 1980)

Jan Zwartkruis	1978–81
Rob Baan	1981
Kees Rijvers	1981–84
Rinus Michels	1984–85
Leo Beenhakker	1985–86
Rinus Michels	1986–88
Thijs Libregts	1988–90
Nol de Ruiter	1990
Leo Beenhakker	1990
Rinus Michels	1990–92
Dick Advocaat	1992–95
Guus Hiddink	1995–98
Frank Rijkaard	1998–2000
Louis van Gaal	2000–02
Dick Advocaat	2002–04
Marco van Basten	2004–08
Bert van Marwijk	2008–

MICHELS THE MASTER

Rinus Michels (1928–2005) was named FIFA's Coach of the Century in 1999 for his achievements with the Netherlands and Ajax. The former Ajax and Netherlands striker took over the manager's job at his old club in 1965 and began creating the side that would dominate European football in the early 1970s. Michels built the team around Johan Cruyff – as he later did with the national side – and introduced the concept known as "Total Football". He moved to Barcelona after Ajax's 1971 European Cup victory, but he was called back to mastermind the Netherlands' 1974 FIFA World Cup bid. Nicknamed "The General", he was known as a disciplinarian who could impose order on the many different factions within the Dutch dressing room. Michels used that skill to great effect after taking over the national team again for their 1988 UEFA European Championship campaign. In the finals, the Dutch beat England and the Republic of Ireland to reach the last four, then knocked out hosts West Germany, before beating the Soviet Union 2-0 in the final. Michels tookcharge for a third spell as manager when the Netherlands reached the semi-finals of Euro 92. He retired straight after the tournament.

CRUYFF THE MAGICIAN

Johan Cruyff's footballing achievements have made him the most famous living Dutchman. Cruyff (born in Amsterdam on 25 April 1947) was the catalyst for the rise of both Ajax and the national team. As one Dutch paper wrote before the 1974 FIFA World Cup final: "Cruyff woke up the Netherlands and took us to a world-class level." His great opponent, Franz Beckenbauer, said: "He is the best player to have come from Europe." Cruyff joined Ajax as a ten-year-old and made his league debut at 17. He led them to eight championships and the European Cup three years in a row. He and coach Rinus Michels also developed the style of playing known as "Total Football", which became a trademark for club and country. Cruyff made his national debut, against Hungary, on 7 September 1966. He scored 33 goals in 48 appearances and captained his country 33 times. He was named Player of the Tournament in the 1974 FIFA World Cup finals and was voted European Player of the Year three times.

NETHERLANDS' HOT STREAK

Going into the 2010 FIFA World Cup final, the Netherlands had won all 14 games of their campaign – eight in qualifying and six in South Africa. This run of 14 consecutive competitive victories, dating back to September 2008, equalled a record set by France from September 2002 to June 2004. The Dutch route to the final was also the ninth time a team got there with a 100 per cent record in games up to and including the semi-final. Under captain **Giovanni van**  **Bronckhorst** (left) and with **Wesley Sneijder** in top form, the Netherlands matched Brazil's 2002 FIFA World Cup achievement of six victories in a row. Their run to the final also extended their unbeaten run to a Dutch record of 25 games. The Netherlands' last defeat before the final was to Australia, 2-1 in a September 2008 friendly.

AMSTERDAM ARENA

Construction work on the Netherlands' major venue, started in 1993. The project cost £100m and the stadium was opened on 14 August 1996. It has been Ajax's home ground ever since and was also one of the main venues when the Netherlands co-hosted Euro 2000. The unusual spelling was adopted after a complaint by a nightclub of the same name.

THE MISSING LINK

Johan Cruyff remains one of the most influential figures in Dutch football. His negotiations with the Dutch Federation to become national coach before the 1994 FIFA World Cup finals broke down and he twice refused offers by Van Basten to step down and become his assistant.

LUCKY RINUS

In 1974, Rinus Michels succeeded Frantisek Fadrhonc, the Czech who had steered the Dutch through the FIFA World Cup qualifiers, as the Netherlands coach with Fadrhonc becoming his assistant. The Netherlands were fortunate to qualify on goal difference. Belgium's Jan Verheyen had a "winner" disallowed for offside in the final qualifier in Amsterdam. TV replays showed the Russian referee had made a mistake. Had the goal stood, Belgium would have advanced at the Netherllands' expense.

GOALS GALORE

Only four players have scored five goals in a game for the Netherlands: Jan Vos, as Finland were crushed 9-0 in July 1912; Leen  Vente, in a 9-3 defeat of Belgium in March 1934; **John Bosman**, in an 8-0 home trouncing of Cyprus in October 1987; and Marco Van Basten, in an 8-0 win in Malta in December 1990. Bosman scored three separate hat-tricks for the Dutch, as did Mannes Francken, Beb Bakhuys and Faas Wilkes. Two of Wilkes' trebles were scored in 1946 – the third came a full 13 years later.

PATIENT VAN BASTEN

The Netherlands manager's job is one of the most precarious in world football. The longest-serving manager in the modern era is Marco van Basten. He was appointed on 29 July 2004 and resigned in June 2008 after the Netherlands' quarter-final elimination from Euro 2008.

VAN BASTEN'S TOURNAMENT

Marco van Basten was the hero of the Netherlands'  1988 UEFA European Championship success. He netted a hat-trick to see off England in the group games, scored a semi-final winner against West Germany, and then cracked a spectacular flying volley to clinch a 2-0 victory over the Soviet Union in the final. The Dutch forward also starred in Italy's Serie A with AC Milan, and was twice the league's top scorer before persistent ankle trouble ended his career prematurely.

HERO HAPPEL

Ernst Happel is second only to Rinus Michels for his coaching achievements with Dutch teams. The former Austria defender made history by steering Feyenoord to the European Cup in 1970 – the first Dutch side to win the trophy. He was drafted in to coach the Netherlands at the 1978 FIFA World Cup finals after guiding Belgian side Brugge to the European Cup final. In Johan Cruyff's absence, Happel drew the best from Ruud Krol, Johan Neeskens and Arie Haan as the Netherlands reached the final before losing in extra-time to Argentina in Buenos Aires.

HANGING AROUND

Sander Boschker waited a long time for his full introduction to international football, but set two Dutch records when finally coming on as a second-half substitute against Ghana in a June 2010 friendly. At the age of 39 years and 256 days, he was not only the oldest Dutchman to win his first cap – but also the oldest Dutch international ever. That remains his only cap . . . so far.

FLYING FEAR DENIED BERGKAMP MORE CAPS

Dennis Bergkamp would have won many more than 79 caps, but for his fear of flying. Bergkamp refused to board aircraft after the Netherlands squad were involved in a bomb hoax incident during the 1994 FIFA World Cup in the United States. He missed away games for the Netherlands and his clubs unless he could reach them by road, rail or boat.

DIFFERENT SIDES OF SNEIJDER

Wesley Sneijder was hoping to achieve an unprecedented quintuple when his Netherlands team took on Spain in the 2010 FIFA World Cup final. No footballer had ever before won the FIFA World Cup in the same season as a domestic league and cup double and the UEFA Champions League or European Cup – let alone adding the FIFA World Cup Golden Boot. Sneijder won the 2009–10 treble with his club side, Internazionale, before only just missing out on the FIFA World Cup and the Golden Boot. Despite his FIFA World Cup final heartbreak, Sneijder did enjoy some romantic solace six days after defeat to Spain, when he married Dutch actress and TV presenter Yolanthe Cabau van Kasbergen.

"NETHERLANDS ON TOUR"

The great Milan side of the late 1980s were often known as "Netherlands on tour" because of their Dutch stars – Ruud Gullit, Marco van Basten and Frank Rijkaard. All three players were key figures in the Netherlands' 1988 UEFA European Championship victory, and they were equally important in Milan's 1989 and 1990 European Cup wins. Gullit and van Basten both scored twice in the 1989 victory over Steaua Bucharest. Rijkaard scored the only goal against Benfica a year later.

NEESKENS'S EARLY GOAL

The Netherlands took a first-minute lead in the 1974 World Cup without a West German player having touched the ball. The Dutch built a move of 14 passes from the kick-off and Johan Cruyff was tripped in the box by Uli Hoeness. Johan Neeskens converted the first penalty in a World Cup final history . . . but they still went on to lose.

NETHERLANDS' DOUBLE LOSERS

Nine Netherlands players were on the losing side in both the 1974 (2-1 to West Germany) and 1978 (3-1 to Argentina) FIFA World Cup finals. Jan Jongbloed, Ruud Krol, Wim Jansen, Arie Haan, Johan Neeskens, Johnny Rep and Rob Rensenbrink started both games. Wim Suurbier started in 1974 and was a substitute in 1978. Rene Van der Kerkhof was a sub in 1974 and started in 1978.

KEEPING IN WITH THE IN–LAWS

Midfield enforcer **Mark van Bommel** was left out of coach Marco van Basten's Dutch squad for the 2008 UEFA European Championship, but was ever-present at the 2010 FIFA World Cup. Van Basten's replacement Bert van Marwijk is his father-in-law: van Bommel being married to van Marwijk's daughter Andra.

THE WINNING CAPTAIN

With his distinctive dreadlocks, Ruud Gullit cut a swathe through world football through the 1980s and '90s. Twice a European Cup winner with AC Milan and a former European Footballer of the Year, he will always be remembered fondly by the Dutch fans as being the first man in a Netherlands shirt to lift a major trophy – the 1988 UEFA European Championship.

DE BOER BOYS SET RECORD

Twins Frank and Ronald De Boer hold the record for the most games played by brothers together for the Netherlands. Frank won 112 caps, while Ronald won 67.

TOP SCORERS

1	Patrick Kluivert	40
2	Dennis Bergkamp	37
3	Ruud van Nistelrooy	35
=	Faas Wilkes	35
5	Johann Cruyff	33
=	Abe Lenstra	33
7	Bep Bakhuys	28
8	Klaas-Jan Huntelaar	26
=	Kick Smit	26
10	Marco van Basten	24

TOP CAPS

1	Edwin Van der Sar	130
2	Frank De Boer	112
3	Gio Van Bronckhorst	106
4	Philip Cocu	101
5	Rafael van der Vaart	90
6	Clarence Seedorf	87
7	Marc Overmars	86
8	Aaron Winter	84
9	Ruud Krol	83
10	Dennis Bergkamp	79
=	Patrick Kluivert	79

BRAVING THE PAIN

Dutch defender **Khalid Boulahrouz** insisted on playing in his country's 2008 UEFA European Championship quarter-final against Russia despite the death of his prematurely-born baby daughter Anissa just days earlier. He and his team-mates all wore black armbands in her honour during the game.

NETHERLANDS' EURO STARS

Three Dutch players have won the European Footballer of the Year award: Johan Cruyff, Ruud Gullit and Marco Van Basten. Cruyff picked up the award in 1971, 1973 and 1974; Gullit was honoured in 1987, and Van Basten was chosen in 1988, 1989 and 1992.

SIXTH SENSE

Maarten Stekelenburg, Edwin van der Sar's successor as the Netherlands' first-choice goalkeeper, impressed many with his performances at the 2010 FIFA World Cup, conceding just six goals in seven games – two of them penalties. His rise is all the more startling because he is deaf in one ear. He also has the unenviable distinction of being the first Dutch international goalkeeper to be shown a red card. On 6 September 2008, in a 2-1 friendly defeat against Australia in Eindhoven, he was sent off for fouling Josh Kennedy.

EARLY DAYS

The Netherlands played their first international against Belgium in Brussels on 30 April 1905. Eddy de Neve scored all the goals in the Netherlands' 4-1 win. The Dutch and their Belgian neighbours have been arch-rivals ever since.

ALL-TIME LEADING SCORER

Born in Amsterdam on 1 July 1976, centre-forward Patrick Kluivert made his Netherlands debut in 1994. In the following ten years he made 79 appearances for the national side, scoring an all-time Dutch record 40 goals.

NETHERLANDS – MODERN GREATS

The Netherlands have been one of the strongest nations in world football for the past 35 years. The Dutch "Total Football" team – led by Johan Cruyff – reached the 1974 FIFA World Cup final, only to lose 2-1 to West Germany. Four years later, the Dutch lost the final against Argentina, 3-1 in extra-time in Buenos Aires. In between, they reached the UEFA European Championship semi-finals in 1976. Coach Rinus Michels steered the Netherlands to their one major honour, in 1988, when they beat the Soviet Union 2-0 in the UEFA European Championship final. They had gained revenge over West Germany for the 1974 defeat by winning 2-1 in the semi-finals. Before reaching the 2010 FIFA World Cup final, the Dutch suffered a series of semi-final setbacks: they lost the 1998 FIFA World Cup semi-final on penalties to Brazil, and were also beaten in UEFA European Championship semi-finals in 1992, 2000 and 2004.

"TOTAL FOOTBALL"

The Netherlands' 1974 FIFA World Cup finalists played a revolutionary style of football described as "Total Football" ("totaalvoetbal"), which Rinus Michels and Johan Cruyff had pioneered at Ajax. The game was based on quick passing and fluid movement, with players frequently interchanging positions. Hence full-backs Wim Suurbier and Ruud Krol often appeared in attack and midfielder Johan Neeskens was a frequent scorer with well-timed breaks from midfield.

DUTCH CLOGS

The Netherlands became the first team to be shown as many as nine cards during a single FIFA World Cup match, when they received eight yellows, including a lenient one for **Nigel de Jong**'s chest-high challenge on Xabi Alonso, and a red during the 2010 final against Spain. The Netherlands were also involved in the FIFA World Cup game with the most cards: their second-round defeat to Portugal four years earlier, when 20 cards were shown in total – 16 yellows and four reds.

NETHERLANDS SO CLOSE

The Netherlands came within a post's width of winning the 1978 FIFA World Cup final. A Rob Rensenbrink shot bounced off an upright in the last minute of normal time. It was 1-1 after 90 minutes and Argentina won 3-1 in extra-time, shattering Dutch final dreams for the second FIFA World Cup in a row.

PENALTY PLAGUE

Missed penalties have become a nightmare for the Netherlands, causing their downfall in several major tournaments. The jinx started in the Euro 92 semi-final when Peter Schmeichel saved Marco van Basten's kick, enabling Denmark to win the penalty shoot-out. the Netherlands lost their Euro 96 quarter-final to France 5-4 on penalties and, two years later, went down 4-2 to Brazil in a FIFA World Cup semi-final shoot-out. Worse followed when the Dutch co-hosted Euro 2000. They missed two penalties in normal time in the semi-final against Italy. Then Italy keeper Francesco Toldo saved two spot-kicks to eliminate the Dutch in the shoot-out.

KEY PLAYER

Maintaining harmony has often been a tricky task for Dutch coaches at major international tournaments – but Bert Van Marwijk managed to do so at the 2010 FIFA World Cup, despite rumoured tension between several of his star starters. When not conducting his team from the touchline, Van Marwijk could occasionally be found playing the piano in the lobby of the squad's Johannesburg hotel.

VAN DER SAR TOPS THE LOT

Goalkeeper **Edwin van der Sar** (born in Voorhout, on 29 October 1970) is the Netherlands' most-capped player, having made 130 appearances for the national side. He joined Ajax in 1990 and helped them win the European Cup five years later. He made his Netherlands debut on 7 June 1995, against Belarus, and was their first-choice keeper for 13 years. He quit international football after the Netherlands' elimination at Euro 2008, but new coach Bert van Marwijk persuaded him to return briefly after injuries to his successors, Maarten Stekelenburg and Henk Timmer. Van der Sar has also won the UEFA Champions League with Manchester United, as well as spending spells with Juventus and Fulham.

GOING DUTCH FULL-TIME

Professionalism was not introduced into Dutch football until 1954. The Netherlands' emergence as a major power came even later, after Ajax and Feyenoord decided to go full-time professional in the early 1960s. Until then, even stars such as Ajax left winger Piet Keizer – who worked in a tailor's – had part-time jobs outside the game.

BEST AND WORST

The Netherlands' record win is 9-0, which they have achieved twice. The first time came against Finland at the Stockholm Olympics on 4 July 1912. The second time was when they thrashed Norway in a FIFA World Cup qualifier in Rotterdam on 1 November 1972. The Dutch suffered their worst defeat on 21 December 1907, when they lost 12-2 to England's amateurs at Darlington!

VAART LOVER

Attacking midfielder Rafael van der Vaart started the 2010 FIFA World Cup final on the Dutch substitutes' bench – but finished it not only as a replacement captain for Giovanni van Bronckhorst but also filling in as an emergency centre-back following the dismissal of John Heitinga. Tottenham Hotspur's subsequent summer signing, who grew up living what he called "the gypsy life" in a caravan, was one of the Netherlands' most admired and exciting players – though perhaps outperformed in the glamour stakes by his model and TV presenter wife Sylvie.

⚽ SPAIN

Spain is home to some of the strongest club sides in Europe (boasting a total of 13 European Cup/UEFA Champions Leagues between them) and has produced some of the biggest names in the sport. For years, as major tournament failures became the depressing norm (the 1964 UEFA European Championship triumph apart), *La Roja* were considered the world game's major underachievers. But that started to change in 2008, in the UEFA European Championship final, when Spain beat Germany 1-0 to give the country its first taste of international success for 44 years and a first-ever top position in the Coca-Cola/FIFA World Rankings. Fast forward to 2010, and the 1-0 defeat of Holland in the FIFA World Cup™ final cemented Spain's place as the world's No. 1 football nation.

⚽ THREE AND EASY

Only three players have scored for Spain in three separate FIFA World Cup final tournaments – Raul (in 1998, 2002 and 2006), Julio Salinas (1986, 1990 and 1994) and Fernando Hierro (1994, 1998 and 2002). The latter is also Spain's third top scorer despite spending a large part of his career as a defender.

⚽ DOUBLING UP

Spain's 2010 FIFA World Cup triumph made them the first country since West Germany, in 1974, to lift the trophy as the reigning European champions. When France combined the two titles, they did it the other way around, by winning the 1998 FIFA World Cup and then the UEFA European Championship two years later.

⚽ KEEPING IT CLEAN

Spanish goalkeeper **Iker Casillas** kept clean sheets in all seven of his country's knockout-round matches across the 2008 UEFA European Championship and the 2010 FIFA World Cup. The team scored four goals in three games at Euro 2008 and four in four in South Africa.

GROUNDS FOR APPEAL

No single country has provided more venues when hosting a FIFA World Cup finals than the 17 stadiums – in 14 cities – used by Spain in 1982. The 2002 tournament was played at 20 different venues but ten were in Japan and ten in South Korea. The 1982 competition was the first FIFA World Cup to be expanded from 16 to 24 teams. The final was played in Madrid's Estadio Santiago Bernabeu.

RIGHT SAID FRED

When Spain came back from 2-0 and then 3-2 down to win 4-3 in Madrid in May 1929, they became the first non-British team to beat England. Spain's victory, in the Estadio Metropolitano, came with the help of their English coach Fred Pentland, who had moved to Spain in 1920. He had most success with Athletic Bilbao, leading them to league and cup doubles in 1930 and 1931 – and inflicting Barcelona's worst-ever defeat, a 12-1 rout in 1931.

SWOON IN JUNE

The date 22 June has been an unfortunate one for Spain, especially when it comes to penalty shoot-outs. They lost on spot-kicks on this date to Belgium in the 1986 FIFA World Cup, England in the 1996 UEFA European Championship and South Korea in the 2002 World Cup. But their luck changed on 22 June 2008, when they beat Italy on penalties in the quarter-finals of the UEFA European Championship, after the game had ended in a 0-0 draw. The win also marked Spain's first victory over Italy in a competitive match since 1920.

AFTER THE PARTY

Newly-crowned world champions Spain slumped to a surprise 4-0 defeat by Portugal in a November 2010 friendly despite starting with 10 of the 11 players who began the 2010 FIFA Cup final against the Netherlands, with only **David Silva** coming in for Pedro. The loss was Spain's heaviest since going down 6-2 at home to Scotland in 1963. Manager Vicente del Bosque's Spanish team had lost also 4-1 to Argentina in September 2010. That was the first time the reigning world champions had conceded four goals in one game since Brazil lost 5-1 to Belgium in 1963.

MAJOR TOURNAMENTS

FIFA WORLD CUP™:
13 appearances – winners 2010

UEFA EUROPEAN CHAMPIONSHIP:
Eight appearances – winners 1964, 2008

FIRST INTERNATIONAL:
Spain 1 Denmark 0 (Brussels, Belgium, 28 August 1920)

BIGGEST WIN:
Spain 13 Bulgaria 0 (Madrid, 21 May 1933)

BIGGEST DEFEAT:
Italy 7 Spain 1 (Amsterdam, Holland 4 June 1928); England 7 Spain 1 (London, England, 9 December 1931)

RED ALERT

Spain refused to play in the first UEFA European Championship in 1960, in protest at having to travel to the Soviet Union, a Communist country. But they changed their minds four years later, not only hosting the tournament but also winning it – by beating the visiting Soviets 2-1 in the final. Spain were captained by Fernando Olivella and managed by Jose Villalonga, who had been the first coach to win the European Cup, with Real Madrid in 1956.

WISE HEAD, OLD SHOULDERS

Luis Aragones became the oldest coach to win the UEFA European Championship when Spain won the 2008 tournament, a month short of his 70th birthday. Aragones, a former centre-forward and known only as "Luis" during his playing days, had lined up for Spain in the run-up to the 1964 finals, but had to watch the team win the competition from the sidelines after being left out of the squad. During his time as national coach between 2004 and 2008, the so-called "Wise Man of Hortaleza" won more matches than any other Spanish boss – 38. Aragones, born in Hortaleza, Madrid on 28 July 1938, spent most of his playing career with Atletico Madrid, where he was surprisingly appointed as club coach (at the surprisingly young age of 36) immediately after retiring in 1974.

TORRES! TORRES!

Fernando Torres originally wanted to be a goalkeeper as a child, before becoming a striker. Torres, born in Madrid on 20 March 1984, was only 19 when he was made captain of his boyhood heroes Atletico Madrid. He has a knack for scoring the only goal in tournament finals – most famously in the 2008 UEFA European Championship, for Spain against Germany in Vienna. He had already achieved the feat in the Under-16 UEFA European Championships in 2001 and for the Under-19s the following year. Torres became the most expensive Spanish footballer ever when Chelsea paid €58.5million to sign him from fellow English club Liverpool in January 2011 – eight months after his international strike partner David Villa cost Barcelona €40million in joining from Valencia.

TOP CAPS

1	Andoni Zubizarreta	126
2	Iker Casillas	119
3	Raul	102
4	Xavi	101
5	Carles Puyol	94
6	Fernando Hierro	89
7	Xabi Alonso	84
=	Fernando Torres	84
9	Jose Antonio Camacho	81
10	Rafael Gordillo	75

TOP SCORERS

1	David Villa	46
2	Raul	44
3	Fernando Hierro	29
4	Fernando Morientes	27
5	Emilio Butragueno	26
=	Fernando Torres	26
7	Alfredo Di Stefano	23
=	Julio Salinas	23
9	Michel	21
10	Telmo Zarra	20

HAPPY HERNANDEZ

Relentlessly precise passer **Xavi Hernandez** has proved himself a more than worthy heir to Pep Guardiola at the heart of the Barcelona and Spain midfields. As well as winning the UEFA Champions League with his club in 2006 and 2009, he was voted Player of the Tournament when Spain won the 2008 UEFA European Championship and also starred as they claimed the FIFA World Cup crown two years later. Xavi finished third in the 2010 FIFA Ballon d'Or voting, behind club mates Lionel Messi and Andres Iniesta. Yet he came close to leaving Barcelona for Italy's AC Milan when aged just 17 – though Xavi was not keen on the proposed move and later expressed his relief at staying in Spain.

VICTORY MARCH

Centre-back Carlos Marchena became the first footballer to go 50 internationals in a row unbeaten, when he played in Spain's 3-2 victory over Saudi Arabia in May 2009 – one more than Brazil's 1950s and 1960s winger Garrincha. Marchena was a member of Spain's successful 2010 FIFA World Cup squad, ending the tournament on 54 consecutive internationals without defeat. Marchena's 57-game unbeaten run came to an end when Argentina beat Spain 4-1 in September 2010.

BEST CAS SCENARIO

No man has captained Spain more often than **Iker Casillas**, who took his appearances with the armband to 54 while leading his country to glory in the 2010 FIFA World Cup final against Holland. The previous record of 50 was also held by a goalkeeper, Andoni Zubizarreta, who appeared for Spain at the 1986, 1990, 1994 and 1998 FIFA World Cups. Casillas broke the record in the second-round 1-0 win over Portugal, in Cape Town.

VILLA FILLS HIS BOOTS

David Villa became Spain's all-time top scorer in FIFA World Cups with his first-round goal against Chile, his sixth overall across the 2006 and 2010 tournaments – then knockout-round strikes against Portugal and Paraguay took his World Cup tally to eight. Emilio Butragueno, Fernando Hierro, Fernando Morientes and Raul had each scored five FIFA World Cup goals for Spain. Villa also became the first Spaniard to miss a penalty in a FIFA World Cup match, when he missed the chance of a hat-trick against Honduras by shooting his spot-kick wide. Spain had scored their previous 14 FIFA World Cup penalties, not counting shoot-outs. Villa pulled ahead of Raul in Spain's all-time scoring stakes with a brace against the Czech Republic in March 2011.

THE RAUL THING

Former Real Madrid striker **Raul Gonzalez Blanco** – known as Raul – is not only Spain's most prolific international goalscorer, with 44 goals in 102 games, he also tops the scoring charts for both the European Cup, with 66 goals, and Real Madrid – after passing Alfredo Di Stefano's tally of 309 club goals during the 2008–09 season. Raul scored seven goals for Spain in just four days in March 1999 – four in a 9-0 thrashing of Austria, followed by three as San Marino were crushed 6-0, but he was controversially left out of Spain's Euro 2008-winning squad by coach Luis Aragones, who condemned the player's lack of success in big international tournaments. Raul also missed out on FIFA World Cup glory in 2010 and, as a club free agent, joined German club Schalke 04 a few weeks after the FIFA World Cup final. Football and family are closely entwined for the man born in Madrid on 27 June 1977 – he celebrates each goal by kissing his wedding ring, a gesture reserved for his wife, Mamen Sanz.

GIFT OF THE FAB

Arsenal's **Cesc Fabregas** became Spain's youngest-ever FIFA World Cup player – and the country's youngest international for 70 years – when he came on as a substitute against Ukraine at the 2006 FIFA World Cup aged 19 years 41 days. Despite wearing the name "Fabregas" on the back of his Arsenal shirt, he is better known in Spain as simply "Cesc".

TRI-NATIONS

Ladislav Kubala played for not one, not two, but three different countries – though he never appeared in the finals of a major international tournament. Despite being born in Budapest on 10 June 1927, he made his international debut for Czechoslovakia in 1946 – winning five more caps for the country of his parents' birth. He then appeared three times for birthplace Hungary after moving back to the country in 1948, before playing 19 games for Spain after leaving Hungary as a refugee and securing a transfer to Barcelona in 1951.

FIT FOR PURPOSE

Luis Suarez played through injury for Spain in the 1964 UEFA European Championship final – luckily for his team-mates, since he set up both goals in a 2-1 triumph. He was named European Footballer of the Year in 1960 – the only Spanish-born player to have taken the prize.

⚽ TREASURE CHEST

The Spanish first division goalkeeper who concedes the fewest goals per game each season is awarded the Zamora Trophy. This is named after legendary keeper **Ricardo Zamora**, who played 46 times for Spain between 1920 and 1936 – including the legendary 4-3 win over England in Madrid in 1929. Zamora was the first Spanish star to play for both Barcelona and Real Madrid. Later he was league title-winning coach of ... Atletico Madrid.

⚽ LUCKY JUAN

Only one player has failed to score in a FIFA World Cup penalty shoot-out with a spot-kick that would have won the game had it gone in: Spain's Juan Carlos Valeron, whose effort went wide against Republic of Ireland in 2002. The shoot-out score was 2-1 in Spain's favour, with just an Irish attempt to follow, when he missed – but his team went on to win anyway.

⚽ LEADING LIGHTS

Spain have become experts in holding on to a lead, winning 43 games in a row having opened the scoring – including all six of their victories at the 2010 FIFA World Cup. The last team to go a goal down to Spain but end up winning the game were Northern Ireland, securing a 3-2 success in a Euro 2008 qualifier in September 2006.

⚽ SPANISH LEAGUE CHAMPIONSHIPS

Real Madrid	**31**
Barcelona	**21**
Atletico Madrid	**9**
Athletic Bilbao	**8**
Valencia	**6**
Real Sociedad	**2**
Deportivo de la Coruna	**1**
Sevilla	**1**
Betis	**1**

⚽ TOP OF THE WORLD

Spain rose to the top of the FIFA world rankings for the first time in July 2008, after winning the UEFA European Championship co-hosted by Austria and Switzerland. They became only the sixth team to reach the No. 1 spot and the first to do so without ever having won the FIFA World Cup.

⚽ SUPER PED

Spanish winger **Pedro** is the only player to have scored in six separate official club tournaments in one calendar year, managing to hit the net for Barcelona in Spain's Primera Liga, Copa del Rey and Super Cup in 2009, as well as the UEFA Champions League, UEFA European Super Cup and FIFA Club World Cup. He was also in the starting line-up for the 2010 FIFA World Cup final – less than two years after being a member of the Barcelona reserve team in Spain's third division and needing new club manager Pep Guardiola's intervention to prevent him being sent home to Tenerife.

SEMI PRECIOUS

Centre-back **Carles Puyol**'s thumping header not only gave Spain victory in their 2010 FIFA World Cup semi-final – it was also the country's first win over Germany in four FIFA World Cup matches. West Germany had won 2-1 in both 1966 and 1982, before a 1-1 draw at the 1994 tournament. But Spain's 1-0 win in 2010 was a repeat of their triumph over Germany in the UEFA European Championship final two years earlier. Nineteen members of the two 2010 FIFA World Cup squads had played in that Euro 2008 showdown, 11 Spanish and eight German.

MORE THAN JUST A CLUB

Barcelona, founded in 1899 by a Swiss businessman Hans Gamper, prides itself on being "more than a club". The club's famous blue and purple resisted the march of commercialism for more than a century until 2006, when the club signed a deal with (and gave money to) the United Nations Children's Fund (UNICEF) in exchange for using the charity's logo on its shirts.

PERFECT PICHICHI

The annual award for top scorer in La Liga is called the "Pichichi" – the nickname of Rafael Moreno, a striker for Athletic Bilbao between 1911 and 1921. He scored 200 goals in 170 games for the club, and once in five matches for Spain. Pichichi, who often took the field wearing a large white cap, died suddenly in 1922, aged just 29.

MAIN STADIUMS

Name	City	Capacity
Camp Nou	Barcelona	98,772
Santiago Bernabeu	Madrid	80,354
Estadio de la Cartuja	Seville	72,000
Vicente Calderon	Madrid	57,200
Lluis Companys	Barcelona	56,000
Mestalla	Valencia	55,000
Manuel Ruiz de Lopera	Seville	52,500
Ramon Sanchez Pizjuan	Seville	45,500
San Mames	Bilbao	40,000
Manuel Martinez Valero	Elche	38,750

THE VULTURE

Born in the Spanish capital and a star for Real for over a decade, **Emilio Butragueno** was a man made in Madrid. Nicknamed The Vulture for his predatory instincts in the penalty area, he made 69 appearances for the Spanish national side, scoring 26 goals.

WHO CAN TELMO

Telmo Zarraonaindia, commonly known as "Zarra", scored a Spanish championship record of 251 goals in 277 games for Athletic Bilbao between 1940 and 1955 – and 20 goals in 20 games for Spain, between 1945 and 1951. He was nicknamed the "finest head in Europe after Churchill".

FIFA FIRST

Real Madrid were the only club formally represented at FIFA's first meeting in Paris in 1904 – though the club was then known simply as Madrid FC. Spanish clubs, such as Real Madrid and Real Betis, dropped the word "Real" – meaning "Royal" – from their names during the Second Spanish Republic, between 1931 and 1939.

BELGIUM

For eight decades Belgium failed to produce a side capable of challenging for the game's greatest prizes. Then came the golden period: runners-up at the 1980 UEFA European Championship; semi-finalists at the 1986 FIFA World Cup™; and regular qualifiers – and even contenders – for major tournaments. Recent times have been tougher, and a nation hopes that failure to qualify for UEFA Euro 2004 and 2008 and the FIFA World Cup™ in 2006 and 2010 does not signal a slide back into darker times.

TOP CAPS

1	Jan Ceulemans	96
2	Eric Gerets	86
=	Franky van der Elst	86
4	Enzo Scifo	84
5	Timmy Simons	82
6	Paul van Himst	81
7	Bart Goor	78
8	Georges Grun	77
9	Lorenzo Staelens	70
=	Marc Wilmots	70

SIXTH SENSE

By qualifying for the 2002 FIFA World Cup, Belgium became the first country to reach six successive tournaments without benefiting once from being either hosts or defending holders. But although they beat reigning champions Argentina at the 1982 finals, they would lose to the same opposition – eventual champions – in the semi-finals four years later.

TOP SCORERS

1	Paul van Himst	30
=	Bernard Voorhoof	30
3	Marc Wilmots	28
4	Joseph Mermans	27
5	Raymond Braine	26
=	Robert De Veen	26
7	Wesley Sonck	24
8	Jan Ceulemans	23
=	Marc Degryse	23
10	Henri Coppens	21

CONSOLATION FOR KEEPER

The Lev Yashin Award (for the best goalkeeper at a FIFA World Cup) was introduced in 1994. The first recipient was Belgium goalkeeper **Michel Preud'homme**, despite his country only making it as far as the second round.

MOTHER'S BOY

Not many footballers turn down a move to AC Milan, but Jan Ceulemans did just that, after seeking the advice of his mum. Belgium's most-capped player (he played 96 times for his country) spent the bulk of his career with Club Brugge, but is best remembered by fans for his contributions to three consecutive FIFA World Cup campaigns. Belgium's finest performance came in finishing fourth at the 1986 tournament in Mexico, when midfielder and captain Ceulemans scored three goals. Born in Lier on 28 February 1957, he retired from international football after the 1990 FIFA World Cup – and later, between 2005 and 2006, returned to Club Brugge as manager.

SWINE FEVER

Only Paul van Himst and Bernard Voorhoof have scored more goals for Belgium than **Marc Wilmots,** nicknamed "The Bull from Dongelberg" and "The Fighting Pig" during his playing days before he became the country's assistant coach. Wilmots's achievements on the field included scoring the winning penalty for Germany's Schalke when they beat Italy's Internazionale in a 1997 UEFA Cup final shoot-out. His route to helping guide his country's national team after hanging up his boots was an unusual one, via politics and a brief term as a Belgian senator.

SPECS APPEAL

Many footballers wear contact lenses, but Belgium captain Jef Jurion was notable in the late 1950s and early 1960s for wearing a pair of specially made glasses during the matches he played.

GOLDEN NOT-SO-OLDIE

Fernand Nisot held the record for being the youngest-ever international footballer for 60 years. He made his Belgium debut in 1911 aged 16 years and 19 days.

CLUB MATES

Belgium ended a 1964 match against Holland with a team entirely made up of Anderlecht players, after Liege goalkeeper Guy Delhasse was substituted by Anderlecht's Jan Trappeniers.

LIMITED KOMPANY

Belgium won Olympic bronze in 1900 and gold 20 years later, but they just missed out on a medal at the 2008 Beijing Games, when they lost to Brazil in the bronze medal play-off. Star player **Vincent Kompany** missed the match after being summoned back to Europe by his German club Hamburg.

HE'S OUR GUY

Belgium's longest-serving, and most successful, coach was **Guy Thys,** who led them to the final of the 1980 UEFA European Championships and to the semi-finals of the FIFA World Cup six years later. He served 13 years in the job – from 1976 to 1989 – then returned to the role just eight months after stepping down, to take his country to the 1990 FIFA World Cup.

ALL CHANGE AT THE TOP

Belgium went through four different coaches in the 13 months from April 2009 to May 2010. Rene Vandereycken's three-year reign came to an end on 7 April 2009, during a disappointing World Cup qualification campaign – but successor Franky Vercauteren lasted just four months. Dutch coach Dick Advocaat took over in October 2009 but quit the following April, after five matches, to be replaced by Georges Leekens – who was himself returning to the job he filled from 1997 to 1999. During his own playing days Leekens was a hard-tackling defender nicknamed "Mac The Knife".

BULGARIA

The glory days of the "golden generation" apart – when Bulgaria finished fourth at the 1994 FIFA World Cup™ in the United States, sensationally beating defending champions Germany 2-1 in the quarter-finals – a consistent pattern emerges with Bulgarian football. Regular qualifiers for the game's major competitions, and the birthplace of some of the sport's biggest names (such as Hristo Stoichkov and Dimitar Berbatov), the country has too often failed to deliver on the big occasions and make its mark on world football.

TOP CAPS

1	Borislav Mikhailov	102
2	Stiliyan Petrov	101
3	Hristo Bonev	96
4	Krassimir Balakov	92
5	Dimitar Penev	90
6	Martin Petrov	89
7	Radostin Kishishev	88
8	Hristo Stoichkov	83
9	Nasko Sirakov	82
10	Zlatko Yankov	80

A NATION MOURNS

Bulgaria lost two of its most popular footballing talents in a June 1971 car crash that killed strikers Georgi Asparukhov, aged 28, and Nikola Kotkov, aged 32. Asparukhov scored 19 goals in 50 internationals, including Bulgaria's only goal of the 1966 FIFA World Cup finals in a 3-1 defeat by Hungary.

MOB RULES

Manchester United and Bulgaria centre-forward **Dimitar Berbatov** claims to have learned English by watching the *Godfather* movies. Berbatov joined United from Tottenham in 2008 for a club and Bulgarian record fee of £30.75m. Before joining Spurs, he had been a member of the Bayer Leverkusen side who narrowly missed out on a treble in 2002. They lost in the final of both the UEFA Champions League and the German cup and finished runners-up in the German Bundesliga. Berbatov surprised and disappointed fans back home when he announced his international retirement aged just 29, in May 2010, having scored a national-record 48 goals in his 78 appearances for Bulgaria.

MAYOR WITH NO HAIR

Balding **Yordan Letchkov** headed the winning goal against holders and defending champions Germany in the 1994 FIFA World Cup quarter-final in the United States. At the time, he played for German club Hamburg. He later became mayor of Sliven, the Bulgarian town where he was born in July 1967.

SEE YOU LATER, LOTHAR

Bulgaria spoiled what could have been another landmark day in the illustrious career of Lothar Matthaus. The Germany captain opened the scoring against Bulgaria in their 1994 FIFA World Cup quarter-final, only for Hristo Stoichkov and Yordan Letchkov to score and clinch a place in the semi-finals. The match was Matthaus' 21st at FIFA World Cups, equalling the previous record. But he showed he harboured no grudge by accepting the job of Bulgaria coach in September 2009, only the second foreigner to take the role. Matthaus replaced Stanimir Stoilov who had resigned after two defeats in Bulgaria's opening 2012 UEFA European Championship qualifiers.

GO FOURTH AND MULTIPLY

The so-called "Golden Generation" of 1994 was the only Bulgarian side to win a match at a FIFA World Cup finals – finishing fourth after beating Greece, Argentina, Mexico and Germany. Bulgaria had only just qualified for the tournament, thanks to Emil Kostadinov's last-minute goal in Paris that knocked out Gerard Houllier's France.

ALL–ROUNDER ALEKSANDAR

Defender Aleksandar Shalamanov played for Bulgaria at the 1966 FIFA World Cup, six years after representing his country as an alpine skier at the Winter Olympics. He also went to the 1964 Olympics as an unused member of the volleyball squad. Shalamanov was voted Bulgaria's best sportsman in 1967 and 1973.

TOP SCORERS

1	Dimitar Berbatov	48
2	Hristo Bonev	47
3	Hristo Stoichkov	37
4	Emil Kostadinov	26
5	Ivan Kolev	25
=	Petar Zhekov	25
7	Atanas Mihaylov	23
=	Nasko Sirakov	23
9	Dimitar Milanov	20
10	Georgi Asparukhov	19
=	Dinko Dermendzhiev	19
=	Martin Petrov	19

STAN THE BURGER VAN MAN

Stiliyan Petrov – nicknamed "Stan" by fans of his English club Aston Villa – was applauded on to the field when he became Bulgaria's first outfield player to reach 100 caps, against Switzerland in March 2011. The midfielder and Bulgaria captain has been playing in Britain since 1999, when he joined Scottish giants Celtic as a 20-year-old – but had to fight hard against a bout of homesickness. He later revealed that his English only improved when he started work behind the counter of a Scottish friend's burger van. Petrov said: "Some of the customers used to stare, thinking: 'That looks like Stiliyan Petrov, but it can't be.' But soon I started to understand things better."

HRISTO'S HISTORY

Hristo Stoichkov, born in Plovdiv, Bulgaria, on 8 February 1968, shared the 1994 FIFA World Cup Golden Boot, awarded to the tournament's top scorer, with Russia's Oleg Salenko. Both scored six times, though Stoichkov became the sole winner of that year's European Footballer of the Year award. Earlier that same year, he had combined up-front with Brazilian Romario to help Barcelona reach the final of the UEFA Champions League. Earlier in his career he was banned for a year after a brawl during the 1985 Bulgarian cup final between CSKA Sofia and Levski Sofia. Stoichkov won trophies with clubs in Bulgaria, Spain, Saudi Arabia and the United States before retiring as a player in 2003.

HEAD BOY

Bulgaria's most-capped player is **Borislav Mikhailov**, born in Sofia on 12 February 1963, who sometimes wore a wig while playing and later had a hair transplant. After retiring in 2005, he was appointed president of the Bulgarian Football Union. His father Bisser was also a goalkeeper and Boris's own son, Nikolay, signed for Liverpool in 2007. All three have played for Levski Sofia.

CROATIA

Croatia's distinctive red-and-white chequered jersey has become one of the most recognized in world football – just ask England. Croatia broke English hearts not once but twice in the UEFA Euro 2008 qualifying tournament. First Croatia beat England 2-0 in Zagreb and then they shocked them 3-2 at Wembley to secure qualification. Croatia's subsequent march to the quarter-finals at UEFA Euro 2008 confirmed their status as a football power. though they will hope to use the Euro 2012 qualifiers to get over the disappointment of failing to qualify for the 2010 FIFA World Cup™.

TOP SCORERS

1	Davor Suker	45
2	Eduardo da Silva	19
=	Darijo Srna	19
4	Niko Kranjcar	15
=	Goran Vlaovic	15
6	Niko Kovac	14
=	Ivica Olic	14
8	Zvonimir Boban	12
=	Ivan Klasnic	12
=	Mladen Petric	12

BILIC BEAT

Shortly after becoming Croatia manager, the guitar-playing **Slaven Bilic** and his rock band released a single, "Vatreno Ludilo" ("Fiery Madness"), which recalled the team's progress during the 1998 FIFA World Cup and went to No. 1 in the Croatian charts. Fashion-conscious Bilic also sports a diamond-studded earring. Bilic, who is also a qualified lawyer, had said he intended to step down as Croatia coach after the 2012 UEFA European Championship, ending six years in charge.

LUKA LOOPY

Luka Modric scored the fastest penalty in UEFA European Championship history: his fourth-minute strike was the only goal of Croatia's first-round victory against co-hosts Austria at the 2008 tournament. But he would miss one of the spot-kicks as Croatia lost a shoot-out to Turkey in the quarter-finals. His much-loved status back home remains unaffected, though, as the diminutive Tottenham Hotspur playmaker – dubbed "the Croat Cruyff", and not just because he wears the number 14 – is now widely seen as one of the world's most skilful midfielders.

HAPPY OPENINGS

Few national teams have been as successful in their infancy as Croatia. Formerly part of Yugoslavia, in their very first senior competition as an independent country, UEFA Euro 96, Croatia reached the quarter-finals, then came third at the 1998 FIFA World Cup, where they became known as the "golden generation". Since becoming eligible to participate in 1993, Croatia qualified for every FIFA World Cup, except for 2010, and missed only one UEFA European Championship.

SUPER SUKER

Striker Davor Suker won the Golden Boot for being top scorer at the FIFA World Cup in 1998, scoring six goals in seven games as Croatia finished third. His strikes included the opening goal in Croatia's 2-1 semi-final defeat to eventual champions France, and the winner in a 2-1 triumph over Holland in the third-place play-off. Suker, by far his country's leading scorer of all time, had hit three goals at the UEFA European Championship in 1996 – including an audacious long-distance lob over Denmark goalkeeper Peter Schmeichel.

DEER DARIJO

Darijo Srna is Croatia's second-top-scorer of all time despite playing many games as a right-back or wing-back. He has a tattoo on his calf in the shape of a deer, the Croatian word for which is "srna". He also has a tattoo on his chest – the name of his brother Igor, who has Down's syndrome and to whom he dedicates each goal he scores.

THE KIDNEYS ARE ALL RIGHT

Striker Ivan Klasnic returned to international duty with Croatia despite suffering kidney failure in early 2007. A first attempt at a transplant failed when his body rejected a kidney donated by his mother, but follow-up surgery – using a kidney from his father – proved successful. He recovered enough to play for Croatia again in March 2008 and represented his country in that summer's UEFA European Championship, scoring twice – including a winning goal against Poland.

GOOD AND BAD

Croatia's joint highest-scoring victories were the 7-0 wins over Andorra in 2006 and Australia in 1998. Croatia's worst defeat in the modern era was a 5-1 loss to England in London, in September 2009, during the qualifiers for the FIFA World Cup.

FAMILY AFFAIR

Niko Kranjcar is the son of former Croatian coach Zlatko Kranjcar, but it wasn't always an easy affiliation. "Two days before he became Croatia's head coach everyone said I should get a call-up," Niko once said. "Then when Dad picked me for UEFA Euro 2004 suddenly it was because I was his son."No such problems for the **Kovac brothers, Robert and Niko**, both of whom are part of Croatian footballing folklore. The siblings were born in Berlin but are proud Croats. Both brothers have now hung up their boots at international level, though Robert went on for a year after Niko retired from Croatian duty.

TOP CAPS

1	Dario Simic	100
2	Josip Simunic	85
3	Robert Kovac	84
4	Niko Kovac	83
5	Stipe Pletikosa	82
=	Darijo Srna	82
7	Robert Jarni	81
8	Ivica Olic	73
9	Davor Suker	69
10	Niko Kranjcar	64

EXPORT SPECIALISTS

Nearly all of Croatia's national team squad play for overseas clubs. Of the 23 selected against Romania in February 2009, only five of the squad were home-based.

DOUBLE IDENTITY

Robert Jarni and Robert Prosinecki both have the rare distinction of playing for two different countries at different FIFA World Cup tournaments. They both represented Yugoslavia in 1990, in Italy, then newly independent Croatia eight years later in France. Full-back Jarni actually played for both Yugoslavia and Croatia in 1990, then only Yugoslavia in 1991, before switching back – and permanently – to Croat colours in 1992 after the country officially joined UEFA and FIFA. He retired with 81 caps for Croatia, seven for Yugoslavia.

CZECH REPUBLIC

The most successful of the former Eastern Bloc countries, as Czechoslovakia they finished as runners-up in the 1934 and 1962 FIFA World Cup™ competitions, and then shocked West Germany in a penalty shoot-out to claim the UEFA European Championship in 1976. Playing as the Czech Republic since 1994, they came agonizingly close to victory at UEFA Euro 96, and lost out in the semi-finals at UEFA Euro 2004. Recent times have been tougher, and although one of Europe's stronger nations the Czechs did not qualify for the 2010 FIFA World Cup™.

EURO-VER AND OVER AND OVER AGAIN

Vladimir Smicer, now the general manager of the Czech national team, is one of only four players to score at three different UEFA European Championship tournaments – along with Germany's Jurgen Klinsmann, France's Thierry Henry and Portugal's Nuno Gomes. Smicer struck at the finals in 1996, 2000 and 2004. Perhaps his other greatest achievement came in his final game for English club Liverpool, scoring as a second-half substitute as the team came back from 3-0 down to beat AC Milan in the 2005 UEFA Champions League final. Smicer's wife Pavlina is the daughter of former Czechoslovakia striker Ladislav Vizek, who won footballing gold with his country at the 1980 summer Olympics but was sent off against France at the FIFA World Cup two years later.

CHIP WITH EVERYTHING

One of the most famous penalties ever taken was Antonin Panenka's decisive spot-kick for Czechoslovakia against West Germany in the final of the 1976 UEFA European Championship, giving the Czechs victory in the shoot-out. Despite the tension, and the responsibility resting on him, Panenka cheekily chipped the ball into the middle of the goal – as goalkeeper Sepp Maier dived to the side. That style of spot-kick is now widely known as a "Panenka", and has been replicated by the likes of France's Zinedine Zidane, in the 2006 FIFA World Cup final.

POPULAR KAREL

UEFA Euro 96 gave the frizzy-haired **Karel Poborsky** the perfect platform to take his career to new heights as he helped the Czech Republic reach the final and then sealed a dream move to Manchester United. His lob against Portugal in the quarter-finals was rated as one of the finest opportunist goals in the tournament's history. His 118 appearances is a record for his country.

CECH CAP

Goalkeeper **Petr Cech** has worn a protective cap while playing ever since suffering a fractured skull during an English Premier League match in October 2006. He later added a chin protector after a facial operation following a training accident.

GETTING IVAN

Ivan Hasek not only won a half-century of caps for Czechoslovakia but also captained the country at the 1990 FIFA World Cup in Italy – and he has kept busy since retiring as a player. Not content with simply taking over as president of the Czech football association in June 2009, he became national team manager the following month after Petr Rada's sacking. He held this role for just three months and five games – three wins and two draws – before handing over to assistant coach and Italia 90 team-mate Michal Bilek, preferring to focus on his presidential duties instead. Under Hasek, the Czech Republic did equal their biggest-ever margin of victory, with a 7-0 win over San Marino – including a national-record four goals in one game by Milan Baros, who sits second on the Republic's all-time leading scorers list and was Golden Boot winner at the 2004 UEFA European Championship.

PASSING THE PUC

The final of the 1934 FIFA World Cup was the first to go into extra-time, with Czechoslovakia ultimately losing 2-1 to hosts Italy despite taking a 76th-minute lead through Antonin Puc. Puc was Czechoslovakia/the Czech Republic's top international scorer from when he retired in 1938 until he was passed, first by Jan Koller, 67 years later, and, latterly, by Milan Baros.

WALK–OUT

Belgium's 1920 victory in the Olympic Games was overshadowed when Czechoslovakia walked off the pitch after half an hour in protest following what they saw as biased refereeing. Czechoslovakia are the only team to have been disqualified in the history of Olympic football.

THE CANNON COLLECTS

Pavel Nedved's election as European Footballer of the Year in 2003 ended an impatient wait for fans in the Czech Republic who had seen a string of outstanding players overlooked since Josef Masopust had been honoured back in 1962. Masopust, a midfield general, had scored the opening goal in the FIFA World Cup final that year before Brazil hit back to win 3-1 in the Chilean capital of Santiago. Years later, Masopust was remembered by Pele and nominated as one of his 125 greatest living footballers. At club level, Masopust won eight Czechoslovak league titles with Dukla Prague, the army club. He was also the winner, in 1962, of the first Czech Golden Ball as domestic footballer of the year. It was another day and in another age. Masopust was presented with his award before the kick-off of a European Cup quarter-final with Benfica – with a minimum of fuss. Years later, Masopust said: "Eusebio just shook hands with me, I put the trophy in my sports bag and went home on the tram."

TOP SCORERS

1	Jan Koller	55
2	Milan Baros	39
3	Antonin Puc	34
4	Zdenek Nehoda	31
5	Pavel Kuka	29
6	Oldrich Nejedly	28
=	Josef Silny	28
8	Vladimir Smicer	27
9	Adolf Scherer	22
=	Frantisek Svoboda	22

TOP CAPS

(Czechoslovakia and Czech Republic)

1	Karel Poborsky	118
2	Jan Koller	91
=	Pavel Nedved	91
4	Zdenek Nehoda	90
5	Pavel Kuka	87
6	Jiri Nemec	84
7	Milan Baros	81
=	Petr Cech	81
=	Vladimir Smicer	81
10	Tomas Ujfalusi	80

TEN OUT OF TEN

Giant striker **Jan Koller** zs Czech football's all-time leading marksman with 55 goals in 91 appearances. Koller scored on his senior debut against Belgium and struck ten goals in ten successive internationals. He scored six goals in each of the 2000, 2004 and 2008 UEFA European Championship qualifying campaigns. He began his career with Sparta Prague, who converted him from goalkeeper to goalscorer. Then, in Belgium, he was top scorer with Lokeren, before scoring 42 goals in two league title-winning campaigns with Anderlecht. Later, with Borussia Dortmund in Germany, he once went in goal after Jens Lehmann was sent off and kept a clean sheet – having scored in the first half.

DENMARK

Denmark have been playing international football since 1908, but it was not until the mid-1980s that they became competitive at the game's major tournaments. The country's crowning moment came in 1992 when, after being called up as a replacement just ten days before the start of the tournament, they walked away with the UEFA European Championship crown, shocking defending world champions West Germany 2-0 in the final. They may not have been able to repeat that success, but remain a significant player in the world game.

TOP CAPS

1	Peter Schmeichel	129
2	Jon Dahl Tomasson	112
3	Thomas Helveg	108
=	Dennis Rommedahl	108
5	Michael Laudrup	104
6	Morten Olsen	102
7	Martin Jorgensen	100
8	Thomas Sorensen	92
9	John Sivebaek	87
10	Jan Heintze	86

GOLDEN GLOVES

 Peter Schmeichel was rated as the world's best goalkeeper in the early 1990s, winning many club honours with Manchester United and, famously, the UEFA European Championship with his native Denmark.

NO. 100 FOR 100

Martin Jorgensen became the first Danish footballer to play at three different FIFA World Cups when he captained the side at the 2010 tournament, having also appeared in 1998 and 2002. Although Jorgensen had decided to retire after those finals, he was stranded on 99 caps. As a result, he reversed his decision to retire and went on to make his 100th appearance for Denmark in a friendly against the Czech Republic on 17 November 2010. To mark the event, he wore shirt No. 100. The 2010 finals also took winger Dennis Rommedahl to 99 international appearances – but he kept playing to pass 100 during qualifiers for the 2012 UEFA European Championship.

DANISH DYNAMITE

Denmark's 6-1 defeat of Uruguay in the 1986 FIFA World Cup finals first-round group stage in Neza, Mexico, ranks among the country's finest performances. Sadly, Denmark's adventure was ended by Spain in the last 16, losing 5-1 after a horrendous back pass by Manchester United's Jesper Olsen allowed the Spanish to open the scoring. The Danes had already been hampered by the loss to suspension of playmaker Frank Arsesen, sent off during their final first-round group game, a victory over eventual runners-up West Germany. The side – popularly known as "Danish Dynamite" – was captained by future national coach Morten Olsen and managed by Sepp Piontek, a German who became the Danish national team's first professional coach when appointed in 1979. Michael Laudrup, a star member of the classic mid-1980s side, described them as "Europe's answer to Brazil".

LEADERSHIP STYLE

Morten Olsen captained Denmark at the 1986 FIFA World Cup and later became the first Dane to reach a century of caps, eventually stepping down from the national team with four goals in 102 international appearances between 1970 and 1989. After he retired from playing all football that year, he switched to coaching, first at club level with Brondby, FC Koln and Ajax Amsterdam, before taking on the job as Danish national coach in 2000 and leading them to the 2002 and 2010 FIFA World Cups. Denmark's 2-1 defeat to England in a February 2011 friendly was his 116th international in charge – taking him past the previous record set between 1979 and 1990 by his former national team boss Sepp Piontek.

PENALTY REDEMPTION

Former Dundee, Celtic and Brondby midfielder **Morten Wieghorst** is the only player to be sent off twice while playing for Denmark – yet has also received a special award for fair play. His first international red card came just three minutes after entering the field as a substitute, against South Africa in the 1998 FIFA World Cup. He was again dismissed after coming on as a sub against Italy in the 2000 UEFA European Championship, though this time he managed a whole 28 minutes of action - and scored a goal in Denmark's 3-2 victory. But the other side of his character was shown during a Carlsberg Cup match against Iran in February 2003, when he deliberately missed a penalty. The spot-kick had been awarded after Iranian defender Jalal Kameli Mofrad had picked the ball up, thinking wrongly that a whistle from the crowd was actually the referee blowing for half-time. The International Olympic Committee later presented Wieghorst with a special fair play prize for deliberately striking his penalty wide – a gesture which looked all the more sporting since Denmark went on to lose the game 1-0.

TOP SCORERS

1	Poul Nielsen	52
=	Jon Dahl Tomasson	52
3	Pauli Jorgensen	44
4	Ole Madsen	42
5	Preben Elkjaer-Larsen	38
6	Michael Laudrup	37
7	Henning Enoksen	29
8	Michael Rohde	22
=	Ebbe Sand	22
10	Brian Laudrup	21
=	Flemming Povlsen	21
=	Allan Simonsen	21

QUICK DRAW

Ebbe Sand scored the fastest FIFA World Cup goal ever scored by a substitute, when he netted a mere 16 seconds after coming on to the pitch in Denmark's clash against Nigeria at the 1998 FIFA World Cup.

CHRISTIAN YOUTH

Denmark fielded the youngest player at the 2010 FIFA World Cup: 18-year-old Ajax midfielder **Christian Eriksen**, who came on as substitute against Holland and Japan. He had made his international debut against Austria in March 2010, becoming Denmark's fourth-youngest international of all time.

THE UNEXPECTED IN 1992

Few football fans are ever likely to forget June 1992, Denmark's finest hour, when their team managed to win the UEFA European Championship. Denmark had not qualified for the final round in Sweden, but ten days before the opening match UEFA asked them to take the place of Yugoslavia, who were thrown out of the tournament in the wake of international sanctions over the Balkan War. The Danes had come second in their qualifying group, behind Yugoslavia, and they took over their spot at the tournament proper. Expectations were minimal, but then the inconceivable happened. Relying heavily on goalkeeper Peter Schmeichel, his defence, and the creative spark of Brian Laudrup, Denmark crafted one of the biggest shocks in modern football history by winning the tournament, culminating in a 2-0 victory over world champions Germany. Their victory was all the more remarkable in that Brian's brother Michael, their finest player, quit during the qualifying competition after falling out with coach Richard Moller Nielsen. He revived his international career in 1993, only for Denmark to fail to qualify for the subsequent FIFA World Cup in the United States.

BROTHERS IN ARMS

Brian (left) and **Michael Laudrup** are among the most successful footballing brothers of modern times. As well as making a combined 186 international appearances, they played across Europe at club level. Michael (104 caps, 37 goals) played in Italy with Lazio and Juventus and in Spain with Barcelona and Real Madrid. Brian (82 caps, 21 goals) starred in Germany with Bayer Uerdingen and Bayern Munich, Italy with Fiorentina and Milan, Scotland for Rangers and England for Chelsea.

GREECE

There is no argument about Greece's proudest footballing moment – their shock triumph at the 2004 UEFA European Championship, one of the game's greatest international upsets. Guided by their long-serving German coach Otto Rehhagel, it was only the Greeks' second appearance at a UEFA Euro finals – while the 2010 tournament in South Africa marked just their second qualification for a FIFA World Cup™.

TOP SCORERS

1	Nikos Anastopoulos	29
2	Angelos Charisteas	24
3	Dimitris Saravakos	22
4	Mimis Papaioannou	21
5	Theofanis Gekas	20
6	Nikos Machlas	18
7	Demis Nikolaidis	17
8	Panagiotis Tsalouchidis	16
9	Giorgos Sideris	14
10	Nikos Liberopoulos	13

SIMPLY THEO BEST

Theodoros "Theo" Zagorakis – born near Kavala on 27 October 1971 – was captain of Greece when they won the UEFA European Championship in 2004 and the defensive midfielder was also given the prize for the tournament's best player. He is the most-capped Greek footballer of all time, with 120 caps. But it was not until his 101st international appearance – 10 years and five months after his Greek debut – that he scored his first goal for his country, in a FIFA World Cup qualifier against Denmark, in February 2005. He retired from international football after making a 15-minute cameo appearance against Spain in August 2007.

PARTY CRASHERS

Shock UEFA Euro 2004 winners Greece became the first team to beat both the holders and the hosts on the way to winning either a UEFA European Championship or FIFA World Cup. In fact, they beat hosts Portugal twice – in both the tournament's opening game and the final, with a quarter-final victory over defending champions France in between.

SOT'S NEW

At 18 years and 46 days old, **Sotiris Ninis** became Greece's youngest scorer on his international debut, in a 2-0 friendly win over Cyprus in May 2008 – just 18 months after he had been happy to be working as a ballboy for his club side Panathinaikos. The second half of the 2006–07 season brought a stunning breakthrough for the attacking midfielder, who made his club debut, became a Greek team's youngest player in any UEFA club competition and then inspired Greece to a runners-up finish in the UEFA U-19s European Championship. The Albanian-born player was voted most valuable player of the summer 2007 tournament – making his first full international call-up only a matter of time.

ALL WHITE NOW

The surprise triumph at UEFA Euro 2004 brought a major change to Greek international football – they switched the national team's kit from blue to white. The former colours had been used since the Hellenic Football Federation was formed in 1926 but the success of Otto Rehhagel's men in their second kit prompted a permanent change of colours.

⚽ TOP CAPS

1	Theodoros Zagorakis	120
2	Giorgios Karagounis	105
3	Angelos Basinas	100
4	Stratos Apostolakis	95
5	Antonios Nikopolodis	90
6	Angelos Charisteas	85
7	Konstantinos Katsouranis	80
8	Dimitris Saravakos	78
9	Stelios Giannakopoulos	77
=	Tasos Mitropoulos	77

⚽ DIMI MORE

Striker **Dimitrios Salpingidis** not only struck the only goal of Greece's 2010 FIFA World Cup qualifying play-off against Ukraine, sealing their place in South Africa. He also then became the first Greek ever to score at a FIFA World Cup, with a 44th-minute deflected strike in the 2-1 Group B triumph over Nigeria.

⚽ WHEN EXPERIENCE DOESN'T COUNT

Ioannis Fetfatzidis, already nicknamed "the Greek Messi", had just seven Greek Superleague matches for Olympiacos to his name when he made his full international debut as a 19-year-old against Latvia in October 2010.

⚽ PEAK POINTS

Greece set a record for UEFA European Championship qualifiers when they notched up 31 points from 12 games in reaching the 2008 finals. The previous best was France's 24, albeit from four matches fewer, ahead of the 2004 tournament.

⚽ HONESTY PAYS

Greece's 500th goal in international football was scored by Demis Nikolaidis at Manchester's Old Trafford in October 2001, giving them an unexpected 2–1 lead away to England in a final 2002 FIFA World Cup qualifier – although David Beckham would go on to equalize with a famous last-minute free-kick. In March the following year, striker Nikolaidis was formally acclaimed by the International Committee for Fair Play for admitting to the referee that he handled the ball when scoring for AEK Athens in the final of the Greek Cup. His team still won the match, and the trophy.

⚽ BACK DOWN WITH A BUMP

Three countries have failed to qualify for the FIFA World Cup two years after winning the UEFA European Championship – Czechoslovakia (who took the title in 1976), Denmark (1992) and Greece (2004). Otto Rehhagel's Greece team got their 2006 FIFA World Cup qualification campaign off to the worst possible start, losing 2–1 to minnows Albania just two months after being crowned shock European champions. His side had also lost their first two matches of qualifying for UEFA Euro 2004, but reached the tournament after winning their final six.

⚽ SIXTEEN–YEAR WAIT

After failing to find the net during all three games at the 1994 FIFA World Cup finals – the only European country to exit that World Cup without scoring – Greece finally opened their account when they next qualified, in 2010. A 2-1 win over Nigeria gave them their first goals – and first points. But despite that victory, thanks to **Vasileios Torosidis**'s decisive goal, defeats to South Korea and Argentina meant Otto Rehhagel's men failed to make the second round.

⚽ KING OTTO

German coach **Otto Rehhagel** became the first foreigner to be voted "Greek of the Year" in 2004, after leading the country to glory at that year's UEFA European Championship. He was also offered honorary Greek citizenship. His nine years in charge after being appointed in 2001 made him Greece's longest-serving international manager. The UEFA Euro 2004 triumph was the first time a country coached by a foreigner had triumphed at either the UEFA European Championship or FIFA World Cup. Rehhagel was aged 65 at UEFA Euro 2004, making him the oldest coach to win the UEFA European Championship – though that record was taken off him four years later, when 69-year-old Luis Aragones lifted the trophy with Spain.

HUNGARY

For a period in the early 1950s, Hungary possessed the most talented football team on the planet. They claimed Olympic gold in Helsinki in 1952, inflicted a crushing first-ever Wembley defeat on England the following year, and entered the 1954 FIFA World Cup™, unbeaten in almost four years, as firm favourites to win the crown. They lost to West Germany in the final and Hungary's footballing fortunes on the world stage have never been the same again.

TOP SCORERS

1	Ferenc Puskas	84
2	Sandor Kocsis	75
3	Imre Schlosser-Lakatos	59
4	Lajos Tichy	51
5	Gyorgy Sarosi	42
6	Nandor Hidegkuti	39
7	Ferenc Bene	36
8	Gyula Zsengeller	32
=	Tibor Nyilasi	32
10	Florian Albert	31

TOP CAPS

1	Jozsef Bozsik	101
2	Laszlo Fazekas	92
3	Gyula Grosics	86
4	Ferenc Puskas	85
5	Imre Garaba	82
6	Gabor Kiraly	81
=	Sandor Matrai	81
8	Ferenc Sipos	77
9	Laszlo Balint	76
=	Ferenc Bene	76
=	Mate Fenyvesi	76

RETURN TO SANDOR

An estimated 1,000 success-starved fans thronged Budapest airport in October 2009 to welcome home the players and staff behind perhaps Hungary's finest footballing feat in decades. The country's youngsters clinched a surprise third place at that autumn's FIFA World U-20 Championship, beating Costa Rica on penalties in a play-off. Then-Liverpool striker Krisztian Nemeth scored the decisive spot-kick, having hit the late extra-time winner against Italy in the quarter-finals. Only Ghana and beaten finalists Brazil performed better. The reward for coach **Sandor Egervari** was promotion to the same role with the full international side the following summer. Egervari had been assistant coach the last time Hungary competed in a FIFA World Cup finals, in 1986.

GOING FOREIGN

Englishman Jimmy Hogan was a hero in Hungary for coaching the virtues of pure football in the 1920s. He was even the Hungarian Federation's guest of honour following the 1953 victory over England. The value of new ideas from abroad was still being maintained into the new century under Erwin Koeman, one of Holland's UEFA European champions in 1988.

GOLDEN HEAD

Sandor Kocsis, top scorer in the 1954 FIFA World Cup finals with 11 goals, was so good in the air he was known as "The Man with the Golden Head". In 68 internationals he scored an incredible 75 goals, including a record seven hat-tricks. His tally included two decisive extra-time goals in the 1954 FIFA World Cup semi-final against Uruguay, when Hungary had appeared to be on the brink of defeat.

GALLOPING MAJOR

Ferenc Puskas was one of the greatest footballers of all time, scoring a remarkable 84 goals in 85 international matches for Hungary and 514 goals in 529 matches in the Hungarian and Spanish leagues. Possessing the most lethal left-foot shot in the history of football, he was known as the "Galloping Major" – by virtue of his playing for the army team Honved before joining Real Madrid and going on to play for Spain. During the 1950s he was top scorer and captain of the legendary "Mighty Magyars" (the nickname given to the Hungarian national team), as well as of the army club Honved.

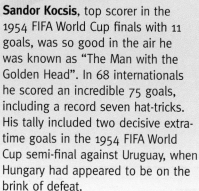

HUNGARY FOR IT

Hungary's 6-3 win over England at Wembley in 1953 remains one of the most significant international results of all time. Hungary became the first team from outside the British Isles to beat England at home, a record that had stood since 1901. The Hungarians had been undefeated for three years and had won the Olympic tournament the year before, while England were the so-called "inventors" of football. The British press dubbed it "The Match of the Century". In the event, the match revolutionized the game in England, Hungary's unequivocal victory exposing the naivete of English football tactics. England captain Billy Wright later summed up the humiliation by saying: "We completely underestimated the advances that Hungary had made, and not only tactically. When we walked out at Wembley ... I looked down and noticed that the Hungarians had on these strange, lightweight boots, cut away like slippers under the ankle bone. I turned to big Stan Mortensen and said: 'We should be all right here, Stan, they haven't got the proper kit.'"

EUROPEAN PIONEERS

While Argentina's match against Uruguay in July 1902 was the first international outside the British Isles, Hungary's 5-0 defeat to Austria in Vienna three months later was Europe's first between two non-UK sides. Ten of Hungary's first 16 internationals were against Austria, with the Hungarians winning four, drawing one and losing five. In total, Hungary have won 66, drawn 30 and lost 40 against their Austrian neighbours.

GLORIOUS FAILURE

Hungary were runaway favourites to win the 1954 FIFA World Cup in Switzerland. They arrived for the finals having been unbeaten for four years. In the first round they thrashed West Germany 8-3, despite finishing with ten men after skipper Ferenc Puskas injured an ankle.

GOODISON LESSON

In the 1966 FIFA World Cup, Hungary gave Brazil a footballing lesson at Goodison Park, running out 3-1 winners before their progress was stopped by the Soviet Union in the quarter-finals. It was Brazil's first defeat in the FIFA World Cup since the 1954 quarter-finals, when they had lost 4-2 to ... Hungary.

YEARS OF PLENTY

Hungary's dazzling line-up of the early 1950s was known as the "Aranycsapat" – or "Golden Team". They set a record for international matches unbeaten, going 31 consecutive games without defeat between May 1950 and their July 1954 FIFA World Cup final loss to West Germany – a run that included clinching Olympic gold at Helsinki in Finland in 1952. That 31-match tally has been overtaken since only by Brazil and Spain. Hungary in the 1950s also set a record for most consecutive games scoring at least one goal – 73 matches – while their average of 5.4 goals per game at the 1954 FIFA World Cup remains an all-time high for the tournament.

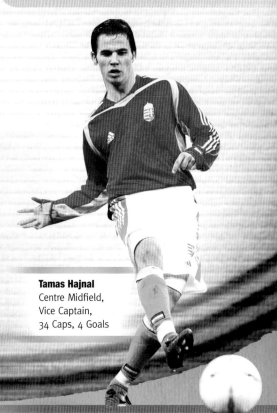

Tamas Hajnal
Centre Midfield,
Vice Captain,
34 Caps, 4 Goals

HIGH FLYERS

1938 – Hungary reach the FIFA World Cup final in France, losing 4-2 to Italy.
1953 – Hungary become the first team from outside the British Isles to beat England at home, winning 6-3 at Wembley.
1954 – Hungary reach the FIFA World Cup final in Switzerland and, despite being odds-on favourites, lose 3-2 to West Germany.
1964 – Hungary reach the semi-finals of UEFA European Championship in Spain.
1965 – Ferencvaros become Hungary's first, and to date only, European club winner, lifting the Inter-Cities Fairs (UEFA) Cup.
1972 – Hungary reach the semi-finals of UEFA European Championships in Belgium, before losing 1-0 to the Soviet Union.
1986 – The last time Hungary qualify for the FIFA World Cup finals – in Mexico.

NORTHERN IRELAND

Northern Ireland have played as a separate country since 1921 (before that there had been an all-Ireland side). They have qualified for the FIFA World Cup™ finals on three occasions: in 1958 (when they became the smallest country to reach the quarter-final stage), 1982 (when they reached the second round) and 1986.

GEORGE BEST

One of the greatest players never to grace a FIFA World Cup, **George Best** (capped 37 times by Northern Ireland) nevertheless won domestic and European honours with Manchester United – including both a European Champions Cup medal and the European Footballer of the Year award in 1968. He also played in the United States, Hong Kong and Australia before his "final" retirement in 1984.

GIANT JENNINGS

Pat Jennings's record 119 appearances for Northern Ireland also stood at one stage as an international record. The former Tottenham Hotspur and Arsenal goalkeeper made his international debut – aged just 18 – against Wales on 15 April 1964, and played his final game in the 1986 FIFA World Cup, against Brazil, on his 41st birthday.

"PETER THE GREAT"

Former Manchester City and Derby County striker Peter Doherty, one of the most expensive players of his era, won the English league and FA Cup as a player, and earned 19 caps for Northern Ireland in a career interrupted by World War Two. His late goal to earn a 2-2 draw in 1947 ensured Northern Ireland avoided defeat against England for the first time. As manager, he led Northern Ireland to the quarter-finals of the 1958 FIFA World Cup – Northern Ireland remain the smallest country ever to reach that stage of the competition. They were defeated 4-0 by France, who went on to finish third.

OH DANNY BOY

Northern Ireland's captain at the 1958 FIFA World Cup was Tottenham Hotspur's cerebral **Danny Blanchflower** – the first twentieth-century captain of an English club to win both the league and FA Cup in the same season, in 1960–61. When asked the secret of his national team's success in 1958, he offered the explanation: "Our tactic is to equalize before the others have scored." More famously, he offered the philosophy: "The great fallacy is that the game is first and foremost about winning. It's nothing of the kind. The game is about glory. It's about doing things in style, with a flourish, about going out and beating the other lot, not waiting for them to die of boredom."

AGE OLD QUESTION

Sam Johnston is the youngest player to have played for any Ireland national team. He was 15 years and 154 days old when he turned out for the old combined team (before the founding of the Irish Free State) in 1882. He also scored in his second game, making him Ireland's youngest-ever goalscorer, too.

TOP SCORERS

1	David Healy	35
2	Colin Clarke	13
=	Billy Gillespie	13
4	Gerry Armstrong	12
=	Joe Bambrick	12
=	Iain Dowie	12
=	Jimmy Quinn	12
8	Billy Bingham	10
=	Johnny Crossan	10
=	Jimmy McIlroy	10
=	Peter McParland	10

TOP CAPS

1	Pat Jennings	119
2	Mal Donaghy	91
3	Sammy McIlroy	88
4	Maik Taylor	87
5	Keith Gillespie	86
6	David Healy	85
7	Aaron Hughes	76
8	Jimmy Nicholl	73
9	Michael Hughes	71
10	David McCreery	67

MAKING YOUR MIND UP

Footballers born in Northern Ireland can choose to represent the neighbouring Republic of Ireland if they wish, based on family or religious connections – as did Manchester United's Derry-born midfielder Darron Gibson in 2007. Initially it appeared he might be joined in switching by two more Northern Irish-born players, Tony Kane and **Michael O'Connor** – but they have since decided they want to play for Northern Ireland and not the Republic after all. Kane was fielded by both the Republic of Ireland and Northern Ireland Under-21 teams while awaiting his first full international call-up, while O'Connor made his senior Northern Ireland debut in 2008.

HERO HEALY

Northern Ireland's record goalscorer **David Healy** has scored more than double the amount of international goals than the next highest player on the list. He scored two goals on his debut against Luxembourg on 23 February 2000, and scored all three as Northern Ireland stunned Spain 3-2 in a qualifier for UEFA Euro 2008 on 6 September 2006.

YOUNG GUN

Norman Whiteside became the then-youngest player at a FIFA World Cup finals (beating Pele's record) when he represented Northern Ireland in Spain in 1982 aged 17 years and 41 days. He went on to win 38 caps, scoring nine goals – before injury forced his retirement aged just 26.

HOME OWNERSHIP

Northern Ireland remain the reigning holders of the British Home Championship, a title contested annually by England, Scotland, Wales and Northern Ireland from 1883–84 to 1983–84. The last tournament ended with all four teams level on four points, after each winning once, drawing once and losing once – but Billy Bingham's Northern Ireland were the only side with a positive goal difference. A new "Nations Cup" contested by Northern Ireland, Scotland, Wales and the Republic of Ireland began in 2011, with organizers hoping to tempt England to join a resurrected British Home Championship in 2013.

BINGHAM'S DOUBLE

Billy Bingham was a key player on the right wing in Northern Ireland's 1958 FIFA World Cup run, and managed the national side to FIFA World Cup qualification in 1982 and 1986 – the only time the country has made it to consecutive tournaments.

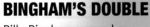

NORWAY

Although they played their first international, against Sweden, in 1908 and qualified for the 1938 FIFA World Cup™, it would take a further 56 years, and the introduction of a direct brand of football, before Norway reappeared at a major international tournament. Success in such competitions has been rare, they have never progressed beyond the second round, but Norway retains the distinction of being the only nation in history never to have lost to Brazil.

BRAZIL RESISTANCE

Norway are the only nation never to have lost – so far – to Samba kings Brazil, enjoying a record of two victories and two draws. Their most memorable match against Brazil came in the first round of the 1998 FIFA World Cup, when Norway triumphed 2-1 against a side who would go on to reach that year's final. Norway actually went a goal down, but came back to win thanks to strikes in the last seven minutes from **Tore Andre Flo** and Kjetil Rekdal.

GOALS FOR EITHER IVERSEN

Steffen Iversen scored the only goal of Norway's only win at a UEFA European Championship – against Spain at the tournament in 2000. Iversen's father Odd had previously been one of the country's leading strikers, hitting memorable strikes in unexpected victories over Yugoslavia in a 1966 FIFA World Cup qualifier and away to France ahead of the 1970 tournament. Odd scored a total of 19 times in 45 games for Norway between 1967 and 1979. Steffen equalled his father's international scoring tally with a hat-trick against Malta in November 2007 – then scored his next two goals against Iceland the following September. He was still playing for Norway in 2011, aged 34, having reached 79 caps for his 21 goals.

YOUR BOYS TOOK A HELL OF A BEATING

Bjorge Lillelien's famous commentary after Norway beat England 2-1 in a qualifier for the 1982 FIFA World Cup remains one of the iconic moments of European football. A commentator from 1957 until just before his death from cancer in 1987, he concentrated on winter sports and football. Roughly translated, it sounded as follows: "Lord Nelson, Lord Beaverbrook, Sir Winston Churchill, Sir Anthony Eden, Clement Attlee, Henry Cooper, Lady Diana, Maggie Thatcher, can you hear me? Your boys took a hell of a beating." Although the commentary was for Norwegian radio, it soon made its way to an English audience and has achieved cliché status. In 2002, Lillelien's words were designated the greatest piece of sports commentary ever by the *Observer* newspaper's sports supplement. Such is its place in British sporting culture, parodies of the commentary have been written to celebrate a vast array of domestic sporting victories.

BACK FROM THE DEAD

Former Norway, Wimbledon and Lillestrom midfielder Stale Solbakken – who became coach of 1FC Köln in May 2011 – had agreed to take charge of the Norway national team from 2012 onwards. All this is quite an achievement for a man who, in 2001, died for seven minutes. He was 33 when he suffered a heart attack during an FC Copenhagen training session and the paramedics, who discoverd his heart had stopped beating, declared him clinically dead. They were able to revive him in an ambulance, but Solbakken – who was found to have been born with a heart defect – had a pacemaker fitted, retired as a player and turned to coaching.

TOP CAPS

1	Thorbjorn Svenssen	104
2	Henning Berg	100
3	Erik Thorstvedt	97
4	Oyvind Leonhardsen	86
=	John Arne Riise	86
6	Kjetil Rekdal	83
7	John Carew	82
8	Erik Mykland	78
9	Svein Grondalen	77
=	Steffen Iversen	77

TOP SCORERS

1	Jorgen Juve	33
2	Einar Gundersen	26
3	Harald Hennum	25
4	Tore Andre Flo	23
=	Ole Gunnar Solskjaer	23
6	John Carew	22
=	Gunnar Thoresen	22
8	Steffen Iversen	21
9	Jan Age Fjortoft	20
10	Odd Iversen	19
=	Oyvind Leonhardsen	19
=	Olav Nilsen	19

ERIK THE VIKING

Goalkeeper **Erik Thorstvedt** was among the Norway footballers taking part at the 1984 Olympic Games in Los Angeles, when they qualified as late replacements after tournament boycotts by Iron Curtain countries Poland and East Germany. He was also a key member of the team who qualified for Norway's first FIFA World Cup since 1938, in 1994, and played a Norwegian goalkeeping record of 97 internationals between 1982 and 1996. But his career at English club Tottenham Hotspur could not have got off to a worse start. Less than five minutes into his 1989 debut against Nottingham Forest – broadcast live on television – he dropped the ball to gift Nigel Clough the opening goal of a 2-1 defeat for Spurs. Despite the blunder, Thorstvedt became hugely popular at the north London club and earned himself the affectionate nickname "Erik The Viking". He played in goal when Spurs lifted the 1991 FA Cup at Wembley – this time beating Forest 2-1. Another Norwegian international goalkeeper played for Spurs later that same decade: Espen Baardsen, the US-born son of Norwegian parents, who decided to retire aged 25 and become a successful City businessman instead.

LONG STAY TRAVELLERS

Norway's best finish at an international tournament was the bronze medal they clinched at the 1936 Summer Olympics in Berlin, having lost to Italy in the semi-finals but beaten Poland 3-2 in a medal play-off thanks to an Arne Brustad hat-trick. That year's side has gone down in Norwegian football history as the "Bronselaget", or "Bronze Team". But they had entered the tournament with low expectations and were forced to alter their travel plans ahead of the semi-final against Italy on 10 August – Norwegian football authorities had originally booked their trip home for the previous day, not expecting to get so far. Italy beat Norway 2-1 in extra-time not only in that summer's Olympic semi-final, but also in the first round of the FIFA World Cup two years later – going on to win both tournaments.

BOOT CAMPER

Egil Olsen, one of Europe's most eccentric coaches, was signed up for a surprise second spell as national manager when Norway put their faith in the direct-football specialist along the road towards the 2010 FIFA World Cup finals in South Africa – 15 years after he had led the unfancied Scandinavians to the 1994 finals. That had been Norway's first finals appearance since 1938 and they followed it up by beating Brazil in the first round in France in 1998, making a hero out of the man in Wellington boots who guided his country to an impressive No. 2 in FIFA's official rankings. Before answering his country's call for a second stint as manager, Olsen's last job had been as manager of Iraq but he left after only three months in charge. Remarkably, in his first match back at the helm for Norway, he masterminded a 1-0 win away to Germany with his route-one tactics. But life was not quite as happy for Olsen during his time at Wimbledon in the 1999–2000 Premier League season. The Norwegian, a firm believer in sports science, imposed a zonal marking system, which he was convinced would work. Critics held it responsible for Wimbledon's collapse in the second half of the season.

POLAND

The history of Polish football is [illegible] highs and depressing lows [illegible] success [illegible] 1974 and [illegible] were followed by failure to qualify for [illegible] tournaments [illegible] to the UEFA European Championship for the first time in 2008 and will co-host the tournament (with Ukraine) in 2012.

STAYING ON LATER THAN LATO

Record-breaking Polish stalwart **Michal Zewlakow** bowed out of international football on familiar turf, even though his country were playing an away game. The versatile defender's 102nd and final appearance for his country was a goalless friendly in Greece in March 2011, at the Karaiskakis stadium in Piraeus where he used to play club football for Olympiacos. Zewlakow had overtaken Grzegorz Lato's appearances record for Poland in his previous match, an October 2010 friendly against Ecuador. Already he had already helped make footballing history for his homeland when he and brother Marcin, a striker, became the first twins to line up together for Poland, against France in February 2000. Marcin would end his international career with 25 appearances and five goals.

TOP SCORERS

1	Wlodzimierz Lubanski	48
2	Grzegorz Lato	45
3	Kazimierz Deyna	41
4	Ernest Pol	39
5	Andrzej Szarmach	32
6	Gerard Cieslik	27
7	Zbigniew Boniek	24
8	Ernest Wilimowski	21
9	Dariusz Dziekanowski	20
10	Roman Kosecki	19
=	Eusebiusz Smolarek	19

COOL KEEPER

What is it with Polish goalkeepers? The country's outfield players may not always be household names worldwide, but Jerzy Dudek (Liverpool), Artur Boruc and Lukasz Zaluska (both Celtic), **Lukasz Fabianski** and Wojciech Szczesny (both Arsenal), and Tomasz Kuszczak (Manchester United) have all played roles at four of Britain's most successful clubs.

STAR SIGN LEO

Leo Beenhakker became the first foreigner to coach Poland when he took charge in July 2006. In a career spanning more than 30 years, Beenhakker has coached Holland and Saudi Arabia, as well as Trinidad and Tobago. He also won three Spanish league titles with Real Madrid from 1987–89 and two Dutch league titles with Ajax in 1980 and 1990. The silver-haired Dutchman underlined his workaholic reputation in the spring of 2009 by taking up an extra role as consultant back home with Feyenoord. His Dutch job became his full focus later that year when he was sacked by Poland.

O COME, O COME, EMMANUEL

Poland were the first European country to qualify for the 2002 FIFA World Cup in South Korea and Japan, largely thanks to the eight goals scored by striker **Emmanuel Olisadebe** – setting a Polish record for a FIFA World Cup qualifying campaign. Nigerian-born Olisadebe had been awarded Polish citizenship during a successful four-year stint at Polonia Warsaw. He was actually given special permission by the president of Poland to become a citizen a year before completing the official qualification period.

TOP CAPS

1	Michal Zewlakow	102
2	Grzegorz Lato	100
3	Kazimierz Deyna	97
4	Jacek Krzynowek	96
=	Jacek Bak	96
6	Wladyslaw Zmuda	91
7	Antoni Szymanowski	82
8	Zbigniew Boniek	80
9	Wlodzimierz Lubanski	75
10	Tomasz Waldoch	74

POLE DANCING

Three is Poland's lucky football number. The years 1974 and 1982 stand out in the annals of the country's sport because, on both occasions, the Poles came third at the FIFA World Cup. In 1974, with their lightning speed and team chemistry, they were almost unstoppable after upsetting England in qualifying. Memorably, when they played hosts West Germany, the pitch was half-flooded and the Poles, who needed a win to reach the final, wanted the game postponed. Instead, in miserably wet conditions, Gerd Muller scored a late German winner. In 1982, in Spain, only Grzegorz Lato, Andrzej Szarmach, Marek Kusto and Wladyslaw Zmuda remained from the 1974 squad. But the exciting mix of veterans and youngsters were no match for Italy in the semi-finals, losing 2-0.

FIVE ASIDE

Poland had five different goalscorers when they beat Peru 5-1 at the 1982 FIFA World Cup: **Wlodzimierz Smolarek**, Grzegorz Lato, Zbigniew Boniek, Andrzej Buncol and Wlodzimierz Ciolek. The feat was not repeated until Phillip Cocu, Marc Overmars, Dennis Bergkamp, Pierre van Hooijdonk and Ronald de Boer gave Holland a 5-0 victory over South Korea at the 1998 FIFA World Cup.

BONIEK

Zbigniew Boniek, arguably the best player Poland has ever produced, earned a place among football's legends for his role in the country's progress to third place at the 1982 FIFA World Cup. However, his absence from the tournament's semi-final will go down as one of the great "what ifs" of the competition. Robbed of their star forward through suspension, could Poland have upset both Italy and the odds and reached the final? Instead they lost 2-0.

SUPER ERNEST

Ernest Wilimowski wrote his name into FIFA World Cup history in 1938 when he scored four goals but still finished on the losing side. Poland went down 6-5 after extra-time to Brazil in a first-round tie in Strasbourg.

PUNCTUALITY PUNISHMENT

Kazimierz Gorski was the coach – once-capped as a player – who led Poland to third place at the 1974 FIFA World Cup, having won gold at the Olympics in Munich, Germany, two years earlier. While winning a reputation for closeness with his players, Gorski could also be ruthless – key player Adam Musial was dropped from the team for a second-round game against Sweden at the 1974 tournament as punishment for turning up 20 minutes late to training. Poland still won the game, 1-0.

LATO'S MISSION

Grzegorz Lato, one of Poland's finest-ever players, became president of the country's football federation in 2008, promising to clean up the sport as Poland gears up to co-host the 2012 UEFA European Championships with Ukraine. "I am determined to change the image of Polish football, to make it transparent and pure," said Lato, a legend in the 1970s and '80s and the top scorer at the 1974 FIFA World Cup (with seven goals).

PORTUGAL

Portugal's first experience of international competition almost ended in triumph. Inspired by Eusebio, they marched through to the semi-finals of the 1966 FIFA World Cup™, only to lose to eventual champions England. A standout performance in the 1984 UEFA European Championship apart, more than 30 years would pass before Portugal enjoyed such giddy heights again. A "golden" generation of players arrived on the scene and since the turn of the century Portugal have become a consistent force on the world football stage.

TOP CAPS

1	LUIS Filipe Madeira FIGO	127
2	FERNANDO Manuel Silva COUTO	110
3	RUI Manuel Cesar COSTA	94
4	Pedro Miguel Resendes "PAULETA"	88
5	SIMAO Pedro Fonseca SABROSA	85
6	JOAO Manuel VIEIRA PINTO	81
7	VITOR Manuel Martins BAIA	80
=	CRISTIANO RONALDO dos Santos Aveiro	80
9	RICARDO Alexandre Martins PEREIRA	79
10	Nuno Miguel Soares "NUNO GOMES"	77

GOODISON GLORY

At the 1966 FIFA World Cup Portugal beat North Korea 5-3 in an incredible quarter-final at Everton's Goodison Park. The sensational Eusebio spurred an amazing comeback after the Koreans had gone 3-0 ahead in the first 25 minutes. He scored four goals to take Portugal to the semi-finals in their first-ever FIFA World Cup appearance. Despite the tears that flowed after defeat to eventual winners England, Portugal rallied to claim third place with a **2-1 victory over the Soviet Union.**

TOP SCORERS

1	Pedro Miguel Resendes "PAULETA"	47
2	EUSEBIO da Silva Ferreira	41
3	LUIS Filipe Madeira FIGO	32
4	Nuno Miguel Soares "NUNO GOMES"	29
5	RUI Manuel Cesar COSTA	26
=	CRISTIANO RONALDO dos Santos Aveiro	26
7	JOAO Manuel VIEIRA PINTO	23
8	Tamagnini Baptista "NENE"	22
=	SIMAO Pedro Fonseca SABROSA	22
10	Rui Manuel Trinidade JORDAO	15
=	Fernando Baptista de Seixas PEYROTEO de Vasconcelo	15
=	HELDER Manuel Marques POSTIGA	15

CLOUD NINE

Scoring nine goals in one match against Leca, eight goals in one match against Boavista, six goals in a game three times, five goals in a game 12 times and four goals in a game 17 times, Fernando Baptista Peyroteo is one of the most prolific goalscorers in world football history. He scored an astonishing 330 goals in 197 Portuguese league games (1.68 goals a game) between 1937 and 1949, and 15 goals in just 20 games for the national side.

THE BLACK PANTHER

Born in Mozambique, **Eusebio** da Silva Ferreira was named Portugal's "Golden Player" to mark UEFA's 50th anniversary in 2004. Signed by Benfica in 1960 at the age of 18, he scored a hat-trick in only his second game – against Santos in a friendly tournament in Paris – outshining the opponents' young star, Pele. He helped Benfica win the second of their European Cups in 1962, was named European Footballer of the Year in 1965, and led Portugal to third place in the 1966 FIFA World Cup, finishing the tournament as top scorer with nine goals. A phenomenal striker, Eusebio scored 320 goals in 313 appearances in the Portuguese league, won the first European Golden Boot in 1968 (and earned a second in 1973). His 41 goals for Portugal – in 64 matches – has been bettered only by Pauleta, who scored 47, but in 24 more appearances.

AT SIXES AND SEVENS

Six different players were on the scoresheet in Portugal's 7-0 victory over North Korea at the 2010 FIFA World Cup: Raul Meireles, Simao, Hugo Almeida, Tiago (who scored twice), Liedson and captain Cristiano Ronaldo. That tally has only been outdone by the seven who shared Yugoslavia's nine goals without reply against Zaire at the 1974 FIFA World Cup. The goals by Simao and **Cristiano Ronaldo** meant they emulated Pauleta in scoring for Portugal at two separate FIFA World Cups.

CRISTIANO RONALDO

Cristiano Ronaldo dos Santos Aveiro got his second name because his father was a great fan of US President Ronald Reagan. Despite growing up a Benfica fan, Ronaldo began his career with local rivals Sporting before moving to Manchester United in 2003. He enjoyed a fantastic season in 2008, winning the Premier League, the Champions League, the Golden Boot in the Premier League and Europe, and capping it all by becoming the second Portuguese player (after Luis Figo) to win the FIFA World Player of the Year award. He became the most expensive footballer ever when Real Madrid paid £80 million to sign him from Manchester United in 2009.

THE FAMOUS FIVE

Eusebio, Mario Coluna, Jose Augusto, Antonio Simoes, and Jose Torres were the "Fabulous Five" in Benfica's 1960s Dream Team, who made up the spine of the Portuguese national side at the 1966 FIFA World Cup. Coluna (the "Sacred Monster"), scored the vital third goal in the 1961 European Cup final and captained the national side in 1966. Jose Augusto, who scored two goals in the opening game against Hungary, went on to manage the national side and later the Portuguese women's team. Antonio Simoes (the "Giant Gnome" – just 1.58 metres/5ft 3in tall) made his debut for Portugal and Benfica in 1962, aged just 18. Jose Torres – the only one of the five not to win the European Cup (though he played in the defeats in both 1963 and 1968) – scored the winner against Russia in the 1966 third-place match, and went on to manage the national side to their next appearance at the FIFA World Cup finals in 1986.

KOREA OPPORTUNITIES

Portugal scored seven goals in four matches at the 2010 FIFA World Cup, all against North Korea in a 7-0 Group G trouncing. It was the joint third-biggest winning margin in a FIFA World Cup finals. Added to the 5-3 triumph over them in a 1966 quarter-final, it means almost one-third of Portugal's 39 FIFA World Cup goals have been scored against North Korea.

HAPPY HUNDREDTH BIRTHDAY

Portugal celebrated the 100th birthday of their modern-day republic by bringing newly crowned world champions Spain back down to earth with a bump, in a specially-arranged friendly international in November 2010. The match was held not only to mark the national anniversary, but also to celebrate the two countries' union in an ultimately-unsuccessful bid to co-host the 2018 FIFA World Cup. Yet there was little equality about the 90 minutes of match action, with Portugal sweeping to a 4-0 triumph – slight consolation for Spain's second-round victory over them at The 2010 FIFA World Cup five months earlier. Portugal's manager this time around was not sacked World Cup coach Carlos Queiroz but former international midfielder **Paulo Bento**. Queiroz served two stints in charge of the national team, as well as leading Portugal's "Golden Generation" team to glory at the FIFA U-20 World Cup in 1989 and 1991.

REP. OF IRELAND

It took a combination of astute management and endless searching through ancestral records before the Republic of Ireland finally qualified for the finals of a major tournament, at the 20th time of asking. But ever since Jack Charlton took the team to UEFA Euro 88, Ireland have remained one of Europe's most dangerous opponents.

KEANE CARRY—ON

Roy Keane stormed out of Ireland's preparation for the 2002 FIFA World Cup in Japan and Korea, heading home before the tournament had even started. Keane's career with Ireland began against Chile on 22 May 1991. He played in all four Ireland's matches at the 1994 FIFA World Cup in the United States, including the shock 1-0 defeat of Italy. Originally appointed captain by Mick McCarthy, Keane returned to the Irish set-up after McCarthy resigned – but announced his international retirement after Ireland failed to qualify for the 2006 FIFA World Cup. His final game was a 1-0 defeat to France on 7 September 2005.

CHAMPION CHARLTON

Jack Charlton became a hero after he took Ireland to their first major finals in 1988, defeating England 1-0 in their first game at the UEFA European Championship. Even better was their first FIFA World Cup finals two years later, where the unfancied Irish lost out only to hosts Italy in the quarter-finals.

KILBANE KEEPS ON AND ON

Only England's Billy Wright, with 70, has played more consecutive internationals than **Kevin Kilbane**, whose 109th Republic of Ireland cap against Macedonia in March 2011 was also his 65th in a row, covering 11 years and five months. The versatile left-sider – nicknamed "Zinedine Kilbane" by fans – was given a rest for Ireland's next game three days later, though, a friendly against Uruguay.

ROBBIE KEEN

The Republic of Ireland's all-time scoring record was taken over by much-travelled striker **Robbie Keane** in October 2004 and he has been adding to it ever since – not least with last-minute equalisers against both Germany and Spain at the 2006 FIFA World Cup. He marked the final game at the old Lansdowne Road with a hat-trick against San Marino in November 2006 – then, four years later, marked the inaugural game at the revamped replacement ground, now known as the Aviva Stadium, with his 100th cap against Argentina. Ireland's 2-1 win over Macedonia in March 2011 was Keane's 41st appearance as captain – equalling the record set in the 1980s and 1990s by Andy Townsend. He followed this up with two more matches as skipper, as Ireland beat Northern Ireland and Scotland in the British-based Carling Nations Cup – scoring three goals across the two games, taking his overall tally to 49, before his brace against Macedonia in June 2011 took him to 51. These made him the first player from the British Isles to score a helf-century of international goals, and past England's 49-goal top scorer Bobby Charlton.

CROKE PARK

Croke Park is the traditional Dublin home of the Gaelic Athletic Association and banned "foreign" sports ... until Ireland were given special permission to play their qualifiers for UEFA Euro 2008 there while their traditional home, Lansdowne Road, was being renovated.

GILES PILES UP THE JOBS

Jack Charlton is Ireland's longest-serving manager, with nine years in the job between 1986 and 1995. But Johnny Giles's stint as boss, between 1973 and 1980, also deserves recognition, since he was still playing club football throughout his reign – for Leeds United, West Bromwich Albion, Philadelphia Fury and finally Shamrock Rovers. Despite his national team duties, that seven-year stint included being a key member of Leeds's 1973–74 English league championship squad and serving as player-manager of both West Brom and Rovers.

CAPTAIN ALL-ROUND

Johnny Carey not only captained Matt Busby's Manchester United to the English league title in 1952, he also captained both Northern Ireland (nine caps) and later the Republic of Ireland (27 caps). He went on to manage the Republic of Ireland between 1955 and 1967.

HOORAY FOR RAY

Ray Houghton may have been born in Glasgow and spoke with a Scottish accent, but he scored two of Ireland's most famous goals. A header gave the Republic a shock 1–0 win over England at UEFA Euro 88 in West Germany and, six years later, his long-range strike was the only goal of the game against eventual finalists Italy, in the first round of the 1994 FIFA World Cup in the USA.

MORE FOR MOORE

Paddy Moore was the first player ever to score four goals in a FIFA World Cup qualifier when Ireland came from behind to draw 4-4 with Belgium on 25 February 1934. Don Givens became the only Irishman to equal Moore's feat when he scored all four as Ireland beat Turkey in October 1975.

CROSSING THE CODES

Cornelius "Con" Martin was a Gaelic footballer whose passion for soccer resulted in his expulsion from the Gaelic Athletic Association. His versatility meant he was as good at centre-half as he was in goal, both for club (Aston Villa) and country. He played both in goal and outfield for the fledgling Irish national team, scoring a penalty in the 2-0 victory over England at Goodison Park in 1949 – in what was England's first home defeat to a non-British opponent.

TOP CAPS

1	Shay Given	113
2	Kevin Kilbane	110
3	Robbie Keane	108
4	Steve Staunton	102
5	Niall Quinn	91
6	Tony Cascarino	88
7	Damien Duff	87
8	Paul McGrath	83
9	Packie Bonner	80
10	Ray Houghton	73

TOP SCORERS

1	Robbie Keane	51
2	Niall Quinn	21
3	Frank Stapleton	20
4	John Aldridge	19
=	Tony Cascarino	19
=	Don Givens	19
7	Noel Cantwell	14
8	Gerry Daly	13
=	Jimmy Dunne	13
10	Ian Harte	11

ROMANIA

The history of Romanian football is littered with a series of bright moments – they were one of four countries (with Brazil, France and Belgium) to appear in the first three editions of the FIFA World Cup™ – followed by significant spells in the doldrums – since 1938 they have qualified for the finals of the tournament only four times in 14 attempts. The country's football highlight came in 1994 when, inspired by Gheorghe Hagi, they reached the quarter-finals of the FIFA World Cup™.

CEMETERY SENTRY

It was second time luckier for former international striker **Victor Piturca** when he coached Romania at the 2008 UEFA European Championship in Austria and Switzerland, even though they were eliminated in the first round. He had previously been manager when the country qualified for the 2000 UEFA European Championship, but was forced out of the job before the tournament itself following arguments with big-name players such as Gheorghe Hagi. Piturca's cousin Florin Piturca was also a professional footballer but died aged only 27 in 1978. Florin's father and Victor's uncle Maximilian, a cobbler, not only built a mausoleum for Florin but also slept at night in the cemetery until his own death in 1994.

TERRIFIC TRIO

Gheorghe Hagi, **Florin Raducioiu** and Ilie Dumitrescu lit up the FIFA World Cup in the United States in 1994. Together they scored nine of Romania's ten goals (Raducioiu four, Hagi three, Dumitrescu two). All three successfully converted their penalties in the quarter-final shoot-out against Sweden, but misses from Dan Petrescu and Miodrag Belodedici sent the Romanians crashing out. All three made big-money moves for the following 1994–95 season: Hagi went from Brescia to Barcelona, Dumitrescu from Steaua Bucharest to Tottenham Hotspur, and Raducioiu went from warming the bench at Milan to the first team at Espanyol.

YELLOW PERIL

Despite topping Group G ahead of England, Colombia and Tunisia at the 1998 FIFA World Cup, Romania's players of that tournament might perhaps be best-remembered for the collective decision to dye their hair **blond** ahead of their final first-round game. The newly bleached Romanians struggled to a 1-1 draw against Tunisia, before being knocked out 1-0 by Croatia in the second round.

THE "HERO OF SEVILLE"

Helmuth Duckadam, the "Hero of Seville", will always be remembered for saving four consecutive penalties as Steaua Bucharest became the first Eastern European side to win the European Cup, beating Barcelona in a shoot-out in 1986. A rare blood disease forced him to retire from the game in 1991, after which he became a stopper of a different kind as a major in the Romanian Border Police.

TOP SCORERS

1	Gheorghe Hagi	35
2	Iuliu Bodola	31
=	Adrian Mutu	31
4	Anghel Iordanescu	26
5	Viorel Moldovan	25
6	Ladislau Boloni	23
7	Rodion Camataru	22
8	Dudu Georgescu	21
=	Florin Raducioiu	21
10	Stefan Dobay	20
=	Ilie Dumitrescu	20

TOP CAPS

1	Dorinel Munteanu	134
2	Gheorghe Hagi	125
3	Gheorghe Popescu	115
4	Ladislau Boloni	108
5	Dan Petrescu	95
6	Bogdan Stelea	91
7	Michael Klein	90
8	Marius Lacatus	84
9	Mircea Rednic	83
10	Bogdan Lobont	78

BORDER CROSSING

Some 14 footballers played for both Romania, during the 1930s, and Hungary, during the 1940s – the most prolific being striker Iuliu Bodola, who scored 30 goals in 48 games for Romania, including appearances at the 1934 and 1938 FIFA World Cups, and four in 13 matches for adopted homeland Hungary.

A GOOD NAME

Gheorghe Popescu was a Romanian international defender, born in 1918, who went on to great success as manager of Steaua Bucharest before becoming president of the Romanian Football Association. Gheorghe "Gica" Popescu – no relation – was also a Romanian international defender, born in 1967, who won 115 caps and a string of European club titles, including the now-defunct Cup-Winners' Cup, the UEFA Cup, as well as domestic leagues and cups in Holland, Spain, Romania and Turkey.

CENTURY MAN

Gheorghe Hagi, Romania's "Player of the [20th] Century", scored three goals and was named in the Team of the Tournament in the 1994 FIFA World Cup in the United States, where Romania lost out on penalties to Sweden after a 2-2 draw in the quarter-finals. Hagi made his international debut in 1983, aged just 18, scored his first goal aged 19 (in a 3-2 defeat by Northern Ireland) and remains Romania's top goalscorer with 35 goals in 125 games. Despite retiring from international football after the 1998 FIFA World Cup, Hagi couldn't resist answering his country's call to play in UEFA Euro 2000. Sadly, two yellow-card offences in six minutes in the quarter-final against Italy meant Hagi's final bow on the international stage saw him receive a red card – and leave the field to take an early bath. Farul Constanta, in Hagi's hometown, named their stadium after him in 2000 – but fans stopped referring to it as such after he took the manager's job at rivals Timisoara.

MAJOR TOURNAMENTS

FIFA WORLD CUP™: 7 appearances – quarter-finals 1994
UEFA EUROPEAN CHAMPIONSHIP: 4 appearances – quarter-finals 2000
FIRST INTERNATIONAL: Yugoslavia 1 Romania 2 (Belgrade, Yugoslavia, 8 June 1922)
BIGGEST WIN: Romania 9 Finland 0 (Bucharest, Romania, 14 October 1973)
BIGGEST DEFEAT: Hungary 9 Romania 0 (Budapest, Hungary, 6 June 1948)

MUTU MUTED

Romania have been unfortunate to see arguably their finest player of the 21st century so far banned from the game not just once but twice, for failing drugs tests. The first was a private test carried out on **Adrian Mutu** by his club employers Chelsea in September 2004, which showed traces of cocaine and provoked the English side into sacking him. He was also banned for seven months but did manage to rehabilitate his career in Italy, for Juventus and then Fiorentina. Mutu then tested positive, however, for an outlawed anti-obesity drug, in January 2010, and received a nine-month ban in April that year. He remains the Romania national team's second-highest scorer of all time, with a tally which includes a strike against Italy at the 2008 UEFA European Championship. Romania have only lost once when Mutu has scored.

RUSSIA

Before the break-up of the Soviet Union (USSR) in 1992, the team was a world football powerhouse, winning the first UEFA European Championship in 1960, gold at the 1956 and 1988 Olympic Games, and qualifying for the FIFA World Cup™ on seven occasions. Playing as Russia since August 1992, the good times have eluded them – they were UEFA Euro 2008 semi-finalists, but then failed to advance from the qualifying play-offs to reach the 2010 FIFA World Cup™. Yet Russia has now been chosen as Eastern Europe's first-ever FIFA World Cup™ host country, staging the tournament in 2018.

TOP SCORERS
(Russia only)

1	Vladimir Beschastnykh	26
2	Valeri Karpin	17
=	Alexandr Kerzhakov	17
4	Andrei Arshavin	16
=	Roman Pavlyuchenko	16
6	Dmitri Sychev	15
7	Igor Kolyvanov	12
8	Sergei Kiriakov	10
=	Aleksandr Mostovoi	10
10	Dmitri Radchenko	9
=	Igor Simutenkov	9

YOUNG PROMISE

Igor Akinfeev became post-Soviet Russia's youngest international footballer when he made his debut in a friendly against Norway on 28 April 2004. The CSKA Moscow goalkeeper was just 18 years and 20 days old. The following season would be perhaps just as memorable for him, clinching a domestic league and cup double with his club while also lifting the UEFA Cup as CSKA Moscow became post-Soviet Russia's first side to win a UEFA club trophy. The youngest Soviet-era debutant was Eduard Streltsov, who hit a hat-trick on his debut against Sweden in June 1956, at the age of 17 years and 340 days – then scored another treble in his second game, against India.

TOP CAPS
(Russia only)

1	Viktor Onopko	109
2	Valeri Karpin	72
3	Vladimir Beschastnykh	71
4	Sergei Ignashevich	65
=	Sergei Semak	65
6	Andrei Arshavin	60
7	Aleksandr Anyukov	56
8	Dmitry Alenichev	55
=	Yuri Nikiforov	55
=	Alexei Smertin	55

MONEY MAN

Roman Abramovich, the commodities billionaire behind Chelsea's 21st-century success, has also been instrumental in the resurgence of Russian football at all levels – including the key step of importing Dutchman Guus Hiddink to manage the national side. In 2008, Hiddink took Russia to the semi-finals of the UEFA European Championship (their best post-Soviet performance), where they lost 3-0 to eventual winners Spain. Abramovich also sponsors the "National Academy of Football" in Russia, which helps build training facilities and pitches to support youth football throughout the country.

MAJOR TOURNAMENTS

FIFA WORLD CUP™: 9 appearances (7 as USSR, 2 as Russia) – fourth, 1966
UEFA EUROPEAN CHAMPIONSHIP: 9 appearances (5 as USSR, 1 as CIS 1992, 3 as Russia) – winners 1960 (USSR), semi-finals 2008 (Russia)
FIRST INTERNATIONAL:
Russian Empire: Finland 2 Russian Empire 1 (Stockholm, Sweden, 30 June 1912)
USSR: USSR 3 Turkey 0 (Moscow, 16 November 1924) (final international: Cyprus 0 USSR 3, Larnaca, 13 November 1991)
CIS: USA 0 CIS 1 (Miami, USA, 25 January 1992) (final international: Scotland 3 CIS 0, Norrkoping, Sweden, 18 June 1992)
Russia: Russia 2 Mexico 0 (Moscow, 16 August 1992)
BIGGEST WIN:
USSR: USSR 11 India 1 (Moscow, 16 September 1955); Finland 0 USSR 10 (Helsinki, 15 August 1957)
CIS: El Salvador 0 CIS 3 (San Salvador, 29 January 1992)
Russia: San Marino 0 Russia 7 (San Marino, 7 June 1995)
BIGGEST DEFEAT:
Russian Empire: Germany 16 Russian Empire 0 (Stockholm, Sweden, 1 July 1912)
USSR: England 5 USSR 0 (London, 22 October 1958)
CIS: Mexico 4 CIS 0 (Mexico City, 8 March 1992)
Russia: Portugal 7 Russia 1 (Lisbon, 13 October 2004)

⚽ CAPPING IT ALL

Viktor Onopko, despite being born in the Ukraine, played all his career for the CIS and Russian national football teams. The first of Onopko's 113 international caps (the first four for the CIS) came in a 2-2 draw against England in Moscow on 29 April 1992. He played in the 1994 and 1998 FIFA World Cups, as well as the UEFA European Championship in 1996. He was due to join the squad for the UEFA European Championship in 2004 but missed out through injury. Onopko's club career, spanning 19 years, took him to Shakhtar Donetsk, Spartak Moscow, Real Oviedo, Rayo Vallecano, Alania Vladikavkaz and FC Saturn. He was Russian footballer of the year in 1993 and 1994.

⚽ SUPER STOPPER

FIFA declared **Lev Yashin** to be the finest goalkeeper of the 20th century – naturally, he made it into their Century XI team, too. In a career spanning 20 years, Yashin played 326 league games for Dynamo Moscow – the only club side he ever played for – and won 78 caps for the Soviet Union, conceding on average less than a goal a game (only 70 in total). With Dynamo, he won five Soviet championships and three Soviet cups, the last of which came in his final full season in 1970. He saved around 150 penalties in his long career, and kept four clean sheets in his 12 World Cup matches. Such was Yashin's worldwide reputation, Chilean international Eladio Rojas was so excited at scoring past the legendary Yashin in the 1962 FIFA World Cup that he gave the surprised keeper a big hug with the ball still sitting in the back of the net. Yashin was nicknamed the "Black Spider" for his distinctive black jersey and his uncanny ability to get a hand, arm, leg or foot in the way of shots and headers of all kinds. In 1963, Yashin became the first, and so far only, keeper to be named European Footballer of the Year, the same year in which he won his fifth Soviet championship and starred for the Rest of the World XI in the English FA's Centenary Match at Wembley.

⚽ PUTTING ON THE STYLE

Coach Guus Hiddink picked **Andrei Arshavin** in his Russia squad for the 2008 UEFA European Championship, despite knowing the playmaker would miss the first two of three group games due to suspension. Arshavin had been sent off for a petulant kick at an opponent, in the closing moments of the final qualifier against Andorra. But he proved his worth with starring roles in Russia's first-round victory over Sweden and their 3-1 quarter-final triumph over Holland. Arshavin, who later joined English club Arsenal from 2008 UEFA Cup holders Zenit St Petersburg, is not just a world-class footballer and one of his country's leading scorers, but also a talented draughts player – and a university graduate, having completed a diploma in fashion design.

⚽ GOLDEN BOY

Igor Netto captained the USSR national side to their greatest successes: gold at the 1956 Olympics in Melbourne and victory in the first-ever UEFA European Championship in France in 1960. Born in Moscow in 1930, Netto was awarded the Order of Lenin in 1957, and became an ice hockey coach after retiring from football.

SCOTLAND

A country with a vibrant domestic league and a rich football tradition – it played host to the first-ever international football match, against England, in November 1872 – Scotland have never put in the performances on the international stage to match their lofty ambitions. There have been moments of triumph, such as an unexpected victory over Holland at the 1978 FIFA World Cup™, but far too many moments of despair. They have not qualified for the finals of a major tournament since 1998.

TOP SCORERS

1	Kenny Dalglish	30
=	Denis Law	30
3	Hughie Gallacher	24
4	Lawrie Reilly	22
5	Ally McCoist	19
6	Bob Hamilton	15
=	James McFadden	15
8	Maurice Johnston	14
9	Bob McColl	13
=	Kenny Miller	13

KING KENNY

Kenny Dalglish is Scotland's joint-top international goalscorer (with Denis Law) and remains the only player to have won more than a century of caps for the national side, with 102 in total – 11 more than the next highest cap-winner, goalkeeper Jim Leighton. Despite growing up a Rangers fan (he was born in Glasgow on 4 March 1951), Dalglish made his name spear-heading Celtic's domestic dominance in the 1970s, winning four league titles, four Scottish Cups and one League Cup. He then went on to become a legend at Liverpool, winning a hat-trick of European Cups (1978, 1981 and 1984) and leading the side as player-manager to their first-ever league and cup double in 1986. He later joined Herbert Chapman and Brian Clough as one of the few managers to lead two different sides to the league title – guiding Blackburn Rovers to the summit of English football in 1994–95. For Scotland, Dalglish scored in both the 1978 and 1982 FIFA World Cup finals, netting the first goal in the famous 3-2 victory over eventual runners-up Holland in the 1978 group stages. He played his last international in 1986.

THE LAWMAN

Denis Law is joint top scorer for Scotland with Kenny Dalglish, scoring 30 goals in only 55 games compared with the 102 it took Dalglish to do the same. Law twice scored four goals in a match for Scotland. First against Northern Ireland on 7 November 1962, helping win the British Home Championships. He repeated the feat against Norway in a friendly on 7 November 1963. Law clearly enjoyed playing against Norway, having grabbed a hat-trick in Bergen just five months earlier.

DON'T COME HOME TOO SOON

Scotland have never made it past the initial stages of the finals of an international tournament. They've gone out of the FIFA World Cup on goal difference three times: to **Brazil in 1974**, to eventual runners-up Holland (on goals scored) in 1978 and to the Soviet Union in 1982.

ROOM FOR ONE MORE?

Hampden Park, Scotland's national stadium, boasts the record for the highest-ever football attendance in Europe. The crowd was so huge no one can be quite sure how many squeezed in to watch Scotland v England in 1937, though the official figure is usually quoted as 149,415. Scotland won the British Home Championship tie 3-1, though they ended runners-up to Wales in the overall tournament.

ONE TEAM IN TALLINN

When Scotland travelled to Estonia for a FIFA World Cup qualifier in October 1996, there was only one team in it – literally. The hosts refused to play in protest at kick-off time being brought forward by almost four hours, following a Scottish complaint about the floodlights. At the newly scheduled time, Scotland sent 11 men on to the field at the Kadrioru Stadium in Tallinn, even though there were no opponents. After Billy Dodds and John Collins had dutifully kicked off, Yugoslav referee Miroslav Radoman blew his whistle and formally abandoned the game. FIFA later ordered the game to be replayed in neutral Monaco. It ended goalless, and Scotland went on to reach the 1998 FIFA World Cup in France.

WEIR ON THE BALL

Rugged Rangers centre-back **David Weir** became Scotland's oldest international footballer when he faced Lithuania in a 2012 UEFA European Championship qualifier on 3 September 2010, aged 40 years and 111 days, for his 66th appearance. He was still representing his country three caps and 39 days later, against reigning world and European champions Spain.

TOP CAPS

1	Kenny Dalglish	102
2	Jim Leighton	91
3	Alex McLeish	77
4	Paul McStay	76
5	Tom Boyd	72
6	David Weir	69
7	Christian Dailly	67
8	Willie Miller	65
9	Danny McGrain	62
10	Richard Gough	61
=	Ally McCoist	61

NEW BALLS PLEASE

Lanarkshire-born forward Andy Wilson scored 12 goals in 12 official international football fixtures for Scotland from February 1920 to April 1923, but spent most of his club career across the border – playing for Middlesbrough, Chelsea and Queens Park Rangers, before spending his last two seasons at French club Nimes. He also represented England at bowls.

I HAVEN'T FELT THIS GOOD SINCE ARCHIE GEMMILL SCORED AGAINST HOLLAND

Archie Gemmill scored Scotland's greatest goal on the world stage in the surprise 3-2 victory over Holland at the 1978 FIFA World Cup. He jinked past three defenders before chipping the ball neatly over Dutch goalkeeper Jan Jongbloed. Amazingly, in 2008, this magical moment was turned into a dance in the English National Ballet's "The Beautiful Game".

SHORT–LEASE McLEISH

Former Aberdeen defender, Rangers manager and Scotland's third most-capped player, Alex McLeish also became his country's shortest-reigning full-time manager for four decades when he served just ten months in 2007 before quitting to join English club Birmingham City. But he is statistically the most successful Scotland boss of all time, with a 70 per cent win record – that is, his side won seven of his 10 games in charge. These included an away win over France in a qualifier for the 2008 UEFA European Championship, but Scotland narrowly missed out on reaching the finals.

UNOFFICIAL WORLD CHAMPIONS

One of the victories most cherished by Scotland fans is the **3-2 triumph** over arch-rivals and reigning world champions England, in April 1967 at Wembley – the first time Sir Alf Ramsey's team had lost since clinching the 1966 FIFA World Cup. Scotland's man of the match that day was ball-juggling left-half/midfielder Jim Baxter, while it was also the first game in charge for Scotland's first full-time manager, Bobby Brown. Less fondly recalled is Scotland's 9-3 trouncing by the same opposition at the same stadium in April 1961, which made unfortunate goalkeeper Frank Haffey the butt of a popular joke that did the rounds across the border in England: "What's the time? Nearly 10 past Haffey." The game was Haffey's second – and last – for Scotland.

SERBIA

The former Yugoslavia was one of the strongest football nations in eastern Europe. They reached the FIFA World Cup™ semi-finals in 1930 and 1962, they were also runners-up in the UEFA European Championships of 1960 and 1968. In addition, Yugoslavia's leading club, Red Star Belgrade, remain the only team from eastern Europe to win the European Cup, when they beat Marseille on penalties in the 1991 final.

MAGIC DRAGAN

Yugoslavia's greatest player was Red Star left winger **Dragan Dzajic**, who later went on to become the club's president. He made his international debut at 18, won a national record 85 caps and scored 23 goals. The most important was his last-minute winner against world champions England in the 1968 UEFA European Championship semi-final in Florence, which took Yugoslavia to the final against Italy. Pele said of Dzajic: "He's a real wizard. I'm sorry he's not Brazilian."

TOP CAPS

1	Savo Milosevic	102
2	Dejan Stankovic	96
3	Dragan Stojkovic	84
4	Predrag Mijatovic	73
5	Slavisa Jokanovic	64
=	Sinisa Mihajlovic	64
7	Mladen Krstajic	59
=	Zoran Mirkovic	59
9	Darko Kovacevic	58
10	Dejan Savicevic	56

SAVICEVIC STRIKES

Dejan Savicevic is Serbia's greatest player of the modern era. The attacking midfielder was a key member of **Red Star Belgrade**'s 1991 European Cup-winning team. He also inspired them to three consecutive championships. He moved on to Milan and starred as his new club beat Barcelona 4-0 in the 1994 European Cup final. He created the opening goal, then crashed home a 35-yard volley. Savicevic later became a prominent supporter of the drive for Montenegrin independence from Serbia and has been credited with playing an influential role in the referendum vote on 21 May 2006 that led to the establishment of a separate Montenegrin state.

YUGOSLAVIA HIT BY BOYCOTT

The rivalry between Serbia and Croatia was apparent even in the early days of the old federation. Yugoslavia reached the last four of the inaugural FIFA World Cup in 1930. But they did so without any Croat players, who boycotted the squad for the finals in protest at the new federal association headquarters being located in the Serb capital, Belgrade.

TOP SCORERS

1	Savo Milosevic	37
2	Predrag Mijatovic	28
3	Nikola Zigic	20
4	Dejan Savicevic	19
5	Mateja Kezman	17
6	Dejan Stankovic	15
=	Dragan Stojkovic	15
8	Danko Lazovic	11
9	Slavisa Jokanovic	10
=	Milan Jovanovic	10
=	Darko Kovacevic	10

STAN'S THE MAN

Internazionale midfielder **Dejan Stankovic** is the only footballer to have represented three different countries at separate FIFA World Cups, playing for Yugoslavia in 2002, Serbia and Montenegro in 2006, and Serbia in 2010. His pragmatic comment on his achievement was: "I'm happy with the record, but I'd rather win. It's OK to have been in three World Cups but I would have liked to have better results." Stankovic, Serbia's second-most-capped player, scored twice on his international debut for Yugoslavia in 1998. He has also twice scored memorable volleyed goals from virtually on the halfway line – once for Inter against Genoa, in 2009–10, with a first-time shot from the opposing goalkeeper's clearance, and an almost identical finish against German club FC Schalke 04 in the UEFA Champions League the following season.

SANTRAC LASTS LONGEST

Slobodan Santrac was the first manager of the "new" Yugoslavia. He served the longest term too, between 1994 and 1998, winning 26 of his 43 games in charge. Since Santrac's departure, Serbia have employed Milan Zivadinovic, Vujadin Boskov (twice), Ilija Petkovic (twice), Milovan Doric, Ivan Curkovic, Dejan Savicevic (twice), Spanish coach Javier Clemente, Miroslav Dukic, Radi Antic and current coach **Vladimir Petrovic**. Former Red Star Belgrade and Arsenal midfielder Petrovic had led Serbia U-21s to second place at the 2004 UEFA Under-21 European Championship.

MILORAD'S MILESTONE

The first man to captain and then coach his country at the FIFA World Cup was Milorad Arsenijevic, who captained Yugoslavia to the semi-finals at the inaugural tournament in Uruguay in 1930 and then managed their squad in Brazil 20 years later.

THE WHITE EAGLES

The national team of former Yugoslavia were nicknamed "Plavni" ("Blues") because of their shirt colour. However, Serbia decided to change their colours after Montenegro voted to become independent. They went for red, not blue. The team asked supporters for a new nickname. The broadcaster B92 proposed "Beli Orlovi" ("White Eagles"), taken from the double-headed white eagle on Serbia's national flag. The name was adopted by both the Serb fans and the national association. The national team is now known as "Beli Orlovi" and the Under-21 side is called "Orlici" ("Eaglets").

GOING IT ALONE

After Serbia and Montenegro competed at the 2006 FIFA World Cup, the 2010 tournament was the first featuring Serbia alone following Montenegro's independence. Topping their qualifying group ahead of France, Radomir Antic's Serbian side failed to make it through to the knockout stages in South Africa, despite a single-goal victory over Group D rivals Germany. A Serbian working for an opposing team was partly to blame – Milovan Rajevac was coach of the Ghana side that beat Serbia 1-0 in their first first-round match. Serbia conceded penalties due to inexplicable handballs in their two opening matches of the finals – Zdravko Kuzmanovic was the culprit against Ghana, and **Nemanja Vidic** (for which he was shown a yellow card) against Germany. Ghana converted their kick to win 1-0, but Germany missed theirs and lost by the same score.

SLOVAKIA

Slovakia have finally begun claiming bragging rights over the neighbouring Czech Republic. A Slovak team did play games during the Second World War but then had to wait until post-war Czechoslovakia divided into Slovakia and the Czech Republic in 1993. Slovakia returned to competitive action in qualifiers for the 1996 UEFA European Championship, finishing a promising third in their group. Continuing gradual progress culminated in qualification for their first FIFA World Cup™, in 2010, when Slovakia not only upset the defending champions Italy with a 3–2 win, but also reached the second round.

TOP SCORERS

1	Robert Vittek	23
2	Szilard Nemeth	22
3	Marek Mintal	14
4	Miroslav Karhan	13
5	Peter Dubovsky	12
6	Stanislav Sestak	11
7	Tibor Jancula	9
=	Lubomir Reiter	9
9	Marek Hamsik	8
10	Filip Holosko	7
=	Filip Sebo	7
=	Jaroslav Timko	7
=	Dusan Tittel	7

BEGINNERS' LUCK

Slovakia were the only qualifiers who were making their first FIFA World Cup Finals appearance at the 2010 tournament – and also became the first European debutants in 12 years to avoid defeat in the opening game. **Slovakia drew 1–1 with New Zealand** and were only denied victory by a stoppage-time equalizer. Spain defeated the two previous European debutants, Ukraine 4–0 in 2006 and Slovenia 3–1 in 2002.

HOMEMADE MARIAN

Marian Masny holds the international appearances record for Slovak-born footballers who played for the united Czechoslovakia, earning 75 caps between 1974 and 1982. Masny, from Rybany, was also the second-highest-scoring Slovak during the united Czechoslovakia era. His 18 goals were only bettered by the 22 in 36 matches struck by Vrutky-born Adolf Scherer from 1958 to 1964. Scherer's tally included three at the 1962 FIFA World Cup, when Czechoslovakia finished runners-up. Scherer scored the winner against Hungary in the quarter-finals and Czechoslovakia's final goal in their 3–1 semi-final victory over Yugoslavia.

BROKEN-DOWN KARHAN

Slovakia's defensive midfielder **Miroslav Karhan** helped his country qualify for the 2010 FIFA World Cup, taking his appearances tally to a national-record 95. But an Achilles tendon injury meant the team captain was ruled out of the tournament itself. After returning to action later in 2010, Karhan became the first Slovakia player to pass 100 caps.

CZECH EIGHT

Eight Slovakia players played in Czechoslovakia's triumphant 1976 UEFA European Championship final against West Germany, including captain Anton Ondrus and both their scorers in the 2–2 draw: Jan Svehlik and Karol Dobias. Three of the team's successful penalty-takers in their 5–3 shoot-out win were Slovak-born: Marian Masny, Ondrus and substitute Ladislav Jurkemik. The other Slovaks to feature were Jan Pivarnik, Jozef Capkovic and Jozef Moder. Defender Koloman Gogh was born in what is now the Czech Republic but had Slovak family ties and played most of his club football for Slovan Bratislava in the Slovak capital.

ROBERT THE HERO

Slovakia's **Robert Vittek** became only the fourth player from a country making their FIFA World Cup debut to score as many as four goals in one tournament, at the 2010 event in South Africa. He hit one against New Zealand, two against defending champions Italy, and a late penalty in a second-round defeat to Holland. The previous three players to have done so were Portugal's Eusebio in 1966, Denmark's Preben Elkjaer Larsen in 1986 and Croatia's Davor Suker in 1998. Vittek's last-minute penalty against Holland made him Slovakia's all-time leading scorer with 23 goals, overtaking former Sparta Prague and Middlesbrough striker Szilard Nemeth. His 2010 FIFA World Cup form was all the more striking, since he had failed to score at all in the qualifiers.

OWN GOAL GLORY

The man whose goal sent Slovakia to their first-ever FIFA World Cup Finals actually played for Poland – it was defender Seweryn Gancarczyk's own goal that gave Slovakia a 1–0 win in October 2009 in their final, decisive group three game of the 2010 qualifiers.

TOP CAPS

1	Miroslav Karhan	101
2	Robert Vittek	77
3	Szilard Nemeth	59
4	Stanislav Varga	55
5	Radoslav Zabavnik	53
6	Robert Tomaschek	52
7	Martin Skrtel	49
8	Jan Durica	47
=	Filip Holosko	47
10	Peter Dzurik	45
=	Marek Hamsik	45
=	Miroslav Konig	45
=	Marek Mintal	45

KNOCKING OUT THE NEIGHBOURS

Neighbours Slovakia and the Czech Republic have played each other four times in competitive matches since Czechoslovakia split to form two different nations in 1993. Slovakia won 2–1 at home but lost 3–0 away during qualifiers for the 1998 FIFA World Cup, before being held 2–2 at home and winning 2–1 away during their successful campaign to reach the 2010 FIFA World Cup. The Czech Republic missed out both times.

CARRY ON DOCTOR

All eight of Slovakia's managers since they returned to international football as an independent nation have been homegrown. The first was **Dr Josef Venglos,** who led the team between 1993 and 1995. Venglos had earlier been assistant coach when Czechoslovakia won the 1976 UEFA European Championship, and was Czechoslovakia's manager when the team finished third at the 1980 UEFA European Championship. He was later the first non-British Isles boss in England's top division when taking over at Aston Villa in 1990.

SWEDEN

Eleven appearances at the FIFA World Cup™ finals (with a best result of second, as tournament hosts, in 1958) and three Olympic medals (including gold in London in 1948), bear testament to Sweden's rich history on the world football stage. Recent success has been harder to find, however, with semi-final appearances at the 1992 UEFA European Championship (again as hosts) and the 1994 FIFA World Cup™ the country's best performances in recent years.

GRE-NO-LI OLYMPIC AND ITALIAN GLORY

Having conquered the world by leading Sweden to gold in the 1948 Olympics in London, Gunnar Gren, Gunnar Nordahl and Nils Liedholm were snapped up by AC Milan. Their three-pronged "Gre-No-Li" forward line led the Italian giants to their 1951 scudetto win. Nordahl, who topped the Serie A scoring charts five times between 1950 and 1955, remains Milan's all-time top scorer with 221 goals in 268 games. Gren and Liedholm went on to appear for the Swedish national team in the 1958 FIFA World Cup – where they finished runners-up.

TOP CAPS

1	Thomas Ravelli	143
2	Roland Nilsson	116
3	Bjorn Nordqvist	115
4	Anders Svensson	114
5	Niclas Alexandersson	109
6	Henrik Larsson	106
7	Olof Mellberg	105
8	Patrik Andersson	96
9	Orvar Bergmark	94
10	Teddy Lucic	86

ONE MORE ENCORE, AGAIN!

One of the most famous and decorated Swedish footballers of modern times, **Henrik Larsson** (a star on the club scene with both Celtic and Barcelona) quit international football after the 2002 FIFA World Cup ... and again after the 2006 FIFA World Cup in Germany. He then made a further comeback in the 2010 FIFA World Cup qualifiers. With 37 goals in his 106 appearances, including five in his three FIFA World Cups, fans and officials clamoured for his return each time he tried to walk away. Sweden's failure to qualify for the tournament in 1998 meant that a record-equalling 12 years elapsed between Larsson's first FIFA World Cup finals goal against Bulgaria in 1994 and his last – so far! – with his dramatic equalizer in the 2-2 group-round draw with England in 2006.

TOP-STOPPER RAVELLI

Thomas Ravelli kept goal for Sweden a record 143 times – conceding 143 goals. He saved two penalties in a shoot-out against Romania in the 1994 FIFA World Cup quarter-final to send Sweden into the last four, where they lost 1-0 to Brazil. Sweden went on to finish third, and were also the tournament's highest scorers with 15 goals in all – four more than eventual champions Brazil. Sweden's tally included five for Kennet Andersson, four for Martin Dahlin and three for Tomas Brolin.

IBRA–CADABRA

Temperamental Swedish striker **Zlatan Ibrahimovic** can claim to be the second most expensive footballer of all time – and he has an ego to match. His bold declarations include "There's only one Zlatan" and "I am like Muhammad Ali" – and he once responded to criticism from Norway's John Carew by scoffing: "What Carew does with a football, I can do with an orange." His transfer from Internazionale of Italy to Spain's Barcelona in 2009 was valued at €69 million, including a move by Samuel Eto'o in the other direction. Yet Ibrahimovic stayed just a season in La Liga before returning to Italy – this time with Inter's city rivals AC Milan. He has won consecutive league titles from 2003–04 onwards, in the Netherlands with Ajax Amsterdam, in Italy with Juventus and then Internazionale, and in Spain with Barcelona. The Malmo-born striker chose to play for Sweden despite also qualifying, through his family, for Bosnia and for Croatia – though he has boycotted the national team on several occasions. He ended his latest self-imposed exile to lead the team, as captain, in qualifiers for the 2012 UEFA European Championship. Ibrahimovic's 25 goals for Sweden include a memorably-cheeky, backheeled volley in a 1-1 draw with Italy at the 2004 UEFA European Championship in Portugal. Sweden reached the next round, with Italy missing out, but Ibrahimovic missed a penalty in their quarter-final shoot-out defeat to the Netherlands.

ALLBACK OF THE NET

One of the strangest international goals was scored by Sweden in a European Championship qualifier against Iceland in Gothenburg's Ullevi stadium, in June 2007. The visiting defence stopped playing when they thought Swiss referee Alain Hamer had awarded Sweden a penalty for handball – but there was no whistle and striker **Marcus Allback** raced through on goal to score. It was Allback's second strike of the game and Sweden's fifth – the match ended 5-0 to the hosts.

ONE–MINUTE WONDERS

Sweden's Magnus Erlingmark can claim to have the shortest FIFA World Cup finals career – amounting to nothing more than his appearance as an 89th-minute substitute against Russia, in the first round of the 1994 tournament. His only rival for the unenviable record is Bulgaria's Petar Mikhtarski, another 89th-minute replacement that summer, in his country's second-round victory over Mexico.

GOTHENBURG FLY THE FLAG

Under Sven-Goran Eriksson, IFK Gothenburg became the first Swedish team to win a European tournament when, in 1982, they crushed Hamburg 4-0 on aggregate in the UEFA Cup final.

TOP SCORERS

1	Sven Rydell	49
2	Gunnar Nordahl	43
3	Henrik Larsson	37
4	Gunnar Gren	32
5	Kennet Andersson	31
6	Marcus Allback	30
7	Martin Dahlin	29
8	Agne Simonsson	27
9	Tomas Brolin	26
10	Zlatan Ibrahimovic	25

MANAGER SWAP

The most successful manager Sweden ever had was Englishman **George Raynor**, who led them to Olympic gold in London in 1948 and steered Sweden to third place and the runners-up spot in the 1950 and 1958 FIFA World Cups respectively. Raynor got one over on the country of his birth when Sweden became only the second foreign side to win at Wembley, with a 3-2 victory over England in 1959. Working in the opposite direction, in 2001 Sven-Goran Eriksson left Serie A side Lazio to become England's first foreign coach. He led the side to three consecutive quarter-finals – in the FIFA World Cups of 2002 and 2006 and the 2004 UEFA European Championship in between. Eriksson, however, failed to lead England to a win over his home country, recording three draws (1-1 in a friendly, 2001; 1-1 in a 2002 FIFA World Cup group game; 2-2 in a 2006 FIFA World Cup group game) and one defeat (0-1 in a friendly, 2004).

BROTHERS IN ARMS

The Nordahl brothers – Bertil, Knut and Gunnar – all won gold medals with Sweden in the 1948 Olympics football tournament. All three went on to play in Italy: Bertil with Atalanta, Knut with Roma, while Gunnar became a goalscoring legend at AC Milan before also turning out for Roma. Twins Thomas and Andreas Ravelli continued the brotherly tradition, winning 143 and 41 caps for Sweden respectively.

SWITZERLAND

Switzerland set a record in 2006 when they became the first side in FIFA World Cup™ finals history to depart the tournament without conceding a goal. It sums up the country's football history: despite three FIFA World Cup™ quarter-final appearances (in 1934, 1938 and 1954 – the latter as tournament hosts), Switzerland has failed to establish itself on the international football stage. The country co-hosted the 2008 UEFA European Championship, with Austria, and is better known as being the home of both FIFA and UEFA.

CLEAN SHEET WIPE-OUT

The Swiss national team made history in 2006 by becoming the first – and to date only – team to exit the FIFA World Cup without conceding a single goal in regulation time. However, in the shoot-out defeat to Ukraine in the second round, following a goalless 120 minutes, they failed to score a single penalty and lost 3-0. Despite being beaten three times in the shoot-out, goalkeeper **Pascal Zuberbuhler**'s performances in Germany earned him a Swiss record for consecutive clean sheets at an international tournament.

DERDIYOK AT THE DOZEN

Nineteen-year-old striker **Eren Derdiyok** scored with his very first kick of the ball in international football, 12 minutes after coming on as a substitute against England at Wembley in a February 2009 friendly. But England, under new coach Fabio Capello for the first time, won 2-1.

TOP SCORERS

1	Alexander Frei	42
2	Kubilay Turkyilmaz	34
=	Max Abegglen	34
4	Andre Abegglen	29
=	Jacques Fatton	29
6	Adrian Knup	26
7	Charles Antenen	22
8	Lauro Amado	21
=	Stephane Chapuisat	21
10	Hakan Yakin	20

LLAMA FARMER FREI-ING HIGH

After being compared to a llama by an angry Swiss sports press for spitting at Steven Gerrard at UEFA Euro 2004, Alexander Frei, Switzerland's all-time top scorer, adopted a llama at Basel zoo as part of his apology to the nation. Frei appeared to abandon all hope of adding to his record Swiss goal tally of 42 in 84 games when he announced his retirement from international football in April 2011, blaming abuse from his own fans during recent matches. These included a goalless draw against minnows Malta, when both Frei and team-mate Gokhan Inler missed penalties. Frei was joined in international retirement by strike partner Marco Streller, who had scored 12 goals in 37 games.

CHAMPION CHAPPI

Stephane "Chappi" Chapuisat – the third man to make 100 appearances for Switzerland – was the first Swiss player to win a UEFA Champions League medal when he led the line for Borussia Dortmund in their 3-1 victory over Juventus in 1997. But his most significant contribution in the final was to make way for Lars Ricken, whose goal with his first touch put the game beyond Juventus. Stephane's father, Pierre-Albert Chapuisat, was also a successful Swiss international – earning 34 caps for the national side in the 1970s and 1980s – but he failed to reach the heights of Stephane, who would later add both the Club World Cup and the Swiss super league (while playing for Grasshoppers) to his winners' medal collection.

SWISS GUARD

Switzerland set a FIFA World Cup record in 2010 when they completed nine hours and 10 minutes without conceding a goal, including the 2006 tournament and passing a mark set by Italy. They then held out for a further nine minutes before conceding to Chile's Mark Gonzalez. Ottmar Hitzfeld's men lost that Group H match 1-0 and would fail to advance to the second round – despite conceding no other goals in their three group games.

TEENAGE RAMPAGE

Cristiano Ronaldo, Wayne Rooney, David Silva and Lukas Podolski were among the future world stars who featured at the 2002 UEFA U-17 European Championship – but it was surprise package Switzerland who took home the country's first international trophy, beating France on penalties after a goalless final. Future full internationals Tranquillo Barnetta and Reto Ziegler were among the spot-kick scorers.

ADMIRABLE GELSON

Switzerland shocked European champions and pre-tournament favourites Spain by beating them 1-0 in their first Group H game at the 2010 FIFA World Cup. Midfielder **Gelson Fernandes** scored the only goal at Durban's Moses Mabhida stadium. Yet Spain enjoyed 63 per cent of possession, having 24 shots compared with Switzerland's eight and 12 corners to Switzerland's three. The victory was Switzerland's first over Spain in 19 attempts.

TOP CAPS

1	Heinz Hermann	117
2	Alain Geiger	112
3	Stephane Chapuisat	103
4	Johann Vogel	94
5	Hakan Yakin	87
6	Alexander Frei	84
7	Patrick Muller	81
8	Severino Minelli	80
9	Andy Egli	79
=	Ciriaco Sforza	79

THE ORIGINAL BOLT

Karl Rappan did so much for Swiss football – including founding its first national football fan club – that it is often forgotten that he was Austrian. After a moderately successful career as a player and coach in Austria, Rappan achieved lasting fame as an innovative manager in Switzerland, leading the national side in the 1938 and 1954 FIFA World Cups, as well as securing league titles and cups as manager of Grasshopper-Club, FC Servette and FC Zurich. He developed a flexible tactical system – which allowed players to switch positions depending on the situation and putting greater pressure on their opponents. This revolutionary new idea became known as the "Swiss bolt", and helped the unfancied hosts defeat Italy on the way to the quarter-finals of the 1954 FIFA World Cup, before losing out to Rappan's home country, Austria. An early advocate of a European league, Rappan eventually settled for the simpler knockout tournament, the Intertoto Cup, which he helped devise and launch in 1961. Rappan was, until Kobi Kuhn, Switzerland's longest-serving and statistically most successful manager, with 29 victories in 77 games in charge.

"MERCI KOBI"

Former Swiss international player and manager, **Jakob "Kobi" Kuhn**, was left close to tears as his players unfurled a "thank you" banner at the end of his final game as Swiss national manager – the 2-0 victory over Portugal in the final group game of UEFA Euro 2008. How times have changed for Kuhn: while now a much-loved elder statesmen of the Swiss game, when Kuhn was just 22 years old, he was sent home from the 1966 FIFA World Cup for missing a curfew. He was then banned from the national side for a year. The shoe was on the other foot when Kuhn had to send Alexander Frei home from UEFA Euro 2004 after the centre-forward spat at England's Steven Gerrard. Kuhn spent most of his playing career, where he was described as playing "with honey in his boots", with FC Zurich, winning six league titles and five Swiss Cups. He played 63 times for the national side, scoring five goals. He then worked his way up through the ranks of the Swiss national team, leading first the Under-18s, then the Under-21s and finally the senior national team. He retired, aged 64, with a record of 32 victories, 18 draws and 23 defeats in 73 matches as Swiss coach.

TURKEY

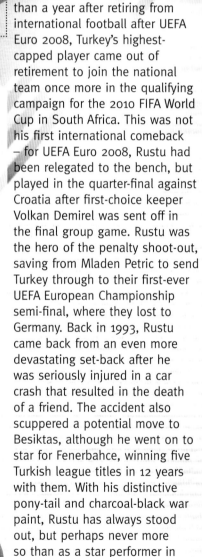

Galatasaray's defeat in the 2000 UEFA ...
in the 2000 UEFA ...
Turkish football ... has
... qualified ...
1950, when they ...
consistently ...
Since 2000 ...
their ...
place finish at the ...
Cup" in 2002 and ...
and a semi-final appearance at
the 2008 UEFA European
Championship.

HAT-TRICK HERO

Turkey captain **Tuncay Sanli** became the first Turkish player to score a hat-trick in the UEFA Champions League when he scored all of Fenerbahce's goals in their 3-0 defeat of Manchester United in Istanbul in 2004. He has also notched up two hat-tricks for the national side, against Switzerland on 16 November 2005 (final score 4-2) and in another 4-2 victory, this time over Austria, on 19 November 2008.

OLD GOLD

The last FIFA World Cup "golden goal" was scored by Turkey substitute Ilhan Mansiz, in the 94th minute of their 2002 quarter-final against Senegal – giving his side a 1-0 win, on their way to finishing third overall. The "golden goal" rule was abandoned ahead of the 2006 FIFA World Cup, which went back to two guaranteed 15-minute periods of extra-time if a knockout fixture ended level after 90 minutes.

QUICK OFF THE MARK

Hakan Sukur scored the fastest-ever FIFA World Cup finals goal – taking only 11 seconds to score Turkey's first goal in their third-place play-off match against South Korea at the 2002 FIFA World Cup. Turkey went on to win the game 3-2 to claim third place, their finest-ever performance in the competition. His total of 51 goals (in 112 games) is more than double his nearest competitor in the national team ranking. His first goal came in only his second appearance, as Turkey beat Denmark 2-1 on 8 April 1992. He went on to score four goals in a single game twice – in the 6-4 win over Wales on 20 August 1997 and in the 5-0 crushing of Moldova on 11 October 2006.

GUESS WHO'S BACK?

Rustu Recber doesn't know the meaning of the word "quit". Less than a year after retiring from international football after UEFA Euro 2008, Turkey's highest-capped player came out of retirement to join the national team once more in the qualifying campaign for the 2010 FIFA World Cup in South Africa. This was not his first international comeback – for UEFA Euro 2008, Rustu had been relegated to the bench, but played in the quarter-final against Croatia after first-choice keeper Volkan Demirel was sent off in the final group game. Rustu was the hero of the penalty shoot-out, saving from Mladen Petric to send Turkey through to their first-ever UEFA European Championship semi-final, where they lost to Germany. Back in 1993, Rustu came back from an even more devastating set-back after he was seriously injured in a car crash that resulted in the death of a friend. The accident also scuppered a potential move to Besiktas, although he went on to star for Fenerbahce, winning five Turkish league titles in 12 years with them. With his distinctive pony-tail and charcoal-black war paint, Rustu has always stood out, but perhaps never more so than as a star performer in Turkey's third-place performance at the 2002 FIFA World Cup finals. He was elected into the Team of the Tournament and was named FIFA's Goalkeeper of the Year.

TWIN TURKS

Hamit Altintop was born 10 minutes before identical twin brother **Halil** – and he has been just about leading the way, throughout their parallel professional footballing careers since their birth in the German city of Gelsenkirchen on 8 December 1982. Both began playing for German amateur side Wattenscheid, before defender-cum-midfielder Hamit signed for FC Schalke 04 in summer 2006 and striker Halil followed suit shortly afterwards. Hamit would stay just a season there, though, before being bought by Bayern Munich. Both helped Turkey reach the semi-finals of the 2008 UEFA European Championship – losing to adopted homeland Germany – though only Hamit was voted among UEFA's 23 best players of the tournament.

FATIH TERIM

Having coached Galatasaray to their UEFA Cup triumph in 2000, **Fatih Terim** put a disappointing year and a half in Italy with Fiorentina and AC Milan behind him to lead Turkey in their amazing run to the 2008 UEFA European Championship semi-finals. Defeat to Portugal in the opening game left the Turks with an uphill task, but stunning successive comebacks against Switzerland and the Czech Republic took them through to the quarter-finals. A 119th-minute goal seemed to have clinched the tie for Croatia, but, as the Croatian players celebrated, "Emperor" Fatih urged his players to get up, pick the ball out of the net and fight on to the very end. They did just that, and Semih Senturk's improbable equalizer took the match to penalties. The semi-final against Germany provided yet another rollercoaster ride, but this time there was no answer to the Germans' last-minute winner. When Fatih said "there is something special about this team" few could disagree.

TOP SCORERS

1	Hakan Sukur	51
2	Tuncay Sanli	22
3	Lefter Kucukandonyadis	21
4	Nihat Kahveci	19
=	Metin Oktay	19
=	Cemil Turan	19
7	Zeki Riza Sporel	15
8	Arif Erdem	11
=	Ertugrul Saglam	11
=	Arda Turan	11

TOP CAPS

1	Rustu Recber	119
2	Hakan Sukur	112
3	Bulent Korkmaz	102
4	Tugay Kerimoglu	94
5	Alpay Ozalan	90
6	Tuncay Sanli	79
7	Ogun Temizkanoglu	76
8	Emre Belozoglu	75
9	Abdullah Ercan	71
10	Oguz Cetin	70

MAJOR TOURNAMENTS

FIFA WORLD CUP™: 2 appearances – 3rd place 2002
UEFA EUROPEAN CHAMPIONSHIP: 3 appearances – semi-finals 2008
FIRST INTERNATIONAL: Turkey 2 Romania 2 (Istanbul, 26 October 1923)
BIGGEST WIN: Turkey 7 Syria 0 (Ankara, 20 November 1949)
Turkey 7 Korea Republic 0 (Geneva, Switzerland, 20 June, 1954)
Turkey 7 San Marino 0 (Istanbul, 10 November 1996)
BIGGEST DEFEAT: Poland 8 Turkey 0 (Chorzow, 24 April 1968)
Turkey 0 England 8 (Istanbul, 14 November 1984)
England 8 Turkey 0 (London, 14 October 1987)

COCA-COLA COLIN

England failed to qualify, but there were two English-born footballers at the 2008 UEFA European Championship – Italy's Simone Perrotta, born just outside Manchester, and the East Londoner formerly called **Colin Kazim-Richards** but known in his adopted homeland of Turkey as Kazim-Kazim. He qualified for Turkey through his mother. Before signing for Turkish giants Fenerbahce in June 2007, he had only played for unfashionable English clubs Bury, Brighton and Hove Albion and Sheffield United. When Brighton bought him from Bury, the transfer fee was paid by Coca-Cola thanks to a competition won by a Brighton fan – meaning Kazim-Richards was duly nicknamed "The Coca-Cola Kid".

UKRAINE

Ukraine has been a stronghold of football in eastern Europe for many years. A steady flow of talent from Ukrainian clubs with a rich European pedigree, such as Dynamo Kiev, provided the Soviet national team with many standout players in the years before independence. Since separating from the Soviet Union in 1991, Ukraine has become a football force in its own right, qualifying for the FIFA World Cup™ for the first time in 2006, reaching the quarter-finals.

MAJOR TOURNAMENTS

FIFA WORLD CUP™: 1 appearance – quarter-finals (2006)
FIRST INTERNATIONAL: Ukraine 1 Hungary 3 (Uzhhorod, Ukraine, 29 April 1992)
BIGGEST WINS: Ukraine 6 Azerbaijan 0 (Kiev, Ukraine, 15 August 2006)
 Andorra 0 Ukraine 6 (Andorra la Vella, Andorra, 14 October 2009)
BIGGEST DEFEATS: Croatia 4 Ukraine 0 (Zagreb, Croatia, 25 March 1995)
 Spain 4 Ukraine 0 (Leipzig, Germany, 14 June 2006)

ROCKET MAN

Andriy Shevchenko beat team-mate **Anatoliy Tymoshchuk**  to become the first Ukrainian footballer to reach a century of international appearances – but the defensive midfielder later overtook Shevchenko and is the country's most-capped player with 104 matches. He also had the rare honour of seeing his name in space, when Ukrainian cosmonaut Yuri Malenchenko launched into orbit wearing a Zenit St Petersburg shirt with "Tymoshchuk" on the back in 2007.

YURI-KA MOMENT

Denys Harmash and Dmytro Korkishko scored the goals against England that gave Ukraine their first major international footballing title, in the final of the 2009 UEFA Under-19 European Championship. The coach was Yuri Kalitvintsev, later assistant to Oleg Blokhin with the senior international side.

HARD START

With the newly independent Ukraine unable to register with FIFA in time for the qualifying rounds for the 1994 FIFA World Cup, many of their stars opted to play for Russia and went to the finals in the United States representing that country. Andrei Kanchelskis, Viktor Onopko, Sergei Yuran and Oleg Salenko could all have played for the new Ukraine side, but decided not to. Ukraine then failed to qualify for an international tournament until the **2006 FIFA World Cup** in Germany, where they lost 3-0 in the quarter-finals to eventual winners Italy.

SUPER SHEVA

In 2004, **Andriy Shevchenko** became the third Ukrainian to win the Ballon D'Or – the first to do so, in 1975, was his 2006 FIFA World Cup coach Oleg Blokhin (second was Igor Belanov in 1986). Shevchenko was the first to win the award since Ukraine's independence from the Soviet Union. Born on 29 September 1976, he was a promising boxer as a youngster, before deciding to focus on football full-time. He has won trophies at every club he's played for, including five titles in a row with Dynamo Kiev, the Serie A and the Champions League with AC Milan, and even two cups in his "disappointing" time at Chelsea. Shevchenko is Ukraine's highest-capped player and leading goalscorer, with 45 goals in 100 games. This includes two at the 2006 FIFA World Cup, where Shevchenko captained his country in their first-ever appearance at a major finals.

LEADING FROM THE FRONT

Oleg Blokhin, Ukraine's manager on their first appearance at the FIFA World Cup finals in 2006, made his name as a star striker with his hometown club Dynamo Kiev. Born on 5 November 1952, in the days when Ukraine was part of the Soviet Union, Blokhin scored a record 211 goals in another record 432 appearances in the USSR national league. He also holds the caps and goals records for the USSR, with 42 goals in 112 games. He led Kiev to two triumphs in the European Cup-Winners' Cup in 1975 and 1986, scoring in both finals, and winning the European Footballer of the Year trophy for his exploits in 1975. Always an over-achiever, Blokhin became the first manager to lead Ukraine to the finals of an international tournament, at the 2006 FIFA World Cup in Germany, where they lost out to eventual winners Italy 3-0 in the quarter-finals after knocking out Switzerland in the second round – also on penalties. Blokhin was renowned for his speed – when Olympic gold medallist Valeriy Borzov trained the Kiev squad in the 1970s, Blokhin recorded a 100 metres time of 11 seconds, just 0.46 seconds slower than Borzov's own 1972 medal-winning run. Blokhin quit as Ukraine manager in December 2007 but returned to the job in April 2011.

REBROV REBORN

Serhiy Rebrov, who retired in 2009, was Andriy Shevchenko's dynamic strike partner for both club and country. The forward pair starred for Dynamo Kiev in the late 1990s before making big-money moves across Europe. Like Shevchenko at Chelsea, Rebrov struggled in London, first at Tottenham Hotspur and then at West Ham United. But after returning to Ukraine in 2005, he earned a late-career recall to the international team – and scored a memorable long-range strike against Saudi Arabia at the 2006 FIFA World Cup. Having dropped back into midfield, he then crossed the border and helped outsiders Rubin Kazan win their first Russian league title in 2008. But Rebrov, a keen amateur radio "ham", remains the Ukrainian Premier League's all-time leading scorer, with 125 goals in 268 games.

TOP SCORERS

1	Andriy Shevchenko	45
2	Serhiy Rebrov	15
3	Sergiy Nazarenko	11
4	Andriy Gusin	9
=	Andriy Vorobey	9
6	Timerlan Huseinov	8
7	Oleg Gusev	7
=	Maksym Kalinichenko	7
9	Viktor Leonenko	6
=	Artem Milevskiy	6
=	Ruslan Rotan	6
=	Andriy Voronin	6

EUROS IN UKRAINE

The 69,000-capacity **Olympic Stadium** in Kiev is scheduled to stage the final of the 2012 UEFA European Championship, a tournament being co-hosted by Ukraine and Poland. The stadium, originally opened in 1923, has been rebuilt and renovated several times since then, and takes its current name from its role in the 1980 Summer Olympics. Although the Games were mostly played in Moscow, Kiev was the setting for seven matches in the Olympic football tournament.

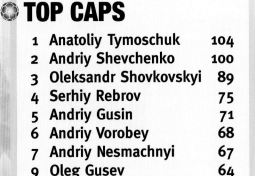

TOP CAPS

1	Anatoliy Tymoschuk	104
2	Andriy Shevchenko	100
3	Oleksandr Shovkovskyi	89
4	Serhiy Rebrov	75
5	Andriy Gusin	71
6	Andriy Vorobey	68
7	Andriy Nesmachnyi	67
9	Oleg Gusev	64
=	Andriy Voronin	64
10	Vladyslav Vashchuk	63

WALES

In a land where rugby union remains the national obsession, Wales have struggled to impose themselves on the world of international football. Despite having produced a number of hugely talented players, Wales have only ever played once in the finals of a major tournament – at the 1958 FIFA World Cup™ finals in Sweden.

GOOD ON RAMSEY

Arsenal midfielder **Aaron Ramsey** became Wales's youngest captain when appointed to the role in March 2011 by new manager Gary Speed. Ramsey was 20 years and 90 days old when he led the side out for the first time, at Cardiff's Millennium Stadium, in a 2012 UEFA European Championship qualifier that ended in a 2-0 win for England. The record had previously been held by centre-back Mike England, 22 years and 135 days old when skipper against Northern Ireland in April 1964. Ramsey had not long returned to full fitness after a potentially career-threatening broken leg suffered while playing for Arsenal against Stoke City in February 2010.

BRICKS TO BRILLIANCE

Goalkeeper **Neville Southall** made the first of his record 92 appearances for Wales in a 3-2 win over Northern Ireland on 27 May 1982. The former hod-carrier and bin man kept 34 clean sheets in 15 years playing for Wales and won the English Football Writers' Player of the Year in 1985 thanks to his performances alongside Welsh captain Kevin Ratcliffe at Everton. In his final match for Wales on 20 August 1997, he was substituted halfway through a 6-4 defeat against Turkey in Istanbul.

WHERE'S OUR GOLDEN BOY?

One of the most skilful and successful players never to appear at the FIFA World Cup, **Ryan Giggs** somehow missed 18 consecutive friendlies for Wales.

HAT-TRICK HERO

Welsh striker **Robert Earnshaw** holds the remarkable record of having scored hat-tricks in all four divisions of English football, the FA Cup, the League Cup, as well as scoring three for the national team against Scotland on 18 February 2004.

TOP CAPS

1	Neville Southall	92
2	Gary Speed	85
3	Dean Saunders	75
4	Peter Nicholas	73
=	Ian Rush	73
6	Mark Hughes	72
=	Joey Jones	72
8	Ivor Allchurch	68
9	Brian Flynn	66
10	Andy Melville	65

TOP SCORERS

1	Ian Rush	28
2	Ivor Allchurch	23
=	Trevor Ford	23
4	Dean Saunders	22
5	Craig Bellamy	18
6	Robert Earnshaw	16
=	Mark Hughes	16
=	Cliff Jones	16
9	John Charles	15
10	John Hartson	14

CAUGHT ON CAMERA

Pioneer movie-makers Sagar Mitchell and James Kenyon captured Wales v Ireland in March 1906, making it the first filmed international football match.

KEEPING UP WITH THE JONESES

Cliff Jones, left-winger for Wales at the 1958 FIFA World Cup and for Tottenham Hotspur's league and cup "Double" winners in 1961, was part of a Welsh footballing dynasty. His father Ivor Jones had previously played for Wales, as did Ivor's brother Bryn. Cliff's cousin Ken, a goalkeeper, was another member of the 1958 FIFA World Cup squad, but never actually played for his country.

YOUNG DRAGON

Gareth Bale became the youngest player to play for Wales when he came on as sub against Trinidad and Tobago on 27 May 2006 aged 16 years and 315 days. The left-back/left-winger put himself on the radar of the world's biggest clubs – and triggered so-called "Bale-mania" – with his dazzling performances for Tottenham Hotspur in the 2010–11 UEFA Champions League season, including a second-half hat-trick in the San Siro stadium against reigning holders Internazionale of Italy.

RUSH FOR GOAL

Ian Rush is Wales's leading goalscorer, with 28 goals in 73 games. His first came in a 3-0 win over Northern Ireland on 27 May 1982; he scored the 28th and final goal in a 2-1 win over Estonia in Tallinn in 1994.

GOSH, IT'S TOSH

John Toshack was a published poet on the side but as a professional footballer he scored 12 goals in 40 games for Wales, in a playing career that also brought him three league championships, one European Cup and two UEFA Cups with Liverpool. After retiring, he coached Swansea City all the way from England's fourth to first division in four seasons, and later served two spells in charge at Real Madrid. During the first, he won the 1989–90 La Liga championship with a team who scored a Spanish league-record 107 goals in 38 games. Toshack lasted just 41 days as Wales manager in 1994 but six years during a second stint, from 2004 to 2010, before being replaced by former international midfielder Gary Speed.

HOME CHAMPIONS

Wales won the Home Championship (an annual competition played between England, Ireland, Scotland and Wales between 1883 and 1984) on 12 occasions, seven outright and five shared.

OTHER TEAMS EUROPE

For the major European football powers, a qualifying campaign for one of the game's major international tournaments would not be the same without an awkward trip to one of the former Eastern Bloc countries or the chance of a goal-fest against the likes of San Marino or Luxembourg. For these countries' players, the thrill of representing their nation is more important than harbouring dreams of world domination.

SELVA SERVICE

San Marino, with a population of under 30,000, is the smallest country to be a member of UEFA. Striker **Andy Selva** is not only San Marino's top scorer, with eight goals, but also the only player to score more than once in recorded senior internationals for the country.

MIXU FORTUNES

Current Finland coach **Mixu Paatelainen** holds the national record for most goals scored in one international, having hit all four in the team's 4-1 home win over San Marino in a December 1994 qualifier for Euro 96. San Marino also provided the opposition for his first game as Finland's national coach in June 2011. Like a former team-mate Jari Litmanen, Paatelainen is the son of a former Finnish international – his father Matti, a striker, scored 11 goals in 47 games for Finland between 1970 and 1977. Mixu has two younger brothers who played professional football too, though neither Mikko nor Markus made the national team. Mikko and Markus were, however, striking partners at Scottish club Cowdenbeath when Mixu was manager in 2005–06.

UNDERDOGS HAVE THEIR DAY

Slovenia were the only unseeded team to win a UEFA qualifying play-off for the 2010 FIFA World Cup, beating Russia on away goals. Slovenia lost 2-1 in Moscow, thanks to substitute Nejc Pecnik's crucial away goal late in the first leg and Ztlatko Dedic scored the only goal in Maribor to give Slovenia victory. With a population of two million and just 429 registered professional players, Slovenia were the smallest nation in the finals.

LIT'S A KNOCK–OUT

Perhaps it's not be too surprising that **Jari Litmanen** should have become a football star – both his parents played for the Lahti-based club Reipas while Litmanen's father Olavi also won five caps for the national team. But Jari's skills and achievements far outstripped them both – and, arguably, any other player the country has produced. It was fitting that Litmanen became the first Finnish player to get his hands on the UEFA European Cup – or Champions League trophy – when his Ajax Amsterdam side beat AC Milan in 1995. Litmanen had left Finland at the age of 21 to make his name and mark with the legendary Dutch club Ajax, inheriting the great Dennis Bergkamp's support-striker role – and number 10 shirt. Litmanen scored in the 1996 UEFA Champions League final, though Ajax lost on penalties to Juventus. He remains the Dutch club's record scorer in European competition, with 24 goals in 44 games. Litmanen joined Barcelona in 1999 and then Liverpool two years later, though his time in England was hampered by a wrist injury he suffered on international duty and he returned to Ajax in 2002. Despite a series of injuries, he remained dedicated to his country, captaining the side between 1996 and 2008, and was still playing and scoring for Finland in 2010 at the age of 39 – having notched up more international goals and games than any other Finn, scoring 32 times in 137 appearances.

GIVING IT UP

Lithuania and Estonia did not bother playing their final group game against each other in the 1934 FIFA World Cup qualifying competition. Sweden had already guaranteed themselves top spot, and the sole finals place available, by beating Lithuania 2-0 and Estonia 6-2.

BEYOND THE IRON CURTAIN

The break-up of the Soviet Union in 1990 led to 15 new footballing nations, though initially Russia played on at the 1992 UEFA European Championship as CIS, or the Commonwealth of Independent States – without the involvement of Estonia, Latvia and Lithuania. In the coming years, UEFA and FIFA approved the creation of separate teams for Russia, Armenia, Azerbaijan, Belarus, Estonia, Georgia, Kazakhstan, Kyrgyzstan, Latvia, Lithuania, Moldova, Tajikstan, Turkmenistan, Ukraine and Uzbekistan. Upheavals in the early 1990s would also fragment the former Yugoslavia into Croatia, Serbia, Bosnia-Herzegovina, Macedonia, Slovenia and Montenegro, while Czechoslovakia split into Slovakia and the Czech Republic.

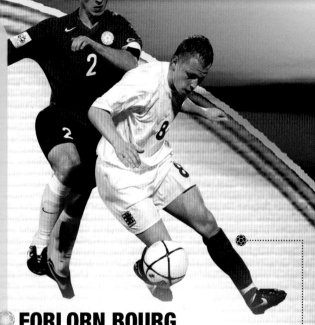

YEAR AFFILIATED TO FIFA

Albania:	1932
Andorra:	1996
Austria:	1905
Belarus:	1992
Bosnia-Herzegovina:	1996
Cyprus:	1948
Estonia:	1923
Faroe Islands:	1988
Finland:	1908
Georgia:	1992
Greece:	1927
Iceland:	1947
Israel:	1929
Kazakhstan:	1994
Latvia:	1922
Liechtenstein:	1974
Luxembourg:	1910
Macedonia:	1994
Malta:	1959
Moldova:	1994
Montenegro:	2007
San Marino:	1988
Slovenia:	1992

FORLORN BOURG

If at first you don't succeed, try and try again – but poor Luxembourg have valiantly tried and failed to qualify for 18 consecutive FIFA World Cup finals. The only time they were not involved was the very first in 1930, when there was no qualification tournament and Luxembourg were not invited to the Finals. The country has had only three victories in FIFA World Cup qualifiers: 4-2 at home to Portugal in October 1961, 2-0 at home to Turkey in October 1972, and 2-1 away to Switzerland in September 2008, when **Alphonse Leweck** scored a late winner.

THE FULL MONTE

Montenegro became the 208th and latest country to be recognized by FIFA, not long after Serbia and Montenegro had competed in the 2006 FIFA World Cup. But the new nation did not become a FIFA or UEFA member in time to compete in qualifiers for the 2008 UEFA European Championships and had to wait until the 2010 FIFA World Cup campaign for their first competitive match – a 2-2 draw at home to Bulgaria, in September 2008.

TRAVELLING MEN

Israel looked like qualifying for the 1958 FIFA World Cup without kicking a ball, because scheduled opponents Turkey, Indonesia and Sudan refused to play them. But FIFA ordered them into a two-legged play-off against a European side – which Israel lost 4-0 on aggregate to Wales. Israel were unfortunate again in the 2006 FIFA World Cup qualifiers, ending the campaign unbeaten – yet failing even to make the play-offs, finishing third in their group behind France and Switzerland. Coach Avram Grant later went on to manage Chelsea, losing the 2008 UEFA Champions League final on penalties to Manchester United. Israel hosted, and won, the 1964 Asian Nations Cup, and qualified for the 1970 FIFA World Cup through a combined Asia/Oceania qualifying competition, but are now members of the European Federation.

SLO STARTERS

The only country to beat Italy on their way to winning the 2006 FIFA World Cup were Slovenia, who triumphed 1-0 in an October 2004 qualifier, thanks to a late goal by centre-back **Bostjan Cesar**. However, Slovenia still missed out on the finals.

AD ENOUGH

Temuri Ketsbaia scored 16 times for Georgia, more than anyone other than 26-goal Shota Arveladze, and was also the first coach to lead a Cypriot side – Anorthosis Famagusta – into the UEFA Champions League before taking over as Georgian national coach in 2009. Yet to many fans – those in England especially – he might be best remembered for his bizarre celebration after scoring a last-minute winner for Newcastle United against Bolton Wanderers in January 1998, when instead of looking pleased he flung off his shirt and furiously kicked out at pitchside advertising hoardings. After receiving the ball when the game kicked off again, he instantly booted it high into the crowd.

MORE SIND AGAINST

Austria's star player **Matthias Sindelar** refused to play for a new, merged national team when Germany annexed Austria in 1938. Sindelar, born in modern-day Hungary in February 1903, was the inspirational leader of Austria's so-called Wunderteam of the 1930s. He scored 27 goals in 43 games for Austria, who went 14 internationals unbeaten between April 1931 and December 1932, won the 1932 Central European International Cup and silver at the 1936 Olympics. During a special reunification match between the Austrian and German teams in Vienna in April 1938, Sindelar disobeyed orders and scored a spectacular solo goal. Austria went on to win 2-0 in a game which might have been expected to end in a diplomatic draw. Sindelar was mysteriously found dead from carbon monoxide poisoning in his Vienna apartment in January 1939.

HAPPY ELVIR

Elvir Bolic holds the goal-scoring record for Bosnia-Herzegovina, striking 24 times in 52 games since the country began playing internationals in 1996 – though his caps record has now been overtaken by Zvjezdan Misimovic. Bolic was also the man who ended Manchester United's 40-year unbeaten record at home in European competition, the only goal of the game for Turkish side Fenerbahce during a Champions League tie at Old Trafford in October 1996.

REIM AND REASONING

Before being overtaken by Latvia's Vitalijs Astafjevs, the European record for most international appearances was held by another Baltic veteran – Estonian holding midfielder Martin Reim scored 14 goals in 157 games for his country between June 1992 and June 2009. Yet he could even have closed in on an unprecedented double-century of international appearances, had he not missed 40 games following a dispute with Latvia's Dutch manager Jelle Goes between 2004 and 2007. He retired from international football after matching the 150-cap record of Germany's Lothar Matthaus in February 2007 but was persuaded to return by new national boss Viggo Jensen. His 157th and final match was a testimonial he was awarded against Equatorial Guinea on 6 June 2009, a day that was also said to mark the centenary of football in Estonia.

THE GUD SON

Iceland striker **Eidur Gudjohnsen** made history on his international debut away to Estonia in April 1996, by coming on as a substitute for his own father, Arnor Gudjohnsen. Eidur was 17 at the time, his father 34 – though both were disappointed they did not get to play on the pitch at the same time. The Icelandic Football Association thought they would get a chance to do so in Iceland's next home game, but Eidur was ruled out by an ankle injury and the opportunity never arose again.

VITAL VITALIJS

Midfielder Vitalijs Astafjevs put Latvia on the map when he became the most-capped European footballer of all time, with 167 appearances for his country – including three at the 2004 UEFA European Championship. He also scored 16 goals for Latvia. Astafjevs made his international debut in 1992, the year the Latvian football team was revived after independence following the break-up of the Soviet Union. He was still playing for his country at the age of 38 in November 2009, when a friendly against Honduras allowed him to overtake Estonian Martin Reim's record for most European caps.

MOST INTERNATIONAL APPEARANCES

Albania:	Foto Strashoka	73
	Altin Lala	73
Andorra:	Oscar Sonejee	87
Austria:	Andreas Herzog	103
Belarus:	Aleksandr Kulchy	89
Bosnia-Herz.:	Zvjezdan Misimovic	57
Cyprus:	Ioannis Okkas	102
Estonia:	Martin Reim	157
Faroe Islands:	Oli Johannesen	83
Finland:	Jari Litmanen	137
Georgia:	Levan Kobiashvili	96
Iceland:	Runar Kristinsson	101
Israel:	Arik Benado	94
Kazakhstan:	Ruslan Baltyiev	73
Latvia:	Vitalijs Astafjevs	167
Liechtenstein:	Mario Frick	99
Luxembourg:	Jeff Strasser	98
Macedonia:	Goce Sedloski	100
Malta:	David Carabott	122
Moldova:	Radu Rebeja	74
Montenegro:	Simon Vukcevic	27
San Marino:	Damiano Vannucci	59
Slovenia:	Zlatko Zahovic	80

IF THE CAP FITS, EVEN IF THE SHOES DON'T...

Since playing their first unofficial international in 1993 (a 3-1 win over Iran) and their first FIFA-approved match two years later (a 2-0 defeat to Albania), Bosnia and Herzegovina had never come close to reaching a major international tournament – until Croatian veteran **Miroslav Blazevic** took charge in 2008. He took a side starring playmaker Zvjezdan Misimovic and striker Edin Dzeko to the brink of the 2010 FIFA World Cup, only narrowly losing a play-off to Portugal – an impressive run he credited to a pair of "lucky" shoes he was given by the mayor of Zagreb and kept wearing even though they were two sizes too small. Superstitious Blazevic had previously insisted on wearing a white scarf when coach of Dinamo Zagreb and a French gendarme's cap when leading Croatia to third place at the 1998 FIFA World Cup.

BARREN SPELLS

Malta are the only European team to have failed to score a single goal in two separate FIFA World Cup qualification campaigns, drawing blanks throughout the build-up to the 1978 and 2010 tournaments – covering six games the first time around, but 10 ahead of the 2010 finals. Six more sides have endured similar goalless streaks in qualifiers: Liechtenstein (across eight games ahead of the 2002 tournament), San Marino (eight games, 1998), Cyprus (four games, 1966), Israel (four games, 1954), Finland (three games, 1938) and Lithuania (one game, 1934).

BASKET CASE

Captain **Rashad Sadygov** not only secured Azerbaijan's biggest win in their history when he scored the only goal against Turkey in a Euro 2012 qualifier in October 2010 – he was also delivering a blow against the country where he was making his living. Having previously played for Turkish top-flight side Kayserispor, he had since moved on to rivals Eskisehirspor. Not every transfer has worked out well for Sadygov – he missed the transfer deadline when signing for Azeri side PFC Neftchi in 2006, so he decided to play basketball for a season to keep himself fit until allowed to resume football.

DARK ERA

Macedonian striker **Darko Pancev** had to wait 15 years to receive his European Golden Boot award for the 1990–91 season, when he scored 34 goals for European Cup winners Red Star Belgrade. Organizers originally suspended the competition between 1991 and 1996, due to disagreements about goal tallies in Cyprus – but eventually agreed to hand Pancev his prize in August 2006. The unlucky European top scorers from 1992 to 1996 were Scotland's Ally McCoist (twice), Welshman David Taylor, Armenian Arsen Avetisyan and Georgian Zviad Endeladze.

MOST INTERNATIONAL GOALS

Albania:	Alban Bushi	14
Andorra:	Ildefons Lima	7
Austria:	Toni Polster	44
Belarus:	Maxim Romashchenko	20
Bosnia-Herz.:	Elvir Bolic	22
Cyprus:	Michalis Konstantinou	32
Estonia:	Andres Oper	36
Faroe Islands:	Rogvi Jacobsen	10
Finland:	Jari Litmanen	32
Georgia:	Shota Arveladze	26
Iceland:	Eidur Gudjohnsen	24
Israel:	Mordechai Spiegler	33
Kazakhstan:	Ruslan Baltiev	13
Latvia:	Maris Verpakovskis	28
Liechtenstein:	Mario Frick	16
Luxembourg:	Leon Mart	16
Macedonia:	Goran Pandev	23
Malta:	Michael Mifsud	26
Moldova:	Serghei Clescenco	11
Montenegro:	Mirko Vucinic	11
San Marino:	Andy Selva	8
Slovenia:	Zlatko Zahovic	35

TU-WHIT TWO-NIL

Finland's adopted lucky mascot is an eagle-owl called "Bubi" that occasionally swoops down on the Helsinki Olympic Stadium during international matches – making his debut during a 2-0 UEFA European Championship qualifier win over Belgium in June 2007 and holding up the game for several minutes as he flew about the pitch and perched on goalposts. The eagle owl was later voted the Finnish capital's "Resident of the Year".

HIGH LIFE

At 64°09'N, Reykjavik, in Iceland, is the northernmost city to host a FIFA World Cup match – though so far only in qualifiers. The northernmost FIFA World Cup finals venue is Sandviken in Sweden, at 60°37'N – while Christchurch in New Zealand (43°32'S) holds the record for southernmost FIFA World Cup venue, with the finals record held by Mar del Plata in Argentina (38°01'S).

BOHEMIAN RHAPSODY

Striker **Josef "Pepi" Bican** is, for many Austrian fans, the most prolific goalscorer of all time. Some authorities put his total tally in officially recognized matches at 805 goals, higher in the rankings than Romario, Pele and Gerd Muller. Bican played for Austrian clubs Rapid Vienna and Admira in the 1930s, but the bulk of his strikes came for Czech-based Slavia Prague between 1937 and 1948. He also scored 19 goals in 19 games for Austria from 1933 to 1936, before switching citizenship and hitting 21 in 14 matches for Czechoslovakia between 1938 and 1949. Although he reached the semi-finals of the 1934 FIFA World Cup with Austria, an administrative error meant he was not registered with his new country in time for the 1938 tournament. He also played one international match for a representative Bohemia and Moravia side in 1939, scoring a hat-trick.

PRISTINA CONDITION

Tough-tackling Albania captain Lorik Cana was born in Pristina, Kosovo, and family connections meant he had the choice of playing for Albania, France or Switzerland when he began his international career after impressive performances for Paris Saint-Germain. Cana, who later played club football for Marseille, Sunderland and Galatasaray, opted to represent Albania – as did his father Agim Cana, who won Albanian caps in the 1980s while also playing for FK Pristina, Dinamo Zagreb and Lausanne-Sport.

LIVING HAND TO FOOT

The part-time international footballers of the Faroe Islands have a motley collection of day jobs – and other sporting achievements. Bobble hat-wearing goalkeeper Jens **Martin Knudsen,** man of the match in their shock 1-0 win over Austria in 1989, made his living as a forklift truck driver – while also winning a national gymnastics title and playing handball. Team-mates who have also played both football and handball include journalist/musician Uni Arge, the Faroes' fourth-top-scorer, and third-placed John Petersen.

LAT'S ENTERTAINMENT

After Austria, who had finished top of their qualifying group, were annexed by Germany prior to the 1938 FIFA World Cup, **Latvia** – who had finished as runners-up behind the Austrians – hoped to take their place, but were overlooked and the tournament went ahead with 15 teams instead of 16. After spending the years between 1940 to 1991 as part of the Soviet Union, Latvia finally qualified for their first major finals in 2004, defeating Turkey in a play-off to reach the UEFA European Championship finals.

RECORD WINS

Albania:	5-0	v Vietnam (A, December 2003);
	6-1	v Cyprus (H, August 2009)
Andorra:	2-0	v Belarus (H, April 2000);
	2-0	v Albania (H, April 2002)
Austria:	9-0	v Malta (H, April 1977)
Belarus:	5-0	v Lithuania (H, June 1998)
Bosnia-Herzegovina:	7-0	v Estonia (H, September 2008)
Cyprus:	5-0	v Andorra (H, November 2000)
Estonia:	6-0	v Lithuana (H, July 1928)
Faroe Islands:	3-0	v San Marino (H, May 1995)
Finland:	10-2	v Estonia (H, August 1922)
Georgia:	7-0	v Armenia (H, March 1997)
Iceland:	9-0	v Faroe Islands (H, July 1985)
Israel:	9-0	v Chinese Taipei (A, March 1988)
Kazakhstan:	7-0	v Pakistan (H, June 1997)
Latvia:	8-1	v Estonia (A, August 1942)
Liechtenstein:	4-0	v Luxembourg (A, October 2004)
Luxembourg:	6-0	v Afghanistan (A, July 1948)
Macedonia:	11-1	v Liechtenstein (A, November 1996)
Malta:	7-1	v Liechtenstein (H, March 2008)
Moldova:	5-0	v Pakistan (A, August 1992)
Montenegro:	3-0	v Kazakhstan (H, May 2008)
San Marino:	1-0	v Liechtenstein (H, April 2004)
Slovenia:	7-0	v Oman (A, February 1999)

RECORD DEFEATS

Albania:	0-12	v Hungary (A, September 1950)
Andorra:	1-8	v Czech Republic (A, June 2005);
	0-7	v Croatia (A, October 2006)
Austria:	1-11	v England (H, June 1908)
Belarus:	0-5	v Austria (A, June 2003)
Bosnia-Herzegovina:	0-5	v Argentina (A, May 1998)
Cyprus:	0-12	v West Germany (A, May 1969)
Estonia:	2-10	v Finland (A, August 1922)
Faroe Islands:	0-7	v Yugoslavia (A, May 1991);
	0-7	v Romania (A, May 1992);
	0-7	v Norway (H, August 1993);
	1-8	v Yugoslavia (H, October 1996)
Finland:	0-13	v Germany (A, September 1940)
Georgia:	0-5	v Romania (A, April 1996);
	1-6	v Denmark (A, September 2005)
Iceland:	2-14	v Denmark (A, August 1967)
Israel*:	1-7	v Egypt (A, March 1934)
Kazakhstan:	0-6	v Turkey (H, June 2006);
	0-6	v Russia (A, May 2008)
Latvia:	0-12	v Sweden (A, May 1927)
Liechtenstein:	1-11	v Macedonia (H, November 1996)
Luxembourg:	0-9	v England (H, October 1960);
	0-9	v England (A, December 1982)
Macedonia:	0-5	v Belgium (H, June 1995)
Malta:	1-12	v Spain (A, December 1983)
Moldova:	0-6	v Sweden (A, June 2001)
Montenegro:	0-4	v Romania (A, May 2008)
San Marino:	0-13	v Germany (H, September 2006)
Slovenia:	0-5	v France (A, October 2002)

* Played under the British Mandate of Palestine.

NO-SCORE ANDORRA

Since playing their first international on New Year's Day 1996 – a 6-1 home defeat to Estonia – Andorra have won only three matches, two of them friendlies. Their only competitive triumph was a 1-0 success over Macedonia in an October 2004 FIFA World Cup qualifying match, when left-back **Marc Bernaus** struck the only goal of the game. Perhaps their lack of strength should come as no surprise – the principality is the sixth-smallest country in Europe, with a population of just 71,822 and they have played their most high-profile games, against England, across the Spanish border in Barcelona.

GEORGIA ON MY MIND

Dynamo Tbilisi, from Georgia, and Zalgiris Vilnius, from Lithuania, played out a 2-2 draw in May 1990 in a game later categorized as an international match between the clubs' two countries. The fixture is now regarded as Georgia's first international, even though the country did not become independent from Russia for another 11 months.

CAUGHT SHORT

If Montenegro are scoring, then fans can "put their shirt" on captain and all-time leading scorer **Mirko Vucinic** being among the goals. He celebrated scoring the winner against Switzerland in a Euro 2012 qualifier by removing not his top, but his shorts – and wearing them on his head, antics that earned him a yellow card. Vucinic had previously celebrated a goal for his Italian club side by taking off both his shorts and his shirt, revealing another AS Roma shirt underneath.

MASSIMO BETTER BLUES

Massimo Bonini was unable to inspire a win or even a draw as San Marino manager between 1996 and 1998. But his playing career was far more effective, including seven years, 192 matches and three Serie A league titles at Italian giants Juventus during the 1980s. Bonini played all 90 minutes of Juventus's 1-0 victory over Liverpool in the 1985 UEFA European Cup final – making him the only San Marino footballer to lift the trophy, or even feature at such a high-flown footballing occasion. Although born in San Marino, he had played for Italy's Under-21s team because FIFA did not officially recognize his homeland until 1990 – after which he was able to win 19 caps for San Marino and was later voted the country's all-time greatest player.

SOUTH AMERICA

South America provided the first hosts of the FIFA World Cup™ and the first official world champions. They now claim nine successes in total (Brazil five, Argentina and Uruguay two each), and the two FIFA World Cup™ finalists from 1930 – Uruguay and Argentina – are now hoping to co-host the centenary tournament in 2030. The continent boasts fans with a unique cultural tradition whose fervour can turn a football match into a carnival.

Argentina's Andres d'Alessandro was South American Footballer of the Year in 2010. The 2004 Olympic gold medallist was recalled to national team duty after a five-year absence.

ARGENTINA

Copa America champions on 14 occasions, FIFA Confederations Cup winners in 1992, Olympic gold medallists in 2004 and 2008 and, most treasured of all, FIFA World Cup™ winners in 1978 and 1986: no country has won as many international titles as Argentina. The country has a long and rich football history (the first Argentine league was contested in 1891) and has produced some of the greatest footballers ever to have played the game.

FRINGE PLAYERS

Daniel Passarella was a demanding captain when he led his country to glory at the 1978 World Cup. He was the same as coach. After taking over the national side in 1994, he refused to pick anyone unless they had their hair cut short – and ordered striker Claudio Caniggia to get rid of his "girl's hair".

BAT'S MY BOY

One 1986 FIFA World Cup winner was succeeded by another: Diego Maradona was replaced as Argentina coach by **Sergio Daniel Batista** after the 2010 FIFA World Cup. Former defensive midfielder Batista, initially appointed as a caretaker manager, got off to the perfect start when his team beat Ireland 1–0 then thrashed newly-crowned world champions Spain 4–1. He had previously coached Argentina to Olympic gold at the 2008 Summer Olympics in Beijing, China.

WORTH WAITING FOR

Argentina's national stadium, "El Monumental" in Buenos Aires, hosted its first game in 1938. But the original design was not completed until 20 years later – largely thanks to the £97,000 River Plate received for a transfer fee from Juventus for Omar Sivori. The stadium is a must-see stop on the itinerary of many global football tourists, for the "Superclasico" derby between hosts River Plate and cross-city rivals Boca Juniors.

BOTTOMS UP

Perhaps the most predictable thing about **Diego Maradona**'s spell as Argentina's coach has been its unpredictability. He was banned from football for two months for his foul-mouthed criticism of journalists after his side finally clinched a place at the 2010 FIFA World Cup. The prospect of being abused did not deter hordes of journalists from flocking to his press conferences in South Africa, meaning attendance had to be made ticket-only. Eccentric elements of his squad's World Cup training sessions included Maradona puffing on cigars while issuing instructions – or bending over and inviting players to aim shots at his backside.

BEGINNER'S LUCK

The youngest FIFA World Cup coach was Juan Jose Tramutola, just 27 years and 267 days old when Argentina opened their 1930 campaign by beating France 1-0. Argentina went on to reach the final, only to lose 4-2 to Uruguay – with both sides providing their own choice of ball for each of the halves.

THE KIDS ARE ALL RIGHT

Argentina's youngsters have won the FIFA World Under-20 Championship a record six times, most recently in 2005 and 2007. Sergio Aguero and Mauro Zarate scored the goals in a 2-1 final win over the Czech Republic, when Canada hosted the tournament in 2007.

NUMBERS GAME

Argentina's FIFA World Cup squads of 1978 and 1982 were given numbers based on alphabetical order, rather than positions, which meant the No. 1 shirt was worn by midfielders Norberto Alonso in 1978 and Osvaldo Ardiles in 1982. The only member of the 1982 squad whose shirt number broke the alphabetical order was No. 10, Diego Maradona.

TARNISHED GOLD

Despite winning Olympics football gold in 2004 and 2008 – with **Javier Mascherano** becoming the first male footballer since 1928 to collect two Olympic golds – Argentina surprisingly failed to qualify for the 2012 tournament in London. South America's two places went instead to Brazil and Uruguay, based on performances at the 2011 South American Youth Championship staged in Peru. Argentina finished third in the final group of six.

A ROUND DOZEN

Argentina were responsible for the biggest win in Copa America history, when five goals by Jose Manuel Moreno helped them thrash Ecuador 12-0 in 1942. The much-travelled Moreno won domestic league titles in Argentina, Mexico, Chile and Colombia.

CHINA IN YOUR HAND

In an unusual move, the two 2008 Olympics football finalists Argentina and Nigeria were allowed to take two drinks breaks during the match, which was watched by 89,102 spectators. The game was played in stifling heat in Chinese host city Beijing. **Angel Di Maria** scored the only goal for Argentina, allowing them to retain the title they won in Athens – for the first time – four years earlier.

DO YOU COME HERE OFTEN?

Argentina and Uruguay have played each other more often than any other two nations – 177 matches, including the first international played outside the UK, in 1901. Argentina won that one, 3-2, in the Uruguayan capital Montevideo, and have led the way ever since – winning 81 games, compared to Uruguay's 53, with 43 draws.

MAJOR TOURNAMENTS

FIFA WORLD CUP™: 15 appearances – Winners (2) 1978, 1986

COPA AMERICA: 38 appearances – Winners (14) 1921, 1925, 1927, 1929, 1937, 1941, 1945, 1946, 1947, 1955, 1957, 1959, 1991, 1993

CONFEDERATIONS CUP: Three appearances – Winners (1) 1992

FIRST INTERNATIONAL: Uruguay 2 Argentina 3 (Montevideo, Uruguay, 16 May 1901)

BIGGEST WIN: Argentina 12 Ecuador 0 (Montevideo, Uruguay, 22 January 1942)

BIGGEST DEFEAT: Czechoslovakia 6 Argentina 1 (Helsingborg, Sweden, 15 June 1958); Bolivia 6 Argentina 1, La Paz, Bolivia, 1 April 2009

GLOBAL GLORY

The old Intercontinental Cup, contested by the club champions of Europe and South America until 2004, was won most often by Argentine sides, who triumphed nine times. Boca Juniors took three titles, Independiente two, with single successes for Estudiantes, Racing Club, River Plate and Velez Sarsfield.

SPOT-KICK FLOP

If at first you don't succeed, try and try again – unfortunately Martin Palermo missed all three penalties he took during Argentina's 1999 Copa America clash with Colombia. The first hit the crossbar, the second flew over the bar, and the third was saved. Colombia won the match 3-0.

NO-GO ROA

Carlos Roa's penalty-saving heroics made it the end of the FIFA World Cup for England in 1998, when his Argentina side triumphed in their second-round shoot-out – victory secured when he palmed away David Batty's spot-kick. Yet Roa believed the real end of the world would come at the dawn of the new millennium in 2000. The devout Seventh Day Adventist church-goer quit football to spend a year in isolated retreat, preparing for the apocalypse. When he discovered life went on, he returned to football and joined Spanish side Real Mallorca. But his insistence on not playing on Saturday evenings helped rule him out of contention for Argentina's 2002 FIFA World Cup squad – and a rematch with England. Discussing his year out, he later insisted: "The break did me good."

WINNING TOUCH

Midfielder Marcelo Trobbiani played just two minutes of FIFA World Cup football – the last two minutes of the 1986 final, after replacing winning goalscorer Jorge Burruchaga. Trobbiani touched the ball once, a backheel. The former Boca star ended his international career with 15 caps and one goal to his name.

TOP SCORERS

1	Gabriel Batistuta	56
2	Hernan Crespo	36
3	Diego Maradona	34
4	Luis Artime	24
5	Leopoldo Luque	22
=	Daniel Passarella	22
7	Jose Sanfilippo	21
=	Herminio Masantonio	21
9	Mario Kempes	20
10	Norberto Mendez	19
=	Jose Manuel Moreno	19
=	Rene Pontoni	19

SECOND TIME LUCKY

Luisito Monti is the only man to play in the the FIFA World Cup final for two different countries. The centre-half, born in Buenos Aires on 15 May 1901 but with Italian family origins, was highly influential in Argentina's run to the 1930 final. They lost the game 4-2 to Uruguay – after Monti allegedly received mysterious pre-match death threats. Following a transfer to Juventus the following year, he was allowed to play for Italy and was on the winning side when they beat Czechoslovakia in the 1934 final. Another member of the 1934 team was Raimundo Orsi, who had also played for Argentina before switching countries in 1929.

DIVINE DIEGO

To many people **Diego Armando Maradona** is the greatest footballer the world has ever seen, better even than Pele. The Argentine legend, born in Lanus on 30 October 1960, first became famous as a ball-juggling child during half-time intervals at Argentinos Juniors matches. He was distraught to be left out of Argentina's 1978 FIFA World Cup squad and was then sent off for retaliation at the 1982 tournament. Maradona, as triumphant Argentina captain in Mexico in 1986, scored the notorious "Hand of God" goal and then a spectacular individual strike within five minutes of each other in a quarter-final win over England. He again captained Argentina to the final in 1990, in Italy – the country where he inspired Napoli to Serie A and UEFA Cup success. He was thrown out of the 1994 FIFA World Cup finals in disgrace after failing a drugs test. Maradona captained Argentina 16 times in FIFA World Cup matches, a record, and was surprisingly appointed national coach in 2008, despite scant previous experience as a manager.

FITTER, JAVIER

Javier Zanetti is Argentina's most-capped player, with 139 international appearances – despite being surprisingly left out of Jose Pekerman's squad for the 2006 FIFA World Cup finals. He returned to the team under Alfio Basile, to overtake Roberto Ayala's record caps tally. Zanetti, who can play at full-back or in midfield, has also played more Serie A matches than any other non-Italian. But he missed out on the FIFA World Cup again in 2010, when he and Esteban Cambiasso were left out by Diego Maradona despite helping Internazionale win the treble of Italian league, Italian Cup and UEFA Champions League in 2009–10.

SUPER MARIO

Mario Kempes, who scored twice in the 1978 FIFA World Cup final and won the Golden Boot, was the only member of Cesar Menotti's squad who played for a non-Argentine club. Playing for Valencia, he had been the Spanish league's top scorer for the previous two seasons.

THE ANGEL GABRIEL

Gabriel Batistuta, nicknamed "Batigol" and Argentina's all-time leading scorer, is the only man to have scored hat-tricks in two separate FIFA World Cups. He scored the first against Greece in 1994 and the second against Jamaica four years later. Hungary's Sandor Kocsis, France's Just Fontaine and Germany's Gerd Muller each scored two hat-tricks in the same FIFA World Cup. Batistuta, born in Reconquista on 1 February 1969, also set an Italian league record during his time with Fiorentina, by scoring in 11 consecutive Serie A matches at the start of the 1994–95 season.

LEO BRAVO

Despite some sparkling performances, **Lionel Messi** somehow failed to score in five games at the 2010 FIFA World Cup. But he did enjoy the achievement of becoming Argentina's youngest-ever captain, when he wore the armband for their final group game against Greece, as regular skipper Javier Mascherano was rested. Before the tournament, coach Diego Maradona had told of struggling to track down Barcelona star Messi on the phone, saying: "He is more difficult to get hold of than US President Barack Obama."

TOP CAPS

1	Javier Zanetti	139
2	Roberto Ayala	115
3	Diego Simeone	106
4	Oscar Ruggeri	97
5	Diego Maradona	91
6	Ariel Ortega	87
7	Gabriel Batistuta	78
8	Juan Pablo Sorin	76
9	Americo Gallego	73
=	Juan Sebastian Veron	73

SAINTED PALERMO

Veteran striker **Martin Palermo** waited 10 years between international appearances before being called up again by his former Boca Juniors team-mate Diego Maradona in 1999. He justified the surprise recall with a stoppage-time winner in the penultimate qualifier against Peru, prompting Maradona to take a celebratory dive in rain-sodden mud on the touchline and then hail it as "the miracle of St Palermo". Palermo also became his country's oldest-ever FIFA World Cup scorer, at the 2010 tournament in South Africa. He was 36 years and 227 days old when he came on as a substitute in the first round against Greece and completed the scoring in a 2-0 victory – a year and 358 days older than Maradona was when scoring against the same country 16 years earlier.

BRAZIL

No country has captured the soul of the game to the same extent as Brazil. The country's distinctive yellow-shirted and blue-shorted players have thrilled generations of football fans, have produced some of the game's greatest moments, and no FIFA World Cup™ tournament would be the same without them. Brazil – the nation that gave birth to Pele, Garrincha, Zico, Ronaldo and Kaka – are the only team to have appeared in the finals of every FIFA World Cup™, and have won the competition a record-breaking five times.

SLIM OLYMPIC PICKINGS

Despite two silver medals (1984 and 1988) and two bronzes (1996 and 2008), Brazil have still not won Olympic gold in the men's football – the only official FIFA-approved competition the country has never won. But they will get another go in London in 2012, after qualifying along with fellow South Americans Uruguay, thanks to Brazil's triumph at the 2011 South American Youth Championship in Peru. Sao Paulo playmaker **Lucas** scored a hat-trick in the final game of that tournament, a 6–0 trouncing of Uruguay.

CLOSE ENCOUNTERS

Brazil have been involved in many memorable games. Their 3-2 defeat to Italy in 1982 is regarded as one of the classic games in FIFA World Cup finals history. Paolo Rossi scored all three of Italy's goals with Brazil coach Tele Santana much criticized for going all out in attack when only a 2-2 draw was needed. Brazil's 1982 squad, with players such as **Socrates**, Zico and **Falcao**, is considered one of the greatest teams never to win the tournament. In 1994, a 3-2 win over the Netherlands in the quarter-finals – their first competitive meeting in 20 years – was just as thrilling, with all the goals coming in the second half.

FIERCEST RIVALS

Brazil's oldest club classic is Fluminense versus Botafogo in Rio de Janeiro. The clubs faced each other for the first time on 22 October 1905, when Fluminense won 6-0. One particular match stirred a controversy that lasted 89 years. The two teams disagreed on the result of the 1907 championship, whose title was disputed up to 1996 ... when they finally decided to share it.

BRAZIL'S RECORD

FIFA WORLD CUP™	19 appearances (every finals)
Matches (97)	W67, D15, L15, GF210, GA88
Winners (5)	1958, 1962, 1970, 1994, 2002
Runners-up (2)	1950, 1998
Third place (2)	1938, 1978
Fourth place (1)	1974
COPA AMERICA	32 appearances
Winners (8)	1919, 1922, 1949, 1989, 1997, 1999, 2004, 2007
CONFEDERATIONS CUP	Six appearances
Winners (3)	1997, 2005, 2009
FIRST INTERNATIONAL	Argentina 3 Brazil 0 (Buenos Aires, 20 September 1914)
BIGGEST WIN	Brazil 14 Nicaragua 0 (Mexico City, 17 October 1975)
HEAVIEST DEFEAT	Uruguay 6 Brazil 0 (Chile, 18 September 1920)

LAND OF FOOTBALL

No country is more deeply identified with football success than Brazil, who have won the FIFA World Cup a record five times – in 1958, 1962, 1970, 1994 and 2002. They are also the only team never to have missed a FIFA World Cup finals and are favourites virtually every time the competition is staged. After winning the trophy for a third time in Mexico in 1970, Brazil kept the **Jules Rimet Trophy** permanently. Sadly, it was stolen from the federation's headquarters in 1983 and was never recovered. Brazilians often refer to their country as "o país do futebol" ("the country of football"). It is the favourite pastime of youngsters, while general elections are often held in the same year as the FIFA World Cup, with critics arguing that political parties try to take advantage of the nationalistic surge created by football and bring it into politics. Charles Miller, the son of a Scottish engineer, is credited with bringing football to Brazil in 1894. Yet the sport would only truly become Brazilian when blacks were able to play at the top level in 1933. At first, because of the game's European origin, it was the sport of Brazil's urban white elite. However, it quickly spread among the urban poor as Brazilians realized the only thing they needed to play was a ball, which could be substituted inexpensively with a bundle of socks, an orange, or even a cloth filled with paper.

CAPTAIN TO COACH

Brazil's 1994 FIFA World Cup-winning captain **Dunga** was appointed national coach in 2006 despite having no previous management experience. He led the team to 2007 Copa America and 2009 FIFA Confederations Cup success. But he lost his job after Brazil were knocked out of the 2010 FIFA World Cup in a 2-1 quarter-final defeat to the Netherlands. Dunga – real name Carlos Caetano Bledorn Verri, but widely known by the Portuguese for "Dopey" – had already faced criticism back home for his team's defensive style and decisions not to take Ronaldinho, Adriano or Alexandre Pato to South Africa.

CUP FLOPS DROPPED

Only four players from Brazil's 2010 FIFA World Cup squad made the cut when new coach **Mano Menezes** picked 23 men for the first game of his reign, the August 2010 match against the USA. Brazil won 3–0, captained by Robinho – one of the few survivors from the South Africa tournament, along with Daniel Alves, Ramires and Thiago Silva.

BLOWING HOT AND COLD

A rare FIFA World Cup to be played in winter conditions put Brazil through more extremes than most, in South Africa in 2010. The *Selecao* opened their campaign in 3°C conditions at Johannesburg's Ellis Park stadium, though later faced Portugal in 25°C heat on the coast, in Durban.

EYE FOR GOAL

Centre-forward **Tostao** – full name Eduardo Goncalves de Andrade – was one of the stars of Brazil's legendary 1970 FIFA World Cup-winning team but almost did not make the tournament. He had suffered a detached retina when hit in the face by a football the previous year, prompting some doctors' warnings that he should be left out. Tostao eventually retired at the age of 26 in 1973, after another eye injury, and went to work as a doctor instead. His 1970 team-mate Pele also experienced failing eyesight.

TOP CAPS

1	Cafu	142
2	Roberto Carlos	125
3	Claudio Taffarel	101
4	Djalma Santos	98
=	Ronaldo	98
6	Lucio	97
7	Gilmar	94
8	Gilberto Silva	93
9	Pele	92
=	Rivelino	92

LEADING BRAZILIAN FIFA WORLD CUP™ MARKSMEN

1	Ronaldo	(top scorer in 2002)	15
2	Pele		12
3	Ademir	(top scorer in 1950)	9
=	Jairzinho	(the only player to score in every match played at a FIFA World Cup, in 1970)	9
=	Vava	(joint-top scorer in 1962)	9
6	Leonidas	(top scorer in 1938)	8
=	Rivaldo		8
7	Careca		7
8	Bebeto		6
=	Rivelino		6

TOP SCORERS

1	Pele	77
2	Ronaldo	62
3	Romario	55
4	Zico	52
5	Bebeto	39
6	Rivaldo	34
7	Jairzinho	33
8	Ademir	32
=	Ronaldinho	32
=	Tostao	32

THE KING

Pele is considered by many as the greatest player of all time, a sporting icon *par excellence* and not only for his exploits on the pitch. When, for instance, he scored his 1,000th goal, Pele dedicated it to the poor children of Brazil. He began playing for Santos at the age of 15 and won his first FIFA World Cup two years later, scoring twice in the final. Despite numerous offers from European clubs, the economic conditions and Brazilian football regulations at the time allowed Santos to keep hold of their prized asset for almost two decades, until 1974. All-time leading scorer of the Brazilian national team, he is the only footballer to be a member of three FIFA World Cup-winning teams. Despite being in the Brazilian squad at the start of the 1962 tournament, an injury suffered in the second match meant he was not able to play on and, initially, he missed out on a winner's medal. However, FIFA announced in November 2007 that he would be awarded a medal retrospectively. After the disastrous 1966 tournament, when Brazil fell in the first round, Pele said he did not wish to play in the FIFA World Cup again. He was finally talked round and ended up, in 1970, playing a key role in what is widely considered as one of the greatest sides ever. Since his retirement in 1977, Pele has been a worldwide ambassador for football, as well undertaking various acting roles and commercial ventures.

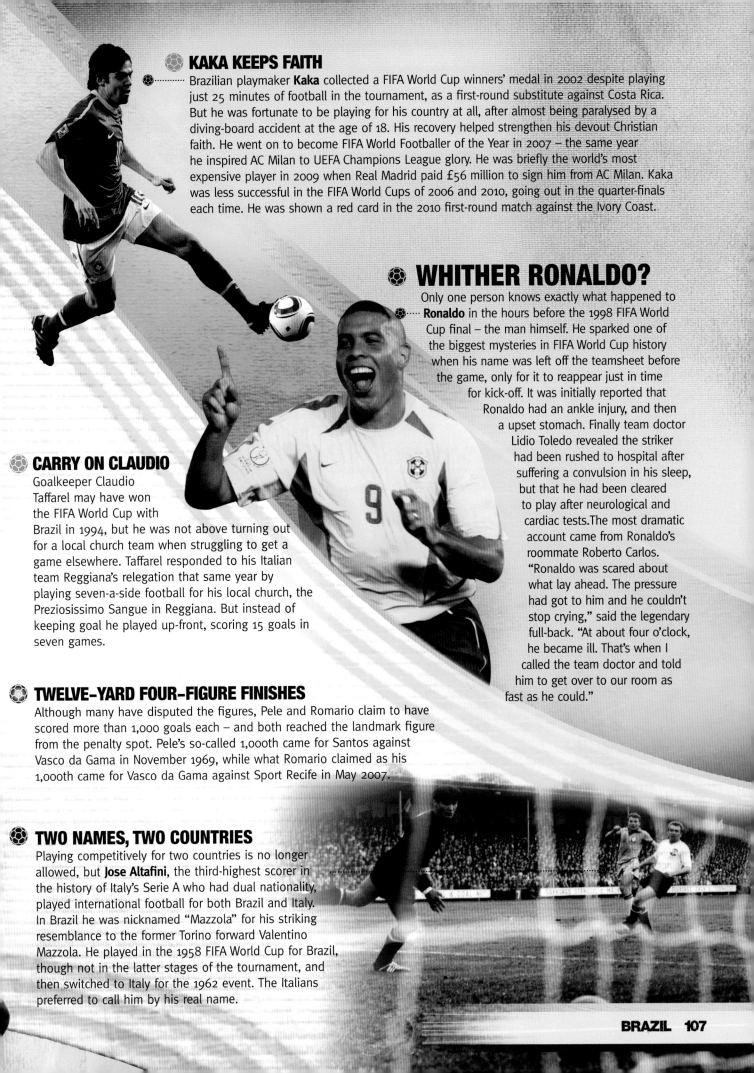

KAKA KEEPS FAITH

Brazilian playmaker **Kaka** collected a FIFA World Cup winners' medal in 2002 despite playing just 25 minutes of football in the tournament, as a first-round substitute against Costa Rica. But he was fortunate to be playing for his country at all, after almost being paralysed by a diving-board accident at the age of 18. His recovery helped strengthen his devout Christian faith. He went on to become FIFA World Footballer of the Year in 2007 – the same year he inspired AC Milan to UEFA Champions League glory. He was briefly the world's most expensive player in 2009 when Real Madrid paid £56 million to sign him from AC Milan. Kaka was less successful in the FIFA World Cups of 2006 and 2010, going out in the quarter-finals each time. He was shown a red card in the 2010 first-round match against the Ivory Coast.

WHITHER RONALDO?

Only one person knows exactly what happened to **Ronaldo** in the hours before the 1998 FIFA World Cup final – the man himself. He sparked one of the biggest mysteries in FIFA World Cup history when his name was left off the teamsheet before the game, only for it to reappear just in time for kick-off. It was initially reported that Ronaldo had an ankle injury, and then a upset stomach. Finally team doctor Lidio Toledo revealed the striker had been rushed to hospital after suffering a convulsion in his sleep, but that he had been cleared to play after neurological and cardiac tests.The most dramatic account came from Ronaldo's roommate Roberto Carlos. "Ronaldo was scared about what lay ahead. The pressure had got to him and he couldn't stop crying," said the legendary full-back. "At about four o'clock, he became ill. That's when I called the team doctor and told him to get over to our room as fast as he could."

CARRY ON CLAUDIO

Goalkeeper Claudio Taffarel may have won the FIFA World Cup with Brazil in 1994, but he was not above turning out for a local church team when struggling to get a game elsewhere. Taffarel responded to his Italian team Reggiana's relegation that same year by playing seven-a-side football for his local church, the Preziosissimo Sangue in Reggiana. But instead of keeping goal he played up-front, scoring 15 goals in seven games.

TWELVE-YARD FOUR-FIGURE FINISHES

Although many have disputed the figures, Pele and Romario claim to have scored more than 1,000 goals each – and both reached the landmark figure from the penalty spot. Pele's so-called 1,000th came for Santos against Vasco da Gama in November 1969, while what Romario claimed as his 1,000th came for Vasco da Gama against Sport Recife in May 2007.

TWO NAMES, TWO COUNTRIES

Playing competitively for two countries is no longer allowed, but **Jose Altafini**, the third-highest scorer in the history of Italy's Serie A who had dual nationality, played international football for both Brazil and Italy. In Brazil he was nicknamed "Mazzola" for his striking resemblance to the former Torino forward Valentino Mazzola. He played in the 1958 FIFA World Cup for Brazil, though not in the latter stages of the tournament, and then switched to Italy for the 1962 event. The Italians preferred to call him by his real name.

CHILE

Chile were one of four founding members of CONMEBOL, South America's football confederation, in 1916. They played in the first match at a South American football championship – losing the opener of the unofficial 1910 tournament 3–0 to Uruguay – an they played in the first official Copa America in 1916. Never winners, they have been runners-up on four occasions, in 1955, 1956, 1979 and 1987. Their greatest glory was hosting – and taking third place at – the 1962 FIFA World Cup™.

TOP SCORERS

1	Marcelo Salas	37
2	Ivan Zamorano	34
3	Caros Caszely	29
4	Leonel Sanchez	23
5	Jorge Aravena	22
6	Humberto Suazo	18
=	Juan Carlos Letelier	18
8	Enrique Hormazabal	17
9	Jaime Ramirez Banda	12
=	Alberto Fouilloux	12
=	Hugo Eduardo Rubio	12
=	Alex Sanchez	12
=	Raul Toro	12

HAPPY ANNIVERSARY

Chile went exactly 48 years between victories at a FIFA World Cup. Their long wait ended in South Africa in 2010 as **Jean Beausejour** scored the only goal of their Group H game against Honduras on 16 June. On 16 June 1962, when they were the tournament's hosts, Chile overcame Yugoslavia in the third-place play-off, also 1–0 (Eladio Rojas scoring). They endured seven defeats and six draws in between. The win over Honduras in Nelspruit was also Chile's first victory in the FIFA World Cup outside of South America.

CENTRE-BACK'S HAT-TRICK

The first player to be named South American Footballer of the Year three times was not Pele, Garrincha or Diego Maradona but Chilean centre-back **Elias Figueroa**, who took the prize in three consecutive years from 1974 to 1976 while playing for Brazilian club Internacional. The only players to emulate such a hat-trick were Brazil's Zico, in 1977, 1981 and 1982, and Argentina forward Carlos Tevez, in 2003, 2004 and 2005. Two more Chileans have won the award: Marcelo Salas in 1997 and Matias Fernandez in 2006. Outside of Brazil and Argentina, the most winners of the prize have come from Chile and Paraguay, with five apiece. Although Figueroa started and ended his playing career in Chile, he also played for clubs in Brazil, Uruguay and the US, while also representing his country for 16 years from 1966 to 1982 – including FIFA World Cup appearances in 1966, 1974 and 1982.

⚽ GOING LOCO FOR 'EL LOCO'

Despite being from Argentina, **Marcelo Bielsa** is a folk hero across Chile after he coached the country to the 2010 FIFA World Cup – and reached the second round with a refreshing team blend, attacking instincts and tactical innovation. Nicknamed "El Loco" and "the last romantic", Bielsa – who coached Argentina to the country's first ever Olympic Games football gold medal in 2004 – said he would resign after his ally Harold Mayne-Nicholls was defeated in elections for the presidency of the Chilean football association. Although the election result was overturned, Bielsa stuck to his guns, and resigned in February 2011.

⚽ SALAS DAYS

Chile's all-time leading scorer **Marcelo Salas** formed a much-feared striking partnership with Ivan Zamorano during the late 1990s and early 21st century. Salas scored four goals as Chile reached the second round of the 1998 FIFA World Cup in France despite not winning a game. The Temuco-born striker later spent two years in international retirement, from 2005 to 2007, but returned for the first four games of qualification for the 2010 FIFA World Cup. His contribution included both Chile goals in a 2-2 draw with Uruguay on 18 November 2007, but his international career ended for good three days later, with a 3-0 defeat to Paraguay.

⚽ SURFACE APPEAL

Football helped keep up the spirits of 33 Chilean miners trapped underground for 69 days after an explosion at a mine in the Atacama desert on 5 August 2010. The men were initially given up for dead, but after news of their survival emerged, supplies sent underground included footage of Chile's 2-1 defeat to Ukraine in a friendly on 7 September. Some of the rescued miners played "keepy-uppies" with footballs on finally emerging into daylight at the surface and, two weeks later, played an exhibition match against their rescuers. The miners lost 3-2 in the 40-minute friendly, when the opposition's goalscorers included the president of Chile, Sebastian Pinera. Football clubs from across the world sent souvenirs and messages of support, and miners were invited to guests at games staged at Manchester United's Old Trafford in England and Real Madrid's Estadio Bernabeu in Spain.

⚽ LUCKY LEO

Leonel Sanchez holds the Chilean record for international appearances, scoring 23 goals in 84 games. But he was lucky to remain on the pitch for one of them. Sanchez escaped an early bath despite punching Italy's Humberto Maschio in the face during their so-called "Battle of Santiago" clash at the 1962 FIFA World Cup, when English referee Ken Aston could have sent off more than just the two players he did dismiss. Sanchez, a left-winger born in Santiago on 25 April 1936, finished the tournament as one of its six four-goal leading scorers – along with Brazilians Garrincha and Vava, Russian Valentin Ivanov, Yugoslav Drazan Jerkovic and Hungarian Florian Albert.

TOP CAPS

1	Leonel Sanchez	84
2	Nelson Tapia	73
3	Alberto Fouilloux	70
=	Marcelo Salas	70
5	Ivan Zamorano	69
=	Fabian Estay	69
7	Javier Margas	63
8	Miguel Ramirez	62
9	Clarence Acuna	61
10	Juan Carlos Letelier	57

URUGUAY

Uruguay was the first country to win a FIFA World Cup™, and they remain the smallest – boasting a population of under four million. Yet their footballers won the game's greatest prize in both 1930 and 1950, the second time shocking hosts and favourites Brazil. Until a fourth-place finish at the 2010 FIFA World Cup™, recent times had been less productive, though only Argentina can match Uruguay's 14 triumphs in the Copa America.

TOP SCORERS

1	Hector Scarone	31
2	Diego Forlan	29
3	Angel Romano	28
4	Oscar Miguez	27
5	Sebastian Abreu	26
6	Pedro Petrone	24
7	Carlos Aguilera	23
8	Fernando Morena	22
9	Jose Piendibene	20
10	Severino Varela	19

HAPPY ANNIVERSARY

A so-called "Mundialito", or "Little World Cup", was staged in December 1980 and January 1981 to mark the 50th anniversary of the FIFA World Cup – and, as in 1930, Uruguay emerged triumphant. The tournament was meant to involve all six countries who had previously won the tournament, though 1966 champions England turned down the invitation and were replaced by 1978 runners-up Holland. Uruguay beat Brazil 2-1 in the final, a repeat of the scoreline from the two teams' final match of the 1950 FIFA World Cup. The Mundialito-winning Uruguay side was captained by goalkeeper **Rodolfo Rodriguez**, still his country's most capped player, and coached by Roque Maspoli, who had played in goal in that 1950 final.

FORLAN HERO

Diego Forlan was the stand-out Uruguayan star of the 2010 FIFA World Cup. He scored five goals – including three from outside the penalty area, making him the first player to do so at a FIFA World Cup since Germany's Lothar Matthaus in 1990. He also hit the crossbar with a long-range free-kick, the final touch of Uruguay's 3-2 defeat to Germany in the third-place play-off. Forlan went into the 2010 tournament having just scored a late winner for Atletico Madrid, against Fulham, in the 2009–10 UEFA Europa League final. Uruguay's fourth-placed finish in South Africa meant Diego fared better than his father Pablo, who played in the Uruguay team knocked out in the first round of the 1974 FIFA World Cup.

DIFFERENT BALL GAME

Uruguay were the inaugural hosts – and the first winners – of the FIFA World Cup in 1930, having won football gold at the Olympics of 1924 in Paris and 1928 in Amsterdam. Among the players who won all three of those titles was forward Hector Scarone, who remains Uruguay's all-time top scorer with 31 goals in 52 internationals. They beat arch-rivals Argentina 4-2 in the 1930 final, in a game which used two different footballs – Argentina's choice in the first half, in which they led 2-1, before Uruguay's was used for their second-half comeback.

TOP CAPS

1	Rodolfo Rodriguez	79
2	Diego Forlan	76
3	Fabian Carini	74
4	Enzo Francescoli	72
=	Alvaro Recoba	69
6	Pablo Gabriel Garcia	68
=	Angel Romano	68
8	Carlos Aguilera	65
9	Jorge Barrios	61
=	Paolo Montero	61

TEACHER KNOWS BEST

Uruguay were the last of 32 teams to clinch qualification for the 2010 FIFA World Cup, needing a play-off against Central America contenders Costa Rica. But despite finishing fifth in the 10-team South America league table, Uruguay went on to finish fourth at the tournament itself – higher than all their continental rivals, including Brazil and Argentina. Their manager throughout qualifying and in South Africa was former schoolteacher **Oscar Washington Tabarez**, nicknamed "The Maestro" and also the man in charge when Uruguay had reached the second round of the 1990 FIFA World Cup.

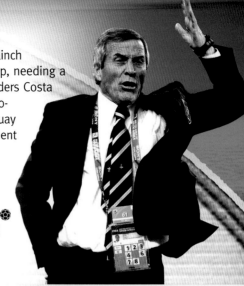

LUCKY LUIS

Striker **Luis Suarez** made a dramatic intervention in his own penalty area in the last moments of Uruguay's quarter-final against Ghana at the 2010 FIFA World Cup in South Africa. He handled the ball on the line, preventing a certain Ghana goal, in the last minute of extra-time. After receiving a straight red card, he was distraught as he headed down the tunnel at Johannesburg's Soccer City stadium – only to dance in delight when Asamoah Gyan's penalty crashed into the crossbar. After the match finished 1-1, Uruguay won 4-2 on penalties, though they were without the suspended Suarez for the semi-final against Holland. Suarez was widely condemned for his actions but did receive some solace from his Ajax Amsterdam club-mate Maarten Stekelenburg. The Dutch goalkeeper sent Suarez a text message congratulating him on his "save".

BOYS IN BLUE

Uruguay's 3-2 home loss to Argentina, in Montevideo on 16 May 1901, was the first international match outside the UK. The second, on 20 July 1902, ended 6-0 to Argentina – still the Celeste's heaviest loss. They have played each other another 176 times in official internationals – a world record – Uruguay winning 53, Argentina 80, and 43 draws. Before an agreed kit-swap in 1910, Uruguay often wore vertical light-blue and white stripes and arch-rivals Argentina would don pale-blue shirts.

OLE, FRANCESCOLI

Until Diego Forlan passed him in 2011, no outfield player had represented Uruguay more often than **Enzo Francescoli** (72 caps) – and few can have taken the field quite so gracefully as the playmaker whose club career included stints with River Plate in Argentina, Racing and Marseille in France and Cagliari and Torino in Italy. His international swansong for Uruguay brought Copa America glory in 1995, when he starred as both midfielder and emergency striker and also scored one of Uruguay's spot-kicks in their penalty shoot-out final victory over Brazil. Among Francescoli's high-profile fans was Zinedine Zidane, who later named his first-born son Enzo.

TRAVEL SICKNESS

Despite winning the 1930 FIFA World Cup, Uruguay turned down the chance to defend their crown four years later, when the tournament was held in Italy. Uruguayan football authorities were unhappy that only four European countries had made the effort to travel to Uruguay and take part in 1930.

GOING CARACAS FOR FOOTBALL

Baseball and boxing may have held more sway with Venezuelans in recent decades but football fever has been on the rise in the twenty-first century – given a big boost by the country staging its first Copa America in 2007. This not only saw extravagant investment in new stadia but also Venezuela's first Copa America victory since 1967 – and unprecedented progress into the knock-out stages. Juan Arango, a popular success in Spain with La Liga club RCD Mallorca, scored Venezuela's goal in the 4–1 quarter-final defeat to Uruguay. Venezuela followed this relative breakthrough by finishing eighth out of ten in South America's qualification campaign for the 2010 FIFA World Cup, above Bolivia and Peru.

NATIONAL STADIUMS

Bolivia:
Estadio Hernando Siles, La Paz (45,000 capacity)

Chile:
Estadio Nacional, Santiago (63,379)

Colombia:
Estadio El Campin, Bogota (48,600)

Ecuador:
Estadio Olimpico Atahualpa, Quito (40,948)

Paraguay:
Estadio Defensores del Chaco, Asuncion (36,000)

Peru:
Estadio Nacional, Lima (45,574)

Venezuela:
Estadio Polideportivo de Pueblo Nuevo, San Cristobal (38,755)

BOLIVIA LEAVE IT LATE

Bolivia have only ever won the Copa America once, but did so in dramatic and memorable style when playing host in 1963. They were the only team to finish the competition unbeaten in all six matches, topping the league table. But they almost threw away glory on the competition's final day, twice squandering two-goal leads against Brazil. Bolivia led 2–0 before being pegged back to 2–2, then saw a 4–2 advantage turn to 4–4. But Maximo Alcocer scored what proved to be Bolivia's winning goal with four minutes remaining.

SIX AND OUT

Bolivia and El Salvador have both played the most FIFA World Cup finals matches without managing to win even once – six each. At least Bolivia did achieve a goalless draw against South Korea in 1994. But they went a record five successive FIFA World Cup finals matches without scoring a goal, across the 1930 and 1994 tournaments, before **Erwin Sanchez** put an end to their barren spell in a 3-1 defeat to Spain in their final 1994 fixture. The unwanted record was equalled at the 2010 FIFA World Cup, by both Honduras and New Zealand. Honduras drew twice and lost once in 1982, then drew once and lost twice in 2010. New Zealand lost all three matches in 1982 then drew all three in 2010.

HOME SECURITY

Colombia are the only country to go through a Copa America tournament without conceding a goal, when they hosted and won the cup for the first and only time in 2001. Their striker **Victor Aristazabal** ended the tournament as top scorer, with six goals, but the only goal of the final against Mexico came from defender Ivan Cordoba. Colombia's hosting rights were put in jeopardy due to security fears – they prompted Argentina to withdraw – but after pondering a move to Venezuela, South American football's governing body, CONMEBOL, decided to keep it in Colombia.

COOL DUDAMEL

Venezuela suffered a series of hefty beatings during qualifiers for the 1998 FIFA World Cup – ending up with no wins and 13 defeats in 16 games, scoring 13 and conceding 41 goals. Their losses included 4–1 to Peru, 6–1 against Bolivia and 6–0 versus Chile, for whom Ivan Zamorano scored five. But Venezuelan goalkeeper Rafael Dudamel did enjoy a moment of joy against Argentina in October 1996, scoring direct from a free-kick with three minutes left. His side still lost the match 5–2.

A FIRST FOR ECUADOR

LDU Quito, based in the Ecuador capital, became the first and to date only team from the country to claim an international title when they won the Copa Libertadores in 2008. They beat Brazilian side Fluminense 3-1 on penalties in the final – after the two legs had ended 5-5 on aggregate. LDU went on to lose to Manchester United in the final of the FIFA Club World Cup later in the year.

TIM'S TIME

Peru were coached at the 1982 FIFA World Cup by Tim, who had been waiting an unprecedented 44 years to return to the FIFA World Cup finals – after playing once as striker for his native Brazil in the 1938 tournament.

BIGGEST DEFEATS

Brazil 10 Bolivia 1
(10 April 1949)

Brazil 9 Colombia 0
(24 March 1997)

Argentina 12 Ecuador 0
(22 January 1942)

Argentina 8 Paraguay 0
(20 October 1926)

Brazil 7 Peru 0
(26 June 1997)

Argentina 11 Venezuela 0
(10 August 1975)

HIGH LIFE

Bolivia and Ecuador play their home internationals at higher altitudes than any other teams on earth. Bolivia's showpiece Estadio Hernando Siles stadium, in the capital La Paz, is 3,637 metres (11,932ft) above sea level, while Ecuador's main Estadio Olimpico Atahualpa, in Quito, sits 2,800 metres (9,185ft) above sea level. Opposing teams have complained that the rarefied nature of the air makes it difficult to breathe, let alone play, but a FIFA ban on playing competitive internationals at least 2,500 metres (8,200ft) above sea level, first introduced in May 2007, was amended a month later – adjusting the limit to 3,000 metres (9,840ft) and allowing Estadio Hernando Siles to be used as a special case. The altitude ban was suspended entirely in May 2008. FIFA had changed its mind after protests by Bolivia, Ecuador and other affected nations Colombia and Peru. Other campaigners to overturn the law included Argentina legend Diego Maradona. He may have regretted his decision. In March 2009 **Bolivia scored a 6-1 home win against Argentina** in a FIFA World Cup qualifier. The Argentina coach was ... Maradona.

BIGGEST WINS

Bolivia 7 Venezuela 0
(22 August 1993)

Argentina 0 Colombia 5
(5 September 1993)

Colombia 5 Uruguay 0
(6 June 2004)

Colombia 5 Peru 0
(4 June 2006)

Ecuador 6 Peru 0
(22 June 1975)

Paraguay 7 Bolivia 0
(30 April 1949)

Hong Kong 0 Paraguay 7
(17 November 2010)

Peru 9 Ecuador 1
(11 August 1938)

Venezuela 6 Puerto Rico 0
(26 December 1946)

ABOVE–PAR PARAGUAY

In their eighth appearance at a FIFA World Cup, Paraguay topped their first-round group for the first time in 2010. Not only that, they went on to reach a later stage of the tournament than ever before, the quarter-finals, before narrowly losing 1-0 to Spain. Their penalty shoot-out victory over Japan in the second round (**Oscar Cardozo**, No. 7 converting the decisive kick) meant four South American countries made the quarter-finals – outnumbering the three European nations for the first time. That said, there were no quarter-finals in 1930, 1950, 1974, 1978 or 1982.

BOTERO'S ERA

Bolivia failed to reach the 2010 FIFA World Cup but did pull off one of the most eye-catching results of the qualifying campaign – a 6–1 thrashing of Argentina, who had previously been unbeaten under new coach Diego Maradona. The 1 April 2009 game in La Paz made an April fool of Maradona but a national icon of striker **Joaquin Botero,** who hit a hat-trick. But the 31-year-old announced his international retirement just a month later, bowing out on 48 caps and with a Bolivian-record 20 goals.

ETCHEVERRY BRIEF APPEARANCE

Marco Etcheverry – nicknamed "El Diablo" – went from saint to sinner during Bolivia's 1994 FIFA World Cup adventure. His goals proved crucial in helping the country qualify for only their second FIFA World Cup, their first since 1950 – most notably in a 2–0 victory over eventual champions Brazil and a 3–1 win over Uruguay. But he began the tournament itself as a substitute, due to a niggling injury, and then lasted just three minutes of the opening match against Germany before being sent off for kicking Lothar Matthaus.

ELITE CUB

Peru forward Teofilo Cubillas became the first player to twice end a FIFA World Cup finals with at least five goals – he scored five apiece in 1970 and 1978, though failed to win the Golden Boot on either occasion. Germany's Miroslav Klose emulated the achievement by scoring five in 2002 and the same tally four years later, the same year he picked up the Golden Boot award.

MOST INTERNATIONAL GOALS

Bolivia	Joaquin Botero	20
Colombia	Adolfo Valencia	31
Ecuador	Agustin Delgado	31
Paraguay	Jose Saturnino Cardozo	25
Peru	Teofilo Cubillas	26
Venezuela	Giancarlo Maldonado	20

MOST INTERNATIONAL CAPS

Bolivia	Luis Cristaldo	93
	Marco Sandy	93
Colombia	Carlos Valderrama	111
Ecuador	Ivan Hurtado	167
Paraguay	Carlos Gamarra	110
Peru	Roberto Palacios	127
Venezuela	Jose Manuel Rey	110

TOP GOALS: PARAGUAY

1	Jose Saturnino Cardozo	25
2	Roque Santa Cruz	21
3	Julio Cesar Romero	13
=	Saturnino Arrua	13
5	Carlos Gamarra	12
=	Gerardo Rivas	12
7	Miguel Angel Benitez	11
8	Salvador Cabanas	10
=	Aurelio Gonzalez	10
=	Carlos Humberto Paredes	10
=	Juan Bautista Villalba	10

RENE HIGUITA

Eccentric goalkeeper **Rene Higuita** managed to score three goals for his country and also performed a famous, and acrobatic, "scorpion kick" save at Wembley in September 1995, hurling himself into the air and flicking away a Jamie Redknapp shot with the heels of both feet. He played for Colombia at the 1990 FIFA World Cup, but missed the 1994 FIFA World Cup finals due to a seven-month jail sentence for his involvement in a kidnapping and then tested positive for cocaine in November 2004.

FIVE-STAR PARAGUAY

The South American Footballer of the Year award dates back to 1971 and has been dominated by players from Brazil and Argentina. However, five Paraguayan players have won the award, all since 1985 – and the honours have come roughly every five years. The first was attacking midfielder Romerito (Julio Cesar Romero) – the only Paraguayan named in Pele's top 125 living players in 2004 – who claimed the prize in 1985. Five years later, it went to Raul Vicente Amarilla who, although Paraguayan, did not win a cap for his country (he had won two Spanish Under-21 caps when playing club football over there). Prolific goalscoring goalkeeper Jose Luis Chilavert won the award in 1996 and he was followed by two strikers, Jose Cardozo, in 2002, and Salvador Cabanas, in 2007.

⚽ IVAN THE ADMIRABLE

Ecuador defender Ivan Hurtado is South America's most-capped footballer, playing 167 games since making his debut in 1992. Including five goals, he was one of Ecuador's most influential players at their first FIFA World Cup finals, in 2002, and captained them as they reached the second round four years later.

⚽ MEDELLIN MURDER

Tragic Colombian defender Andres Escobar, 27, was shot dead outside a Medellin club 10 days after scoring an own goal in a 1994 FIFA World Cup first-round match against the United States. Colombia lost the game 2-1 and were eliminated from a tournament some observers – including Pele – had tipped them to win.

⚽ MARKSMAN SPENCER

Ecuador's greatest player of all time is arguably prolific striker **Alberto Spencer,** even though he played much of his club football in Uruguay. Spencer holds the record for most goals in South America's Copa Libertadores club championship, scoring 54 times between 1960 and 1972 and lifting the trophy three times with Uruguay's Penarol. He also scored four goals in 11 games for Ecuador and once in four appearances for Uruguay. Spencer was nicknamed "Magic Head" and was even praised as a better header of the ball than Pele – the tribute coming from Pele himself.

⚽ TOP CAPS: PARAGUAY

1	Carlos Gamarra	110
2	Denis Caniza	99
3	Roberto Acuna	97
4	Celso Ayala	85
5	Jose Saturnino Cardozo	82
6	Roberto Fernandez	78
=	Justo Villar	78
8	Juan Bautista Torales	77
9	Paulo Da Silva	76
10	Roque Santa Cruz	75

⚽ SAFE HANDS OSCAR

Keeping clean sheets for Colombia all the way through the 2001 Copa America was **Oscar Cordoba,** who went on to become his country's most-capped goalkeeper – with 73 appearances between 1993 and 2006.

⚽ HIGHS AND LOWS FOR LOLO

Teodoro "Lolo" Fernandez scored six goals in two games for Peru at the 1936 Summer Olympics in Berlin, including five in a 7–3 defeat of Finland and another in a 4–2 extra-time victory over Austria. But Peru were outraged when the Austrians claimed that fans invading the pitch included one brandishing a gun – and even more upset when Olympics officials ordered the match to be replayed. Peru withdrew from the tournament in protest, with Colombia joining them in sympathy, while Austria went on to claim silver. But Fernandez and his teammates had a happier ending at the Copa America three years later, with Peru crowned champions and Fernandez finishing top scorer with seven goals. Only Teofilo Cubillas, with 26 goals in 81 games, has scored more for Peru than Fernandez's 24 from 32 appearances.

CANIZA CAN DO

Centre-back and captain Denis Caniza, 36, became the first Paraguayan to play at four different FIFA World Cups, with his one appearance against New Zealand during the 2010 tournament. He has also now played more FIFA World Cup matches than any other Paraguayan, taking his tally to 12 – and his total cap count to 99. Caniza had retired from international football after the 2006 FIFA World Cup, but was persuaded to return by new coach Gerardo Martino the following year.

AFRICA

Even before the likes of Cameroon, Nigeria and, latterly, Senegal and Ghana began to reach the closing stages of FIFA World Cups™, Africa had been giving the world some of its most eye-catchingly skillful and powerful players. While footballers from across Africa now star in the globe's biggest league and cup competitions, the continent became the sustained focus of attention in 2010 when its fans welcomed the FIFA World Cup™ finals to the Rainbow Nation of South Africa.

Samuel Eto'o (9) has been one of the most feared strikers in European club football for many years. The Cameroon star is the Africa Cup of Nations' most prolific goalscorer ever.

FAWZI'S FIRST

Abdelrahman Fawzi became the first African footballer to score at a FIFA World Cup, when he pulled a goal back for Egypt against Hungary in the first round of the 1934 tournament – then scored an equalizer eight minutes later, to make it 2-2 at half-time. Egypt went on to lose the match 4-2, and would not return to the finals for another 56 years.

PLAY–OFF PIQUE

Morocco's qualification for the 1970 FIFA World Cup ended a 36-year African exile from the finals. No African countries played at the 1966 FIFA World Cup in Africa, with 16 possible candidate countries all boycotting the event because FIFA wanted the top African team to face a side from Asia or Oceania in a qualification play-off.

SUDDEN DEATH IN SUDAN

As if the North African rivalry between Algeria and Egypt were not intense enough, qualifiers for the 2010 FIFA World Cup pitted them against one another not once, not twice – but three times. A 2-0 win for Egypt against Algeria – including a stoppage-minute goal by Emad Moteab – in their scheduled second qualifier meant they ended the final African phase level on points, goal difference and goals scored. A one-off play-off match, hosted in neutral Sudan, was held – and Algeria's **Antar Yahia** (right) scored the only goal of the game, taking Algeria to the finals for the first time in 24 years. Both countries' governments felt compelled to call for calm, amid allegations that the Algerian team bus and Egyptian fans had come under attack ahead of the crucial matches.

AGELESS ALI

Tunisian goalkeeper **Ali Boumnijel** played in all three of his country's games at the 2006 FIFA World Cup – making him the oldest player to feature in Germany that summer, as well as only the fifth man over the age of 40 to play at a FIFA World Cup. Boumnijel conceded six goals in those three matches, against Saudi Arabia (two, in a 2-2 draw), Spain (three, in a 3-1 defeat) and Ukraine (one, in a 1-0 loss).

REDS IN A ROW

When Antar Yahia was sent off for a second bookable offence, three minutes into stoppage-time of Algeria's 1-0 defeat to the USA at the 2010 FIFA World Cup, it was not only the latest red card shown in any World Cup game not featuring extra-time. It also meant at least one player had been sent off on eight consecutive days of the 2010 tournament – a record run for any FIFA World Cup.

ANTAR THE STAR

Antar Yahia had been the hero of Algeria's 2010 FIFA World Cup qualifying campaign, scoring the winning goal in a play-off against arch-rivals Egypt. The defender was actually born in France, in 1982, and played for the French under-18s before switching to Algeria in 2004, scoring on his debut for the country's under-23s.

MOROCCAN ROLL

Morocco remain the only North African country to reach the second round of a FIFA World Cup, though they were knocked out, 1-0, by eventual finalists West Germany. It was in Mexico in 1986 that Morocco were the first African team to top a FIFA World Cup group, finishing above England, Poland and Portugal. Crucial was their 3-1 victory over Portugal in their final group game, following goalless draws against the other two teams – including an England side who lost captain Bryan Robson to a dislocated shoulder and vice-captain Ray Wilkins to a red card. **Abderrazak Khairi** scored two of the goals against Portugal, while Lothar Matthaus's winning strike for Germany came with just three minutes remaining.

NORTH AFRICAN COUNTRIES' BEST FIFA WORLD CUP™ PERFORMANCES

ALGERIA: First round 1982, 1986, 2010
EGYPT: First round 1934, 1990
MOROCCO: Second round 2006
TUNISIA: First round 1978, 1998, 2002, 2006

NORTH AFRICAN COUNTRIES' FIFA WORLD CUP™ QUALIFICATIONS

ALGERIA: 3 (1982, 1986, 2010)
EGYPT: 2 (1934, 1990)
MOROCCO: 4 (1970, 1986, 1994, 1998)
TUNISIA: 4 (1978, 1998, 2002, 2006)

NORTH AFRICA: TOP FIFA WORLD CUP™ GOALSCORERS

Salah Assad (Algeria) 2
Salaheddine Bassir (Morocco) 2
Abdelrahman Fawzi (Egypt) 2
Abdeljalil Hadda (Morocco) 2
Abderrazak Khairi (Morocco) 2

NO WAITING GAME

Morocco's 2-1 defeat to Saudi Arabia in 1994 was one of the last two games to be played simultaneously at a FIFA World Cup, without falling on a final match-day of a group. Belgium were beating Holland 1-0 at the same time, with every team in Group F having still one game to play. At later tournaments, every match has been played separately until the climactic two fixtures of any group.

HOMEGROWN HERO

Of the six African countries at the 2010 FIFA World Cup, Algeria's was the only squad with an African coach – **Rabah Saadane**, in his fifth separate stint in charge since 1981. He previously led his country to the 1986 FIFA World Cup in Mexico, where they were also eliminated in the first round. Along with Honduras, the Algeria team of 2010 were one of only two countries failing to score a single goal. However, they did concede just twice in their three games: 1-0 defeats to Slovakia and the USA, and a surprise goalless draw with England – Algeria's first-ever FIFA World Cup clean sheet.

MOKHTAR RUNS AMOK

Egypt had to play only two matches to qualify for the 1934 FIFA World Cup, becoming the first African representatives at the tournament. Both games were against a Palestine side under the British mandate – and the Egyptians won both games handsomely, 7-1 in Cairo and 4-1 in Palestine. Captain and striker Mahmoud Mokhtar scored a hat-trick in the first leg, a brace in the second. Turkey were also meant to contest qualifiers against the two sides, but withdrew, leaving the path to the finals free for Egypt.

TUNISIA IN TUNE

Tunisia became the first African team to win a match at a FIFA World Cup finals, when they beat Mexico 3-1 in Rosario, Argentina, in 1978 – thanks to goals from Ali Kaabi, Nejib Ghommidh and Mokhtar Dhouib. While they share with Morocco the North African record of reaching four different FIFA World Cups, they are the only nation from that part of the continent to qualify for three finals in a row – in 1998, 2002 and 2006. Among the players to feature in all three tournaments were 2006 captain Riadh Bouazizi, Hatem Trabelsi and **Radhi Jaidi**.

NORTH AFRICA NATIONAL RECORDS

THANKS, PAL

Hungarian Pal Titkos became the first foreign coach to win the CAN Africa Cup of Nations when he led Egypt to their second triumph in 1959. One Briton has achieved the feat: English-born former Wales manager **Mike Smith** coached Egypt to the title in 1986.

FOUNDING FATHERS

The Confederation of African Football was officially established by a meeting in the Sudanese capital Khartoum, in the city's Grand Hotel on 7 February 1957 – three days before the first Africa Cup of Nations kicked off in the same city. Representatives of Sudan, South Africa, Ethiopia and Egypt were present at the first assembly, and Egypt's Abdel Aziz Salem became CAF's first president.

OFFICIAL INFLUENCE

The first African to referee a FIFA World Cup final was Morocco's **Said Belqola**, who controlled the 1998 climax in which hosts France beat Brazil 3-0. Perhaps his most notable moment was sending off France's **Marcel Desailly** in the 68th minute – brandishing only the third red card to be shown in a FIFA World Cup final. Belqola was 41 at the time. He died from cancer just under four years later.

HITTING THE TOP 10

Egypt's record-breaking third successive Africa Cup of Nations triumph in February 2010 helped propel them to 10th place in the official FIFA rankings. Nigeria are the only African country to have reached any higher, hitting fifth in April 1994.

SUDAN IMPACT

After two second-place and one third-place finishes, Sudan became the third and last of the ACN Africa Cup of Nations founders to lift the trophy, when they beat Ghana in the 1970 final. Hosts Sudan left it late to reach the final, with two goals from El-Issed – the second 12 minutes into extra-time – seeing off Egypt. The same player scored the only goal of the final, after 12 minutes.

NORTH AFRICA: SELECTED TOP GOALSCORERS

ALGERIA: Abdelhafid Tasfaout 34
EGYPT: Hossam Hassan 69
LIBYA: Tarik El Taib 14
MOROCCO: Salaheddine Bassir 25
SUDAN: Haytham Tambal 26
TUNISIA: Francileudo Santos 22

SORE LOSERS

Libya could claim the record for highest-scoring victory by an African side, having racked up a 21-0 lead over Oman during the Arab Nations Cup in April 1966. But the Oman players walked off with 10 minutes remaining, in protest at Libya being awarded a penalty, and played no further part in the competition. Libya's goal tally included nine for Ahmed Ben Suwed, seven for Ali Al-Baski and four for Mahmoud Al-Jahani. Mahmoud Zand got the other. Ahmed Ben Suwed and Ali Al-Baski subsequently scored five apiece in a 13-0 trouncing of North Yemen – yet still Libya only ended the tournament in third place, after losing their semi-final to hosts Iraq.

HALFWAY TO A HUNDRED

Amr Zaki and Ahmad Fathy scored the goals as the Confederation of African Football celebrated their 50th anniversary with a friendly between Egypt and Sweden in February 2007 – and a 2-0 victory for the reigning African champions.

HEAD–TO–HEAD

The international career of Algeria's leading scorer **Abdelhafid Tasfaout** came to an end at the 2002 Africa Cup of Nations – though it could have been a lot worse. Tasfaout was knocked out by a collision with Mali defender Boubacar Diarra which caused him to swallow his tongue, prompting fears he might not even survive – though, thankfully, he did recover. Tasfaout, who played French league football for six years, scored 34 goals in 62 games for Algeria between 1990 and 2002.

GOING UP IN FLAMES

Key CAF documents were initially kept at the Sudan Football Association's HQ in Khartoum, but within just a few months of the federation's founding, a blaze broke out there and destroyed them – prompting the CAF to set up official home in the Egyptian capital Cairo instead.

NORTH AFRICA: SELECTED TOP APPEARANCES

ALGERIA: Mahieddine Meftah 107
EGYPT: Ahmed Hassan 173
LIBYA: Tarik El Taib 77
MOROCCO: Abdelmajid Dolmi 124
SUDAN: Haitham Mustafa 102
TUNISIA: Sadok Sassi 110

NEW TUNISIAN

Tunisia's all-time top scorer was not born there – in fact, he did not even visit the place until his late teens. But Brazilian-born **Francileudo Santos** eventually accepted Tunisian citizenship at the age of 24 in 2004, four years after completing a two-year spell at the country's leading club Etoile du Sahel. Within weeks of officially turning Tunisian, he was helping his new nation not only host but win the 2004 Africa Cup of Nations – scoring four goals, including the opener in the final against Morocco. A knee injury restricted him to just 11 minutes' action at the FIFA World Cup two years later, but he recovered to reclaim his place in the Tunisian first 11 and now boasts a tally of 22 international goals in 40 games.

MAD FOR 'MADIBA'

Apart from the Dutch and Spanish sides competing in the 2010 FIFA World Cup final, one of the star attractions in Johannesburg's Soccer City stadium on 11 July 2010 was South Africa's legendary former president **Nelson Mandela**. The frail 91-year-old – known affectionately by his tribal name of "Madiba" – was driven on to the pitch before the game in a golf cart and given a rapturous reception by the crowd. It marked his one and only public appearance at the tournament. Mandela had hoped to attend the opening ceremony and game on 11 June, but was mourning the death of his 13-year-old great-granddaughter in a car crash the previous evening. He had been a high-profile presence at the FIFA vote in 2004 which awarded South Africa hosting rights for 2010.

SUB–SAHARAN AFRICAN COUNTRIES' BEST FIFA WORLD CUP™ PERFORMANCES

ANGOLA: First round 2006
CAMEROON: Quarter-finals 1990
GHANA: Quarter-finals 2010
IVORY COAST: First round 2006, 2010
NIGERIA: Second round 1994, 1998
SENEGAL: Quarter-finals 2002
SOUTH AFRICA: First round 1998, 2002, 2010
TOGO: First round 2006
ZAIRE/CONGO DR: First round 1974

SUB–SAHARAN AFRICAN COUNTRIES' FIFA WORLD CUP™ QUALIFICATIONS

CAMEROON: 6 (1982, 1990, 1994, 1998, 2002, 2010)
NIGERIA: 4 (1994, 1998, 2002, 2010)
SOUTH AFRICA: 3 (1998, 2002, 2010)
GHANA: 2 (2006, 2010)
IVORY COAST: 2 (2006, 2010)
ANGOLA: 1 (2006)
SENEGAL: 1 (2002)
TOGO: 1 (2006)
ZAIRE/CONGO DR: 1 (1974)

GOING FOR A SONG

Two players have been sent off at two separate FIFA World Cups: Cameroon's Rigobert Song, against Brazil in 1994 and Chile four years later, and France's Zinedine Zidane – red-carded against Saudi Arabia in 1998 and against Italy in the 2006 final. Song's red card against Brazil made him the youngest player to be dismissed at a FIFA World Cup – he was just 17 years and 358 days old. Song, born in Nkanglikock on 1 July 1976, is Cameroon's most-capped player, with 137 appearances – including winning displays in the 2000 and 2002 finals of the Africa Cup of Nations. He has been joined in the national team by his nephew, Arsenal utility player Alexandre Song Billong.

LIONS TAMED

Cameroon's third and final game at the 2010 FIFA World Cup, a 2-1 defeat to Holland, made them the first African country to play as many as 20 FIFA World Cup matches. But there was little to celebrate this time around – the "Indomitable Lions", coached by Frenchman Paul Le Guen, had already become the first team eliminated from the 2010 competition.

JOLLY ROGER

Cameroon striker **Roger Milla**, famous for dancing around corner flags after each goal, became the FIFA World Cup's oldest scorer against Russia in 1994 – aged 42 years and 39 days. He came on as substitute during that tournament with his surname handwritten, rather than printed, on the back of his shirt. Milla, born in Yaounde on 20 May 1952, had retired from professional football for a year before Cameroon's president, Paul Biya, persuaded him to join the 1990 FIFA World Cup squad. His goals in that tournament helped him win the African Footballer of the Year award for an unprecedented second time – 14 years after he had first received the trophy. He finally ended his international career after the 1994 FIFA World Cup in the United States, finishing with 102 caps and 28 goals to his name.

BROTHERS AT ARMS

Two Boateng brothers were on the pitch at the same time when Germany played Ghana at the 2010 FIFA World Cup – but on opposing sides, a FIFA World Cup first. Jerome was playing left-back for Germany, while elder half-brother **Kevin-Prince** was in the Ghana midfield – having officially switched nationality just a month before the tournament. Both were born in the German capital Berlin, and have the same German mother but different Ghanaian fathers. Kevin-Prince had an extra effect on the 2010 FIFA World Cup in South Africa, through his tackle on German captain Michael Ballack in the May 2010 FA Cup final in England. Ballack was so badly injured that he had to be substituted and missed the World Cup altogether.

HORN OF AFRICA

Colombian pop star Shakira sang the official 2010 FIFA World Cup anthem, which she performed at both an official tournament-opening concert and the closing ceremony. But perhaps an even more distinctive sound that summer was the din of the vuvuzelas – the plastic horns that have been a feature of South African football matches since the 1980s and were a must-have for many fans attending FIFA World Cup fixtures. Some players – including Argentina's Lionel Messi and Portugal's Cristiano Ronaldo – complained that the constant drone was distracting, though others such as England's Jamie Carragher and Holland's Wesley Sneijder spoke up in the horns' defence. FIFA and the South African tournament organizers resisted calls for the instruments to be banned, while some television channels made technical arrangements to turn down the vuvuzelas' volume.

HENRI AND IVORY

The Ivory Coast were widely considered unfortunate to go out in the first round of their first FIFA World Cup, in 2006, having been drawn in the "group of death" alongside Argentina and Holland. A side starring **Didier Drogba**, Didier Zokora and brothers Kolo and Yaya Toure was managed by Frenchman Henri Michel, who was coaching at a fourth FIFA World Cup with a fourth different country. He had previously led France in 1986, Cameroon in 1994 and Morocco in 1998. Only Bora Milutinovic and Carlos Alberto Parreira have taken more different teams to FIFA World Cups. The same "group of death" nickname was given to the Ivory Coast's group in 2010, when they faced Brazil, Portugal and North Korea, and again finished third.

RATOMIR GETS IT RIGHT

Ghana went through four different managers during qualifiers for the 2006 FIFA World Cup, with Serbian coach Ratomir Dujkovic finally clinching the country a place at the finals for the very first time. He led them through the whole of 2005 unbeaten, winning a FIFA prize for being the most-improved team of the year. Ghana were the only African country to make it through the first round of both the 2006 and 2010 FIFA World Cups, despite having the youngest average age of any squad each time. They were again coached by a Serb in 2010, this time Milovan Rajevac.

SUB–SAHARAN AFRICAN COUNTRIES: TOP FIFA WORLD CUP™ GOALSCORERS

Roger Milla (Cameroon) 5
Asamoah Gyan (Ghana) 4
Papa Bouba Diop (Senegal) 3
Samuel Eto'o (Cameroon) 3
Daniel Amokachi (Nigeria) 2
Emmanuel Amunike (Nigeria) 2
Shaun Bartlett (South Africa) 2
Henri Camara (Senegal) 2
Aruna Dindane (Ivory Coast) 2
Didier Drogba (Ivory Coast) 2
Patrick Mboma (Cameroon) 2
Benni McCarthy (South Africa) 2
Sulley Muntari (Ghana) 2
Francois Omam-Biyik (Cameroon) 2

'BAFANA BAFANA' BACK 'BAGHANA BAGHANA'

Despite missing injured midfielder Michael Essien, Ghana were the only African side to survive the first round of the 2010 FIFA World Cup – and received exuberant support from home fans in South Africa as they reached the quarter-finals. Ghana's footballers, traditionally known as the "Black Stars", were renamed "Africa's Stars" by some – or "BaGhana BaGhana", playing on South Africa's nickname "Bafana Bafana", which means "The Boys, The Boys".

HOT DROG

Didier Drogba may have been raised in France but he was born in Ivory Coast and remains one of the African country's favourite sons for his actions both on and off the pitch. The Chelsea striker and Ivory Coast captain has a record 45 goals in 72 international appearances for the Elephants. He has been credited with influence off the pitch, too, when he called for a ceasefire in the civil-war-torn nation. He also pushed for an Africa Cup of Nations qualifier against Madagascar in June 2007 to be moved from the capital Abidjan to rebel army stronghold Bouake, in an effort to encourage reconciliation. Drogba, a two-time CAF African Footballer of the Year, captained the Ivory Coast team at the two FIFA World Cups they have reached, in 2006 and 2010.

SUB–SAHARAN AFRICA: SELECTED TOP GOALSCORERS

ANGOLA: Akwa 36
BOTSWANA: Dipsy Selolwane 11
CAMEROON: Samuel Eto'o 44
GHANA: Abedi "Pele" Ayew 33
IVORY COAST: Didier Drogba 45
MOZAMBIQUE: Tico-Tico 27
NAMIBIA: Gervatius Uri Khob 12
NIGERIA: Rashidi Yekini 37
SENEGAL: Henri Camara 31
SOUTH AFRICA: Benni McCarthy 32
SWAZILAND: Sibusiso Dlamini 26
ZIMBABWE: Peter Ndlovu 38

KNOCKED OUT ON PENALTIES

Botswana goalkeeper and captain Modiri Marumo was sent off in the middle of a penalty shoot-out against Malawi in May 2003, after punching the opposing goalkeeper Philip Nyasulu in the face. Botswana defender Michael Mogaladi had to go in goal for the rest of the shoot-out, which Malawi won 4-1.

FIFTEEN LOVE

Fifteen-year-old Samuel Kuffour became the youngest footballer to win an Olympic medal when Ghana took bronze at the 1992 Olympics in Barcelona – 27 days before his 16th birthday.

EAGLETS SOAR

The first African country to win an official FIFA tournament was Nigeria, when their "Golden Eaglets" beat Germany 2-0 in the final of the 1985 World Under-17 Championships.

ANGOLAN GOALS

Angola lost their first match against former colonial masters Portugal 6-0 in 1989. Their second meeting, 12 years later, was abandoned as Portugal led 5-1, after Angola had four players sent off and another, Helder Vicente, carried off injured.

GENEROUS GEORGE

In 1995 Liberia's George Weah became the first African to be named FIFA World Player of the Year, an award that recognized his prolific goalscoring exploits for Paris Saint-Germain and AC Milan. That same year he added the European Footballer of the Year and African Footballer of the Year prizes to his collection. Weah not only captained his country, but often funded the team's travels – though he remains the only FIFA World Player of the Year whose country has never qualified for a FIFA World Cup. After retiring in 2003 after 60 caps and 22 international goals, he moved into politics and ran unsuccessfully for the Liberian presidency in 2005.

UNFULFILLED PROMISE

Zambia have never qualified for a FIFA World Cup, but caused a sensation when they beat Italy 4-0 in a group game at the 1988 Olympics in Seoul. **Kalusha Bwalya** scored a hat-trick and later revealed the Italians had rudely snubbed his team before the game – but were pleading for autographs afterwards. Tragedy struck on 27 April 1993. Zambia were in a strong position to reach the 1994 FIFA World Cup but lost their coach and 18 of their players when the military plane carrying them crashed in Gabon on its way to a qualifier in Senegal, killing everyone on board. Olympic hero Bwalya had missed the flight because he was playing for Dutch team PSV Eindhoven at the time.

SUB–SAHARAN AFRICA: SELECTED TOP APPEARANCES

ANGOLA: Akwa 80
BOTSWANA: Dipsy Selolwane 34
CAMEROON: Rigobert Song 135
GHANA: Abedi "Pele" Ayew 73
IVORY COAST: Didier Zokora 78
MOZAMBIQUE: Dario 88
NAMIBIA: Johannes Hindjou 69
NIGERIA: Mudashiru Lawal 86
SENEGAL: Henri Camara 99
SOUTH AFRICA: Aaron Mokoena 99
SWAZILAND: Mlungisi Ngubane 91
ZIMBABWE: Peter Ndlovu 100

DRAMATIC TURNAROUNDS

Ghana managed to concede three goals in a minute to world champions Germany in an April 1993 friendly. Ghana had been 1-0 up with 20 minutes left, before losing the game 6-1. In the 1989 FIFA World Youth Championships, Nigeria were 4-0 down with 25 minutes left in their quarter-final against the Soviet Union – but hit back to draw 4-4 before winning 5-3 on penalties.

SOUTH LONDON SOUTH AFRICANS

English club Charlton Athletic featured four South African-born players in the 1950s – though **Eddie Firmani** would play three internationals for Italy, while John Hewie earned 19 caps for Scotland. Firmani went on to play for Sampdoria, Internazionale and Genoa, becoming the first man to score a century of league goals in both England and Italy.

ASIA & OCEANIA

Asia carved out a major place in footballing history in 2002 when South Korea and Japan were the first co-hosts of a FIFA World Cup™ – and the South Koreans marked the moment by also becoming Asia's first semi-finalists, losing to Germany, then to Turkey in the third-place play-off. There have been further good showings since then, not only by South Korean and Japan, but also by North Korea and new Asian confederation recruits Australia – while the billion-plus populations of India and China must surely leave their mark on world football in years to come.

Asian Footballer of the Year in 2010, Australia's Sasa Ognenovski (right) was uncapped when he left Adelaide United for South Korea's Seongnam Ilhwa Chunma in 2009.

AUSTRALIA

Victims, perhaps, of an overcomplicated qualifying system that has limited the country's FIFA World Cup™ finals appearances, and hampered by its geographical isolation that, in the early years, saw other sports prosper in the country at football's expense, it has taken many years for Australia to establish itself on the world football map. However, driven by a new generation of players, many based with top European clubs, the Socceroos delivered for the first time at the 2006 FIFA World Cup™. They are the No. 1 ranked team in Asia.

NATIVE HERO

Harry Williams holds a proud place in Australian football history as the first Aboriginal player to represent the country in internationals. He made his debut in 1970 and was part of the first Australian squad to compete at a FIFA World Cup finals, in West Germany in 1974.

LUCKY NUMBER

The No. 2 shirt is the only one to have been on the field for Australia for all 900 minutes of their three FIFA World Cup campaigns. In 1974 it was worn by Doug Utjesenovic and in both 2006 and 2010 by Lucas Neill.

TOP CAPS

1	Alex Tobin	87
2	Paul Wade	84
3	Mark Schwarzer	78
4	Tony Vidmar	76
5	Brett Emerton	75
6	Scott Chipperfield	68
7	Peter Wilson	64
8	Attila Abonyi	61
9	John Kosmina	60
=	Stan Lazaridis	60

TOP SCORERS

1	Damian Mori	29
2	John Aloisi	27
3	Attila Abonyi	25
=	John Kosmina	25
4	Tim Cahill	21
=	Archie Thompson	21
5	David Zdrilic	20
6	Graham Arnold	19
9	Ray Baartz	18
10	Gary Cole	17
=	Brett Emerton	17
=	Aurelio Vidmar	17

SOCCEROOS MAKE IT AT LAST

The Australian national team – nicknamed the "Socceroos" – have been buoyed by massive support over the past decade. Their FIFA World Cup battles – culminating in a run to the last 16 in the 2006 finals – have established football among the nation's most popular sports. For many years, the game had languished behind cricket, the two rugby codes and Aussie rules football in the public imagination. Football had been kept alive by immigrants – first from Britain, then by arrivals from Italy, Greece and the former Yugoslavia. But the nation rallied round for the 1998 FIFA World Cup qualifying play-off final against Iran, which the Socceroos lost on away goals. Four years later, Australia lost another play-off, this time to Uruguay, 3-1 on aggregate.

CAHILL MAKES HISTORY

Tim Cahill netted Australia's first-ever FIFA World Cup finals goal when he scored an 84th-minute equalizer against Japan in Kaiserslautern on 12 June 2006. Cahill added another five minutes later and John Aloisi struck in stoppage time to give the Socceroos a 3-1 win – their only victory in the finals. Australia later lost 2-0 to Brazil and drew 2-2 with Croatia to qualify from their group.

BET ON BRETT

Brett Holman's goal against Ghana, in a 1-1 draw at the 2010 tournament, made him Australia's youngest marksman at a FIFA World Cup. He was 26 years 84 days old at the time, 105 days younger than Tim Cahill had been when striking against Japan in 2006. Holman added to his tally five days later, when Australia beat Serbia 2-1. Cahill himself was also on the scoresheet, though goal difference meant Australia failed to reach the second round.

AUSTRALIA'S SHOOT-OUT RECORD

Australia are the only team to reach the FIFA World Cup finals via a penalty shoot-out – in the final qualifying play-off in November 2005. They had lost the first leg 1-0 to Uruguay in Montevideo. Marco Bresciano's goal levelled the aggregate score, which remained 1-1 after extra-time. Goalkeeper **Mark Schwarzer** made two crucial saves as Australia won the shoot-out 4-2, with John Aloisi scoring the winning spot-kick.

COME TO A LAND DOWN UNDER

After reaching the quarter-finals of their first AFC Asian Cup in 2007 and finishing runners-up to Japan four years later, Australia will want to make it third time lucky at the 2015 tournament – especially as the country will be playing host this time. Australia was the only country to bid for staging rights.

AUSTRALIA RECORDS

Honours: Oceania champions 1980, 1996, 2000, 2004
First international: v New Zealand (lost 3-1), Auckland, 17 June 1922
Biggest win: 31-0 v American Samoa, Coffs Harbour, 11 April 2001
Biggest defeat: 7-0 v Croatia, Zagreb, 6 June 1998

THREE-CARD TRICK

Graham Poll, in 2006, was not the first referee at a FIFA World Cup to show the same player three yellow cards. It happened in another game involving Australia, when their English-born midfielder Ray Richards was belatedly sent off against Chile at the 1974 FIFA World Cup. Reserve official Clive Thomas, from Wales, informed Iranian referee Jafar Namdar he had booked Richards three times without dismissing him. Richards played four unwarranted minutes before eventually receiving his marching orders.

OLD ALLEGIANCES STILL MATTER

Many Australian-born players chose to play for their parents' countries rather than for Australia – Joey Didulica, Anthony Seric and Josip Simunic (Croatia), Sasa Ognenovski (Macedonia) and Sasa Ilic (Serbia). Simunic even played for Croatia against Australia in the 2006 FIFA World Cup finals – and was famously sent off after being shown three yellow cards by English referee Graham Poll. Bologna-born Italy striker Christian Vieri grew up in Australia, but his Aussie-born brother Max represented the Socceroos.

KEWELL THE TOPS

Harry Kewell (born on 22 September 1978) is widely regarded as Australia's best-ever player. The left winger has scored 13 goals in 39 international appearances, including the equalizer against Croatia that took Australia to the last 16 of the 2006 FIFA World Cup finals. Kewell has enjoyed a successful club career with Leeds United, Liverpool and Galatasaray. He is also the only Australian-born player to gain a Champions League winner's medal, with Liverpool in 2005. He endured an unhappier time at the 2010 FIFA World Cup, when he lasted just 22 minutes before being red-carded for handball against Ghana – the 150th sending-off in the history of the finals.

⚽ JAPAN

The past two decades have seen great breakthroughs for Japanese football. Until the first professional league was introduced in 1993, clubs had been amateur and football was overshadowed in Japan's affections by other sports such as baseball, martial arts, table tennis and golf. Even more significantly, Japan co-hosted the 2002 FIFA World Cup™ – where the team reached the second round for the first time. And AFC Asian Cup wins in 1992, 2000, 2004 and 2011 were celebrated keenly as proof of surging standards.

⚽ TOP SCORERS

1	Kunishige Kamamoto	75
2	Kazuyoshi Miura	55
3	Hiromi Hara	37
4	Takuya Takagi	27
5	Kazushi Kimura	26
6	Shunsuke Nakamura	24
7	Naohiro Takahara	23
8	Masashi Nakayama	21
=	Shinji Okazaki	21
10	Teruki Miyamoto	19

⚽ NAKATA BLAZES THE TRAIL

Hidetoshi Nakata ranks among Japan's best-ever players. The midfielder set up all three goals in a 3-2 FIFA World Cup qualifying play-off win over Iran in November 1997. Nakata moved to Perugia in Italy after the 1998 finals, becoming the first Japanese player to star in Europe, and won a Serie A championship medal with Roma in 2001. He was followed abroad by international team-mates such as Shinji Ono, who joined Feyenoord in the Netherlands, and midfielder Shunsuke Nakamura, whose European employers included Reggina in Italy, Celtic in Scotland and Espanyol in Spain. Nakata started in three FIFA World Cup finals tournaments, making ten appearances and scoring one goal – the second in a 2-0 win over Tunisia that took Japan to the last 16 in 2002. Nakata won 77 caps and scored 11 goals, before surprisingly retiring from all forms of football after the 2006 FIFA World Cup, aged just 29.

⚽ POLITICAL FOOTBALL

Japan were surprise bronze medallists in the football tournament at the 1968 summer Olympics in Mexico City, and star striker **Kunishige Kamamoto** finished top scorer overall with seven goals. He remains Japan's all-time leading scorer, with 76 goals in 75 matches. Since retirement, he has combined coaching with being elected to Japan's parliament and serving as vice-president of the country's football association.

⚽ TAKE TWO FOR TAKESHI

Former international defender Takeshi Okada was Japan's coach for both the 1998 and 2010 FIFA World Cups. Three foreign coaches had been in charge in between – Frenchman Philippe Troussier, Brazilian Zico and Bosnian Ivica Osim. Okada stepped down for a second time after the 2010 FIFA World Cup, expressing an ambition to later become a farmer. He said: "When it rains, I'll read a book, and when it's fine, I'll work on the farm."

TOP CAPS

1	Masami Ihara	122
2	Yoshikatsu Kawaguchi	116
3	Yuji Nakazawa	110
4	Yasuhito Endo	106
5	Shunsuke Nakamura	98
6	Kazuyoshi Miura	89
7	Junichi Inamoto	82
=	Alessandro Santos	82
9	Satoshi Tsunami	78
10	Hidetoshi Nakata	77
=	Seigo Narazaki	77

YOU'RE BARRED

Japan achieved their first-ever FIFA World Cup victory on foreign soil at the 2010 tournament in South Africa, and reached the knock-out stages for the first time away from home as well. Their penalty shoot-out against Paraguay in the second round was the first in FIFA World Cup history that did not feature at least one European country. The shoot-out was the first of the 2010 tournament and the 21st overall. Paraguay won 5–3 on penalties after the match had ended goalless after extra-time. Japanese full-back Yuichi Komano was the only taker to miss, hitting the bar with his spot-kick.

THREE AND IN

Japan's 3–1 Group E **victory over Denmark in Bloemfontein** at the 2010 FIFA World Cup made them the first Asian side to score three times in one FIFA World Cup match since North Korea's 5–3 defeat to Portugal in their 1966 quarter-final. Japan's goals came from Keisuke Honda, Yasuhito Endo and Shinji Okazaki. Honda and Endo both scored directly from free-kicks, the first time a team has managed such a double in one FIFA World Cup game since Yugoslavia hit three when beating Zaire 9–0 in 1974.

TROUSSIER STEERS JAPAN TO VICTORY

Parisian-born Philippe Troussier was named Asia's Coach of the Year in 2000 after leading Japan to a 1–0 victory over Saudi Arabia in the Asian Cup final in Lebanon. He also steered the Japanese to their best-ever FIFA World Cup finish, on home soil in 2002, when they lost 1–0 to Turkey in the last 16 – even if that achievement was overshadowed by Guus Hiddink's success with semi-finalists and co-hosts South Korea.

DATING GAME

Japan have opened three of their four FIFA World Cup finals campaigns on the same date, 14 June – losing 1–0 to Argentina in 1998, beating Tunisia 2–0 in 2002 and **defeating Cameroon 1–0** in 2010. The only exception was their 2006 campaign, when they kicked off on 12 June and took the lead against Australia through Shunsuke Nakamura – only to concede three goals in the final six minutes and stoppage-time.

JAPANESE GOAL GLUT

No team have scored more goals in one AFC Asian Cup tournament than Japan's 21 in six games on their way to winning the title for the second time, in Lebanon in 2000 – though the final against Saudi Arabia was settled with just a single goal, by Shigeyoshi Mochizuki. Nine different players scored for Japan during the tournament – including Akinori Nishizawa and Naohiro Takahara, who each managed five – while their team-mate Ryuzo Morioka scored once in his own net. Japan's most emphatic victory of the tournament came in the first round, 8–1 against Uzbekistan, with both Nishizawa and Takahara hitting hat-tricks.

SOUTH KOREA

"Be the Reds!" was the rallying cry of South Korea's fervent fans as they co-hosted the 2002 FIFA World Cup™ – and saw their energetic team become the first Asian side to reach the semi-finals, ultimately finishing fourth. South Korea also won the AFC Asian Cup the first two times it was staged. South Korea could well claim to be the continent's leading football side, even if AFC Asian Cup triumphs have been thin on the ground since then. The country's professional K-League is making progress and South Korean teams have won the Asian club championship nine times in total, more than any other nation's.

TOP SCORERS

1	Cha Bum-Kun	55
2	Hwang Sun-Hong	50
3	Park Yi-Cheon	36
4	Kim Jae-Han	33
5	Choi Soon-Ho	30
6	Huh Jung-Moo	29
=	Kim Do-Hoon	29
8	Choi Yong-Soo	27
=	Lee Tae-Ho	27
10	Lee Dong-Gook	25

HIDDINK THE SOUTH KOREAN HERO

Dutchman **Guus Hiddink** is Asia's most successful national coach. The former PSV Eindhoven and Holland coach took charge of South Korea in late 2000. He changed the team approach, and experimented in friendlies because, as co-hosts, they had automatically qualified for the 2002 FIFA World Cup. Home fans and media hoped South Korea might make it out of the first round for the first time ever. They far exceeded all expectations, topping their group, eliminating Italy in the second round and reaching the semi-finals with a shoot-out win over Spain, where they lost 1–0 to Germany, then went down 3–2 in the third-place play-off against Turkey. Fourth place was still the best-ever finish for an Asian team. Hiddink was rewarded by becoming the first foreigner to be made an honorary South Korean citizen, and the stadium at Gwangju was renamed in his honour.

SPIDER CATCHER

Goalkeeper **Lee Woon-Jae** – nicknamed "Spider Hands" – made himself a nation's hero by making the crucial penalty save that took co-hosts South Korea into the semi-finals of the 2002 FIFA World Cup. He blocked Spain's fourth spot-kick, taken by winger Joaquin in a quarter-final shoot-out. Lee, who also played in the 1994, 2006 and 2010 FIFA World Cups, provided more penalty saves at the 2007 AFC Asian Cup – stopping three spot-kicks in shoot-outs on South Korea's way to third place. He played in goal in every one of South Korea's qualifiers for the 2010 FIFA World Cup – a campaign Huh Jung-Moo's side went through without a single defeat, the continent's only team to do so.

KIM'S TREBLE SUCCESS

South Korea midfielder Kim Joo-Sung is the only player to have won the Asian Footballer of the Year award three times – and in successive years, from 1989 to 1991. He played in three FIFA World Cup finals tournaments but never progressed beyond the group stages. He won 77 caps, scoring 14 goals, and was one of the first South Korean players to make a mark abroad, joining Bundesliga side Bochum in 1992 and staying for two seasons.

⚽ TOP CAPS

1	Hong Myung-Bo	136
2	Lee Woon-Jae	132
3	Lee Young-Pyo	126
4	Yoo Sang-Chul	122
5	Cha Bum-Kun	121
6	Kim Tae-Young	104
7	Hwang Sun-Hong	103
8	Park Ji-Sung	100
9	Kim Nam-Il	96
10	Choi Soon-Hoo	95
=	Ha Seok-Ju	95

HWANG'S THE MAN

A rare veteran among South Korea's young guns at the 2002 FIFA World Cup was 33-year-old **Hwang Sun-Hong**, after Cha Bum-Kun the only other player to score a half-century of goals for the country. His 50th goal came in the 2–0 win over Poland that clinched South Korea's place in the second round. Hwang had also played in the 1990 and 1994 FIFA World Cups, but missed the 1998 event through injury.

HONG SETS FIFA WORLD CUP™ RECORD

South Korea defender **Hong Myung-Bo** was the first Asian footballer to appear in four consecutive FIFA World Cup finals tournaments. He played all three games as South Korea lost to Belgium, Spain and Uruguay in 1990. He scored twice in three appearances in 1994 – his goal against Spain sparking a Korean fightback from 2–0 down to draw 2–2. In 1998 he started all three group games as South Korea were eliminated at the group stage. Four years later, on home soil, he captained South Korea to fourth place in the finals, the best-ever performance by an Asian team – and he was also voted third-best player of the tournament, taking the Bronze Ball individual prize. Hong's total of 16 appearances in the FIFA World Cup is also a record for an Asian player. He later became coach of the South Korea Under-20 squad.

CHA BOOM AND BUST

Even before South Korea made their FIFA World Cup breakthrough under Guus Hiddink, the country had a homegrown hero of world renown – thunderous striker **Cha Bum-Kun**, known for his fierce shots and suitable nickname "Cha Boom". He helped pave the way for more Asian players to make their name in Europe by signing for German club Eintracht Frankfurt in 1979 and later playing for Bundesliga rivals Bayer Leverkusen. His achievements in Germany included two UEFA Cup triumphs – with Frankfurt in 1980 and with Leverkusen eight years later – while his performances helped make him a childhood idol for future German internationals such as Jurgen Klinsmann and Michael Ballack. His record 55 goals for the national team, in 121 appearances, included a seven-minute hat-trick against Malaysia in the 1977 Park's Cup tournament – levelling the score after South Korea had been trailing 4–1. "Cha Boom" later served as national coach, winning 22, losing 11 and drawing eight during his time in charge between January 1997 and June 1998 – but there was an unhappy ending when he was sacked two games into the 1998 FIFA World Cup, after South Korea's 5–0 beating by the Netherlands.

OTHER ASIAN COUNTRIES

The lesser-known Asian footballing nations represent the true backwaters of world football. These may well be the countries in which true football obsession has yet to take hold, but competition between, and achievements by, these teams are no less vibrant. The regions are the home to many of the game's record-breakers – from the most goals in a single game to the most career appearances – and some of these records may never be broken.

SAUDIS MAKE FLYING START

Saudi Arabia reached the last 16 in their first FIFA World Cup finals appearance in 1994. **Saeed Owairan's** winner against Belgium enabled them to finish level on points with the Netherlands in Group F. Sami Al-Jaber and Fuad Amin had scored in a 2-1 win over Morocco, after the Saudis lost their opening game 2-1 to the Dutch. They lost 3-1 to Sweden in the last 16. Substitute Fahad Al-Ghesheyan scored in the 85th minute after the Swedes led 2-0. Kennet Andersson grabbed Sweden's decisive third goal three minutes later. The Saudis have failed to advance beyond the group stages in their three subsequent appearances.

IRAN TOP SCORERS

1	Ali Daei	109
2	Karim Bagheri	50
3	Ali Karimi	36
4	Javad Nekounam	26
5	Gholam Hossein Mazloomi	19
=	Farshad Pious	19
7	Ali Asghar Modir Roosta	18
8	Vahid Hashemian	15
9	Alireza Vahedi Nikbakht	14
10	Mehdi Mahdavikia	13
=	Ali Parvin	13
=	Hassan Rowshan	13

THREE AND OUT

Only Japan, with four, have won the AFC Asian Cup more often than three-times champions Saudi Arabia and Iran. But Iran are the sole country to have lifted the trophy three times in a row – though they have failed to reclaim their continental crown since 1976, despite four third-place finishes.

IRAN'S WINNING RUN

Iran won all 13 matches across their hat-trick of AFC Asian Cup triumphs in 1968, 1972 and 1976 – and their 8–0 win over South Yemen in 1976 remains a tournament record. Among the players who enjoyed repeat success was Homayoun Behzadi, who scored in all four games in 1968 and was again on the winning side four years later. Iran's manager in 1976 was Heshmat Mohajerani, who also led the team to the football quarter-finals of that year's Summer Olympics in Montreal before steering Iran to their first-ever FIFA World Cup in 1978. Iran's captain at the tournament in Argentina was midfielder Ali Parvin – who had scored the only goal of the 1976 AFC Asian Cup final against Kuwait.

RANK OUTSIDERS

North Korea only narrowly lost their first game of the 2010 FIFA World Cup, 2-1 to Brazil – **Ji Yun-Nam** scoring late on for the Koreans. The match was between the tournament's highest- and lowest-ranked qualifying teams. Brazil were in first place in the FIFA rankings, while North Korea were 105th.

IRAN TOP CAPS

1	Ali Daei	149
2	Javad Nekounam	118
3	Ali Karimi	112
4	Mehdi Mahdavikia	111
5	Hossein Kaebi	89
6	Karim Bagheri	87
7	Hamidreza Estili	82
8	Javad Zarincheh	80
9	Ahmad Reza Abedzadeh	79
=	Mohammad Nosrati	79

APPEARANCES IN THE FIFA WORLD CUP™ FINALS

Saudi Arabia	4	(1994, 1998, 2002, 2006)
Iran	3	(1978, 1998, 2006)
New Zealand	2	(1982*, 2010*)
North Korea	2	(1966, 2010)
China	1	(2002)
Indonesia*	1	(1938)
Iraq	1	(1986)
Israel	1	(1970)
Kuwait	1	(1982)
United Arab Emirates	1	(1990)

* Indonesia played in the 1938 FIFA World Cup as Dutch East Indies

SHAKEN SHEIKH

Kuwait have qualified for the FIFA World Cup just once, in 1982 – though they made a memorable appearance when they almost walked off the field in protest at a decision. Kuwait's chief Olympic official, **Sheikh Fahad Al-Ahmed,** even stomped on to the pitch in Valladolid, Spain, when France's Alain Giresse scored a goal that would have given les Bleus a 4–1 ahead. The Kuwaitis claimed they had heard a whistle and stopped playing and ultimately convinced referee Myroslav Stupar to disallow the strike. The game still finished 4–1 to France, though, and Kuwait were eliminated in the first round.

IRAN STOP AT 19

Iran hold the record for the highest score in an Asian zone FIFA World Cup qualifier. They thrashed Guam 19-0 in Tabriz on 24 November 2000. **Karim Bagheri** scored six goals and Ali Karimi four. Future national coach Ali Daei and Farhad Majidi both netted three. This was two goals better than Iran's previous highest qualifying win – 17-0 against the Maldives on 2 June 1997, when Bagheri scored seven times. Two days after their 19-goal thrashing, Guam crashed 16-0 to Tajikistan.

PALESTINE THE PIONEERS

Palestine, then under British rule, were the first Asian team to enter the FIFA World Cup qualifiers. They lost 7-1 away to Egypt on 16 March 1934. They lost the return match at home on 6 April, 4-1. Four years later, they were eliminated by Greece, who won 3-1 in Tel Aviv and 1-0 at home.

CHINA YET TO REALIZE POTENTIAL

China, the world's most populous nation, have qualified just once for the FIFA World Cup finals, in 2002. They topped their final qualifying group by eight points from the United Arab Emirates, but coach Bora Milutinovic's team slumped in the finals, failing to score a goal in defeats by Costa Rica (2-0), Brazil (4-0) and Turkey (3-0).

WORLD'S WORST

On the same day that Brazil and Germany contested the FIFA World Cup final on 30 June 2002, the two lowest-ranked FIFA countries were also taking each other on. Asian side Bhutan ran out 4–0 winners over CONCACAF's Montserrat, in a match staged in the Bhutan capital Thimphu. The winning side's captain, striker Wangay Dorji, scored a hat-trick.

ON THE UP

The best Asian countries have become familiar figures at recent FIFA World Cup finals tournaments. Co-hosts South Korea and Japan both gave a good account of themselves in 2002 – with the South Koreans achieving Asia's best-ever finish, losing in the semi-finals. Saudi Arabia and Iran have been powerful forces, too, and the Asian Federation was strengthened by new members, Australia, after 2006. North Korea set the standard for Asian hopefuls in 1966 when they reached the quarter-finals in their first tournament appearance. They overcame teams from Asia, Africa and Oceania to qualify, beating Australia 9-2 on aggregate in a final play-off. Asia had four guaranteed places at the 2010 finals in South Africa, with the chance of a fifth but Bahrain, the fifth-placed team in the qualifiers, lost a play-off to Oceania winners New Zealand.

AI–DEAYEA CAPS THEM ALL

Saudi goalkeeper Mohamed Al-Deayea had to choose between football and handball as a youngster. He was persuaded by his elder brother Abdullah to pick football. He made 181 appearances for his country, the first coming against Bangladesh in 1990, the last against Belgium in May 2006. He also appeared in the FIFA World Cup finals tournaments of 1994, 1998 and 2002. He played his last finals game in a 3-0 defeat by the Republic of Ireland on 11 June 2002 and was recalled to the squad for the 2006 finals, although he did not play.

HAPPY DAEI

Iran striker **Ali Daei** became the first footballer to score a century of international goals, when his four in a 7-0 defeat of Laos on 17 November 2004 took him to 102. He ended his career having scored 109 times for Iran in 149 internationals between 1993 and 2006 – though none of his goals came during FIFA World Cup appearances in 1998 and 2006. He is also the all-time leading scorer in the AFC Asian Cup, with 14 goals, despite failing ever to win the tournament. His time as national coach was less auspicious – he lasted only a year from March 2008 to March 2009 before being fired, as Iran struggled in qualifiers for the 2010 FIFA World Cup.

KUWAIT IN GOLD

Kuwait's one and only AFC Asian Cup triumph came in 1980, when they also hosted the tournament. They beat South Korea 3-0 in the final – having lost by the same scoreline, to the same opponents, in a first-round group game. Faisal Al-Dakhil was Kuwait's hero in the final, scoring two of their goals, his fourth and fifth of the tournament. He had also struck what proved to be the winner in a 2–1 semi-final victory over Iran.

BARCA'S BEST

The first Asian footballer ever to play for a European club remains the all-time leading scorer for Spanish giants Barcelona – the best part of a century on. Paulino Alcantara, from the Philippines, scored 357 goals in 357 matches for Barcelona between 1912 and 1927, having made his debut aged just 15 – another club record. Alcantara, who was born in the Philippines but had a Spanish father, played internationals for Catalonia, Spain and his native Philippines – for whom he featured in a record 15–2 trouncing of Japan in 1917. Alcantara became a doctor after retiring from football at the age of 31, though he did briefly manage Spain in 1951.

ASIAN FOOTBALLER OF THE YEAR

Year	Player	Country
1988	Ahmed Radhi	Iraq
1989	Kim Joo-Sung	Soutwh Korea
1990	Kim Joo-Sung	South Korea
1991	Kim Joo-Sung	South Korea
1992	not awarded	
1993	Kazuyoshi Miura	Japan
1994	Saeed Owarain	Saudi Arabia
1995	Masami Ihara	Japan
1996	Khodadad Azizi	Iran
1997	Hidetoshi Nakata	Japan
1998	Hidetoshi Nakata	Japan
1999	Ali Daei	Iran
2000	Nawaf Al Temyat	Saudi Arabia
2001	Fan Zhiyi	China
2002	Shinji Ono	Japan
2003	Mehdi Mahdavikia	Iran
2004	Ali Karimi	Iran
2005	Hamad Al-Montashari	Saudi Arabia
2006	Khalfan Ibrahim	Qatar
2007	Yasser Al-Qahtani	Saudi Arabia
2008	Server Djeparov	Uzbekistan
2009	Yasuhito Endo	Japan
2010	Sasa Ognenovski	Australia

THE JONG TURNING

North Korea's star striker at the 2010 FIFA World Cup, **Jong Tae-Se**, sobbed when their anthem was played before the first game against Brazil, but he had never actually visited the country he was playing for. Jong was born in Japan, where he continues to play his club football for Kawasaki Frontale, and has parents who are South Korean citizens. But he chose to pursue his family right to a North Korean passport.

AFC ASIAN CUP ALL-TIME TOP SCORERS

1	Ali Daei (Iran)	14
2	Lee Dong-Gook (South Korea)	10
3	Naohiro Takahara (Japan)	9
4	Jassem Al-Houwaidi (Kuwait)	8
5	Behtash Fariba (Iran)	7
=	Hossein Kalani (Iran)	7
=	Choi Soon-Ho (South Korea)	7
=	Faisal Al-Dakhil (Kuwait)	7
9	Yasser Al-Qahtani (Saudi Arabia)	6
=	Alexander Geynrikh (Uzbekistan)	6

PAK STRIKE MAKES HISTORY

North Korea's **Pak Doo Ik** earned legend status by scoring the goal that eliminated Italy from the 1966 FIFA World Cup finals. The shockwaves caused by the victory were comparable to those caused by the United States' 1-0 win over England in 1950. Pak netted the only goal in the 42nd minute at Middlesbrough on 19 July. North Korea thus became the first Asian team to reach the quarter-finals. Pak, an army corporal, was promoted to sergeant after the victory and later became a gymnastics coach.

ASIA PRESSES ON

The best Asian players have become famous around the world over the past decade. FIFA's decision to expand the World Cup finals – and allocate more places to Asian teams – gave those stars the chance to shine on an international stage. Hidetoshi Nakata, Japan's general of the 1998 finals, led the way to success in Europe, soon followed by his colleague Shinji Ono to Feyenoord, and, more recently, by midfielder Shunsuke Nakamura. Iran's top scorer, Ali Daei, made a name for himself in Germany with Hertha Berlin while Iranian winger, or midfielder, Mehdi Mahdavikia was twice voted "Player of the Year" by Hamburg's supporters. South Korean midfielder Park Ji-Sung won the UEFA Champions League with Manchester United and was a semi-finalist with PSV Eindhoven, alongside international team-mate Lee Young-Pyo.

A LONG JOURNEY FOR A BEATING

The first Asian country to play in a FIFA World Cup finals was Indonesia, who as the Dutch East Indies played in France in 1938. The tournament was a straight knockout and, on 5 June in Reims, Hungary beat them 6-0, with goals from Gyorgy Sarosi, Gyula Zsengeller (two each), Vilmos Kohut and Geza Toldi.

AFC ASIAN CUP–WINNING COACHES

1956	**Lee Yoo-Hyung**	(South Korea)
1960	**Wi Hye-Deok**	(South Korea)
1964	**Gyula Mandl**	(Israel)
1968	**Mahmoud Bayati**	(Iran)
1972	**Mohammad Ranjbar**	(Iran)
1976	**Heshmat Mohajerani**	(Iran)
1980	**Carlos Alberto Parreira**	(Kuwait)
1984	**Khalil Al-Zayani**	(Saudi Arabia)
1988	**Carlos Alberto Parreira**	(Saudi Arabia)
1992	**Hans Ooft**	(Japan)
1996	**Nelo Vingada**	(Saudi Arabia)
2000	**Philippe Troussier**	(Japan)
2004	**Zico**	(Japan)
2007	**Jorvan Vieira**	(Iraq)
2011	**Alberto Zaccheroni**	(Japan)

OWAIRAN'S MAGIC GOAL

Saudi Arabia forward Saeed Owairan scored the finest goal of the 1994 FIFA World Cup finals. He dribbled for more than 50 yards, beating five challenges, to hit the winner against Belgium on 29 June. His goal helped the Saudis to reach the last 16 in their finals debut. Owairan scored 24 goals in 50 matches for Saudi Arabia between 1991 and 1998.

AL-JABER TO THE FORE

Sami Al-Jaber (born on 11 December 1972 in Riyadh) became only the second Asian player to appear in four FIFA World Cup finals tournaments when he started against Tunisia in Munich on 14 June 2006. He scored in a 2-2 draw, his third goal in nine appearances at the finals. Al-Jaber played only one game in 1998 before he was rushed to hospital with a burst appendix, which ruled him out of the competition. He became Saudi Arabia's record scorer, with 44 goals in 163 matches.

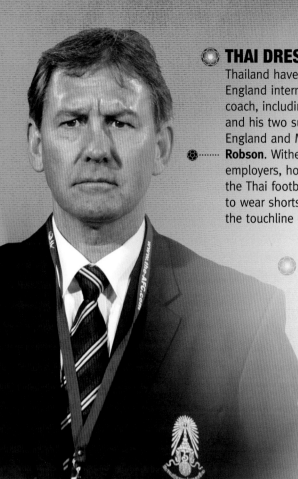

THAI DRESS CODE

Thailand have made a habit of appointing former England internationals as the national team's coach, including ex-Aston Villa striker Peter Withe and his two successors, Peter Reid and former England and Manchester United captain **Bryan Robson**. Withe's style did not always impress his employers, however – he was briefly suspended by the Thai football federation because he preferred to wear shorts rather than a formal suit while on the touchline during games.

FOREIGN DOUBLE AGENT

Brazilian Carlos Alberto Parreira is the only coach to win the AFC Asian Cup twice – and he did so with two different countries. His Kuwait side won in 1980 and he got his hands on the trophy again eight years later, this time in charge of Saudi Arabia.

LOCAL COACHES MAKE THEIR MARK

Three more native-born Asian national team coaches have been named Asia's Coach of the Year. The first, in 2001, was Nasser Al-Johar, who steered Saudi Arabia through to the 2002 FIFA World Cup finals, two points clear of Iran in the decisive qualifying group. Adnan Hamad followed him three years later, leading Iraq to the Asian Cup quarter-finals, little more than a year after the US invasion. The 2007 winner was Uzbekistan's Rauf Inileyev, who guided his country to the 2007 Asian Cup quarter-finals, beating China 3-0 on the way.

HIGHEST ... AND LOWEST

The highest attendance for an Asian team in a home FIFA World Cup qualifier was the 130,000 who watched Iran draw 1-1 with Australia in the Azadi Stadium, Tehran, on 22 November 1997. The game was the first leg of a final playoff for the last place in the 1998 finals. Iran advanced on away goals after drawing the second leg 2-2 in Melbourne. The lowest attendance was the "crowd" of 20 that turned out for Turkmenistan's 1-0 win over Taiwan, played in Amman, Jordan, on 7 May 2001.

HUGE FOLLOWING FOR FOOTBALL IN CHINA

China's national team boasts a massive fan base – as was demonstrated when they reached the FIFA World Cup finals for the only time in 2002. Between their qualification on 19 October 2001 and their opening game of the finals against Costa Rica on 4 June 2002, an estimated 170 million new TV sets were sold throughout China! TV audiences for the team's three matches regularly topped 300 million, even though China lost all three matches and failed to score a goal.

PAK CARRIES THE FLAME

North Korea's hero of the 1966 FIFA World Cup finals, **Pak Doo Ik**, is still much admired by his countrymen. He was chosen as one of the 56 people to carry the Olympic torch across North Korea on its way to the 2008 Beijing Olympics. He was also the oldest – a sprightly 70.

CHINA'S 4X4

Four teams carry the name of China. The China national team receives most attention, but Hong Kong (a former British colony) and Macau (a former Portuguese colony) both retain their autonomous status for football – as Hong Kong China and Macau China respectively. Meanwhile, the independent island state of Taiwan competes in the FIFA World Cup and other competitions as Chinese Taipei.

UAE KO ZAGALLO

Brazilian great Mario Zagallo, who won the FIFA World Cup as both player and manager, coached the United Arab Emirates when they qualified for their one and only FIFA World Cup finals in 1990. But despite his success in the Asian qualifiers, he was sacked on the eve of the FIFA World Cup itself. Zagallo was replaced by Polish coach Bernard Blaut, whose UAE team lost all three matches at Italia 90. Other big names to have managed the UAE over the years include Brazil's Carlos Alberto Parreira (another FIFA World Cup winner with Brazil), England's Don Revie and Roy Hodgson, Ukraine's Valery Lobanovsky and Portugal's Carlos Queiroz.

SOVIET REPUBLICS FIND NEW HOME

The break-up of the former Soviet Union swelled the ranks of the Asian Confederation in the early 1990s. Former Soviet republics Kazakhstan, Kyrgyzstan, Tajikistan, Turkmenistan and Uzbekistan all joined in 1994, though the Kazaks switched to UEFA in 2002. **Uzbekistan** have been the most successful, reaching the Asian Cup quarter-finals in 2007. Australia are the AFC's the 46th – and newest – members, entering the confederation on 1 January 2006, a few months after East Timor had become the 45th.

DOUBLE AGENT

Although North Korea's Kim Myong-Won usually plays as a striker, he was named as one of three goalkeepers in the country's 23-man squad for the 2010 FIFA World Cup. FIFA told North Korea he would only be able to play in goal, rather than outfield, though he failed to make it on to the pitch in any form during his country's three Group G matches.

THE ISRAEL ISSUE

Israel is, geographically, an Asian nation. It hosted – and won – the Asian Cup in 1964. But, over the years, many Asian confederation countries refused to play Israel on political grounds. When Israel reached the 1970 FIFA World Cup finals they came through a qualifying tournament involving two Asian nations – Japan and South Korea – and two from Oceania – Australia and New Zealand. In 1989, Israel topped the Oceania group, but lost a final play-off to Colombia for a place in the 1990 finals. They switched to the European zone qualifiers in 1992 and have been a full member of the European federation, UEFA, since 1994.

ASIAN CUP WINNERS

The Asian Cup is Asia's continental championship

Year	Winners
1956	South Korea
1960	South Korea
1964	Israel
1968	Iran
1972	Iran
1976	Iran
1980	Kuwait
1984	Saudi Arabia
1988	Saudi Arabia
1992	Japan
1996	Saudi Arabia
2000	Japan
2004	Japan
2007	Iraq
2011	Japan

FROZEN OUT

Mongolia went 38 years without playing a single international between 1960 and 1998 and still barely stages any action, whether international or domestic, due to below-freezing conditions between October and June.

OCEANIA

Football in Oceania can claim some of the most eye-catching football statistics – though not necessarily in a way many there would welcome, especially the long-suffering goalkeepers from minnow islands on the end of cricket-style scorelines. The departure to the Asian Football Confederation of Australia, seeking more testing competition, was a morale blow – but benefited New Zealand out on the pitch. The finals tournament of the 2010 FIFA World Cup™ was the first to feature both Australia and New Zealand.

⚽ TOP CAPS: NEW ZEALAND

1	Ivan Vicelich	71
2	Simon Elliott	68
3	Vaughan Coveny	64
4	Ricki Herbert	61
5	Chris Jackson	60
6	Brian Turner	59
7	Duncan Cole	58
=	Steve Sumner	58
9	Chris Zoricich	57
10	Ceri Evans	56

⚽ KAREMBEU THE FIFA WORLD CUP WINNER

Christian Karembeu, born in New Caledonia, is the only FIFA World Cup winner to come from the Oceania region. He started for France in their 3-0 final victory over Brazil on 12 July 1998. The defensive midfielder had earlier begun against Denmark (group), Italy (quarter-finals) and Croatia (semi-finals). He played 53 times for France, scoring one goal, and was also a double European Champions League Cup winner with Real Madrid in 1998 in 2000.

⚽ RYAN'S SISTER

New Zealand's captain **Ryan Nelsen** flew back from Blackburn in England to his native city of Christchurch in March 2011 after the city was devastated by an earthquake. Nelsen was worried for the safety of his family, especially his pregnant sister Stephanie Martin – but after being "knocked down" by the 6.3-magnitude quake, she successfully and safely gave birth to a healthy baby boy. Nelsen was free to spend some time back home due to a red card and three-match suspension in the English Premier League.

⚽ LATE DANE

After losing all three of their games at the 1982 tournament, centre-back **Winston Reid**'s stoppage-time header against Slovakia in their 2010 opener gave New Zealand a 1-1 draw – and their first-ever point at a FIFA World Cup. Reid had only made his New Zealand debut less than a month earlier, having lived in Denmark since the age of ten and taken up Danish citizenship.

⚽ TOP SCORERS: NEW ZEALAND

1	Vaughan Coveny	28
2	Steve Sumner	22
3	Brian Turner	21
4	Jock Newall	17
=	Shane Smeltz	17
6	Keith Nelson	16
7	Grant Turner	15
8	Darren McClennan	12
=	Michael McGarry	12
=	Wynton Rufer	12

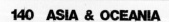

RETURNING RICKI

Ricki Herbert is the only footballer from New Zealand to reach a FIFA World Cup twice – he played left-back at the 1982 tournament in Spain, then coached the country to what is only their second World Cup, in 2010. Qualification second time around came courtesy of a play-off win over Asian Football Confederation representatives Bahrain – though the New Zealand football authorities have been pondering whether to follow Australia in defecting from Oceania and joining the AFC. Herbert, born in Auckland in 1961, combined qualifying for the 2010 FIFA World Cup with coaching New Zealand-based club Wellington Phoenix, who play in Australia's A-League.

SHANE IN SEVENTH HEAVEN

New Zealand striker **Shane Smeltz** has come a long way in his football career. Born on 29 September 1981, in Germany, he played for a few clubs in Australia and New Zealand as a youngster before moving to England in 2005. Smeltz won his first full international cap in April 2006, when he was playing for AFC Wimbledon, who were then in the third tier of English non-league football, effectively the seventh level of the domestic game.

PIERRE'S PERFECT START

The very first goal of the 2010 FIFA World Cup was scored, in qualifying, by New Caledonia's Pierre Wajoka – the only strike of an August 2007 match against Tahiti, the country of his birth.

BAD LUCK OF THE DRAW

Despite featuring at only their second-ever FIFA World Cup – and first since 1982 – New Zealand did not lose a game in South Africa in 2010. They drew all three first-round matches, against Slovakia, Italy and Paraguay. The three points were not enough to secure a top-two finish in Group F, but third-placed New Zealand did finish above defending world champions Italy. The only other three teams to have gone out despite going unbeaten in their three first-round group games were Scotland in 1974, Cameroon in 1982 and Belgium in 1998.

LAUGHING ALL THE WAY TO THE BANK

New Zealand went to the 2010 FIFA World Cup with four amateur players in their 23-man squad. Midfielder **Andy Barron**, who works as an investment adviser at a bank in Wellington, even made it on to the pitch as a stoppage-time substitute against reigning world champions Italy.

BUSY NICKY

Nicky Salapu was the unfortunate goalkeeper who conceded an international-record 31 times, as his American Samoa team lost 31-0 to Australia in April 2001. Just two days earlier, Australia had crushed Tonga 22-0. Passport problems meant American Samoa were denied several of their best players for the Australia game and included three 15-year-olds in a line-up that had an average age of just 18. Depite this, they managed to keep the game goalless ... for the first 10 minutes. In his eight international appearances, Salapu conceded 91 goals – with just one in his opposite number's net, scored by Natia Natia, in a 9-1 defeat to Vanuatu in May 2004. Midfielder Natia's goal was American Samoa's first in a FIFA World Cup qualifier. The country's only victory, over Wallis and Futana in 1983, came before they were officially recognized by FIFA in 1998. Wallis and Futana – a tiny Polynesian island, a French colony, 800km west of American Samoa – remain unrecognized by world football's governing body.

THE WHITE STUFF

New Zealand's national football team is known as the "All-Whites" – not just a recognition of their kit colours, but also a counterpoint to the "All-Blacks" nickname of the country's more famous and successful rugby union side.

CONCACAF

Mexican fans provide the colour and the waves, America the pizzazz and the Caribbean countries plenty of joyous vibrancy – the CONCACAF region, covering the Caribbean, Central and North America, is increasingly following football as eagerly as anywhere else. Mexicans have long been among the most enthusiastic FIFA World Cup™ followers, all the way back to the inaugural finals in 1930. And Mexico was, in 1970 and 1986, the first nation to host the finals twice.

Despite qualifying for every FIFA World Cup finals since 1990, the USA and stars, such as Landon Donovan (right, against Ghana), get more media interest from abroad than at home.

MEXICO

Mexico may well be the powerhouse of the CONCACAF region and are regular qualifiers for the FIFA World Cup™ – they did not play in the finals of the tournament on just three occasions (1934, 1974 and 1982) – but they have always struggled to impose themselves on the international stage. Two FIFA World Cup™ quarter-final appearances (both times as tournament hosts, in 1970 and 1986) represent their best performances to date. A football-mad nation expects more.

TOP SCORERS

1	Jared Borgetti	46
2	Cuauhtemoc Blanco	39
3	Carlos Hermilloso	35
=	Luis Hernandez	35
5	Enrique Borja	31
6	Zague	30
7	Luis Flores	29
=	Luis Garcia	29
=	Hugo Sanchez	29
10	Benjamin Galindo	28

VICTOR HUGO

Jared Borgetti may hold the record as Mexico's all-time leading scorer, but perhaps the country's most inspirational striker remains **Hugo Sanchez,** famed for his acrobatic bicycle-kick finishes and somersaulting celebrations. Sanchez played for Mexico at the 1978, 1986 and 1994 FIFA World Cups and would surely have done so had they qualified in 1982 and 1990. During spells in Spain with Atletico Madrid and Real Madrid he finished as La Liga's top scorer five years out of six between 1985 and 1990. The highlight of his disappointing term as Mexico coach, from 2006 to 2008, was finishing third at the 2007 Copa America.

MAKING HIS MARQUEZ

Rafael Marquez set a FIFA World Cup appearance  record for Mexico when playing in the 2010 second-round defeat to Argentina. That game took him to 12 games in the competition, one more than former goalkeeper Antonio Carbajal and also two other members of the 2010 squad – forward Cuauhtemoc Blanco and midfielder Gerardo Torrado.

HERNANDEZ HEADS THE FINALS LIST

Luis Hernandez's four goals in 1998 make him Mexico's highest-ever scorer in a FIFA World Cup finals tournament. Hernandez netted twice in Mexico's 3-1 group win over South Korea. His last-minute equalizer also earned them a 2-2 draw against Holland. Hernandez, nicknamed "The Matador", gave his side the lead against Germany in the last 16, before late goals by Jurgen Klinsmann and Oliver Bierhoff eliminated the Mexicans.

TOP CAPS

1	Claudio Suarez	178
2	Pavel Pardo	148
3	Jorge Campos	131
4	Alberto Garcia Aspe	127
5	Cuauhtemoc Blanco	121
=	Ramon Ramirez	121
=	Gerardo Torrado	121
8	Oswaldo Sanchez	99
9	Rafael Marquez	98
10	Carlos Hermosillo	90

LITTLE PEA FROM A POD

Javier Hernandez's goal for Mexico against France, in Polokwane on 17 June 2010 made him the third generation of his family to play at a FIFA World Cup. Hernandez – nicknamed "Chicharito", or "Little Pea" – is the son of Javier Hernandez who reached the quarter-finals with Mexico in 1986 and the grandson of Tomas Balcazar, a member of the country's 1954 squad. Balcazar also scored against France at his FIFA World Cup – and like his grandson was aged 22 when he did so. Another Mexican pair were the first grandfather-grandson pairing to each play at the finals. Luis Perez represented Mexico in 1930 in Uruguay. His grandson Mario Perez played for Mexico, on home turf, 40 years later.

FAMILY SPLIT

Winger **Giovani dos Santos** was distraught when Mexico's 30-man preliminary squad was reduced to 23 for the 2010 FIFA World Cup – though not for the obvious reason. He actually made the cut, and played in all four of Mexico's matches, but his brother Jonathan dos Santos was left out by coach Javier Aguirre.

MEXICO RECORDS

First international:
won 3-2 v Guatemala,
Guatemala City,
1 January 1923
Biggest win:
13-0 v Bahamas,
Toluca, 28 April 1987
Biggest defeat: 8-0 v
England, Wembley, 10 May 1961
CONCACAF champions: 1965, 1971, 1977, 1993, 1996, 1998, 2003
Confederations Cup winners: 1999

MEXICO BEATS EARTHQUAKE

Mexico stepped in to host the 1986 FIFA World Cup finals after the original choice, Colombia, pulled out in November 1982. FIFA chose Mexico as the replacement venue because of its stadiums and infrastructure, still in place from the 1970 finals. The governing body turned down rival bids from Canada and the United States. Mexico had to work overtime to be ready for the finals, after the earthquake of 19 September 1985, which killed an estimated 10,000 people in central Mexico and destroyed many buildings in Mexico City.

SUAREZ SETS OUTFIELD RECORD

Mexico defender **Claudio Suarez** is the world's most-capped outfield player, with 178 caps. He ranks second only to Saudi Arabia goalkeeper Mohamed Al-Deayea, who has 181 caps. Suarez – nicknamed "The Emperor" – played in all of Mexico's four games in 1994 and 1998. He missed the 2002 finals because of a broken leg, but was included in the squad for the 2006 finals at the age of 37, although he did not play.

ROSAS NETS HISTORIC PENALTY

Mexico's Manuel Rosas scored the first penalty ever awarded in the FIFA World Cup finals when he converted a 42nd-minute spot-kick in his country's match against Argentina in 1930. Rosas scored again in the 65th minute, but it was too little too late for the Mexicans: they crashed to a 6-3 defeat.

AGUIRRE IN CHARGE AGAIN

Mexico coach **Javier Aguirre** has had two spells in charge. Aguirre, known as "The Basque" because of his ancestry, guided Mexico to the last 16 in 2002. He returned in place of Sven-Goran Eriksson on 3 April 2009, after the Swede was sacked following Mexico's 3-1 defeat by Honduras in a FIFA World Cup qualifier for South Africa 2010. Aguirre announced his resignation after Mexico were eliminated from the 2010 tournament by Argentina.

UNITED STATES

Some of the game's biggest names – from Pele to David Beckham – may well have graced the United States' domestic league over the years, and the country may well be one of only 15 countries to have been granted the honour of hosting a FIFA World Cup™, but football is still very much a minority sport in the world's most powerful country. However, following a series of impressive performances on the world stage, the hope is that the situation will soon change.

TOP SCORERS

1	Landon Donovan	45
2	Eric Wynalda	34
3	Brian McBride	30
4	Joe-Max Moore	24
5	Bruce Murray	21
6	Clint Dempsey	19
7	DaMarcus Beasley	17
=	Earnie Stewart	17
9	Cobi Jones	15
10	Marcelo Balboa	13
=	Hugo Perez	13

ARENA'S MEN REACH LAST EIGHT

The US's best performance in the modern FIFA World Cup finals came in 2002 when they reached the last eight. Coach Bruce Arena's side beat Portugal 3-2, drew 1-1 with South Korea and lost 3-1 to Poland to qualify in second place from Group D. **Brian McBride** and Landon Donovan scored in a 2-0 win over Mexico in the last 16. They lost 1-0 to Germany in the quarter-finals. The squad featured many players with European experience – **Brad Friedel**, Kasey Keller, Claudio Reyna, McBride, Donovan, DaMarcus Beasley and Cobi Jones. Arena was later succeeded by his assistant Bob Bradley after the US were eliminated at the group stage of the 2006 finals in Germany.

LANDON HOPE AND GLORY

The USA's all-time leading scorer **Landon Donovan** was the undoubted star of their 2010 FIFA World Cup campaign. He scored three goals in four matches, including a stoppage-time winner against Algeria that meant his side finished top of Group C. His four displays at the tournament meant he has now featured in 13 FIFA World Cup matches for the USA, two ahead of compatriots Earnie Stewart and Cobi Jones. His successful penalty in a second-round defeat to Ghana also made him the USA's all-time top scorer in the competition, with five goals – one more than 1930 hat-trick hero Bert Patenaude.

CALIGIURI'S SHOT MAKES HISTORY

The US's FIFA World Cup qualifying win in Trinidad, on 19 November 1989, is regarded as a turning point in the country's football history. The team included just one full-time professional, Paul Caligiuri, of (West) German second division club Meppen. He scored the only goal of the game with a looping shot after 31 minutes to take the US to their first finals for 40 years. Trinidad's goalkeeper, Michael Maurice, claimed to have been blinded by the sun, but the win raised the profile of the US team hugely, despite a first-round elimination in the 1990 FIFA World Cup. It also provided the impetus for the professional organization of the US squad. Caligiuri said: "It was the single most important game we ever won."

BOB'S YOUR FATHER

Coach **Bob Bradley**'s USA team were surprise winners of Group C at the 2010 FIFA World Cup, a place above seeded favourites England. This was the first time the country had topped their first-round group since the very first FIFA World Cup in 1930. Bradley picked his son **Michael** for all four USA games at the 2010 tournament, and the midfielder rewarded his father's faith by scoring a late equalizer in the 2-2 Group C draw with Slovenia.

DEMPSEY'S DOUBLE

Clint Dempsey became only the second USA international to score at two different FIFA World Cups when his long-range shot was fumbled into the net by England goalkeeper Robert Green in their 1-1 draw in Rustenburg at the 2010 tournament. Dempsey had previously scored in a 2-1 defeat to Ghana, in the first round in Germany four years earlier. The first American to achieve the feat was striker Brian McBride, who netted against Iran in 1998 and winners against Portugal and Mexico in 2002. Dempsey's feat was emulated by Landon Donovan – a goalscorer against Poland and Mexico in 2002 and against Slovenia, Algeria and Ghana in 2010.

RECORD–BREAKERS

FIFA's choice of the United States to host the 1994 finals was controversial. Critics pointed to US's poor international record, and the lack of a national professional league. But the US made it as far as the last 16, thanks to a 2-1 win over Colombia, before losing 1-0 to eventual winners Brazil. In addition, the total attendance of 3,587,538 set a record for the finals.

TEAM AMERICA'S BRIEF EXPERIMENT

Governing body US Soccer entered the US national side in the NASL as "Team America" for one season in 1983. The experiment was soon dropped when the side finished bottom of the table. Team America struggled from the start because many of the top players preferred to stay with their own clubs. They were rarely able to field a settled side either.

TOP CAPS

1	Cobi Jones	164
2	Jeff Agoos	134
3	Marcelo Balboa	128
4	Landon Donovan	127
5	Claudio Reyna	112
6	Paul Cagliuri	110
7	Eric Wynalda	106
8	Kasey Keller	102
9	Earnie Stewart	101
10	Tony Meola	100
=	Joe-Max Moore	100

ENGLAND STUNNED BY GAETJENS

The US's 1-0 win over England on 29 June 1950 ranks among the biggest surprises in FIFA World Cup history. England, along with hosts Brazil, were joint favourites to win the trophy. The US had lost their last seven matches, scoring just two goals. Joe Gaetjens scored the only goal, in the 37th minute, diving to head Walter Bahr's cross past goalkeeper Bert Williams. England dominated the game, but US keeper Frank Borghi made save after save. Defeats by Chile and Spain eliminated the US at the group stage, but their victory over England remains the greatest result in the country's football history.

KEEPING UP WITH JONES

His dreadlocked hair helped catch the attention, but **Cobi Jones's** raiding runs down the wing also made him one of the host country's most high-profile performers at the 1994 FIFA World Cup. Jones went on to become the USA's most-capped player, with 164 international appearances between 1992 and 2004. When he finally retired from all forms of the game in 2007, his number 13 shirt was officially "retired" by the Los Angeles Galaxy – the first time a Major League Soccer club had honoured a player in such a way. Jones had been with the Galaxy since the MLS was launched in 1996 and later served the club as assistant coach and caretaker manager.

⚽ CONCACAF OTHER TEAMS

Mexico and the United States (with 23 FIFA World Cup™ finals appearances between them) are undoubtedly the powerhouses of the CONCACAF region. Of the other teams to make up the football nations in North and Central America and the Caribbean, only three countries (Costa Rica in 1990, 2002 and 2006), El Salvador (1970 and 1982) and Honduras (1982 and 2010) have qualified for the FIFA World Cup™ finals on more than one occasion.

⚽ COSTA RICA KEEP BATTLING

Costa Rica, spearheaded by **Paulo Wanchope**, have been the most successful of Mexico's Central American neighbours at the FIFA World Cup finals. They qualified in 1990, 2002 and 2006, and reached the last 16 at that first attempt, beating Scotland 1-0 and Sweden 2-1 in their group. They were knocked out by Czechoslovakia, 4-1. In 2002, they beat China 2-0 and drew 1-1 with Turkey but went home after losing 5-2 to Brazil. They again departed at the group stage in 2006, losing all three matches. El Salvador qualified twice, in 1970 and 1982 – but lost all six of their matches, including a 10-1 defeat by Hungary in 1982. Honduras have also qualified twice but gone out in the first round both times. In 1982, they drew 1-1 with Spain and Northern Ireland, but lost 1-0 to Yugoslavia. They didn't score a goal in 2010, losing to Chile and Spain before drawing with Switzerland.

PAVON ... AND ON ... AND ON

Striker **Carlos Pavon**, the only man to play a century of games for Honduras, scored seven goals in their qualifiers to reach the 2010 FIFA World Cup – their first finals since 1982. Yet the veteran, then aged 36, played just 60 minutes of the tournament itself. Pavon, nicknamed "The Shadow", has played club football in seven different countries: Honduras, Mexico, Spain, Italy, Colombia, Guatemala and the United States, where he starred alongside David Beckham for the Los Angeles Galaxy.

WAITING GAMES

Patience is the watchword for many of Central America's smaller nations when it comes to footballing achievement – or even participation. International matches are rare in Montserrat due to the risk of volcanic activity on the 5,000-population Caribbean island. The team has played just 13 international matches in the twenty-first century, none between November 2004 and March 2008. More positively, Puerto Rico finally ended a 14-year wait for a win when they beat Bermuda 2–0 in January 2008, before reaching the second round of CONCACAF's qualifiers for the 2010 FIFA World Cup. The British Virgin Islands were eliminated from those qualifiers despite not losing a game – their two-legged first-round tie against the Bahamas ended 5–5 on aggregate, with the British Virgin Islands knocked out on away goals.

⚽ COSTA RICA WIN WITHOUT A CROWD

The lowest-ever attendance for a CONCACAF FIFA World Cup qualifier was for the Costa Rica–Panama game on 26 March 2005. FIFA ordered the game, staged at the Saprissa Stadium in San Jose, to be played behind closed doors after missiles were thrown at visiting players and the match officials when Mexico won there 2-1 on 9 February. The game was known as "the ghost match". Costa Rica beat Panama 2-1, thanks to a **Roy Myrie** goal in the first minute of stoppage time.

CONCACAF TEAMS IN THE FIFA WORLD CUP™ FINALS

Appearances made by teams from the CONCACAF region at the FIFA World Cup finals

1	Mexico	14
2	US	9
3	Costa Rica	3
4	El Salvador	2
=	Honduras	2
6	Canada	1
=	Cuba	1
=	Haiti	1
=	Jamaica	1
=	Trinidad & Tobago	1

PROUD RECORD

The CONCACAF confederation can boast of having had at least one representative in every FIFA World Cup finals. Mexico and the United States entered the first finals in 1930 – and the US reached the semi-finals before losing to Argentina. Since then, these two have dominated the qualifying competition. Mexico have played in a total of 14 finals tournaments; the USA have in nine, and all of the last six. Other countries have challenged them recently. Costa Rica's third appearance and Trinidad & Tobago's debut at the 2006 FIFA World Cup gave CONCACAF a record four representatives at one tournament. And, at the 2010 FIFA World Cup, Honduras made their second finals appearance.

REGGAE BOYZ STEP UP

In 1998, Jamaica became the first team from the English-speaking Caribbean to reach the FIFA World Cup finals. The "Reggae Boyz", as they were nicknamed, included several players based in England. They were eliminated at the group stage, despite beating Japan 2-1 in their final game with two goals by **Theodore Whitmore**. They had earlier lost 3-1 to Croatia and 5-0 against Argentina.

BROTHERS IN ARMS

Honduras became the first team to field not one, not two, but three siblings at a FIFA World Cup, when they picked defender **Johnny** (left), midfielder **Wilson** (right) and striker **Jerry** (middle) **Palacios** in the 2010 squad. Jerry was a last-minute call-up, as replacement for injured Julio Cesar de Leon. Tottenham Hotspur defensive midfielder Wilson Palacios was perhaps the most famous and acclaimed player in the first Honduras side to reach a FIFA World Cup in 28 years. Like the 1982 side, though, Reinaldo Rueda's men went three games without a win or even a goal. An older brother, Milton Palacios, played 14 times as a defender for Honduras between 2003 and 2006 but was not in the running for the 2010 squad.

CUBA SHOW THE WAY

In 1938, Cuba became the first island state of the CONCACAF region to reach the FIFA World Cup quarter-finals. They drew 3-3 with Romania after extra-time in the first round, then won the replay 2-1 with goals by Hector Socorro and Carlos Oliveira after trailing at half-time. They were thrashed 8-0 by Sweden in the last eight. Haiti were the next Caribbean island to play in the finals, in 1974. They lost all three group games, 3-1 to Italy, 7-0 against Poland and 4-1 to Argentina.

PALACIOS FAMILY PAIN

Another of the Palacios brothers, the youngest, Edwin, was mourned by all the three siblings who went to the 2010 FIFA World Cup. He had been kidnapped in 2007, and his remains were found 18 months later. After hearing the tragic news, Wilson Palacios sat in reception all night in the hotel where Tottenham Hotspur were preparing for a Saturday match, reluctant to disturb anyone – to the amazement of sympathetic manager Harry Redknapp, who found him patiently waiting there in the morning.

TRINIDAD'S FIRST TIME

Trinidad & Tobago reached the FIFA World Cup finals for the first time in 2006 after a marathon qualifying competition that ended with their 1-0 play-off victory in Bahrain. The team, nicknamed the "Socca Warriors", held Sweden 0-0 in their opening game, but lost 2-0 to England and 2-0 to Paraguay.

RUEDA AWAKENING

Colombian-born coach Reinaldo Rueda was granted Honduran citizenship after leading his adopted country to the 2010 FIFA World Cup. The players were also granted an open-top bus tour through the capital Tegucigalpa and an audience with the president after a successful end to CONCACAF qualifiers.

PART 2:
FIFA ALL-TIME RECORDS
WORLD CUP™

Spain became only the eighth winners of the FIFA World Cup™ when they triumphed in South Africa in 2010. However, Brazil remain the record-holders, with five victories inspired by superstars from Pele and Garrincha to Ronaldo and Ronaldinho. Argentina and Uruguay are the other South American winners, with past champions from Europe being England, France, Germany and Italy.

FIFA QUALIFIERS
WORLD CUP™

OCEANIA ADVENTURES

After completing their qualification rounds in Oceania for the 2010 FIFA World Cup, **New Zealand** had to wait 11 months before finally taking on Bahrain – Asia's fifth-best-placed team – in a two-legged play-off for a place in South Africa. The "All Whites" triumphed 1-0 on aggregate in November 2009, but it was another Oceanian team that boasted the best goals-per-game ratio of any country taking part in 2010 qualifiers. The Solomon Islands scored an average of 3.8 times per match, their record boosted by a 12-1 win over American Samoa. England were the next most prolific, managing 3.4 goals per game – and, unlike the unfortunate Solomon Islands, they secured a berth at the finals to boot.

UAE IN A SQUEEZE

The **United Arab Emirates** reached the finals in 1990 by recording just one win and scoring only four goals in the Asian final round. They drew four of their five matches, but beat China 2-1 to qualify in second place behind South Korea.

T&T AT FULL STRETCH

Trinidad and Tobago share the record for the most games played to qualify for a FIFA World Cup finals. They played 20 in reaching the 2006 finals, beginning with 2-0 away and 4-0 home wins over the Dominican Republic in the preliminaries. T&T then finished second behind Mexico at the four-team first group stage to reach the six-team final group. After finishing fourth, they had to play off against Bahrain and won 2-1 on aggregate. Uruguay matched that figure in 2010, with 18 South America group matches and a two-legged play-off.

FIFA OPENS WORLD CUP TO THE WORLD

FIFA has enlarged the World Cup finals twice since 1978, to take account of the rising football nations of Africa and Asia. The rise in interest is reflected in the massive number of sides entering the qualifying competition – 204 for the 2010 event. **João Havelange**, the Brazilian who was president of FIFA from 1974 to 1998, enlarged the organization both to take advantage of commercial opportunities and to give smaller nations a chance. The number of teams in the finals was first increased from 16 to 24 for the 1982 finals in Spain, with an extra place given for Africa and Asia and a chance for a nation from Oceania to reach the finals. The number of finalists was further increased to 32 for the 1998 tournament in France. This decision offered five places to African teams, four to sides from Asia and Oceania and three from North/Central America and the Caribbean. The formula for the 2010 finals in South Africa offered 13 places to Europe, four to South America, five to Africa, plus the hosts; four for Asia, with another for the winners of an Asia v Oceania play-off, in which Oceania's New Zealand beat Asia's Bahrain. CONCACAF (the North and Central American and Caribbean federation) had three spots. The other place was decided by a play-off in which Uruguay, the fifth-placed South American team, saw off Costa Rica, the fourth-placed team in the CONCACAF qualifiers.

EGYPT POINT THE WAY

African teams, such as Cameroon, Tunisia, South Africa and Nigeria, make frequent appearances in the modern FIFA World Cup finals, but for many years, Egypt were the only African nation to have played in the finals. They qualified in 1934, by beating Palestine 7-1 at home and 4-1 away. The next African qualifiers were Morocco, who reached the finals in Mexico 36 years later.

ALL–TIME QUALIFICATIONS BY REGIONAL CONFEDERATION

1	Europe	218
2	South America	74
3	North/Central America & Caribbean	35
4	Africa	34
5	Asia	28
6	Oceania	4

THE FIRST SHOOT–OUT

The first penalty shoot-out in qualifying history came on 9 January 1977 when Tunisia beat Morocco 4-2 on spot-kicks after a 1-1 draw in Tunis. The first game, in Casablanca, had also finished 1-1. Tunisia went on to qualify for the finals.

SPANISH INVINCIBLES

Several countries have qualified for a FIFA World Cup without losing or even drawing a single game. But the **Spain** side who cruised their way through to the 2010 tournament in South Africa were the first to do so while playing as many as 10 matches. Qualifying for the same finals from a smaller group, Holland won eight games out of eight. West Germany also went through eight matches without dropping a point in reaching the 1982 FIFA World Cup in Spain, and Brazil won six out of six in qualifying for the 1970 competition – at which Mario Zagallo's men won another six out of six on their way to lifting the trophy.

MOVING THE FINALS AROUND

After the 1954 and 1958 finals in Europe, FIFA decided that they would be staged alternately in South America and Europe. This lasted until the award of the 1994 tournament to the United States. Things have changed since then. Japan and South Korea were the first Asian hosts in 2002 and in 2010 South Africa were the first hosts from Africa.

THE GROWTH OF THE QUALIFYING COMPETITION

This charts the number of countries entering qualifiers for the FIFA World Cup finals. Some withdrew before playing.

World Cup	Teams entering
Uruguay 1930	-
Italy 1934	32
France 1938	37
Brazil 1950	34
Switzerland 1954	45
Sweden 1958	55
Chile 1962	56
England 1966	74
Mexico 1970	75
West Germany 1974	99
Argentina 1978	107
Spain 1982	109
Mexico 1986	121
Italy 1990	116
USA 1994	147
France 1998	174
Japan/South Korea 2002	199
Germany 2006	198
South Africa 2010	206

HURTADO THE LEADER

Ecuador defender **Ivan Hurtado** has made the most appearances in FIFA World Cup qualifiers. He has played 56 games, including 16 in the 2006 preliminaries. He was Ecuador's youngest-ever international when he made his debut at 17 years 285 days.

THE FASTEST SUBSTITUTION

The quickest substitution in the history of the qualifiers came on 30 December 1980, when North Korea's Chon Byong Ju was substituted in the first minute of his country's home game against Japan.

KOSTADINOV STUNS FRANCE

On 17 November 1993, in the last game of the Group Six schedule, Bulgaria's Emil Kostadinov scored one of the most dramatic goals in qualifying history to deny France a place in the 1994 finals. France seemed to be cruising with the score at 1-1 in stoppage time, but Kostadinov earned Bulgaria a shock victory after David Ginola had lost the ball. The Bulgarians reached the semi-finals of the tournament in the United States, losing 2-1 to Italy.

PALMER BEATS THE WHISTLE

Carl Erik Palmer's second goal in Sweden's 3-1 win over the Republic of Ireland in November 1949 was one of the most bizarre in qualifying history. The Irish defenders stopped, having heard a whistle, while Palmer ran on and put the ball in the net. The goal stood, because the whistle had come from someone in the crowd, not the referee. The 19-year-old forward went on to complete a hat-trick.

BWALYA LEAVES IT LATE

Zambia's **Kalusha Bwalya** is the oldest player to have scored a match-winning goal in a FIFA World Cup qualifying match. The 41-year-old netted the only goal against Liberia on 4 September 2004 after coming on as a substitute. He had also scored in his first qualifier, 20 years previously, in Zambia's 3-0 win over Uganda.

AUSTRALIA'S INCREDIBLE GOAL SPREE

Australia set a FIFA World Cup qualifying record in 2001, one that is unlikely to be beaten, as the Socceroos scored 53 goals in the space of two days. The details:

9 April 2001, Sydney: Australia 22, Tonga 0
Australia scorers: Scott Chipperfield 3, 83 mins; Damian Mori 13, 23, 40; John Aloisi 14, 24, 37, 45, 52, 63; **Kevin Muscat** (No. 2, right) 18, 30, 54, 58, 82; Tony Popovic 67; Tony Vidmar 74; David Zdrilic 78, 90; Archie Thompson 80; Con Boutsiania 87

11 April 2001, Sydney: Australia 31, American Samoa 0
Australia scorers: Boutsiania 10, 50, 84 mins; Thompson 12, 23, 27, 29, 32, 37, 42, 45, 56, 60, 65, 68, 88; Zdrilic 13, 21, 25, 33, 58, 66, 78, 89; Vidmar 14, 80; Popovic 17, 19; Simon Colosimo 51, 81; Fausto De Amicis 55

THOMPSON SETS UNLIKELY MARK

Archie Thompson eased past Iran striker Karim Bagheri's record for the number of goals in a single qualifying match (seven) as Australia thrashed American Samoa 31-0 on 11 April 2001. He netted 13 goals. David Zdrilic also beat Bagheri's total with eight goals. Australia had previously smashed Iran's scoring record two days earlier with a 22-0 victory over Tonga.

THE FASTEST GOAL

Davide Gualtieri, of minnows San Marino, scored the fastest goal in qualifying history when he netted after just nine seconds against England on 17 November 1993. England went on to win 7-1 but still failed to qualify.

MUNICH DISASTER HITS ENGLAND

England's 1958 FIFA World Cup hopes were wrecked by the Munich air disaster on 6 February 1958, which devastated champions Manchester United. Three United players – left-back Roger Byrne, left-half Duncan Edwards and centre-forward Tommy Taylor – had been outstanding in England's unbeaten qualification campaign, with each playing in all four matches. Nineteen-year-old Edwards netted twice and Taylor scored eight goals. Byrne and Taylor died in the crash; Edwards died 15 days later.

A REAL ALL-ROUNDER

West Indian cricket legend Sir Viv Richards can be acclaimed as an all-rounder in more than just the so-called "summer game" alone. He may have more famously helped his country win the cricket World Cup in 1975 and 1979, but he also played football for Antigua and Barbuda in qualifiers for the 1974 FIFA World Cup. Unfortunately, his football side lost all four of the qualifying matches they contested.

RECORD HAT-TRICK

Abdel Hamid Bassiouny of Egypt scored the fastest-ever hat-trick in qualifying history in their 8-2 win over Namibia on 13 July 2001. He netted three times in just 177 seconds between the 39th and 42nd minutes.

YOUNGEST AND OLDEST

The youngest player to appear in the FIFA World Cup qualifiers is Souleymane Mamam of Togo, who was 13 years 310 days when he played against Zambia on 6 May 2001. The oldest was MacDonald Taylor, who was 46 years, 180 days when he played for the Virgin Islands against St Kitts Nevis on 18 February 2004.

DAEI TOPS THE SCORERS

Iran's **Ali Daei** is the all-time top scorer in FIFA World Cup qualifiers. His nine goals in the 2006 qualifying campaign took his total to 30, nine ahead of the previous joint record-holder, Japan's Kazu Miura. Daei also scored seven goals in the 1994 qualifiers, four in the 1998 preliminaries and ten in 2002.

HORST THE FIRST TO GIVE WAY

The first player to be substituted during a FIFA World Cup qualifier was West Germany's **Horst Eckel,** replaced by Richard Gottinger in their 3-0 victory over the short-lived protectorate of Saarland in October 1953. Eckel would go on to play on the right side of midfield in the side that beat Hungary in the 1954 FIFA World Cup final, while Gottinger's delayed appearance against Saarland was his first and last for his country. By the time of the 1958 FIFA World Cup qualifiers, Saarland had been integrated within West Germany.

UNITED STATES LEAVE IT LATE

The latest of all qualifying play-offs took place in Rome on 24 May 1934, when the USA beat Mexico 4-2 to clinch the last slot in the FIFA World Cup finals. Three days later, the Americans were knocked out 7-1 by hosts Italy in the first round of the tournament.

ITALY FORCED TO QUALIFY

Italy are the only host country who have been required to qualify for their own tournament. The 1934 hosts beat Greece 4-0 to go through. FIFA decided that, for the 1938 finals, the holders and the hosts would qualify automatically. That decision was changed for the 2006 finals. Since then, only the hosts have been exempt from qualifying, though South Africa played in the second round of qualifying for 2010. This is because it doubled up as qualifiers for the 2010 Africa Cup of Nations.

TURKEY THROUGH ON LUCK OF THE DRAW

Turkey were the first team to qualify for the FIFA World Cup finals after the drawing of lots. Their play-off against Spain, in Rome on 17 March 1954, ended 2-2. Qualification was decided by a 14-year-old Roman boy, Luigi Franco Gemma. He was blindfolded to draw the lots – and pulled out Turkey, instead of much-fancied Spain.

THE "FOOTBALL WAR"

War broke out between El Salvador and Honduras after El Salvador beat Honduras 3-2 in a play-off on 26 June 1969 to qualify for the 1970 finals. Tension had been running high between the neighbours over a border dispute and there had been rioting at the match. On 14 July, the Salvador army invaded Honduras.

MOST SUCCESSFUL QUALIFYING ATTEMPTS

Italy	13
West Germany/Germany	12
Mexico	12
Spain	12
Argentina	12
Brazil	11
England	11
Belgium	10
Sweden	10
Yugoslavia/Serbia	10
Czechoslovakia/Czech Republic	9
Hungary	9

ENGLAND IN, SCOTLAND OUT

England, led by **Billy Wright**, took part in the FIFA World Cup finals for the first time in 1950. They won their all-British group ahead of Scotland. Both teams thus qualified, but the Scots refused to go to the finals in Brazil because they had only finished second. The Scots subsequently qualified eight times, but have never advanced beyond the first round of the finals.

THIERRY'S TRICKERY

France qualified for the 2010 FIFA World Cup finals thanks to one of the most controversial goals of recent international history. The second leg of their play-off against the Republic of Ireland in November 2009 was 14 minutes into extra-time when striker **Thierry Henry** clearly controlled the ball with his hand, before crossing to William Gallas who gave his side a decisive 2-1 aggregate lead. After Swedish referee Martin Hansson allowed the goal to stand, the Football Association of Ireland first called for the game to be replayed, then asked to be allowed into the finals as a 33rd country – but both requests proved in vain.

ITALY HEAD THE QUALIFYING LIST

Italy have the best qualifying record of any nation. They have qualified 13 times – in 1934, 1954, 1962, 1966, 1970, 1974, 1978, 1982, 1994, 1998, 2002, 2006 and 2010. They were exempt as holders from qualifying in 1938, 1950 and 1986. They were hosts in 1990. They have only once been eliminated in the qualifiers, when they were knocked out by Northern Ireland in 1958.

GOING UNDERCOVER

The Kingdome in Seattle, United States, hosted the first FIFA World Cup qualifier to be played indoors, when the US beat Canada 2-0 in October 1976 – just a few months after the same venue had staged its first rock concert, by Paul McCartney's post-Beatles band Wings, and a religious rally featuring evangelist Billy Graham and country singer Johnny Cash. Canada gained revenge by beating the US 3-0 in a play-off, hosted in Haiti, to reach the next stage of the CONCACAF qualifying round. But only Mexico would go on to represent the continent at the 1978 FIFA World Cup in Argentina.

WALES IN THROUGH THE BACK DOOR

All four British teams have reached the FIFA World Cup finals only once, in 1958. England, Scotland and Northern Ireland all topped their groups, but **Wales** qualified by a roundabout route. They had been eliminated – then were offered a second chance. Israel had emerged unchallenged, for political reasons, from the Asian qualifying section. However, FIFA ruled that the Israelis could not qualify without playing a match and that they must play off against one of the second-placed European teams. Wales were drawn to meet them and qualified by winning both games 2-0.

ARGENTINA'S LONG BOYCOTT

Argentina boycotted the FIFA World Cup for nearly 20 years. They were Copa America holders in 1938, but refused to travel to France because they were upset at being passed over to host the finals. They were also unhappy at being paired with Brazil in a qualifier. They did not take part in the 1950 or 1954 competitions either, after Brazil were chosen to host the 1950 finals. Argentina did not return to FIFA World Cup competition until the qualifiers for the 1958 finals.

FIFA TEAM RECORDS
WORLD CUP™

⚽ SPAIN GAIN

The FIFA World Cup trophy had a new name engraved on it for first time since 1998 when **Spain** beat the Netherlands 1-0 in the 2010 final, in Johannesburg's Soccer City stadium on 11 July. The match was the first final in 32 years to feature two teams who had never won the competition before. The only previous finals featuring two non-former winners were when Argentina beat the Dutch in 1978, Brazil beat Sweden in 1958, West Germany defeated Hungary in 1954, Italy beat Czechoslovakia in 1934 and, of course, Uruguay saw off Argentina in the inaugural 1930 tournament.

⚽ SHARING THE GOALS

France in 1982 and winners Italy, in 2006, supplied the most individual goalscorers during a FIFA World Cup finals tournament – ten. Gerard Soler, Bernard Genghini, Michel Platini, Didier Six, Maxime Bossis, Alain Giresse, Dominque Rocheteau, Marius Tresor, Rene Girard and Alain Couriol netted for France. Alessandro Del Piero, Alberto Gilardino, Fabio Grosso, Vincenzo Iaquinta, Luca Toni, Pippo Inzaghi, Marco Materazzi, Andrea Pirlo, Francesco Totti and Gianluca Zambrotta all scored for Italy, who went on to win the tournament.

⚽ BRAZIL COLOUR UP

Brazil's yellow shirts are famous throughout the world. But the national team wore **white shirts** for each of the first four World Cup tournaments. Brazil's 2-1 defeat by Uruguay, which cost them the 1950 World Cup, came as such a shock to the population that the national association decided to change the team's shirt colours, to try and wipe out the bitter memory.

⚽ SINGING THE BLUES

Spain's 2010 FIFA World Cup triumph – for whom **Xavi** was a star even in an unfamiliar all-blue kit – made them the first team to win the tournament while playing the final in their second kit since England in 1966.

⚽ ITALY KEEP IT TIGHT

Italy set the record for the longest run without conceding a goal at the FIFA World Cup finals. They went five games without conceding at the 1990 finals, starting with their 1-0 group win over Austria. Goalkeeper Walter Zenga was not beaten until Claudio Caniggia scored Argentina's equalizer in the semi-final. And a watertight defence did not bring Italy the glory it craved: Argentina reached the final by winning the penalty shoot-out 4-3.

TODAY EUROPE, TOMORROW THE WORLD

Spain's 2010 trophy-lifting coach **Vicente del Bosque** became only the second manager to have won both the FIFA World Cup and the UEFA Champions League or its previous incarnation, the European Champions' Cup. Marcello Lippi won the UEFA prize with Juventus in 1996, 10 years before his Italy team became world champions. Del Bosque won the UEFA Champions League twice with Real Madrid, in 2000 and 2002, though he was sacked in summer 2003 for "only" winning the Spanish league title the previous season.

DO YOU COME HERE OFTEN?

Germany or West Germany have now played Yugoslavia/Serbia a record-equalling seven times at FIFA World Cup finals, after **Milan Jovanovic's** goal gave Serbia a 1–0 win in Port Elizabeth, South Africa, in the 2010 tournament. Germany enjoyed victories in 1954, 1958, 1974 and 1990, while Yugoslavia won in 1962 and the countries drew in 1998. There have also been seven FIFA World Cup clashes between Brazil and Sweden, though the latter have yet to taste success. Brazil won in 1938, 1950, 1958, 1990 and twice in 1994 – but drew in 1978.

MOST APPEARANCES IN THE FIFA WORLD CUP™ FINAL

1	Brazil	7
=	Germany/West Germany	7
3	Italy	6
4	Argentina	4
5	Netherlands	3
6	Czechoslovakia	2
=	France	2
=	Hungary	2
=	Uruguay	2
10	England	1
=	Spain	1
=	Sweden	1

BRAZIL PROFIT FROM RIMET'S VISION

Jules Rimet, president of FIFA from 1921 to 1954, was the driving force behind the first World Cup, in 1930. The tournament in Uruguay was not the high-profile event it is now, with only 13 nations taking part. The long sea journey kept most European teams away. Only four – Belgium, France, Romania and Yugoslavia – made the trip. Regardless, Rimet's dream had been realized and the FIFA World Cup grew and grew in popularity. Brazil have been the most successful team in the competition's history, winning the trophy five times. They have won more games in the FIFA World Cup finals (67) than any other country, though Germany have now played more games – 99 to Brazil's 97. Italy have won the FIFA World Cup four times and West Germany three. The original finalists, Uruguay and Argentina, have both lifted the trophy twice. England, in 1966, and France, in 1998, have won once, both as hosts, before Spain lifted their first FIFA World Cup in South Africa in 2010.

WHY THE BRITISH TEAMS STAYED OUT

England and Scotland are considered the homelands of football, but neither country entered the FIFA World Cup until the qualifiers for the 1950 finals. The four British associations – England, Scotland, Wales and Northern Ireland – quit FIFA in the 1920s over a row over broken-time (employment compensation) payments to amateurs. The British associations did not rejoin FIFA until 1946.

ONE-TIME WONDERS

Indonesia, then known as the Dutch East Indies, made one appearance in the finals, in the days when the tournament was a strictly knockout affair. On 5 June 1938, they lost 6–0 to Hungary in the first round, and have never qualified for the tournament since.

MOST APPEARANCES IN FIFA WORLD CUP™ FINALS TOURNAMENTS

1	Brazil	19
2	Germany/West Germany	17
=	Italy	17
4	Argentina	15
5	Mexico	14

FIFA WORLD CUP™ STOPS THE WORLD

The FIFA World Cup finals are the biggest sporting event in history. Television was in its infancy when the first finals were held in 1930. The tournament has since become the most popular TV sporting event of all. The 2006 finals were watched by a worldwide audience of 26.3 billion, 0.1 billion fewer than the 2002 finals. In addition to the estimated 700 million fans who watched the 2010 FIFA World Cup final at Soccer City, Johannesburg, between Spain and the Netherlands on televisions around the world, hundreds of thousands of others went to public squares and Fan Fests to watch the match on giant screens.

GOLDEN NARROWS

Before 2010, no country had won five consecutive FIFA World Cup matches by a one-goal margin – but **Arjen Robben** and the Netherlands and became the first, thanks to their 3-2 semi-final victory over Uruguay. Before then, the record rested with Italy, who managed four single-goal wins in a row across the 1934 and 1938 FIFA World Cups. Spain's 1-0 defeat of the Dutch in the 2010 FIFA World Cup was also their fifth consecutive single-goal victory and fourth in the knockout stages.

GERMANY'S GOAL BONANZA

West Germany conceded 14 goals in the 1954 finals, the most ever conceded by the FIFA World Cup winners. But they scored 25 – second most in FIFA World Cup history. Only their victims in the final – Hungary – scored more than the Germans: they netted 27.

EVER RED

England's victory in 1966 was not just the only time they have won the FIFA World Cup – it also now remains the only time the prize has been clinched by a side wearing red shirts in the final. Spain might have emulated England's fashion sense in 2010 but had to wear blue to avoid clashing with the Netherlands' bright orange – they did, however, change back into their usual red to receive the trophy from FIFA president **Joseph S. Blatter**.

THE FEWEST GOALS CONCEDED

FIFA World Cup winners France (1998), Italy (2006) and Spain (2010) hold the record for the fewest goals conceded on their way to victory. All three conceded just two. Spain also now hold the record for fewest goals scored by FIFA World Cup winners. They netted just eight in 2010, below the 11 scored by Italy in 1938, England in 1966 or Brazil in 1994.

SPONSORS MAKE THE FINALS PAY

The 2010 FIFA World Cup was the most lucrative ever, with world football's governing body FIFA pocketing $3.2 million in profits from the event in South Africa. A record 700m viewers tuned in to the final between Spain and the Netherlands – another all-time high.

FEWEST GOALS CONCEDED IN ONE TOURNAMENT:
Switzerland: 0, 2006

MOST GOALS SCORED IN ONE TOURNAMENT
Hungary: 27, 1954

MOST WINS IN ONE TOURNAMENT
Brazil: 7, 2002

MOST GOALS SCORED IN ONE TOURNAMENT
Just Fontaine (France): 13, 1958

MOST CONSECUTIVE MATCHES SCORING A GOAL AT FIFA WORLD CUP™ FINALS

18	Brazil	1930–58
18	Germany	1934–58, 1986–98
17	Hungary	1934–62
16	Uruguay	1930–62
15	Brazil	1978–90
15	France	1978–86

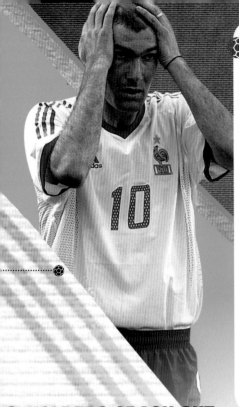

PERFORMANCES BY HOST NATION AT FIFA WORLD CUP™ FINALS

1930	Uruguay	Champions
1934	Italy	Champions
1938	France	Quarter-finals
1950	Brazil	Runners-up
1954	Switzerland	Quarter-finals
1958	Sweden	Runners-up
1962	Chile	Third place
1966	England	Champions
1970	Mexico	Quarter-finals
1974	West Germany	Champions
1978	Argentina	Champions
1982	Spain	Second round
1986	Mexico	Quarter-finals
1990	Italy	Third place
1994	United States	Second round
1998	France	Champions
2002	South Korea	Fourth place
	Japan	Second round
2006	Germany	Third place
2010	South Africa	First round

SAFE EUROPEAN HOME

Spain's triumph at the 2010 FIFA World Cup in South Africa made them the first European team to lift the trophy outside their own continent. After Italian glory in 2006, Spain's success four years later set another first – the first time the prize has gone to different European countries twice in succession. Furthermore, Europe has also now edged ahead of South America in FIFA World Cup wins – 10–9 up, since the inaugural tournament in 1930.

HOLDERS CRASH OUT

France produced the worst performance by a defending FIFA World Cup winner in Japan and South Korea in 2002: they lost their opening game 1-0 to Senegal, drew 0-0 against Uruguay and were eliminated after losing 1-0 to Denmark. They were the first defending champions to be knocked out without scoring a goal. In 2010 Italy emulated France by exiting at the first-round stage, and without winning a match – nor indeed ever taking the lead. At least Italy did achieve two draws – and scored four goals. They opened with a 1-1 draw against Paraguay, needed a penalty to force another 1-1 draw against minnows New Zealand, and they were on their way home after losing 3-2 to Slovakia.

THREE AND OUT

The Netherlands, coached by **Bert van Marwijk** in 2010, became the only country to have reached the final of three FIFA World Cups without managing to lift the trophy once. Their six victories en route to the 2010 final are also more than any other team has managed in one tournament without going on to claim the main prize.

BRAZIL LEAD THE WAY

Brazil scored the most victories in finals tournaments when they won all their seven games in 2002. They began with a 2-1 group win over Turkey and ended with a 2-0 final triumph over Germany. They scored 18 goals in their unbeaten run and conceded on only four occasions.

HOME DISCOMFORT

South Africa became the first host nation to fail to reach the second round of a FIFA World Cup, when staging the 2010 tournament – though their first-round record of one win, one draw and one defeat was only inferior on goal difference to the opening three games played by hosts Spain, in 1982, and the USA, in 1994, both of whom reached the second round. Uruguay's 3–0 victory over South Africa in Pretoria on 16 June 2010 equalled the highest losing margin suffered by a FIFA World Cup host, following Brazil's 5–2 win over Sweden in the 1958 final and Italy's 4–1 trouncing of Mexico in their 1970 quarter-final.

FIFA WORLD CUP™ GOALSCORING

FINE HOST

Siphiwe Tshabalala's goal for South Africa at Soccer City, Johannesburg, in the opening match of the 2010 FIFA World Cup not only gave his team the lead against Mexico – it was also the fifth time the hosts had scored the first goal of a FIFA World Cup. Previous examples were: Ademir, for Brazil in a 4–0 win over Mexico in 1950; Agne Simonsson, for Sweden in a 3–0 win, also against Mexico, in 1958; Paul Breitner, West Germany's only and winning goal against Chile in 1974 (though it was the second game – Brazil and Yugoslavia having played out a goalless draw); and Philipp Lahm, for Germany in a 4–2 defeat of Costa Rica in 2006. Tshabalala's strike was also the fourth time Mexico had let in the opening goal of a FIFA World Cup. As well as Ademir and Simonsson, Mexico conceded the first-ever goal in a FIFA World Cup, scored by France's Lucien Laurent in 1930.

HIGHEST SCORES

The highest-scoring game in the FIFA World Cup finals was the quarter-final between Austria and Switzerland on 26 June 1954. Austria staged a remarkable comeback to win 7-5, with centre-forward **Theodor Wagner** scoring a hat-trick, after trailing 3-0 in the 19th minute. Three other games have produced 11 goals – Brazil's 6-5 win over Poland in the 1938 first round, Hungary's 8-3 win over West Germany in their 1954 group game and the Hungarians' 10-1 rout of El Salvador at the group stage in 1982.

LOW-SCORING SPAIN

Spain won the 2010 FIFA World Cup despite scoring just eight goals in seven games on their way to the title – fewer than any world champions in history, including 11-goal Italy in 1934, England in 1966 and Brazil in 1994. Vicente del Bosque's Spain were also the first team to win 1-0 in all four of their knockout matches. David Villa scored the decisive goal in two of those matches.

GENEROUS OPPONENTS

Germany were the first team to benefit from an opponent scoring an own goal at a FIFA World Cup – Switzerland's Ernst Loertscher put the ball into his own net during Germany's 4–2 win at the 1938 tournament. Germany, or West Germany, have been gifted a record-equalling four own goals in FIFA World Cup history – level with Italy. Mexico, Bulgaria, the Netherlands, Yugoslavia, Portugal and South Korea have all scored two FIFA World Cup own goals apiece – the most recent being perpetrated by Park Chu-Young, in South Korea's 4–1 defeat to Argentina in 2010, three days after Denmark's Daniel Agger gave the Netherlands the lead in another first-round match.

GAGGIA

BALLOT

ZERO TOLERANCE

Paraguay's 0-0 draw and subsequent **penalty shoot-out win** over Japan in the second round at the 2010 FIFA World Cup made it seven goalless draws at the one tournament – equalling the stalemate record set in both 1982 and 2006. Andres Iniesta's late winner for Spain against the Netherlands in the 2010 final meant Brazil against Italy in 1994 is still the only FIFA World Cup final to remain goalless.

THE FASTEST GOAL

Turkey's **Hakan Sukur** holds the record for the quickest goal scored in the FIFA World Cup finals. He netted after 11 seconds against South Korea in the 2002 third-place play-off. Turkey went on to win 3-2. The previous record was held by Vaclav Masek of Czechoslovakia, who struck after 15 seconds against Mexico in 1962.

BIGGEST FIFA WORLD CUP™ FINALS WINS

Hungary 10, El Salvador 1 (15 June 1982)
Hungary 9, South Korea 0 (17 June 1954)
Yugoslavia 9, Zaire 0 (18 June 1974)
Sweden 8, Cuba 0 (12 June 1938)
Uruguay 8, Bolivia 0 (2 July 1950)
Germany 8, Saudi Arabia 0 (1 June 2002)

MOST GOALS IN ONE FIFA WORLD CUP™

Goals	Country	Year
27	Hungary	1954
25	West Germany	1954
23	France	1958
22	Brazil	1950
19	Brazil	1970

MOST GOALS IN FIFA WORLD CUP™ FINALS (MINIMUM 100)

1	Brazil	210
2	Germany/W Germany	206
3	Italy	126
4	Argentina	123

MOST AND LEAST

The most goals scored in a single FIFA World Cup finals tournament is 171, in France in 1998, after FIFA extended the competition to 32 teams and 64 matches for the first time. The highest number of goals per match was recorded in the 1954 finals, with 140 goals in just 26 games at an average of 5.38 goals per game. The lowest average per game came in Italy in 1990, when 115 goals were scored in 52 matches, an average of 2.21 goals per game. The 2010 FIFA World Cup saw 145 goals – at an average of 2.26 per game.

YOUNGEST AND OLDEST

The youngest-ever scorer of a goal in FIFA World Cup finals history is **Pele.** He was 17 years and 239 days old when he notched Brazil's winner against Wales in the 1958 quarter-finals. Cameroon's **Roger Milla** – aged 42 years and 39 days – became the oldest scorer when he netted his country's only goal in a 6-1 defeat by Russia in 1994.

GOING FOR GOLD

Four different players were tied as top scorer at the 2010 FIFA World Cup, but for the first time, the adidas Golden Boot prize was awarded to only one after being decided on goals set up as well as goals scored. Uruguay's Diego Forlan, Spain's David Villa and the Netherlands' Wesley Sneijder missed out on the award, which went instead to Germany's 20-year-old **Thomas Muller.** Like them, he had scored five times, but had also contributed more assists – three, compared with one apiece for Villa, Sneijder and Forlan. Villa received the adidas Silver Boot, because he made his contributions in fewer minutes on the pitch (634) than adidas Bronze Boot recipient Sneijder (652) or Forlan (654).

COMING BACK FOR MORE

Seven footballers have scored goals at FIFA World Cup tournaments 12 years apart, the latest being Mexico's Cuauhtemoc Blanco. His successful penalty against France, in Polokwane in 2010, came a dozen years after his first FIFA World Cup goal, against Belgium, in 1998. Others to have scored across a similar time-span are Brazil's Pele (1958–1970), West Germany's Uwe Seeler (1958–1970), Argentina's Diego Maradona (1982–1994), Denmark's Michael Laudrup (1986–1998), Sweden's Henrik Larsson (1994–2006) and Saudi Arabia's Sami Al-Jaber (1994–2006).

HEAD FOR FIGURES

Arjen Robben's emphatic header against Uruguay, to put the Netherlands 3-1 up in their 3-2 semi-final win at the 2010 FIFA World Cup, was the 2,200th goal ever scored in the competition. **Andres Iniesta**'s winning goal for Spain in that summer's final took the overall FIFA World Cup tally to 2,208.

ROSSI THE ITALY HERO

Paolo Rossi turned from villain to hero as Italy won the 1982 FIFA World Cup. Coach Enzo Bearzot had picked Rossi even though he had only just completed a two-year suspension after a match-fixing scandal. Rossi was criticized for a lack of fitness in the early matches, but he scored a hat-trick against Brazil, two goals as Italy beat Poland in the semi-final, and the opener in their FIFA World Cup final victory over West Germany.

EUSEBIO THE STRIKE FORCE

Portugal's **Eusebio** was the striking star of the 1966 FIFA World Cup finals. Ironically, he would not be eligible to play for Portugal now. He was born in Mozambique, then a Portuguese colony, but now an independent country. He finished top scorer with nine goals, including two as Portugal eliminated champions Brazil and four as they beat North Korea 5-3 in the quarter-finals after trailing 3-0.

FIFA WORLD CUP™ FINALS TOP SCORERS (1930–78)

Maximum 16 teams in finals

Year	Venue	Top Scorer	Country	Goals
1930	Uruguay	Guillermo Stabile	Argentina	8
1934	Italy	Oldrich Nejedly	Czechoslovakia	5
1938	France	Leonidas	Brazil	7
1950	Brazil	Ademir	Brazil	9
1954	Switzerland	Sandor Kocsis	Hungary	11
1958	Sweden	Just Fontaine	France	13
1962	Chile	Garrincha	Brazil	4
		Vava	Brazil	
		Leonel Sanchez	Chile	
		Florian Albert	Hungary	
		Valentin Ivanov	Soviet Union	
		Drazen Jerkovic	Yugoslavia	
1966	England	Eusebio	Portugal	9
1970	Mexico	Gerd Muller	West Germany	10
1974	West Germany	Grzegorz Lato	Poland	7
1978	Argentina	Mario Kempes	Argentina	6

KEMPES MAKES HIS MARK

Mario Kempes was Argentina's only foreign-based player in the hosts' squad at the 1978 finals. Twice top scorer in the Spanish league, Valencia's Kempes was crucial to Argentina's success. Coach Cesar Luis Menotti told him to shave off his moustache after he failed to score in the group games. Kempes then netted two against Peru, two more against Poland, and two decisive goals in the final against the Netherlands.

NO GUARANTEES FOR TOP SCORERS

Topping the FIFA World Cup finals scoring chart is a great honour for all strikers, but few have gained the ultimate prize and been leading scorer. Argentina's Guillermo Stabile started the luckless trend in 1930, topping the scoring charts but finishing up on the losing side in the final. The list of top scorers who have played in the winning side is small: Garrincha and Vava (joint top scorers in 1962), Mario Kempes (top scorer in 1978), Paolo Rossi (1982) and Ronaldo (2002). Gerd Muller, top scorer in 1970, gained his reward as West Germany's trophy winner four years later. Other top scorers, such as Sandor Kocsis, 1954, Just Fontaine, 1958, and Gary Lineker, 1986, have been disappointed in the final stages. Kocsis was the only one to reach the final – and Hungary were defeated. Four players finished tied on five goals at the 2010 FIFA World Cup and one – David Villa – collected a winner's medal, but the Golden Boot went to Germany's Thomas Muller.

STABILE MAKES AN IMPACT

Guillermo Stabile, top scorer in the 1930 FIFA World Cup finals, had never played for Argentina before the tournament. He made his debut – as a 25-year-old – against Mexico because first-choice Roberto Cherro had suffered a panic attack. He netted a hat-trick then scored twice against both Chile and the United States as Argentina reached the final. He struck one of his side's goals in the 4-2 defeat by Uruguay in the final.

SCORING SKIPPERS

Both captains scored when the Netherlands beat Uruguay in their Cape Town semi-final at the 2010 FIFA World Cup in South Africa – **Giovanni van Bronckhorst** for the Dutch, Diego Forlan for Uruguay. This had happened only four times before in FIFA World Cup history.

HURST MAKES HISTORY

England's **Geoff Hurst** became the first and to date only player to score a hat-trick in a FIFA World Cup final when he netted three in the hosts' 4-2 victory over West Germany in 1966. Hurst headed England level after the Germans took an early lead, then scored the decisive third goal with a shot that bounced down off the crossbar and just over the line, according to the Soviet linesman. Hurst hit his third in the last minute. The British TV commentator Kenneth Wolstenholme described Hurst's strike famously with the words: "Some people are on the pitch ... They think it's all over ... It is now!"

TWO OUT OF 10

Only two players wearing the iconic No. 10 shirt have won the Golden Boot at FIFA World Cup finals: Argentina's Mario Kempes in 1978 and England's Gary Lineker eight years later. Dutch No. 10 Wesley Sneijder was in the running for the prize in 2010, but finished second behind Germany's No. 13 Thomas Muller.

ANDRES THE GIANT

Spain's hero in the 2010 FIFA World Cup final was **Andres Iniesta** (right), whose 116th-minute goal was also the latest trophy-winning strike in the tournament's history – not counting penalty shoot-outs, that is.

FIFA WORLD CUP™ FINALS ALL–TIME LEADING GOALSCORERS

	Name	Country	Tournaments	Goals
1	Ronaldo	Brazil	1998, 2002, 2006	15
2	Gerd Muller	West Germany	1970, 1974	14
=	Miroslav Klose	Germany	2002, 2006, 2010	14
3	Just Fontaine	France	1958	13
4	Pele	Brazil	1958, 1962, 1966, 1970	12
5	Sandor Kocsis	Hungary	1954	11
=	Jurgen Klinsmann	W Germany/Germany	1990, 1994, 1998	11
7	Gabriel Batistuta	Argentina	1994, 1998, 2002	10
=	Teofilo Cubillas	Peru	1970, 1978	10
=	Gregorz Lato	Poland	1974, 1978, 1982	10
=	Gary Lineker	England	1986, 1990	10
=	Helmut Rahn	West Germany	1954, 1958	10

THE BRADLEY BUNCH

Michael Bradley's late equalizer for the United States, in their Group C 2-2 draw with Slovenia in June 2010, made him the first person to score a FIFA World Cup goal for a team coached by his own father – in this case, Bob Bradley.

THE GREAT GONZALO

Argentina striker **Gonzalo Higuain** ended an eight-year wait for a FIFA World Cup hat-trick when he scored three in his team's 4-1 victory over South Korea in the first round of the 2010 tournament. The 2006 FIFA World Cup was the only one without a single hat-trick, making Higuain's treble the first for eight years and seven days – since Pauleta scored three in Portugal's 4-0 trouncing of Poland at the 2002 tournament.

PELE SO UNLUCKY

Pele would surely have been the all-time FIFA World Cup top scorer but for injuries. He was sidelined early in the 1962 finals, and again four years later. He scored six goals in Brazil's 1958 triumph, including two in the 5-2 final victory over Sweden. He also netted Brazil's 100th FIFA World Cup goal as they beat Italy 4-1 in the 1970 final.

MULLER'S SCORING HABIT

West Germany's **Gerd Muller** had the knack of scoring in important games. He struck the winner against England in the 1970 quarter-final and his two goals in extra-time against Italy almost carried his side to the final. Four years later, Muller's goal against Poland ensured that West Germany reached the final on home soil. Then he scored the winning goal against the Netherlands in the FIFA World Cup final. He also had a goal disallowed for offside – wrongly, as TV replays proved.

RONALDO SO CONSISTENT

Ronaldo was a consistent scorer in the three FIFA World Cup finals tournaments he played in. He netted four times in 1998, when they were runners-up to France, eight as Brazil won the 2002 tournament – including both goals in the final – and three more in 2006. He became the all-time top scorer when netting Brazil's opener in a 3-0 win over Ghana in the last-16 round at Dortmund on 27 June 2006. As a teenager, Ronaldo had been a member of Brazil's FIFA World Cup winning squad in the United States in 1994, but did not play.

KLINSMANN'S CONTRIBUTION

Jurgen Klinsmann has been an influential force at the FIFA World Cup both as a player and a coach. He scored three goals when West Germany won the FIFA World Cup in 1990, five more – for a unified Germany – in the 1994 finals, and three in 1998. He then coached Germany to the semi-finals in 2006.

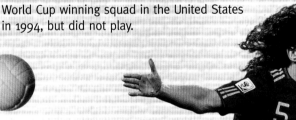

THE POWER OF 73

The goals that proved to be decisive in both semi-finals at the 2010 FIFA World Cup were each scored in the 73rd minute: Arjen Robben's header in the Netherlands' 3–2 win over Uruguay, and **Carles Puyol's** header – the only goal of the game – for Spain against Germany the following evening.

WHO SCORED THE FIRST HAT-TRICK?

For many years, Argentina's Guillermo Stabile was considered the first hat-trick scorer in the FIFA World Cup finals. He netted three in Argentina's 6-3 win over Mexico on 19 July 1930, but has since been superseded by Bert Patenaude of the United States. FIFA changed its records in November 2006, to acknowledge that Patenaude's treble two days earlier, in the Americans' 3-0 win over Paraguay, had been the tournament's first hat-trick.

FIFA WORLD CUP APPEARANCES

Two players, Mexico's Antonio Carbajal and Germany's Lothar Matthaus, have appeared in a record five FIFA World Cup™ final tournaments, but for many players, appearing just once in football's ultimate event is cause enough for dreams. The following pages chart individual appearance records at football's premier competition, from the longest to the shortest, to the greatest time elapsed between FIFA World Cup™ appearances.

YOUNGEST AND OLDEST

Northern Ireland forward Norman Whiteside became the then youngest player to appear in the FIFA World Cup finals when he started against Yugoslavia in 1982, aged just 17 years and 41 days. The oldest player to feature in the tournament was Cameroon forward Roger Milla, who faced Russia in 1994 aged 42 years and 39 days.

THIS IS ENGLAND

England's Premier League (including Chelsea and England's **Frank Lampard**) was the best-represented domestic league at the 2010 FIFA World Cup, with 117 of the 32 squads' 736 players appearing in that competition. Germany's Bundesliga had 84 players, Italy's Serie A 80, Spain's Primera Liga 59, France's Ligue 1 45, the Netherlands' Eredivisie 34 and Japan's J-League 25.

MOST APPEARANCES IN FIFA WORLD CUP™ FINALS

25 Lothar Matthaus (West Germany/ Germany)
23 Paolo Maldini (Italy)
21 Diego Maradona (Argentina)
   Uwe Seeler (West Germany)
   Wladyslaw Zmuda (Poland)

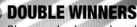

DOUBLE WINNERS

Players who have played on the winning side in two FIFA World Cup finals:

Giovanni Ferrari (Italy), 1934, 1938
Giuseppe Meazza (Italy), 1934, 1938
Pele (Brazil), 1958, 1970
Didi (Brazil), 1958, 1962
Djalma Santos (Brazil), 1958, 1962
Garrincha (Brazil), 1958, 1962
Gilmar (Brazil), 1958, 1962
Nilton Santos (Brazil), 1958, 1962
Vava (Brazil), 1958, 1962
Zagallo (Brazil), 1958, 1962
Zito (Brazil), 1958, 1962
Cafu (Brazil), 1994, 2002

THE "DOUBLE" CHAMPIONS

Franz Beckenbauer and Mario Zagallo are a unique duo. They have both won the FIFA World Cup as a player and a coach. Beckenbauer also had the distinction of captaining West Germany to victory on home soil in 1974. As coach, he steered them to the final in Mexico in 1986 and to victory over Argentina in Italy four years later. He was nicknamed "Der Kaiser" (The Emperor) both for his style and his achievements. Zagallo gained two winners' medals as a player. He was the left-winger in Brazil's triumphant march to the 1958 championship, before playing a deeper role in their 1962 victory. He took over from the controversial Joao Saldanha as Brazil coach three months before the 1970 finals and guided the side to victory in all six of its games, scoring 19 goals and routing Italy 4-1 in the final. Zagallo later filled the role of the team's technical director when Brazil won the FIFA World Cup for a fourth time in 1994.

MOST FIFA WORLD CUP™ FINALS TOURNAMENTS

These players all played in at least four FIFA World Cup finals tournaments.

5   **Antonio Carbajal** (Mexico) 1950, 1954, 1958, 1962, 1966
    Lothar Matthaus (West Germany/Germany) 1982, 1986, 1990, 1994, 1998
4   **Djalma Santos** (Brazil) 1954, 1958, 1962, 1966
    Pele (Brazil) 1958, 1962, 1966, 1970
    Uwe Seeler (West Germany) 1958, 1962, 1966, 1970
    Karl-Heinz Schnellinger (West Germany) 1958, 1962, 1966, 1970
    Gianni Rivera (Italy) 1962, 1966, 1970, 1974
    Pedro Rocha (Uruguay) 1962, 1966, 1970, 1974
    Wladyslaw Zmuda (Poland) 1974, 1978, 1982, 1986
    Giuseppe Bergomi (Italy) 1982, 1986, 1990, 1998
    Diego Maradona (Argentina) 1982, 1986, 1990, 1994
    Enzo Scifo (Belgium) 1986, 1990, 1994, 1998
    Franky van der Elst (Belgium) 1986, 1990, 1994, 1998
    Andoni Zubizarreta (Spain) 1986, 1990, 1994, 1998
    Paolo Maldini (Italy) 1990, 1994, 1998, 2002
    Hong Myung-Bo (South Korea) 1990, 1994, 1998, 2002
    Cafu (Brazil) 1994, 1998, 2002, 2006
    Sami Al-Jaber (Saudi Arabia) 1994, 1998, 2002, 2006
    Denis Caniza (Paraguay) 1998, 2002, 2006, 2010
    Fabio Cannavaro (Italy) 1998, 2002, 2006, 2010
    Thierry Henry (France) 1998, 2002, 2006, 2010
    Rigobert Song (Cameroon) 1994, 1998, 2002, 2010

HOME IS IN CATALONIA

Spanish champions **Barcelona** had more players at the 2010 FIFA World Cup than any other club, with 14 – eight for Spain, including new signing David Villa, with reserve goalkeeper Victor Valdes being the only one not to play. English clubs Chelsea and Liverpool had 12 players apiece in South Africa for the tournament, followed by 11 from Germany's Bayern Munich.

DOUBLE DUTCH, DOUBLE WHAMMY

Arjen Robben and Mark van Bommel suffered an unusual double whammy in the 2009–10 season: they ended on the losing side in both the UEFA Champions League final, for Bayern Munich against Internazionale, and the FIFA World Cup final, for the Netherlands against Spain. Others who have endured similar fates are Oliver Neuville, Bernd Schneider and Carsten Ramelow (for Bayer Leverkusen against Real Madrid, and Germany against Brazil, in 2002) and Thierry Henry (for Arsenal against Barcelona, and France against Italy, in 2006).

IT'S THE SAME OLD SONG

Cameroon's veteran defender **Rigobert Song** played just 17 minutes of the 2010 FIFA World Cup in South Africa, but it did make him the first African to play at four editions of the tournament – nine matches, stretching across 16 years and nine days. He featured in 1994, 1998, 2002 and 2010 – missing the 2006 event because Cameroon failed to qualify. Only three players have enjoyed longer FIFA World Cup careers: Mexicans Antonio Carbajal (spanning 16 years and 25 days) and Hugo Sanchez (16 years, 17 days) and Germany's Lothar Matthaus (16 years, 14 days). Other players for whom the 2010 tournament was their fourth FIFA World Cup were Italy's Fabio Cannavaro (taking his total appearances to 18), France's Thierry Henry (14) and Paraguay's Denis Caniza (10).

MOST FIFA WORLD CUP™ FINALS MATCHES (BY POSITION)

Goalkeeper: Claudio Taffarel (Brazil, 18 matches)
Defence: Cafu (Brazil, 20); Wladyslaw Zmuda (Poland, 21); Fabio Cannavaro (Italy, 18); Paolo Maldini (Italy, 23)
Midfielders: Grzegorz Lato (Poland, 20); Lothar Matthaus (West Germany/Germany, 25); Wolfgang Overath (West Germany, 19); Enzo Scifo (Belgium, 17)
Forwards: Diego Maradona (Argentina, 21); Uwe Seeler (West Germany, 21)

PROSINECKI'S SCORING RECORD

Robert Prosinecki is the only player to have scored for different countries in FIFA World Cup finals tournaments. He netted for Yugoslavia in their 4-1 win over the United Arab Emirates in the 1990 tournament. Eight years later, following the break-up of the old Yugoslavia, he scored for Croatia in their 3-0 group-game win over Jamaica, and then netted the first goal in his side's 2-1 third-place play-off victory over the Netherlands.

QUICKEST SUBSTITUTIONS

The three fastest substitutions in the history of the FIFA World Cup finals have all come in the fourth minute. In each case the player substituted was so seriously injured that he took no further part in the tournament: Steve Hodge came on for Bryan Robson in England's 0-0 draw with Morocco in 1986; Giuseppe Bergomi replaced Alessandro Nesta in Italy's 2-1 win over Austria in 1998; and Peter Crouch subbed for Michael Owen in England's 2-2 draw with Sweden in 2006.

UNHAPPY ENDINGS

For the second FIFA World Cup final in a row, the climactic match of the 2010 tournament featured a footballer not only playing his last international, but the final game of his career. Like Zinedine Zidane in 2006, **Giovanni van Bronckhorst** didn't complete the game four years later – though, unlike the Frenchman, he wasn't sent off but substituted, in the 105th minute. Dutch captain van Bronckhorst had scored a spectacular goal in the 2010 semi-final victory against Uruguay, but finished on the losing side in the final against Spain.

SIMUNIC'S THREE-CARD MATCH

Croatia's Josip Simunic shares (with Ray Richards of Australia in 1974) the record for collecting the most yellow cards in one match at the FIFA World Cup finals – three. He received three yellows against Australia in 2006 before he was sent off by English referee Graham Poll. When Poll showed Simunic his second yellow, he forgot he had already booked him.

LEADING CAPTAINS

Three players have each captained their teams in two FIFA World Cup finals – Diego Maradona of Argentina, Dunga of Brazil and West Germany's Karl-Heinz Rummenigge. Maradona lifted the trophy in 1986, but was a loser four years later. Dunga was the winning skipper in 1994, but was on the losing side in 1998. Rummenigge was a loser on both occasions, in 1982 and 1986. Maradona has made the most appearances as captain at the FIFA World Cup finals, leading out Argentina 16 times between 1986 and 1994.

FASTEST RED CARDS IN THE FIFA WORLD CUP™ FINALS

1 min Jose Batista (Uruguay) v Scotland, 1986
8 min Giorgio Ferrini (Italy) v Chile, 1962
14 min Zeze Procopio (Brazil) v Czechoslovakia, 1938
19 min Mohammed Al Khlaiwi (Saudi Arabia) v France, 1998
Miguel Bossio (Uruguay) v Denmark, 1986
21 min Gianluca Pagliuca (Italy) v Rep of Ireland, 1994

FASTEST YELLOW CARDS IN THE FIFA WORLD CUP™ FINALS

1 min Sergei Gorlukovich (Russia) v Sweden, 1994
Giampiero Marini (Italy) v Poland, 1982
2 min Jesus Arellano (Mexico) v Italy, 2002
Henri Camara (Senegal) v Uruguay, 2002
Michael Emenalo (Nigeria) v Italy, 1994
Humberto Suazo (Chile) v Switzerland, 2010
Mark van Bommel (Netherlands) v Port., 2006

DENILSON STEPS UP FROM THE BENCH

Brazil winger **Denilson** has made the most substitute appearances at the FIFA World Cup finals – 11. He was involved in 12 of Brazil's games at the 1998 and 2002 finals, but started only one, against Norway in 1998. He was a half-time substitute for Leonardo in the 1998 final and came on for Ronaldo in stoppage time of the 2002 final (his last appearance in the finals), when Brazil beat Germany 2-0.

FIRST ELEVEN

In an age of squad numbers, **Brazil** may have pleased some traditionalists when fielding players wearing shirt numbers one to 11 in the starting line-ups for their first two games of the 2010 FIFA World Cup, against North Korea and the Ivory Coast. Kicking off for coach Dunga on each occasion were: 1 Julio Cesar, 2 Maicon, 3 Lucio, 4 Juan, 5 Felipe Melo, 6 Michel Bastos, 7 Elano, 8 Gilberto Silva, 9 Luis Fabiano, 10 Kaka and 11 Robinho. **the Netherlands** managed a similar starting structure for not only their second-round tie against Slovakia, but the final against Spain: 1 Maarten Stekelenburg, 2 Gregory van der Wiel, 3 Johnny Heitinga, 4 Joris Mathijsen, 5 Giovanni van Bronckhorst, 6 Mark van Bommel, 7 Dirk Kuyt, 8 Nigel de Jong, 9 Robin van Persie, 10 Wesley Sneijder and 11 Arjen Robben. Both Brazil and the Netherlands came close to the same feat when they met in the quarter-finals, though both featured a number 13 – Brazil's Dani Alves, in place of 7 Elano, and the Netherlands' Andre Ooijer instead of 4 Joris Mathijsen (Elano and Mathijsen were unavailable through injury).

⚽ **YOUNGEST PLAYERS IN FIFA WORLD CUP™ FINAL**
Pele (Brazil) – 17 years, 249 days, in 1958
Giuseppe Bergomi (Italy) – 18 years, 201 days, in 1982
Ruben Moran (Uruguay) – 19 years, 344 days, in 1950

⚽ **OLDEST PLAYERS IN FIFA WORLD CUP™ FINAL**
Dino Zoff (Italy) – 40 years, 133 days, in 1982
Gunnar Gren (Sweden) – 37 years, 241 days, in 1958
Jan Jongbloed (Netherlands) – 37 years, 212 days, in 1978
Nilton Santos (Brazil) – 37 years, 32 days, in 1962

⚽ **PUZACH THE FIRST SUB**
The first substitute in FIFA World Cup finals history was Anatoli Puzach of the Soviet Union. He replaced Viktor Serebrianikov at half-time of the Soviets' 0–0 draw with hosts Mexico on 31 May 1970. The 1970 tournament was the first in which substitutes were allowed, with two permitted for each side. FIFA increased this to three per team for the

⚽ **FOUR AND OUT**
The most players sent off in one FIFA World Cup finals game is four. Costinha and Deco of Portugal and Khalid Boulahrouz and Gio van Bronckhorst of the Netherlands were sent off by Russian referee Valentin Ivanov in their second-round match in Germany in 2006.

⚽ **CANIGGIA – SENT OFF, WHILE ON THE BENCH…**
Claudio Caniggia of Argentina became the first player to be sent off from the substitutes' bench, during the match against Sweden in 2002. Caniggia was dismissed in first-half stoppage time for dissent towards UAE referee Ali Bujsaim. Caniggia carried on protesting after the referee warned him to keep quiet, so Bujsaim showed him a red card.

⚽ **MALDINI'S MINUTES RECORD**
Lothar Matthaus of West Germany/Germany has started the most FIFA World Cup finals matches – 25. But Italy defender **Paolo Maldini** (left) has stayed on the field for longer, despite starting two games fewer. Maldini played for 2,220 minutes, Matthaus for 2,052. According to the stopwatch, the top four are completed by Uwe Seeler of West Germany, who played for 1,980 minutes, and Argentina's Diego Maradona, who played for 1,938.

⚽ **SHOOT–OUT SAVIOURS**
West Germany's Harald "Toni" Schumacher and Sergio Goycochea of Argentina hold the record for the most penalty shoot-out saves in the finals – four each. Schumacher's saves came over two tournaments – in 1982 and 1986, including the decisive stop in the 1982 semi-final against France. Goycochea made his crucial saves in 1990, first in Argentina's quarter-final win over Yugoslavia and then against Italy to take his team to the final. His four shoot-out saves in one tournament is also a record. The record for the most shoot-out saves in one game is held by Portugal goalkeeper Ricardo. He saved three times to knock out England in the quarter-finals of the 2006 FIFA World Cup.

⚽ **UNBEATEN GOALKEEPERS IN THE FIFA WORLD CUP™ FINALS***

Walter Zenga (Italy)	517 minutes without conceding a goal, 1990
Peter Shilton (England)	502 minutes, 1986–90
Sepp Maier (W Germany)	475 minutes, 1974–78
Gianluigi Buffon (Italy)	460 minutes, 2006
Emerson Leao (Brazil)	458 minutes, 1978
Gordon Banks (England)	442 minutes, 1966

* Pascal Zuberbuhler did not concede a goal in all 390 minutes played by Switzerland in the 2006 FIFA World Cup. Iker Casillas of Spain completed 433 minutes without conceding a goal in 2010.

IKER'S REPEAT PERFORMANCE

Spain's **Iker Casillas** became only the third goalkeeper to save two FIFA World Cup penalties – aside from shoot-outs – and the first to spread them across different tournaments. First he pushed away Ian Harte's spot-kick in a second-round tie against the Republic of Ireland in 2002. Even more impressive was how he caught Paraguayan forward Oscar Cardozo's effort in their 2010 quarter-final. Spain went on to win both matches. The two goalkeepers who had enjoyed such double success before were Poland's Jan Tomaszewski in 1974 and the United States' Brad Friedel in 2002.

NOT THINKING OUTSIDE THE BOX

Italy's Gianluca Pagliuca was the first goalkeeper to be sent off at a FIFA World Cup match when he was dismissed for handball outside his penalty area after 21 minutes against Norway at Giants Stadium, New York, in 1994. Despite sacrificing playmaker Roberto Baggio for goalkeeper Luca Marchegiani, Italy still won 1-0.

ITALY'S ELDER STATESMAN

Dino Zoff became both the oldest player and oldest captain to win the FIFA World Cup when his Italian side lifted the trophy in Spain in 1982. He was 40 years and 133 days old at the time. Alongside him in the team was defender Giuseppe Bergomi, aged 18 years and 201 days, a difference of 21 years and 297 days.

FIVE-STAR CARBAJAL

Antonio Carbajal, of Mexico, is one of only two men to have appeared at five FIFA World Cup finals – the other was Germany's versatile Lothar Matthaus. Carbajal, who played in 1950, 1954, 1958, 1962 and 1966, conceded a record 25 goals in his 11 FIFA World Cup finals appearances – the same number let in by Saudi Arabia's Mohamed Al-Deayea across ten games in 1994, 1998 and 2002. Al-Deayea was a member of the Saudi squad for the 2006 tournament but did not play.

HUMBLE ORIGINS

As recently as 1978, English club Wigan Athletic were playing non-league football in the country's fifth tier. Yet by 2010 they were not only in the top-flight English Premier League, but had two of their players facing each other at that year's FIFA World Cup in South Africa. Even more unusually, Ghana's **Richard Kingson** and Serbia's **Vladimir Stojkovic** were both goalkeepers – and had both spent the season as reserves to Wigan's first-choice Chris Kirkland. Kingson emerged triumphant from the two countries' first-round clash, keeping a clean sheet as Ghana won 1-0.

NUMBER-ONE NUMBER ONES

The Lev Yashin Award was introduced in 1994 for the man voted best goalkeeper of the FIFA World Cup – though a goalkeeper has been picked for an all-star team at the end of every tournament dating back to 1930. The all-star team was expanded from 11 to 23 players in 1998, allowing room for more than one goalkeeper, but returned to 11 players in 2010. Players who were picked for the all-star teams but missed out on the Lev Yashin Award were Paraguay's Jose Luis Chilavert in 1998, Turkey's Rustu Recber in 2002, and Germany's Jens Lehmann and Portugal's Ricardo in 2006. The first Lev Yashin Award was presented to Belgium's Michel Preud'homme, even though he only played four games, conceding four goals, at the 1994 competition – his side were edged out 3-2 by Germany in the second round. Legendary Soviet goalkeeper Lev Yashin, after whom the trophy is named, played in the 1958, 1962 and 1966 FIFA World Cups and was a member of his country's 1970 squad as third-choice keeper and assistant coach – although he was never chosen for a FIFA World Cup team of the tournament. Yashin conceded the only FIFA World Cup finals goal scored directly from a corner-kick, taken by Colombia's Marcos Coll during a 4-4 draw in 1962.

OLIVER'S ARMS

Germany's **Oliver Kahn** is the only goalkeeper to have been voted FIFA's Player of the Tournament, winning the award at the 2002 FIFA World Cup – despite taking a share of the blame for Brazil's winning goals in the final.

RIGHT WAY FOR RICARDO

Spain's Ricardo Zamora became the first man to save a penalty in a FIFA World Cup finals match, stopping Valdemar de Brito's spot-kick for Brazil in 1934. Spain went on to win 3-1.

BROTHERS IN ARMS

Brothers Viktor and Viacheslav Chanov were two of the three goalkeepers in the Soviet Union's 1982 FIFA World Cup squad, but first-choice Rinat Dasayev was preferred to them both throughout. Viktor, eight years younger than Vyacheslav, did make one appearance at the 1986 FIFA World Cup four years later and ended his career with 21 caps. Vyacheslav had to wait until 1984 for his first and only international appearance.

LEADING FROM THE BACK

Iker Casillas became the third goalkeeper to captain his country to FIFA World Cup glory, when Spain became champions in South Africa in 2010. He emulated Italians Gianpiero Combi (in 1934) and Dino Zoff (1982). Casillas was also the first man to lift the trophy after his side had lost their opening match of the tournament.

UNLUCKY BREAK

Goalkeeper Frantisek Planicka broke his arm during Czechoslovakia's 1938 second-round clash against Brazil, but played on, even though the game went to extra-time before ending in a 1-1 draw. Not surprisingly, given the extent of his injury, Planicka missed the replay two days later, which the Czechs lost 2-1, and the goalkeeper of the 1938 FIFA World Cup never added to his tally of 73 caps.

PLAYERS VOTED BEST GOALKEEPER OF THE TOURNAMENT

1930	Enrique Ballestrero (Uruguay)		1978	Ubaldo Fillol (Argentina)
1934	Ricardo Zamora (Spain)		1982	Dino Zoff (Italy)
1938	Frantisek Planicka (Czechoslovakia)		1986	Harald Schumacher (West Germany)
1950	Roque Maspoli (Uruguay)		1990	Sergio Goycoechea (Argentina)
1954	Gyula Grosics (Hungary)		1994	Michel Preud'homme (Belgium)
1958	Harry Gregg (Northern Ireland)		1998	Fabien Barthez (France)
1962	Viliam Schrojf (Czechoslovakia)		2002	Oliver Kahn (Germany)
1966	Gordon Banks (England)		2006	Gianluigi Buffon (Italy)
1970	Ladislao Mazurkiewicz (Uruguay)		2010	Iker Casillas (Spain)
1974	Jan Tomaszewski (Poland)			

BATTERING RAMON

Argentina's 6-0 win over Peru at the 1978 FIFA World Cup aroused suspicion because the hosts needed to win by four goals to reach the final at the expense of arch-rivals Brazil – and Peruvian goalkeeper Ramon Quiroga had been born in Argentina. He insisted, though, that his saves prevented the defeat from being even more embarrassingly emphatic. Earlier in the same tournament, Quiroga had been booked for a foul on Grzegorz Lato after running into the Polish half of the field.

KHUNE LOSES HIS COOL

Host nation South Africa's **Itumeleng Khune** became only the second goalkeeper to be sent off at a FIFA World Cup when he was red-carded during their 3-0 defeat to Uruguay in the 2010 first round. He was penalized for a professional foul on Luis Suarez, also conceding a penalty at the same time. Khune, 22, had been one of the team's best performers in the opening game of the tournament, a 1-1 draw with Mexico.

MORE AND MORA

Luis Ricardo Guevara Mora holds the unenviable record for most goals conceded in just one FIFA World Cup finals match. The 20-year-old had to pick the ball out of the net ten times in El Salvador's thrashing by Hungary in 1982 – and his team-mates managed only one goal of their own in reply. In this game he also set the record for being the youngest goalkeeper to participate in the FIFA World Cup finals.

TONY AWARD

United States goalkeeper **Tony Meola** left the national team after the 1994 FIFA World Cup because he wanted to switch sports and take up American football instead. He failed to make it in gridiron and returned to soccer, but did not play for his country again until 1999. He retired for a second time after reaching a century of international appearances and still holds the record for being the youngest FIFA World Cup captain, having worn the armband for the US's 5-1 defeat to Czechoslovakia in 1990, aged 21 years 316 days.

THREE'S COMPANY

Both Czechoslovakia and Belgium used all three of their goalkeepers at the 1982 FIFA World Cup in Spain – Zdenek Hruska, Stanislav Seman and Karel Stromsik for the Czechs, and Jean-Marie Pfaff, Theo Custers and Jacques Munaron for the Belgians.

PUTTING THE LOVE IN GLOVE

For the third time since it was first handed out five FIFA World Cups ago, the 2010 Golden Glove prize went to the man between the sticks for the newly crowned world champions. Spain captain **Iker Casillas** received the award as best goalkeeper in South Africa, adding it to a winner's medal just as Italy's Gianluigi Buffon had in 2006 and France's Fabien Barthez had in 1998. Casillas's exploits included saving a penalty by catching the ball, in the quarter-final win over Paraguay. He celebrated winning the final by giving a passionate on-air kiss to his TV presenter girlfriend **Sara Carbonero**. Perhaps they were kissing and making up – she had appeared to criticize Casillas when interviewing him in the immediate aftermath of Spain's first game of the competition, a surprise 1-0 defeat to Switzerland.

TOP GOALS

1930	70	(3.89 per match)
1934	70	(4.12 per match)
1938	84	(4.67 per match)
1950	88	(4 per match)
1954	140	(5.38 per match)
1958	126	(3.6 per match)
1962	89	(2.78 per match)
1966	89	(2.78 per match)
1970	95	(2.97 per match)
1974	97	(2.55 per match)
1978	102	(2.68 per match)
1982	146	(2.81 per match)
1986	132	(2.54 per match)
1990	115	(2.21 per match)
1994	141	(2.71 per match)
1998	171	(2.67 per match)
2002	161	(2.52 per match)
2006	147	(2.3 per match)
2010	145	(2.27 per match)
Total	**2,208**	**(2.86 per match)**

THE PETER PRINCIPLE

Peter Shilton became the oldest FIFA World Cup captain when he led England for their 1990 third-place play-off against hosts Italy. He was 40 years and 292 days old as he made his 125th and final appearance for his country – though his day was spoiled by a 2-1 defeat, including a goalkeeping error that gifted Roberto Baggio Italy's opener. Shilton, born in Leicester on 18 September 1949, also played for England at the 1982 and 1986 tournaments. He became captain in Mexico in 1986 after Bryan Robson was ruled out of the tournament by injury and Ray Wilkins by suspension, and featured in one of the FIFA World Cup's all-time memorable moments, when he was out-jumped by Argentina's Diego Maradona for the infamous "Hand of God" goal. Shilton jointly holds the record for most FIFA World Cup clean sheets, with ten – along with France's Fabien Barthez, who played at the 1998, 2002 and 2006 tournaments. Both men made 17 FIFA World Cup finals appearances apiece.

TRADING PLACES

The first goalkeeper to be substituted at a FIFA World Cup was Romania's Stere Adamache, who was replaced by Rica Raducanu 27 minutes into a 3-2 defeat to Brazil in 1970. Romania were 2-0 down at the time.

PLAYING THROUGH THE PAIN BARRIER

The first FIFA World Cup clean sheet was kept by Jimmy Douglas of the United States in a 3-0 win over Belgium in 1930. He followed that up with another, as Paraguay were beaten by the same scoreline – but Argentina proved too good, winning 6-1 in the semi-final. Douglas injured his knee after only four minutes, but had to play on as this occurred in the days before substitutes were allowed.

JAMES (ALMOST) THE FIRST

When England coach Fabio Capello made the late decision to start with Robert Green in goal for their opening match of the 2010 FIFA World Cup against the USA, it looked like back-up shot-stopper **David James** might set an unenviable record – that of being the first player to go to three different FIFA World Cups without seeing any action. James had been an unused reserve goalkeeper at both the 2002 and 2006 tournaments. However, Green's error when allowing Clint Dempsey's equalizer to slip through his hands in the 1-1 draw meant James was called into the England team for their next match against Algeria – and he retained his place for the subsequent group match against Slovenia as well as the round of 16 tie against Germany. Not only was James the oldest player at the 2010 competition but also he became the oldest-ever FIFA World Cup debutant, aged 39 years and 221 days, and he kept a clean sheet in a goalless draw against the Algerians. Nine days later came his final game of the summer – the 4-1 second-round defeat to Germany that also proved to be the last of his 53 England appearances.

FIFA MANAGERS
WORLD CUP™

PERSONAL EXPERIENCE

Eight managers at the 2010 FIFA World Cup had previous World Cup experience as a player: Mexico's Javier Aguirre, Brazil's **Dunga**, New Zealand's Ricki Herbert, Denmark's Morten Olsen, South Korea's Huh Jung-Moo, Argentina's **Diego Maradona**, Slovakia's former Czechoslovakia international Vladimir Weiss and England's Italian coach Fabio Capello. Both Maradona and Dunga had won the trophy, not just as players but as captains, while Maradona and Aguirre had both been red-carded at a FIFA World Cup – Maradona against Brazil in 1982, Aguirre against West Germany four years later.

YOUNG JUAN

Juan Jose Tramutola remains the youngest-ever FIFA World Cup coach, leading Argentina in the 1930 tournament at the age of 27 years and 267 days. Italian Cesare Maldini became the oldest in 2002, taking charge of Paraguay when aged 70 years and 131 days.

DREAM ELEVEN

Luiz Felipe Scolari managed a record 11 FIFA World Cup finals wins in a row, across the 2002 tournament, when he was in charge of Brazil, and 2006, when coach of Portugal. That winning run extends to 12 games if one counts Portugal's victory over England in the 2006 quarter-final, though that was on penalties after a goalless draw.

PUFF DADDIES

The coaches of the two sides appearing at the 1978 FIFA World Cup final were such prolific smokers that an oversized ashtray was produced for Argentina's Cesar Luis Menotti and the Netherlands's Ernst Happel so they could share it on the touchline.

SOCCER SIX

Only one man has gone to six FIFA World Cups as coach: Brazilian **Carlos Alberto Parreira**, whose greatest moment came when he guided Brazil to the trophy for the fourth time in 1994. His second stint as Brazil coach was less successful – they fell in the quarter-finals in 2006. Parreira also led Kuwait (1982), the United Arab Emirates (1990), Saudi Arabia (1998) and hosts South Africa (2010) at the finals. He had stepped down as South Africa coach in April 2008, for family reasons, but returned late the following year. Parreira was once sacked midway through a FIFA World Cup. In 1998 he led Saudi Arabia for the first two of their three games – losing 1-0 to Denmark and 4-0 to France – before receiving his marching orders.

ELDEST STATESMAN OTTO

Otto Rehhagel was not only the oldest coach at the 2010 FIFA World Cup, but the oldest in the competition's history. The German was 71 years 317 days old when his Greece team played their third and final game of the tournament, a 2-0 defeat to Argentina.

CRASHING BORA

Only one tournament behind record-holder Carlos Alberto Parreira, **Bora Milutinovic** has coached at five different FIFA World Cups – with a different country each time, two of them being the hosts. As well as Mexico in 1986 and the United States in 1994, he led Costa Rica in 1990, Nigeria in 1998 and China in 2002. He reached the knockout stages with every country except China – who failed to score a single goal.

DIVIDED LOYALTIES

No coach has won the FIFA World Cup in charge of a foreign country, but several have found themselves taking on their homelands in the FIFA World Cup. These include Brazilian 1958 FIFA World Cup-winning midfielder Didi, whose Peru side lost 4-2 to his home country in 1970. Sven-Goran Eriksson was England coach for their 1-1 draw against his native Sweden in 2002, the same year Frenchman Bruno Metsu led Senegal to a 1-0 opening-match win over France. Former Yugoslavia goalkeeper Blagoje Vidinic endured the most bittersweet moment – he coached Zaire to their first and only FIFA World Cup in 1974, and then had to watch his adopted players lose 9-0 to Yugoslavia.

FIFA WORLD CUP™ – WINNING COACHES

1930	Alberto Suppici
1934	Vittorio Pozzo
1938	Vittorio Pozzo
1950	Juan Lopez
1954	Sepp Herberger
1958	Vicente Feola
1962	Aymore Moreira
1966	Alf Ramsey
1970	Mario Zagallo
1974	Helmut Schon
1978	Cesar Luis Menotti
1982	Enzo Bearzot
1986	Carlos Bilardo
1990	Franz Beckenbauer
1994	Carlos Alberto Parreira
1998	Aime Jacquet
2002	Luiz Felipe Scolari
2006	Marcello Lippi
2010	Vicente del Bosque

SCHON SHINES

West Germany's **Helmut Schon** was coach for more FIFA World Cup matches than any other man – 25, across the 1966, 1970, 1974 and 1978 tournaments. He has also won the most games as a coach, 16 in all – including the 1974 final against the Netherlands. The 1974 tournament was third time lucky for Schon. He he had taken West Germany to second place in 1966 and to third in 1970. Before taking charge of the national side, Schon had worked as an assistant to Sepp Herberger, coach of West Germany's 1954 FIFA World Cup-winning team – Schon was coach of the then-independent Saarland regional side at the time. Dog-lover Schon, born in Dresden on 15 September 1915, scored 17 goals in 16 internationals for Germany between 1937 and 1941. He succeeded Herberger in 1964 and spent 14 years in charge of his country. He was the only coach to win both the FIFA World Cup (1974) and the European Championship (1972).

FIFA WORLD CUP™ REFEREEING

⚽ YEARS OF EXPERIENCE

Spain's Juan Gardeazabal Garay remains the youngest man to referee at a FIFA World Cup, being just 24 years 193 days old when he took charge at the 1958 tournament in Sweden. He also officiated in 1962 and 1966. Englishman George Reader is not only the oldest man to have refereed a FIFA World Cup final – 56 years 236 days old when he ran the effective climax between Brazil and Uruguay in 1950 – but also the oldest referee at any FIFA World Cup. He died on 13 July 1978, exactly 48 years to the day since the very first FIFA World Cup fixture.

⚽ COLLECTIVE RESPONSIBILITY

Two referees originally picked to officiate at the 2010 FIFA World Cup were unfortunate enough to be withdrawn on the eve of the tournament – not for their own errors, but because of their assistants. Algeria's **Mohamed Benouza** and Paraguay's **Carlos Amarilla** were both told the bad news a fortnight before the big kick-off when their compatriot assistant referees failed pre-tournament fitness tests. At least Amarilla had the comfort of having already refereed at the 2006 FIFA World Cup.

⚽ DOUBLE DUTY

Only two men have refereed a FIFA World Cup final and a European Championship final. Italian Sergio Gonella officiated at the 1978 World Cup final between Argentina and the Netherlands, two years after overseeing the European Championship final between West Germany and Czechoslovakia. Swiss official Gottfried Dienst took control of the 1966 FIFA World Cup final, between England and West Germany, and the drawn 1968 European Championship final between Italy and Yugoslavia – Spain's Jose Maria Ortiz de Mendibil was awarded the replay.

BAKU OF THE NET

The official who signalled that Geoff Hurst's controversial extra-time goal for England in the 1966 FIFA World Cup final had crossed the line is often wrongly described as a Russian linesman. In fact, Tofik Bakhramov was from Azerbaijan, so he was officially a Soviet Union linesman. The Azeri national football stadium, in the capital Baku, is now named after him.

⚽ FRENCH CONNECTION

Frenchman **Georges Capdeville**, in charge for Italy's win over Hungary in 1938, is the only man to referee the final in a FIFA World Cup hosted by his own country.

⚽ FIFA WORLD CUP™ FINAL REFEREES

1930	Jean Langenus (Belgium)
1934	Ivan Eklind (Sweden)
1938	Georges Capdeville (France)
1950	George Reader (England)
1954	William Ling (England)
1958	Maurice Guigue (France)
1962	Nikolay Latyshev (USSR)
1966	Gottfried Dienst (Switzerland)
1970	Rudi Glockner (West Germany)
1974	Jack Taylor (England)
1978	Sergio Gonella (Italy)
1982	Arnaldo Cezar Coelho (Brazil)
1986	Romualdo Arppi Filho (Brazil)
1990	Edgardo Codesal (Mexico)
1994	Sandor Puhl (Hungary)
1998	Said Belqola (Morocco)
2002	Pierluigi Collina (Italy)
2006	Horacio Elizondo (Argentina)
2010	Howard Webb (England)

COUPE DU MONDE 1938

WORLDWIDE WEBB

Former Yorkshire policeman **Howard Webb** became the fourth Englishman to referee a
FIFA World Cup final when he was chosen for the 2010 showdown between Spain and the
Netherlands. He had earlier controlled two group games and a second-round tie between
Spain and Chile. The honour came less than two months after he refereed the UEFA
Champions League final between Inter Milan and Bayern Munich, making him the first man
in charge of both World Cup and European Cup final matches in the same summer. Webb
also became the first FIFA World Cup debutant ref to be given the final. At just three days
short of his 39th birthday, Webb was also the youngest FIFA World Cup final referee since
Frenchman Georges Capdeville, who took charge of the 1938 final aged 38 years and
232 days. Even younger was Swedish 28-year-old Ivan Eklind, in 1934.

PROLIFIC OFFICIALS

No referees have run more FIFA World Cup matches than Joel Quiniou and
Benito Archundia. Frenchman Quiniou took charge of eight games across the
1986, 1990 and 1994 tournaments. In the last of these, he became the first
man to referee four matches in one FIFA World Cup – including Italy's semi-
final victory over Bulgaria. Since then, others have officiated in even more
matches in a single FIFA World Cup: Mexico's Archundia and Argentina's
Horacio Elizondo each controlled five games in 2006, as did Uzbekistan's
Ravshan Irmatov in 2010. Elizondo was referee for both the first and final
matches in 2006, emulating the feat of English referee George Reader in
1950. Elizondo's memorable moments included a red card for Zinedine
Zidane following the French star's headbutt on Marco Materazzi in the
2006 final, a red card for England's Wayne Rooney for stamping on Portugal's
Ricardo Carvalho in their quarter-final that summer, and a yellow card for Ghana's Asamoah
Gyan, for taking a penalty against the Czech Republic too quickly. Gyan then missed his
second attempt. After five games in 2006, Archundia was given responsibility for three
matches in 2010 – including the third-place play-off between Germany and Uruguay.

TIME, GENTLEMEN

Welsh referee Clive Thomas disallowed what would have
potentially been a winning goal by Brazil against Sweden
in the 1978 FIFA World Cup. Thomas said he had blown
the final whistle seconds before Zico headed in from a
corner, and the game ended in a 1-1 draw. In contrast,
Israeli referee Abraham Klein tried to blow the final whistle
several times when England played Brazil at the 1970
FIFA World Cup in Guadalajara, but none of the players
appeared to hear him.

NETTO'S NET

Soviet captain Igor Netto persuaded Italian referee Cesare
Jonni to disallow a goal for his own team at the 1962 FIFA
World Cup, pointing out that Igor Chislenko had shot wide
– the ball entered the Uruguayan goal through a hole in
the net. His side still won the first-round match, 2-1.

RED CARD CARTER

Mexican referee **Arturo Brizio Carter** has sent off more players
at FIFA World Cups than any other official. He showed seven
red cards in the six games he controlled at the 1994 and 1998
tournaments – with "victims" including Italy's Gianfranco Zola,
Argentina's Ariel Ortega and France's Zinedine Zidane. His
collection of red cards includes four at the one tournament,
in 1994 – a tally matched by fellow Mexican Felipe Ramos in
2002 and both Russia's Valentin Ivanov and England's Graham
Poll in 2006. France's Joel Quiniou spread six red cards across
the 1986, 1990 and 1994 tournaments while Guatemala's Carlos
Batres showed five in total, in 2002, 2006 and 2010.

ADVANCE BOOKING

Two players have been booked within a minute of kick-off – Italy's Giampiero Marini, against Poland, in 1982, and Russia's Sergei Gorlukovich against Sweden 12 years later. But Uruguayan Jose Batista went one worse in a 1986 first-round match against Scotland, receiving a red card after just 56 seconds for a gruesome foul on Gordon Strachan. His team-mates held on for a goalless draw.

NOT LEADING BY EXAMPLE

The first man to be sent off at a FIFA World Cup was Peru's Placido Galindo, at the first tournament in 1930 during a 3-1 defeat to Romania. Chilean referee Alberto Warnken dismissed the Peruvian captain for fighting.

REPEAT OFFENDERS

France's **Zinedine Zidane** and Brazil's **Cafu** are both FIFA World Cup winners – and both notched up a record six FIFA World Cup cards, though Cafu escaped any reds, while Zidane was sent off twice. Most famously, Zidane was dismissed for headbutting Italy's Marco Materazzi in extra-time of the 2006 final in Berlin – the final match of the Frenchman's career. He had also been sent off during a first-round match against Saudi Arabia in 1998, but returned from suspension in time to help France win the trophy with a sensational two-goal performance in the final. The only other man to have been sent off twice at two different FIFA World Cups is Cameroon's Rigobert Song. When dismissed against Brazil in 1994, he became the FIFA World Cup's youngest red card offender – aged just 17 years and 358 days. He saw red for the second time against Chile in 1998.

VERY EARLY BATHS

Quickfire offenders at the 2010 FIFA World Cup included Algerian striker Abdelkader Ghezzal, booked within a minute of coming on as a substitute against Slovakia and sent off after 15 minutes for his second yellow. Uruguay's young playmaker **Nicolas Lodeiro** lasted just 16 minutes as a substitute against France before becoming the first dismissal of the tournament – receiving one booking for kicking the ball away and a second for a late lunge on Bacary Sagna. But it was Brazilian superstar Kaka – a former FIFA World Footballer of the Year – who left the least time between his first and second yellow cards in one match. He was first booked 85 minutes into a first-round match against the Ivory Coast, before a second yellow – and inevitable red – just three minutes later.

CARDS CLOSE TO CHEST

Only one group in FIFA World Cup finals history has featured no bookings at all – Group 4 in 1970, featuring West Germany, Peru, Bulgaria and Morocco. In contrast, the 2006 FIFA World Cup in Germany was the worst for both red and yellow cards, with 28 dismissals and 345 bookings in 64 matches.

FIFA WORLD CUP™ RED CARDS, BY TOURNAMENT

1930	1
1934	1
1938	4
1950	0
1954	3
1958	3
1962	6
1966	5
1970	0
1974	5
1978	3
1982	5
1986	8
1990	16
1994	15
1998	22
2002	17
2006	28
2010	17

FINAL COUNT

Before 14 yellow cards were shown in the 2010 FIFA World Cup final, the previous 18 finals had featured 40 bookings between them – an average of 2.2 per game. The 15 cards flourished by 2010 final referee Howard Webb – 14 yellows and one red – were nine more than those shown by previous record-holder Romualdo Arppi Filho, who "awarded" Argentina four and West Germany two yellows in the 1986 final.

SOLE CHANCE OF GLORY

India withdrew from the 1950 FIFA World Cup because some of their players wanted to play barefoot but FIFA insisted all players must wear football boots. India have not qualified for the tournament since.

BREAKING COVER

Zaire defender Mwepu Llunga was booked for running out of the wall and kicking the ball away as Brazil prepared to take a free-kick, at the 1974 FIFA World Cup. Romanian referee Nicolae Rainea ignored Llunga's pleas of innocence.

GOOD SON, BAD SON

Cameroon's Andre Kana-Biyik served two suspensions during the 1990 FIFA World Cup. The first came after he was sent off in the opening match against Argentina – six minutes before his brother Francois Omam-Biyik scored the only goal. His second ban came after yellow cards in the final group game against Russia and in the second-round defeat of Colombia.

YELLOW MELO'S RED MIST

Felipe Melo's red card for stamping on Arjen Robben, in Brazil's 2010 FIFA World Cup quarter-final defeat to the Netherlands, means Brazil have now had more players sent off in FIFA World Cup history than any other team – one more than Argentina. Melo was Brazil's 11th dismissal, after Kaka had become the 10th in a first-round victory over the Ivory Coast. Melo could also have gone down as the first player ever to score an own goal and be sent off in the same FIFA World Cup match, but the first Dutch goal was later officially awarded to their own playmaker Wesley Sneijder.

ALL'S FAIR

FIFA World Cup organizers hailed an improvement in fair play between the 2006 tournament in Germany and the event in South Africa four years later. Not only were red cards down from 28 to 17, but also injuries which could be blamed on fouls were reduced from 40 per cent to 16 per cent. There were 260 yellow cards shown in 2010 – down from the all-time record of 345 in 2006 – and eight of those were second yellow cards. Three of those eight (Aleksandar Lukovic of Serbia, **Kaka** of Brazil and Johnny Heitinga of the Netherlands) also received a yellow card in one other match they played.

ELBOWED OUT

Italian defender Mauro Tassotti was given an unprecedented eight-game ban for smashing Spain's Luis Enrique in the face with his elbow in 1994 – an offence missed by match referee Sandor Puhl. Spain lost 2-1 and were further enraged when the Hungarian official was then selected to referee the final.

CAPACITY PLANNING

If current plans are realized and every seat is occupied, the attendances at the finals of the next three FIFA World Cups will be 76,525 at the **Maracanã** in Rio de Janeiro, Brazil, in 2014; 89,368 at the Luzhniki in Moscow, Russia, four years later; and 86,250 at the **Lusail Iconic Stadium** in Lusail, Qatar, in 2022. The smallest proposed capacities at the next three tournaments are 41,375 at Curitina's Arena da Baixada in 2014, 43,702 at the Rostov-on-Don stadium in 2018 and 43,520 at the new Qatar University Stadium in Doha in 2022. FIFA regulations these days insist that any venue staging a FIFA World Cup match must have a capacity of at least 40,000.

TWO'S COMPANY, 300'S A CROWD

The 300 people who were recorded as watching Romania beat Peru 3-1 in 1930 formed the FIFA World Cup finals' smallest attendance, with plenty of room for manoeuvre inside the Estadio Pocitos in Montevideo. A day earlier, ten times as many people are thought to have been there to watch France's 4-1 win over Mexico.

SOUTH AFRICAN SUCCESS

The 2010 FIFA World Cup in South Africa was watched by a total of 3,178,856 spectators, across the 64 matches in 10 different stadiums – the third-highest aggregate attendance in the tournament's history, behind the United States in 1994 and Germany in 2006. The average attendance was 49,670 and though some concerns were raised about patches of empty seats at several games, organizers said they were happy that 92.9 per cent of places were filled.

CITY SLICKER

The capacity of South Africa's 2010 FIFA World Cup showpiece venue, **Soccer City** in Johannesburg, was increased from 78,000 to 84,490. The design of the newly revamped stadium was based on traditional African pottery and nicknamed the Calabash. Soccer City hosted both the opening game and the final – as well as four more first-round fixtures, a second-round clash and a quarter-final.

GENDER EQUALITY

Only two stadiums have hosted the finals of the FIFA World Cup for both men and women. The Rose Bowl, in Pasadena, California, was the venue for the men's final in 1994 – when Brazil beat Italy – and the women's showdown between the victorious US and China five years later, which was watched by 90,185 people. But Sweden's Rasunda Stadium, near Stockholm, just about got there first – though it endured a long wait between the men's final in 1958 and the women's in 1995. Both sets of American spectators got their money's worth, watching games that went into extra-time and which were settled on penalties.

FIFA WORLD CUP™ FINAL ATTENDANCES

Year	Attendance	Stadium	City
1930	93,000	Estadio Centenario	Montevideo
1934	45,000	Stadio Nazionale del PNF	Rome
1938	60,000	Stade Olympique de Colombes	Paris
1950	174,000	Estadio do Maracana	Rio de Janeiro
1954	60,000	Wankdorfstadion	Berne
1958	51,800	Rasunda Fotbollstadion	Solna
1962	68,679	Estadio Nacional	Santiago
1966	98,000	Wembley Stadium	London
1970	107,412	Estadio Azteca	Mexico City
1974	75,200	Olympiastadion	Munich
1978	71,483	Estadio Monumental	Buenos Aires
1982	90,000	Estadio Santiago Bernabeu	Madrid
1986	114,600	Estadio Azteca	Mexico City
1990	73,603	Stadio Olimpico	Rome
1994	94,194	Rose Bowl	Pasadena
1998	80,000	Stade de France	Paris
2002	69,029	International Stadium	Yokohama
2006	69,000	Olympiastadion	Berlin
2010	84,490	Soccer City	Johannesburg

TOURNAMENT ATTENDANCES

Year	Total	Average
1930	434,500	24,139
1934	358,000	21,059
1938	376,000	20,889
1950	1,043,500	47,432
1954	889,500	34,212
1958	919,580	26,274
1962	899,074	28,096
1966	1,635,000	51,094
1970	1,603,975	50,124
1974	1,768,152	46,530
1978	1,546,151	40,688
1982	2,109,723	40,572
1986	2,393,331	46,026
1990	2,516,348	48,391
1994	3,587,538	68,991
1998	2,785,100	43,517
2002	2,705,197	42,269
2006	3,359,439	52,491
2010	3,178,856	49,670
TOTAL	34,108,964	44,182

FAN FESTS FIND FAVOUR

After city centre **"Fan Fests"**, including giant TV screens and food stalls, proved popular at the 2006 FIFA World Cup in Germany, they were staged again in 2010 – not only across South African cities (such as **Durban**, below), but also elsewhere in the world including Rio in Brazil, Rome in Italy, Paris in France and Sydney in Australia. A total of 6,151,823 people visited the Fan Fests for the tournament's 64 games, including 2,634,018 across South Africa and 3,517,805 abroad. German capital Berlin attracted the biggest crowd, with 350,000 flocking to the Fan Fest there to watch Germany's semi-final defeat to Spain.

ABSENT FRIENDS

Only 2,823 spectators turned up at the Rasunda Stadium in Stockholm to see Wales play Hungary in a first-round play-off match during the 1958 FIFA World Cup. More than 15,000 had attended the first game between the two sides, but boycotted the replay in tribute to executed Hungarian uprising leader Imre Nagy.

MORBID MARACANA

The largest attendance for a FIFA World Cup match was at Rio de Janeiro's Maracana for the last clash of the 1950 tournament – though no one is quite sure how many were there. The final tally was officially given as 174,000, though some estimates suggest as many as 210,000 witnessed the host country's traumatic defeat. Tensions were so high at the final whistle, winning Uruguay captain Obdulio Varela was not awarded the trophy in a traditional manner, but had it surreptitiously nudged into his hands. FIFA president Jules Rimet described the crowd's overwhelming silence as "morbid, almost too difficult to bear". Uruguay's triumphant players barricaded themselves inside their dressing room for several hours before they judged it safe enough to emerge. Those spectators, however many there were, were the last to see Brazil play in an all-white kit – the unlucky colours were scrapped and, after a competition was held to find a new national strip, were replaced by the now-familiar yellow and blue.

FIFA STADIUMS & HOSTS

WORLD CUP™

BERLIN CALL

Despite later becoming the capital of a united Germany, then-divided Berlin only hosted three group games at the 1974 FIFA World Cup in West Germany – the host country's surprise loss to East Germany took place in Hamburg. An unexploded World War Two bomb was discovered beneath the seats at Berlin's Olympiastadion in 2002, by workers preparing the ground for the 2006 tournament. Germany, along with Brazil, had applied to host the tournament in 1942, before it was cancelled due to the outbreak of World War Two.

TWIN PEAKS

Five stadiums have the distinction of staging both the final of a FIFA World Cup and the Summer Olympics athletics: Berlin's Olympiastadion (1936 Olympics, 2006 FIFA World Cup); London's Wembley (1948 Olympics, 1966 FIFA World Cup); Rome's Stadio Olimpico (1960 Olympics, 1990 FIFA World Cup); Mexico City's Azteca (1968 Olympics, 1970 and 1986 FIFA World Cups); and Munich's Olympiastadion (1972 Olympics, 1974 FIFA World Cup). The Rose Bowl in Pasadena, California, hosted both the final of the 1994 FIFA World Cup and the 1984 Olympics football tournament, but not the main Olympics track-and-field events.

OLYMPIC NAMES

The stadium hosting the opening match of the 1930 FIFA World Cup had stands named after great Uruguayan footballing triumphs: Colombes, in honour of the 1924 Paris Olympics venue; Amsterdam, after the site where that title was retained four years later; and Montevideo, even though it would be another fortnight before the home team clinched the first FIFA World Cup in their own capital city.

RIO'S MARIO

Most people know Brazil's largest stadium as the Maracana, named after the Rio neighbourhood and a small nearby river. But, since the mid-1960s, the official title has actually been "Estadio Jornalista Mario Filho", after a Brazilian journalist who had helped in the campaign for the stadium to be built.

TERRITORIAL GAINS

History was made twice over when **FIFA** decided in December 2010 which countries would stage the 2018 and 2022 FIFA World Cups. The 2018 vote went in favour of Russia – ahead of Spain/Portugal, Belgium/Netherlands and England – meaning the first FIFA World Cup to be held in Eastern Europe. The tournament will then go to the Middle East for the first time in 2022, after Qatar emerged ahead of rival bids from the USA, Japan, South Korea and Australia.

MEXICAN SAVE

Mexico was not the original choice to host the 1986 FIFA World Cup, but stepped in when Colombia withdrew in 1982 due to financial problems. Mexico held on to the staging rights despite suffering from an earthquake in September 1985 that left approximately 10,000 people dead, but which left the stadiums unscathed. FIFA kept faith in the country, and the **Azteca Stadium** went on to become the first venue to host two FIFA World Cup final matches – and Mexico the first country to stage two FIFA World Cups. The Azteca – formally named the "Estadio Guillermo Canedo", after a Mexican football official – was built in 1960 using 100,000 tonnes of concrete, four times as much as was needed for the old Wembley.

ARCHITECTS' PREROGATIVE

Distinctive and creative elements were added to the stadiums built especially for the 2010 FIFA World Cup in South Africa, including the giraffe-shaped towers at **Nelspruit's Mbombela stadium**, the 350-metre-long arch and rope-swing soaring above **Durban's main arena**, and the white "petals" shrouding the Nelson Mandela Bay stadium in Port Elizabeth.

DIFFERENT DRUMS

An authentic and distinctive South African souvenir was taken home by each player named man of the match at the 2010 FIFA World Cup. The Budweiser-sponsored prize was designed by South African graduate Jonathan Fundudis and based on the design of the traditional African "djembe" drum. Dutch playmaker Wesley Sneijder collected four of the awards, more than any other player. Japan's Keisuke Honda, Portugal's Cristiano Ronaldo, Uruguay's **Diego Forlan** and Spain's Andres Iniesta collected the prize three times each. Iniesta's haul included the honour of being voted the best player of the final against the Netherlands.

UNSUCCESSFUL HOSTING BIDS

1930	Hungary, Italy, Netherlands, Spain, Sweden
1934	Sweden
1938	Argentina, Germany
1950	None
1954	None
1958	None
1962	Argentina, West Germany
1966	Spain, West Germany
1970	Argentina
1974	Spain
1978	Mexico
1982	West Germany
1986	Colombia*, Canada, USA
1990	England, Greece, USSR
1994	Brazil, Morocco
1998	Morocco, Switzerland
2002	Mexico
2006	Brazil, England, Morocco, South Africa
2010	Egypt, Libya/Tunisia, Morocco
2014	None
2018	England, Netherlands/Belgium, Spain/Portugal
2022	Australia, Japan, South Korea, USA

* Colombia won hosting rights for 1986 but later withdrew.

BREAKING THE CODE

Not all the stadiums at the 2010 FIFA World Cup were entirely new constructions – several were old-fashioned mainly rugby venues given enough of a facelift to cope with the new football-led demand. These included Johannesburg's Ellis Park and Pretoria's **Loftus Versfeld**. The Pretoria arena is the usual home ground of popular rugby team the Blue Bulls, though they did play a pre-FIFA World Cup game at Johannesburg's showpiece Soccer City stadium. Soccer City also staged an August 2010 rugby international between the Springboks of South Africa and the All-Blacks of New Zealand.

HOSTS WITH THE MOST

No other single-hosted FIFA World Cup has used as many venues as the 14 spread across Spain in 1982. The 2002 tournament was played at 20 different venues, but ten of these were in Japan and ten in co-host country South Korea.

FIFA WORLD CUP™ PENALTIES

FIFA WORLD CUP™ PENALTY SHOOT-OUTS

Year	Round	120-minute Score	Winners	Shoot-out Score
1982	Semi-final	West Germany 3 France 3	West Germany	5-4
1986	Quarter-final	West Germany 0 Mexico 0	West Germany	4-1
1986	Quarter-final	France 1 Brazil 1	France	4-3
1986	Quarter-final	Belgium 1 Spain 1	Belgium	5-4
1990	Second round	Republic of Ireland 0 Romania 0	Republic of Ireland	5-4
1990	Quarter-final	Argentina 0 Yugoslavia 0	Argentina	3-2
1990	Semi-final	Argentina 1 Italy 1	Argentina	4-3
1990	Semi-final	West Germany 1 England 1	West Germany	4-3
1994	Second round	Bulgaria 1 Mexico 1	Bulgaria	3-1
1994	Quarter-final	Sweden 2 Romania 2	Sweden	5-4
1994	Final	Brazil 0 Italy 0	Brazil	3-2
1998	Second round	Argentina 2 England 2	Argentina	4-3
1998	Quarter-final	France 0 Italy 0	France	4-3
1998	Semi-final	Brazil 1 Netherlands 1	Brazil	4-2
2002	Second round	Spain 1 Republic of Ireland 1	Spain	3-2
2002	Quarter-final	South Korea 0 Spain 0	South Korea	5-3
2006	Second round	Ukraine 0 Switzerland 0	Ukraine	3-0
2006	Quarter-final	Germany 1 Argentina 1	Germany	4-2
2006	Quarter-final	Portugal 0 England 0	Portugal	3-1
2006	Final	Italy 1 France 1	Italy	5-3
2010	Second round	Paraguay 0 Japan 0	Paraguay	5-3
2010	Quarter-final	Uruguay 1 Ghana 1	Uruguay	4-2

TAKING THE FIFTH

Paraguay's 5-3 victory on penalties over Japan, following a goalless draw in their 2010 second-round match, made them the seventh team to score as many as five spot-kicks in a FIFA World Cup shoot-out. They followed West Germany against France in 1982, Belgium against Spain in 1986, the Republic of Ireland against Romania in 1990, Sweden against Romania in 1994, South Korea against Spain in 2002 and Italy against France in the 2006 final. West Germany and Sweden also missed one apiece in their respective shoot-outs.

FIRST IS BEST

Paraguay's defeat of Japan and **Diego Forlan** and Uruguay's win against Ghana in 2010 mean seven straight FIFA World Cup penalty shoot-outs have been won by the team taking the first kick. The last side to go second and win was Spain, against the Republic of Ireland in 2002.

WOE FOR ASAMOAH

Ghana striker **Asamoah Gyan** is the only player to have missed two penalties during match-time at FIFA World Cups. He hit the post with a spot-kick against the Czech Republic during a group game at the 2006 tournament, then struck a shot against the bar with the final kick of extra-time in Ghana's 2010 quarter-final versus Uruguay. Had he scored then, Gyan would have given Ghana a 2–1 win – following Luis Suarez's goal-stopping handball on the goal-line – and a first African place in a FIFA World Cup semi-final. Despite such a traumatic miss, Gyan did then step up to take Ghana's first penalty in the shoot-out, again striking it high – but this time into the back of the net. His team still lost, though, 4–2 on penalties.

FRENCH KICKS

The first penalty shoot-out at a FIFA World Cup finals came in the 1982 semi-final in Seville between West Germany and France, when French takers Didier Six and **Maxime Bossis** were the unfortunate players to miss. The same two countries met in the semi-finals four years later – and West Germany again won, though in normal time, 2-0. The record for most shoot-outs is shared by the 1990 and 2006 tournaments, with four apiece. Both semi-finals in 1990 went to penalties, while the 2006 final was the second to be settled that manner – Italy beating France 5-3 after David Trezeguet struck the crossbar.

⚽ CLOSE SAVES

Just two minutes and three seconds separated the two penalties awarded by Guatemalan referee Carlos Batres in the second-round clash between Paraguay and Spain in 2010 – a FIFA World Cup record. Not only were the spot-kicks given at either end of the pitch in Johannesburg's Ellis Park stadium, but both were saved. First, Spanish goalkeeper Iker Casillas caught Oscar Cardozo's attempt, after the Paraguay striker was fouled by Gerard Pique. Then, after striker David Villa was brought down by Antolin Alcaraz, **Justo Villar** palmed away Xabi Alonso's penalty. Alonso actually scored with his attempt, but Batres ordered a retake due to Spanish encroachment in the area. Spain had scored all 14 of their FIFA World Cup penalties going into the 2010 tournament – excluding shoot-outs – but Alonso's miss came just 12 days after David Villa fired a spot-kick wide against Honduras.

⚽ THREE IN ONE

Argentina's stand-in goalkeeper Sergio Goycochea set a tournament record by saving four shoot-out penalties in 1990 – though West Germany's Harald Schumacher managed as many, across the 1982 and 1986 tournaments. Portugal's Ricardo achieved an unprecedented feat by keeping out three attempts in a single shoot-out, becoming an instant hero in his side's quarter-final win over England in 2006.

⚽ THE PLAYERS WHO MISSED IN SHOOT-OUTS

Argentina: Diego Maradona (1990), Pedro Troglio (1990), Hernan Crespo (1998), Roberto Ayala (2006), Esteban Cambiasso (2006)
Brazil: Socrates (1986), Julio Cesar (1986), Marcio Santos (1994)
Bulgaria: Krassimir Balakov (1994)
England: Stuart Pearce (1990), Chris Waddle (1990), Paul Ince (1998), David Batty (1998), Frank Lampard (2006), Steven Gerrard (2006), Jamie Carragher (2006)
France: Didier Six (1982), Maxime Bossis (1982), Michel Platini (1986), Bixente Lizarazu (1998), David Trezeguet (2006)
Germany/West Germany: Uli Stielike (1982)
Ghana: John Mensah (2010), Dominic Adiyiah (2010)
Italy: Roberto Donadoni (1990), Aldo Serena (1990), Franco Baresi (1994), Daniele Massaro (1994), Roberto Baggio (1994), Demetrio Albertini (1998), Luigi Di Biagio (1998)
Japan: Yuichi Komano (2010)
Mexico: Fernando Quirarte (1986), Raul Servin (1986), Alberto Garcia Aspe (1994), Marcelino Bernal (1994), Jorge Rodriguez (1994)
Netherlands: Phillip Cocu (1998), Ronald de Boer (1998)
Portugal: Hugo Viana (2006), Petit (2006)
Republic of Ireland: Matt Holland (2002), David Connolly (2002), Kevin Kilbane (2002)
Romania: Daniel Timofte (1990), Dan Petrescu (1994), Miodrag Belodedici (1994)
Spain: Eloy (1986), Juanfran (2002), Juan Carlos Valeron (2002), Joaquin (2002)
Sweden: Hakan Mild (1994)
Switzerland: Marco Streller (2006), Tranquillo Barnetta (2006), Ricardo Cabanas (2006)
Ukraine: Andriy Shevchenko (2006)
Uruguay: Maximiliano Pereira (2010)
Yugoslavia: Dragan Stojkovic (1990), Dragoljub Brnovic (1990), Faruk Hadzibegic (1990)

⚽ PENALTY SHOOT-OUTS BY COUNTRY

4	Germany/West Germany (4 wins)	1	Belgium (1 win)
4	Argentina (3 wins, 1 defeat)	1	Bulgaria (1 win)
4	France (2 wins, 2 defeats)	1	Paraguay (1 win)
4	Italy (1 win, 3 defeats)	1	Portugal (1 win)
3	Brazil (2 wins, 1 defeat)	1	South Korea (1 win)
3	Spain (1 win, 2 defeats)	1	Sweden (1 win)
3	England (3 defeats)	1	Ukraine (1 win)
2	Republic of Ireland (1 win, 1 defeat)	1	Uruguay (1 win)
		1	Yugoslavia (1 win)
2	Mexico (2 defeats)	1	Ghana (1 defeat)
2	Romania (2 defeats)	1	Netherlands (1 defeat)
		1	Japan (1 defeat)
		1	Switzerland (1 defeat)

⚽ GERMAN EFFICIENCY

Germany, or West Germany, have won all four of their FIFA World Cup penalty shoot-outs, more than any other team. Their run began with a semi-final victory over France in 1982, when goalkeeper Harald Schumacher was the matchwinner, despite being lucky to stay on the pitch for a vicious extra-time foul on France's Patrick Battiston. West Germany also reached the 1990 final thanks to their shoot-out expertise, this time proving superior to England – as they similarly did in the 1996 European Championships semi-final. Germany were better at spot-kicks than Argentina in their 2006 quarter-final, when goalkeeper **Jens Lehmann** consulted a note predicting the direction the Argentine players were likely to shoot towards. The vital information was scribbled on a scrap of hotel notepaper by Germany's chief scout Urs Siegenthaler. The only German national team to lose a major tournament penalty shoot-out were the West Germans, who contested the 1976 European Championships final against Czechoslovakia – their first shoot-out experience, and clearly an effective lesson, as they have not lost a shoot-out since.

THE UEFA European Championship has gone from being a four-team curiosity, snubbed by major nations, to perhaps the third-biggest sporting event on earth, arguably behind only the FIFA World Cup and the Summer Olympic Games. UEFA, the European football confederation, was founded during the 1954 FIFA World Cup in Switzerland and initially set itself the task of creating a championship for national teams. Many of the major European nations – such as Italy, West Germany and England – refused to take part in the initial competition, launched in 1958, because their national associations feared fixture congestion. So the first finals, featuring four nations, were staged in France and saw the Soviet Union end up as first winners after defeating Yugoslavia in the final in Paris's original Parc des Princes.

Now the map of Europe has changed so remarkably that, while UEFA's membership has more than doubled, the Soviet Union and Yugoslavia no longer exist. The Soviets also reached the second finals in 1964 but lost their crown in the final against their Spanish hosts in the Estadio Bernabeu in Madrid. Spain's playmaker Luis Suarez, from Italy's Internazionale, thus became the first player to win the European Championship and the European Cup in the same season.

In the tournament's early years, the qualifying system was based on a simple two-legged knockout system, but this was amended to a group-based format and then, in 1980, the finals were expanded to eight nations. That year saw West Germany win for a second time, having previously triumphed in 1972. In 1996 the unified Germany extended their record to three titles after beating the Czech Republic (formerly half of Czechoslovakia) with an Oliver Bierhoff extra-time golden goal at Wembley. By then the finals had been expanded again to 16 teams.

History was made in 2000 when Belgium and the Netherlands organized the first co-hosted finals. In 2008, Austria and Switzerland were co-hosts, and Spain won their first major international trophy since that 1964 success. This time Fernando Torres was their goal-scoring hero.

Tournament mascots Slavek (left) and Slavko will provide the happy smiling faces of the UEFA European Championship 2012. They are wearing home colours of the co-hosts Poland and Ukraine, respectively.

UEFA EURO 2012 PREVIEW

For the first time, the 2012 UEFA European Championship will be staged in the old Eastern bloc, with Poland and Ukraine sharing hosting rights. The two nations received automatic qualifications for the tournament, and will play their group matches on home soil. Eight venues will be used, four in Poland and four in Ukraine, with the opening match on 8 June in Warsaw and the final in Kiev on 1 July. It has been almost 30 years, however, since the host nation won the tournament, France winning in Paris in 1984.

THE VENUES

Poland and Ukraine share a common border. Below is a map showing the eight cities which will host games in Euro 2012. From Poznan to Donetsk is approximately, 1,000 miles (1,600km).

UKRAINE

Kiev Olympic Stadium (63,195)
Donetsk Donbass Arena (50,055)
Kharkiv Metalist Stadium (38,500)
Lviv New Stadium (30,000)

POLAND

Warsaw National Stadium (53,224)
Poznan Municipal Stadium, (42,004)
Gdansk PGE Arena (40,818)
Wroclaw Municipal Stadium (40,610)

CITIES OF THE FUTURE

Four cities in each of the host nations were initially chosen to stage matches: Warsaw, Gdansk, Poznan and Wroclaw in Poland, and Kyiv, Lviv, Donetsk and Kharkiv in Ukraine. New stadia are being built in six of the cities, in Warsaw, Gdansk, Wroclaw, Kyiv, Lviv and Donetsk, while Those in Poznan and Kharkiv are undergoing major renovation work.

WATCHING WORLD

European governing body UEFA expects about 1.4 million fans, from not just across their continent but all over the world, to pour into the host nations for Euro 2012. The final should be watched by a sell-out 63,000 crowd and followed by a television audience numbering hundreds of millions, in more than 200 countries. Worldwide viewing figures may even exceed the 287 million who watched Spain beat Germany 1–0 in the Euro 2008 final.

EASTERN PROMISE

Neither Poland nor Ukraine have enjoyed much success in the UEFA European Championships. Poland appeared in their only finals in Portugal in 2004, but they did not get beyond the first round group stage. Ukraine has never qualified for a UEFA Euro finals as an independent state, but Ukraine was a part of the Soviet Union. The USSR won the inaugural tournament in 1960 and lost in the final in 1964, 1972 and 1988.

SLAV-A-GO HEROES

The official slogan of the tournament is "Creating History Together", while the two official cartoon mascots have been given the names **Slavek** (left) and **Slavko.**

SHARE AND SHARE ALIKE

The joint hosting venture by Poland and Ukraine emerged as the winner of a lengthy bidding process, seeing off four other challenges by Italy, Croatia/Hungary, Turkey and Greece.

HOSTS WITH THE MOST

The eight venues in the two countries match the number used when the UEFA European Championships were shared in 2000 (Belgium and the Netherlands) and 2008 (Switzerland and Austria). Only UEFA 2004 in Portugal had more venues (10).

SPANISH INQUISITION

After elegantly capturing not only the 2008 European Championship but also the 2010 FIFA World Cup, Spain are expected to go into Euro 2012 as bookies' favourites to retain their crown – especially as star players such as **David Silva**, Fernando Torres and Andres Iniesta will still be in their 20s. But strong challenges are expected from other contenders such as **Joachim Low's** Germany, who took third place at the 2010 FIFA World Cup thanks to the youthful likes of Mesut Ozil and Thomas Muller; that tournament's beaten finalists the Netherlands; and a rejuvenated France, under new coach Laurent Blanc. Other new coaches appointed following the 2010 FIFA World Cup and hoping to make an impression in 2012 include Italy's Cesare Prandelli, Portugal's Paulo Bento and Russia's Dick Advocaat.

UEFA EUROPEAN CHAMPIONSHIP QUALIFIERS

The UEFA European Championship qualifying competition has become a huge event in its own right, with 50 teams having competed for places alongside hosts Austria and Switzerland at Euro 2008. How times have changed. There was one two-legged qualifying round for the 1960 competition, to reduce the 17 entrants to 16, and none for the 1964 tournament, which saw teams meet each other on a home-and-away basis in the first round. A full-scale qualifying competition was first launched for the 1968 finals, with eight groups of four and one group of three. The number of qualifiers increased in size again during the 1990s as several new associations joined UEFA after the break-ups of the Soviet Union and Yugoslavia and entered the championship for the first time.

QUICK TURNOVER

Germany's Joachim Low and Croatia's **Slaven Bilic**  were the only managers among the eight Euro 2008 quarter-finalists still in the same job when Euro 2012 qualifiers began. Spain's Luis Aragones, the Netherlands' Marco van Basten, Portugal's Luiz Felipe Scolari and Italy's Roberto Donadoni all left their jobs after the 2008 tournament. Turkey's Fatih Terim stepped down in October 2009, to be replaced by Guus Hiddink, who had managed Russia in 2008.

IRISH STAGE FIRST QUALIFIER

The first qualifying game in UEFA European Championship history was played on 5 April 1959, when the Republic of Ireland beat Czechoslovakia 2-0 in Dublin. Seventeen teams entered the inaugural competition, so the total had to be reduced to 16 for the first round. The Czechs went through 4-2 on aggregate, after winning the second leg in Bratislava 4-0 on 10 May.

IRISH VICTORY NOT ENOUGH

West Germany's 1-0 defeat by Northern Ireland in Hamburg on 11 November 1983 was their first-ever home loss in the qualifying competition, but their 2-1 win over Albania in Saarbrucken four days later enabled them to pip Northern Ireland on goal difference for a place in the 1984 finals.

BRITS STAY HOME TO QUALIFY

The four British teams used the Home International Championship of 1966–67 and 1967–68 as a qualifying group for the 1968 finals. FIFA World Cup holders England went through but, at their own request, the British teams have been drawn separately for each subsequent qualifying competition.

GERMANS RUN UP 13

Germany's 13-0 win in San Marino on 6 September 2006 was the biggest victory margin in qualifying history. **Lukas Podolski**  (4), Miroslav Klose (2), Bastian Schweinsteiger (2), Thomas Hitzlsperger (2), Michael Ballack, Manuel Friedrich and Bernd Schneider scored the goals. The previous biggest win was Spain's 12-1 rout of Malta in 1983.

EARLY UPHEAVAL

Eye-catching results in the early stages of qualifying for UEFA Euro 2012 included France's 1–0 home defeat by Belarus and Portugal's 4–4 draw with Cyprus, who equalized in the 87th minute through Andreas Avraam. Fabio Capello's England were held to a goalless draw at Wembley by Montenegro, who had been ranked the lowest of the five teams in Group G.

GERMANY'S WEMBLEY WONDER NIGHT

West Germany's greatest-ever team announced their arrival at Wembley on 29 April 1972, when they beat England 3-1 in the first leg of the UEFA European Championship quarter-finals. Uli Hoeness, Gunter Netzer and Gerd Muller scored the goals. West Germany went on to win the trophy, beating the Soviet Union 3-0 in the final. Their team at Wembley was: Sepp Maier; Horst Hottges, Georg Schwarzenbeck, Franz Beckenbauer, Paul Breitner; Jurgen Grabowski, Herbert Wimmer, Gunter Netzer, Uli Hoeness; Sigi Held, Gerd Muller. Eight of them played in West Germany's 1974 FIFA World Cup final win over Holland.

APPEARANCES IN THE FINALS TOURNAMENT

10	West Germany/Germany
9	Soviet Union/CIS/Russia
8	Holland
	Spain
7	Czech Republic/Czechoslovakia
	Denmark
	England
	France
	Italy
5	Portugal
	Yugoslavia
4	Belgium
	Romania
	Sweden
3	Croatia
	Greece
	Switzerland
	Turkey
2	Bulgaria
	Hungary
	Scotland
1	Austria
	Latvia
	Norway
	Poland
	Republic of Ireland
	Slovenia

HEALY POSTS GOAL RECORD

Northern Ireland forward **David Healy** (No.9 – born in Killyleagh on 5 August 1979) set a new scoring record with 13 goals in the Euro 2008 qualifiers. His tally included hat-tricks against Spain and Liechtenstein. Healy beat the previous record of 12 goals, netted by Croatia's Davor Suker in the qualifiers for UEFA Euro 96. Ole Madsen of Denmark scored 11 goals before the finals tournament in 1964, but qualifying groups were not introduced until two years later.

SERBS YOU RIGHT

The UEFA Euro 2012 qualifier between Group C rivals Italy and Serbia on 12 October 2010 was abandoned after just six minute, following disturbances among Serbian supporters in Genoa's Stadio Luigi Ferraris. UEFA later awarded Italy a 3–0 win.

PANCEV FORCED TO MISS OUT

Yugoslavia's **Darko Pancev** (born in Skopje on 7 September 1965) was top scorer in the qualifiers for Euro 1992 with ten goals. Yugoslavia topped qualifying Group Four, but they were banned from the finals because of their country's war in Bosnia, so Pancev never had the chance to shine. After the break-up of the Yugoslav federation, he went on to become the star player for the new nation of Macedonia.

ANDORRA, SAN MARINO STRUGGLE

Minnows Andorra and San Marino each have yet to win a match in the qualifying competition. Andorra have lost all their 30 games, with a goal difference of six against 88. San Marino have lost all their 46 games, with a goal difference of six against 200!

DUTCH EDGE FIRST PLAY-OFF

The first-ever group qualifying play-off was held on 13 December 1995 at Liverpool's Anfield stadium when the Netherlands beat the Republic of Ireland 2-0 to clinch the final place at Euro 96. **Patrick Kluivert** scored both of the Dutch goals.

PORTUGAL SPURN HOME ADVANTAGE

In 2004, Portugal became the first host nation to reach the final since France 20 years earlier. They were also the first hosts to lose the final, going down 1-0 to Greece in Lisbon on 4 July. France (1984) and Spain (1964) had previously become European champions on home soil.

THREE OFF AS CZECHS ADVANCE

Czechoslovakia's 3-1 semi-final win over Holland in Zagreb, on 16 June 1976, featured a record three red cards. The Czechs' Jaroslav Pollak was dismissed for a second yellow card – a foul on Johan Neeskens – after an hour. Neeskens followed in the 76th minute for kicking **Zdenek Nehoda**. Wim van Hanegem became the second Dutchman dismissed, for dissent, after Nehoda scored the Czechs' second goal with six minutes of extra-time left.

DENMARK'S UNEXPECTED TRIUMPH

Denmark were unlikely winners of UEFA Euro 1992. They had not even expected to take part after finishing behind Yugoslavia in their qualifying group, but they were invited to complete the final eight when Yugoslavia were barred for security fears following the country's collapse. Goalkeeper **Peter Schmeichel** was their hero – in the semi-final shoot-out win over Holland and again in the final against Germany, when goals by John Jensen and Kim Vilfort earned Denmark a 2-0 win.

GERMANS DOMINATE AS COMPETITION TAKES OFF

In 50 years, the UEFA European Championship has grown to become the most important international football tournament, after the FIFA World Cup finals. Only 17 teams entered the first competition, won by the Soviet Union in 1960. Fifty took part in qualifying for the right to join hosts Austria and Switzerland at the 2008 finals. Germany (formerly West Germany) have dominated the tournament, even though they did not enter the first two competitions. They have won three times and finished runners-up on three more occasions. France and Spain have each triumphed twice. Denmark, in 1992, and Greece, in 2004, have been the tournament's surprise winners. Meanwhile, some of Europe's most famous teams have underachieved. Italy have won the trophy only once, on home soil in 1968; whereas England have never even reached the final – their best finish was third place in 1968.

DOMENGHINI RESCUES ITALY

The most controversial goal in the history of the final came on 8 June 1968. Hosts Italy were trailing 1-0 to Yugoslavia with ten minutes left. The Yugoslavs seemed still to be organizing their wall when Angelo Domenghini curled a free-kick past goalkeeper Ilja Pantelic for the equalizer. Yugoslavia protested but the goal was allowed to stand. Italy won the only replay in finals history 2-0, two days later, with goals from Gigi Riva and Pietro Anastasi.

FRANCE BOAST PERFECT RECORD

France, on home soil in 1984, are the only side to win all their matches since the finals expanded beyond four teams. They won them without any shoot-outs, too, beating Denmark 1-0, Belgium 5-0 and Yugoslavia 3-2 in their group, Portugal 3-2 after extra-time in the semi-finals and Spain 2-0 in the final.

CZECHS WIN LONGEST SHOOT-OUT

The longest penalty shoot-out in finals history came in the 1980 third-place play-off between hosts Italy and Czechoslovakia, in Naples on 21 June. The Czechs won 9-8, following a 1-1 draw. After eight successful spot-kicks each, Czech goalkeeper **Jaroslav Netolicka** saved Fulvio Collovati's kick.

FRANCE STRIKE, WITHOUT STRIKERS

France still hold the record for the most goals scored by one team in a finals tournament, 14 in 1984. Yet only one of those goals was netted by a recognized striker – **Bruno Bellone**, who hit the second in their 2-0 final win over Spain. France's inspirational captain, Michel Platini, supplied most of the French firepower, scoring an incredible nine goals in five appearances. He hit hat-tricks against Belgium and Denmark and a last-gasp winner in the semi-final against Portugal. Midfielders Alain Giresse and Luis Fernandez chipped in with goals in the 5-0 win over Belgium. Defender Jean-Francois Domergue gave France the lead against Portugal in the semi-finals, and added another in extra-time after Jordao had put Portugal 2-1 ahead.

GERMANS SET RECORD MARGIN

West Germany's 3-0 win over the Soviet Union in 1972 remains the biggest margin of victory in any final. **Gerd Muller** netted the opening goal in the 27th minute. Midfielder Herbert Wimmer added the Germans' second after 52 minutes and Muller completed the rout six minutes later. All of the past four finals (1996, 2000, 2004 and 2008) have been settled by one-goal margins.

TOP TEAM SCORERS IN THE FINALS

1960	Yugoslavia	6
1964	Spain, Soviet Union,	
	Hungary	4
1968	Italy	4
1972	West Germany	5
1976	West Germany	6
1980	West Germany	6
1984	France	14
1988	Holland	8
1992	Germany	7
1996	Germany	10
2000	France, Holland	13
2004	Czech Republic	9
2008	Spain	12

BIGGEST WINS IN THE FINALS

Holland 6, Yugoslavia 1, 2000
France 5, Belgium 0, 1984
Denmark 5, Yugoslavia 0, 1984
Sweden 5, Bulgaria 0, 2004

SPAIN REFUSE TO MEET SOVIETS

Political rivalries wrecked the planned clash between Spain and the Soviet Union in the 1960 quarter-finals. The fascist Spanish leader, General Francisco Franco, refused to allow Spain to go to the communist Soviet Union – and banned the Soviets from entering Spain. The Soviet Union were handed a walkover on the grounds that Spain had refused to play. Franco relented four years later, allowing the Soviets to come to Spain for the finals. He was spared the embarrassment of presenting the trophy to them, however, as Spain beat the Soviet Union 2-1 in the final.

TOSS FAVOURS HOSTS ITALY

Italy reached the 1968 final on home soil thanks to the toss of a coin. It was the only game in finals history decided in such fashion. Italy drew 0-0 against the Soviet Union after extra-time in Naples on 5 June 1968. The Soviet captain, Albert Shesternev, made the wrong call at the toss – so Italy reached the final where they beat Yugoslavia.

UEFA EUROPEAN CHAMPIONSHIP WINNERS

3	West Germany/Germany (1972, 1980, 1996)
2	France (1984, 2000)
	Spain (1964, 2008)
1	Soviet Union (1960)
	Czechoslovakia (1976)
	Italy (1968)
	Holland (1998)
	Denmark (1992)
	Greece (2004)

DELLAS TIMES IT RIGHT FOR GREECE

Greece scored the only "silver goal" victory in the history of the competition in the UEFA Euro 2004 semi-finals. (The silver goal rule meant that a team leading after the first period of extra-time won the match.) Traianos Dellas headed Greece's winner seconds before the end of the first period of extra-time against the Czech Republic in Porto on 1 July. Both golden goals and silver goals were abandoned for UEFA Euro 2008, and drawn knockout matches reverted to being decided over the full 30 minutes of extra-time, and penalties if necessary.

PLAYER RECORDS

SHEARER TALLY BOOSTS ENGLAND

Alan Shearer is the only Englishman to top the finals scoring chart. Shearer led the scorers with five goals as England went out on penalties to Germany in the Euro 96 semi-final at Wembley. He netted against Switzerland, Scotland and the Netherlands (2) in the group and gave England a third-minute lead against the Germans. Shearer added two more goals at Euro 2000, to stand second behind Michel Platini in the all-time scorers' list.

RICARDO THE SHOOT-OUT DECIDER

Portugal goalkeeper Ricardo was the hero of his side's quarter-final shoot-out win against England in Lisbon on 24 June 2004. The score was 5-5 in the shoot-out – following a 2-2 draw – when Ricardo saved Darius Vassell's spot-kick. The Portugal keeper then coolly struck a penalty-kick past David James to knock England out.

VAN BASTEN LEADS DUTCH CHARGE

The Netherlands' **Marco van Basten** was the striking star of Euro 1988. He scored a hat-trick in the 3-1 win over England and netted a late winner to pip hosts West Germany 2-1 in the semi-finals. His strike in their 2-0 win over the Soviet Union is regarded as the greatest goal ever scored in the final. He met Arnold Muhren's crossfield pass with a spectacular mid-air volley, which flew past keeper Rinat Dassayev for the second Dutch goal.

VONLANTHEN BEATS ROONEY RECORD

The youngest scorer in finals history was Switzerland midfielder **Johan Vonlanthen.** He was 18 years 141 days when he netted in their 3-1 defeat by France on 21 June 2004. He beat the record set by England forward Wayne Rooney four days earlier. Rooney was 18 years 229 days when he scored the first goal in England's 3-0 win over the Swiss.

KIRICHENKO NETS QUICKEST GOAL

The fastest goal in the history of the finals was scored by Russia forward Dmitri Kirichenko. He netted after just 68 seconds to give his side the lead against Greece on 20 June 2004. Russia won 2-1, but Greece still qualified for the quarter-finals – and went on to become shock winners. The fastest goal in the final was Spain midfielder Jesus Pereda's sixth-minute strike in 1964, when Spain beat the Soviet Union 2-1.

ILYIN GOAL MAKES HISTORY

Anatoly Ilyin of the Soviet Union scored the first goal in UEFA European Championship history when he netted after four minutes against Hungary on 29 September 1958. A crowd of 100,572 watched the Soviets win 3-1 in the Lenin Stadium, Moscow. The Soviet Union went on to win the first final, in 1960.

TOP SCORERS IN FINALS HISTORY

1 Michel Platini (France)   9
2 Alan Shearer (England)   7
3 Nuno Gomes (Portugal)
= Thierry Henry (France)
= Patrick Kluivert (Netherlands)
= Ruud van Nistelrooy (Netherlands)   6
7 Milan Baros (Czech Republic)
= Jurgen Klinsmann (W Germany/Germany)
= Marco van Basten (Netherlands)
= Zinedine Zidane (France)   5

BIERHOFF NETS FIRST "GOLDEN GOAL"

Germany's **Oliver Bierhoff** scored the first golden
goal in the history of the tournament when he hit the
winner against the Czech Republic in the Euro 96 final
at Wembley on 30 June. (The golden goal rule meant the
first team to score in extra-time won the match.) Bierhoff
netted in the fifth minute of extra-time. His shot from 20
yards deflected off defender Michal Hornak and slipped
through goalkeeper Petr Kouba's fingers.

PONEDELNIK'S MONDAY MORNING FEELING

Striker Viktor Ponedelnik headed the Soviet Union's extra-time winner to beat
Yugoslavia 2-1 in the first final on 10 July 1960 – and sparked some famous
headlines in the Soviet media. The game in Paris kicked off at 10pm Moscow
time on Sunday. It was running into Monday morning there by the time
Ponedelnik – whose name means "Monday" in Russian – scored. He said:
"When I scored, all the journalists wrote the headline 'Ponedelnik zabivayet v
Ponedelnik' – 'Monday scores on Monday'."

PLATINI SETS FANTASTIC STANDARD

Michael Platini towered over the 1984 finals, setting a scoring record that has yet to be
beaten. France's great attacking midfielder and captain netted nine goals as his side won
the tournament on home soil. Platini opened with France's winner against Denmark, netted
a hat-trick in the 5-0 win over Belgium, then scored all three in a 3-2 win over Yugoslavia.
He produced his most dramatic intervention in the semi-final against Portugal, grabbing
France's decider in the last minute of extra-time. He set his team on the way to a 2-0 victory
over Spain in the final too, when his free-kick squirmed through goalkeeper Luis Arconada's
hands. Some 24 years later, after Platini had become UEFA president, he invited Arconada to
be his special guest at the 2008 final in Vienna ... on this occasion to see Spain win.

VASTIC THE OLDEST

The oldest scorer in finals history is Austria's Ivica Vastic. He was 38 years and
257 days old when he equalized in the 1-1 draw with Poland at UEFA Euro 2008.

TOP SCORERS IN THE FINALS

Year	Scorer	Goals
1960	Francois Heutte (France)	2
	Milan Galic (Yugoslavia)	
	Valentin Ivanov (Soviet Union)	
	Drazan Jerkovic (Yugoslavia)	
	Slava Metreveli (Soviet Union)	
	Viktor Ponedelnik (Soviet Union)	
1964	Ferenc Bene (Hungary)	2
	Dezso Novak (Hungary)	
	Jesus Pereda (Spain)	
1968	Dragan Dzajic (Yugoslavia)	2
1972	Gerd Muller (West Germany)	4
1976	Dieter Muller (West Germany)	4
1980	Klaus Allofs (West Germany)	3
1984	Michel Platini (France)	9
1988	Marco van Basten (Netherlands)	5
1992	Dennis Bergkamp (Netherlands)	3
	Tomas Brolin (Sweden)	
	Henrik Larsen (Denmark)	
	Karlheinz Riedle (Germany)	
1996	Alan Shearer (England)	5
2000	Patrick Kluivert (Netherlands)	5
	Savo Milosevic (Yugoslavia)	
2004	Milan Baros (Czech Republic)	5
2008	David Villa (Spain)	4

MATTHAUS MIRRORS TOURNAMENT GROWTH

The career of Lothar Matthaus straddles the growth of the European Championship. He appeared in four tournaments between 1980 and 2000. He missed Euro 92 because of injury and stayed at home for Euro 96 after falling out with coach Berti Vogts and skipper Jurgen Klinsmann. He had made his entry as a 19-year-old substitute for Bernd Dietz in West Germany's 3-2 group win over the Netherlands in Naples on 14 June 1980. That was the first tournament which involved eight teams and two groups rather than the previous four semi-finalists. He ended his association with the championship at the age of 39, playing for a reunited Germany as they were eliminated 3-0 by Portugal at Euro 2000. By now the tournament had expanded to include 16 teams in four groups. Despite featuring in four tournaments, Matthaus made only 11 appearances in total. He did, however, enter the tournament when it was taking its first steps to expansion and left it when the European Championship had become second only to the FIFA World Cup as football's most important international competition.

BROTHERS IN ARMS

Four pairs of brothers went to Euro 2000: Gary and Phil Neville (England), Frank and Ronald de Boer (Netherlands), Daniel and Patrik Andersson (Sweden) and Belgium's Emile and Mbo Mpenza.

BECKENBAUER'S 100th ENDS IN DEFEAT

West Germany legend Franz Beckenbauer won his 100th cap in the 1976 final against Czechoslovakia. After his side's shoot-out defeat, he played only three more games for his country before retiring from international football.

PORTUGAL TRIO BANNED FOR THE LONGEST

The longest suspensions in the history of the finals were handed out to three Portugal players after their Euro 2000 semi-final defeat by France. Zinedine Zidane's "Golden Goal" penalty infuriated the Portuguese, who surrounded referee Gunter Benko and assistant Igor Sramka. The three Portuguese players – **Abel Xavier**, Nuno Gomes and Paulo Bento – were banned for "physically and verbally intimidating" the officials. Xavier was suspended from European football for nine months. Gomes, who was also sent off, was banned for eight months. Bento received a six-month suspension.

VAN BASTEN SPOILS SHILTON'S DAY

Goalkeeper Peter Shilton is England's most-capped player, with 125 appearances, but he will remember his 100th cap – in Dusseldorf on 15 June 1988 – for all the wrong reasons. Marco van Basten fired a second-half hat-trick past him as the Netherlands beat England 3-1 in their second Group Two game of UEFA Euro 88.

MOST FINALS TOURNAMENTS PLAYED

Six players have appeared in four finals tournaments:

Lothar Matthaus (W Germany/Germany)	1980, 1984, 1988, 2000
Peter Schmeichel (Denmark)	1988, 1992, 1996, 2000
Aaron Winter (Netherlands)	1988, 1992, 1996, 2000
Lilian Thuram (France)	1996, 2000, 2004, 2008
Edwin van der Sar (Netherlands)	1996, 2000, 2004, 2008
Alessandro Del Piero (Italy)	1996, 2000, 2004, 2008

MULLERY THE FIRST TO GO

Wing-half Alan Mullery became the first England player ever to be sent off when he was dismissed in the 89th minute of their 1-0 semi-final defeat by Yugoslavia in Florence on 5 June 1968. Mullery was sent off for a foul on Dobrivoje Trivic, three minutes after Dragan Dzajic had scored Yugoslavia's winner. His dismissal came in England's 424th official international match.

HAGI'S JOURNEY ENDS IN RED

Romania's greatest player, Gheorghe Hagi won the last of his 125 caps in a 2-0 UEFA Euro 2000 quarter-final defeat by Italy on 24 June. However, his international career would end in sad circumstances: he was sent off in the 59th minute for two yellow-card offences. Hagi had previously been booked against Germany and Portugal – and had missed Romania's 3-2 group win over England through suspension.

MOST GAMES PLAYED IN THE FINALS

16	Edwin van der Sar	(Netherlands)
	Lilian Thuram	(France)
14	Luis Figo	(Portugal)
	Nuno Gomes	(Portugal)
	Karel Poborsky	(Czech Republic)
	Zinedine Zidane	(France)

TWO REDS END LONG RUN

After France defender Yvon Le Roux was sent off in the 1984 final, the next two finals tournaments passed without a single red card. That all changed in Spain's bad-tempered 1-1 Group B draw with Bulgaria at Leeds on 9 June 1996. Italian referee Piero Ceccarini sent off Bulgaria's Petr Houbtchev for bringing down Jose Luis Caminero, then dismissed Spain's Antonio Pizzi for a wild tackle on Radostin Kishishev.

ARAGONES THE VETERAN COACH

Luis Aragones, Spain's coach in 2008, is the oldest boss of a European champion team. Aragones (born in Madrid on 28 July 1938) was 29 days short of his 70th birthday when Spain beat Germany 1-0 in the final on 29 June. That was his last match in charge. He had taken over the national team after Euro 2004.

KADLEC FATHER AND SON

Czech defenders Miroslav and Michal Kadlec are the only father and son to have played in the finals. Miroslav (born on 22 June 1964 in Uherske Hradiste) captained the Czech Republic side that finished as runners-up to Germany at Euro 96. He also scored the winning penalty in the semi-final shoot-out against France. Michal (born on 13 December 1984 in Vyskov) made his first appearance as an 80th-minute substitute for Jaroslav Plasil in the Group A game against Turkey in Geneva on 15 June 2008.

SUAREZ GAINS FIRST DOUBLE

The first man to earn winners' medals in the European Championship and the European Cup in the same season was Spain's **Luis Suarez**. He helped Spain beat the Soviet Union 2-1 in the final on 21 June 1964. A few weeks earlier, Suarez had been in the Internazionale team that beat Real Madrid 3-1 in the European Cup final. Four players were in both PSV Eindhoven's 1988 European Cup final victory over Benfica and the Netherlands' UEFA Euro 88 final defeat of Russia. Nicolas Anelka won the Champions League with Real Madrid in 2000 and was in the France squad that won Euro 2000, but he did not appear in the final.

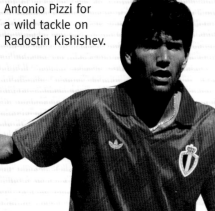

SCIFO THE YOUNGEST

The youngest player to feature in a game at the finals was Belgium midfielder **Enzo Scifo**. He was 18 years 115 days when he appeared in his country's 2-0 win over Yugoslavia on 13 June 1984 and started in all three of Belgium's group games.

MATTHAUS THE OLDEST

The oldest player to appear in a game at the UEFA European Championship finals was Germany's Lothar Matthaus. He was 39 years 91 days when he played in their 3-0 defeat by Portugal on 20 June 2000.

EURO 2008 IN THE INTERNET AGE

The Internet became a massive conduit for public interest for the UEFA Euro 2008 finals. More than 105 million surfers from more than 200 countries visited the dedicated site www.Euro2008.com. The biggest volume of traffic – around 15 per cent – came from the United Kingdom. The greatest number of daily hits was 4.9 million.

NAMES ON THEIR SHIRTS

Players wore their names as well as their numbers on the back of their shirts for the first time at Euro 92. They had previously been identified only by numbers.

EURO 2012 UNDER WAY

Euro 2012 – which features 24 teams for the first time – will be co-hosted by Poland and Ukraine. The opening match will be staged at Poland's National Stadium in Warsaw. Ukraine will host the final, at the Olympic Stadium, Kiev. The other Polish venues are in Gdansk, Poznan and Wroclaw. The Ukrainian venues are at Lviv, Kharkiv and Donetsk.

SPAIN'S RECORD TV AUDIENCE

Spain's UEFA Euro 2008 final win over Germany attracted the largest television audience in the country's history. More than 14 million homes tuned in to the game, and hundreds of thousands more fans watched on giant public screens in squares and parks. The final was shown live in 231 countries around the globe.

ITALY HOSTS TWICE

Italy were the first country to host the finals twice – in 1968 and 1980. They were awarded the finals in 1968 in recognition of the 60th anniversary of the Italian football federation. Belgium have also hosted the finals twice: first, alone, in 1972, and then in partnership with the Netherlands for Euro 2000.

ELLIS BLOWS THE WHISTLE

English referee **Arthur Ellis** took charge of the first UEFA European Championship final between the Soviet Union and Yugoslavia in 1960. Ellis had also refereed the first-ever European Cup final, between Real Madrid and Reims, four years earlier. After he retired from football, he became the "referee" on the British version of the Europe-wide game show *It's a Knock-out*.

GREEKS HAND ALBANIA WALKOVER

When Greece were drawn against Albania in the first round of the 1964 tournament, the Greeks immediately withdrew, handing Albania a 3-0 walkover win. The countries had technically been at war since 1940. The Greek government did not formally lift the state of war until 1987, although diplomatic relations were re-established in 1971.

FINALS HOSTS

1960	France
1964	Spain
1968	Italy
1972	Belgium
1976	Yugoslavia
1980	Italy
1984	France
1988	West Germany
1992	Sweden
1996	England
2000	Netherlands and Belgium
2004	Portugal
2008	Austria and Switzerland

LOW COUNTRIES START DUAL TREND

 In 2000, Belgium and the Netherlands began the trend for dual hosting the UEFA European Championship finals – it was the first time the tournament was staged in more than one country. The opening game was Belgium's 2-1 win over Sweden in Brussels on 10 June. The final was staged in Rotterdam on 2 July. Austria and Switzerland jointly hosted Euro 2008. The opening game was Switzerland's 1-0 defeat by the Czech Republic in Basel on 7 June. The final was staged in Vienna on 29 June.

THUNDERSTORM HAMPERS SEMI–FINAL COVERAGE

UEFA Euro 2008 TV viewers missed much of the dramatic finale to Germany's 3-2 semi-final win over Turkey because of a television blackout. A thunderstorm and high winds in Vienna – where TV operations were based – meant the loss of pictures for several minutes. TV viewers missed both Miroslav Klose's goal that gave Germany a 2-1 lead, and Semih Senturk's equalizer. But coverage was resumed just in time for **Philipp Lahm's** stoppage-time winner.

RECORD FINAL CROWD AT THE BERNABEU

The record attendance for a UEFA European Championship final was the 120,000 who saw Spain beat the Soviet Union 2-1 at the Estadio Santiago Bernabeu in Madrid on 21 June 1964.

TOP TEN TEAMS IN FINALS MATCHES

Team	Pld	W	D	L	F	A
West Germany/Germany	38	19	10	9	55	39
Netherlands	32	17	8	7	55	32
France	28	14	7	7	46	34
Spain	30	13	9	8	38	31
Portugal	23	12	4	7	34	22
Italy	27	11	12	4	27	18
Czechoslovakia/Czech Republic	25	11	5	9	36	32
Soviet Union/CIS/Russia	27	11	5	11	31	36
England	23	7	7	9	31	28
Denmark	24	6	6	12	26	38

THE "ITALIAN JOB"

The 1968 finals in Italy were used as the backdrop to a famous English-language film – *The Italian Job*, starring Michael Caine – about a British gang who use the cover of the finals to stage a daring gold robbery in Turin. The film was released in England on 2 June 1969.

CHAMPIONSHIPS BECOME AN EXTRAVAGANZA

The UEFA European Championship attracts more media attention than any other football tournament for national teams except for the FIFA World Cup finals. Once the UEFA European Championship finals featured four teams and lasted for a few days; now they include 16 teams and the competition has become a three-week extravaganza. The party will last even longer in 2012 when 24 teams will contest the tournament in Poland and Ukraine for the first time. TV viewing figures will almost certainly set new records, while new media – such as the Internet – will play an ever-increasing role in the coverage.

DUTCH TAKE TO THE WATER

The Netherlands celebrated their 1988 triumph in unusual style. The team paraded on a barge through the canals of Amsterdam. A crowd estimated at more than one million greeted them – and many houseboats moored on the canals were damaged by happy fans dancing on their roofs!

PART 4: COPA AMERICA

JET travel has had a revolutionary effect on international sports competition over the past 50 years, but the difficulties of organizing major events in the first half of the 20th century did have some positive effects. FIFA's founding membership in 1904 was entirely European, and though South American nations – such as Brazil, Argentina and Uruguay – were not slow in signing up, the opportunities available to them to play against their European cousins were scarce. Occasional European teams, usually clubs, made sporadic tours to South America, but the time taken and disruption caused by long sea journeys meant that, for example, only four European national teams went to Uruguay to play in the inaugural FIFA World Cup in 1930, and they all sailed on the same vessel.

The South Americans thus had to organize their own international competitions, which led directly to the creation in 1916 of the South American Championship, now known as the Copa America. Communications not being what they are today, even then organization was a far from simple matter – hence many of the initial championships are now considered "unofficial". Further problems arose over competition scheduling which, in later years, often meant that countries were unable to secure the release of their finest players who were contracted to clubs in Europe. The issue of such a player exodus was a particular problem for Argentina in the late 1950s. They won the South American title in 1957 and were considered favourites to win the FIFA World Cup the following year. By then, however, they had lost all their inspirational inside-forward trio – Humberto Maschio, Antonio Valentin Angelillo and Enrique Omar Sivori – to Italian clubs. Eventually the club versus country issue was resolved by FIFA's enforcement of a unified international calendar, which recognized the priority status of the Copa America.

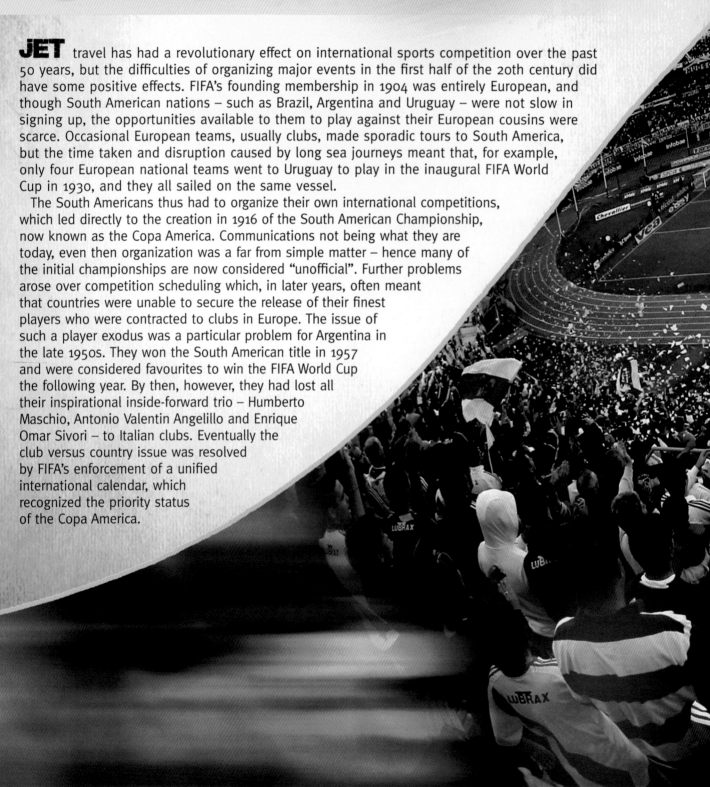

South America's fervid football fans turn venues such as the Momumental in Buenos Aires – the venue for the 2011 Copa America final – into a cauldron of noise and a sea of colour.

COPA AMERICA TEAM RECORDS

LITTLE NAPOLEON

In 1942, Ecuador and their goalkeeper Napoleon Medina conceded more goals in one tournament than any other team, when they let in 31 goals across six games – and six defeats. Three years later he and his team-mates finally managed to keep a clean sheet, in a goalless draw against Bolivia – but still managed to let in another 27 goals in their five other matches.

COLLECTIVE RESPONSIBILITY

Brazil's players shared the goalscoring duties on their way to the 1997 Copa America title, finishing with a record ten scorers: Ronaldo (five goals), Leonardo and Romario (three apiece), Denilson, Djalminha and Edmundo (two each) and Aldair, Dunga, Flavio Conceicao and **Ze Roberto** (one each).

COPA AMERICA WINNERS

1916	Uruguay (league format)
1917	Uruguay (league format)
1919	Brazil 1 Uruguay 0
1920	Uruguay (league format)
1921	Argentina (league format)
1922	Brazil 3 Paraguay 1
1923	Uruguay (league format)
1924	Uruguay (league format)
1925	Argentina (league format)
1926	Uruguay (league format)
1927	Argentina (league format)
1929	Argentina (league format)
1935	Uruguay (league format)
1937	Argentina 2 Brazil 0
1939	Peru (league format)
1941	Argentina (league format)
1942	Uruguay (league format)
1945	Argentina (league format)
1946	Argentina (league format)
1947	Argentina (league format)
1949	Brazil 7 Paraguay 0
1953	Paraguay 3 Brazil 2
1955	Argentina (league format)
1956	Uruguay (league format)
1957	Argentina (league format)
1959	Argentina (league format)
1959	Uruguay (league format)
1963	Bolivia (league format)
1967	Uruguay (league format)
1975	Peru 4 Colombia 1 (on aggregate, after three games)
1979	Paraguay 3 Chile 1 (on aggregate, after three games)
1983	Uruguay 3 Brazil 1 (on aggregate, after two games)
1987	Uruguay 1 Chile 0
1989	Brazil (league format)
1991	Argentina (league format)
1993	Argentina 2 Mexico 1
1995	Uruguay 1 Brazil 1 (Uruguay won 5-3 on penalties)
1997	Brazil 3 Bolivia 1
1999	Brazil 3 Uruguay 0
2001	Colombia 1 Mexico 0
2004	Brazil 2 Argentina 2 (Brazil won 4-2 on penalties)
2007	Brazil 3 Argentina 0

HOSTING RIGHTS BY COUNTRY

Argentina	8	(1916, 1921, 1925, 1929, 1937, 1946, 1959, 1987)
Uruguay	7	(1917, 1923, 1924, 1942, 1956, 1967, 1995)
Chile	6	(1920, 1926, 1941, 1945, 1955, 1991)
Peru	6	(1927, 1935, 1939, 1953, 1957, 2004)
Brazil	4	(1919, 1922, 1949, 1989)
Ecuador	3	(1947, 1959, 1993)
Bolivia	2	(1963, 1997)
Paraguay	1	(1999)
Colombia	1	(2001)
Venezuela	1	(2007)

EXTRA TIME

The longest match in the history of the Copa America was the 1919 final between Brazil and Uruguay. It lasted 150 minutes, 90 minutes of regular time plus two extra-time periods of 30 minutes each.

HOW IT STARTED

The first South American "Championship of Nations", as it was then known, was held in Argentina from 2–17 July 1916, during the country's independence centenary commemorations. The tournament was won by Uruguay, who drew with Argentina in the last match of the tournament. It was an inauspicious beginning. The 16 July encounter had to be abandoned at 0-0 when fans invaded the pitch and set the wooden stands on fire. The match was continued at a different stadium the following day and still ended goalless ... but Uruguay ended up topping the mini-league table and were hailed the first champions. Isabelino Gradin was the inaugural tournament's top scorer. The event also saw the foundation of the South American federation CONMEBOL, which took place a week into the competition on 9 July 1916. From that point on the tournament was held every two years, though some tournaments are now considered to have been unofficial.

SUB–STANDARD

During the 1953 Copa America, Peru were awarded a walkover win when Paraguay tried to make one more substitution than they were allowed. Would-be substitute Milner Ayala was so incensed, he kicked English referee Richard Maddison and was banned from football for three years. Yet Paraguay remained in the tournament and went on to beat Brazil in the final – minus, of course, the disgraced Ayala.

ROTATING RIGHTS

The Campeonato Sudamericano de Selecciones was rebaptized the Copa America from 1975. Between then and 1983 there was no host nation, before CONMEBOL adopted the policy of rotating the right to host the Copa America among the ten member confederations. The first rotation was complete after Venezuela hosted the 2007 edition, with Argentina lined up to play host for the ninth time in 2011.

HISTORY MEN

The Copa America is the world's oldest surviving international football tournament, having been launched in 1916 when the participating nations were Argentina, Bolivia, Brazil, Chile, Colombia, Ecuador, Paraguay, Peru, Uruguay and Venezuela. In 1910, an unofficial South American championship had been won by Argentina, who beat Uruguay 4-1 in the decider – though the final match had been delayed a day after rioting fans burnt down a stand at the Gimnasia stadium in Buenos Aires.

FALLEN ANGELS

Argentina's 1957 Copa America-winning forward trio of Humberto Maschio, Omar Sivori and Antonio Valentin Angelillo became known by the nickname "the angels with dirty faces". At least one of them scored in each of the side's six matches – Maschio finished with nine, Angelillo eight and Sivori three. Argentina's most convincing performance was an opening 8-2 win over Colombia, in which Argentina had scored four goals and missed a penalty within the first 25 minutes. The dazzling displays made Argentina, not eventual winners Brazil, favourites for the following year's FIFA World Cup. Before then, however, Maschio, Sivori and Angelillo had all been lured away to Europe by Italian clubs and the Argentine federation subsequently refused to pick them for the trip to Sweden for the FIFA World Cup. Sivori and Maschio ultimately made it to the FIFA World Cup, in 1962. However, to fury back home, they did so wearing not the light blue-and-white stripes of Argentina, but the Azzurri blue of their newly adopted Italy.

CONSISTENT COLOMBIANS

In 2001, Colombia, who went on to win the trophy for the first and only time in their history, became the only country to go through an entire Copa America campaign without conceding a single goal. They scored 11 goals themselves, more than half of them from six-goal tournament top scorer **Victor Aristazabal**. Keeping the clean sheets was goalkeeper Oscar Cordoba, who had previously spent much of his international career as back-up to the eccentric Rene Higuita. Just a month earlier, Cordoba had won the South American club championship, the Copa Libertadores, with Argentine side Boca Juniors.

TRIUMPHS BY COUNTRY

Uruguay 14 (1916, 1917, 1920, 1923, 1924, 1926, 1935, 1942, 1956, 1959, 1967, 1983, 1987, 1995)
Argentina 14 (1921, 1925, 1927, 1929, 1937, 1941, 1945, 1946, 1947, 1955, 1957, 1959, 1991, 1993)
Brazil 8 (1919, 1922, 1949, 1989, 1997, 1999, 2004, 2007)
Peru 2 (1939, 1975)
Paraguay 2 (1953, 1979)
Bolivia 1 (1963)
Colombia 1 (2001)

MORE FROM MORENO

Argentina were not only responsible for the Copa America's biggest win, but also the tournament's highest-scoring game, when they put 12 past Ecuador in 1942 – to no reply. Jose Manuel Moreno's five strikes in that game included the 500th goal in the competition's history. Moreno, born in Buenos Aires on 3 August 1916, ended that tournament as joint top scorer with team-mate Herminio Masantonio – hitting seven goals. Both men ended their international careers with 19 goals for their country, though Moreno did so in 34 appearances – compared to Masantonio's 21. Masantonio scored four in the Ecuador thrashing.

FAMILIAR FACES

Uruguay have made the most appearances (40), followed by Argentina (38), Chile (35), Paraguay (33), Brazil (32) and Peru (28). Argentina has hosted the Copa America the most times – eight, followed by **Uruguay** (seven) and Chile (six).

FROG PRINCE

Chilean goalkeeper Sergio Livingstone holds the record for most Copa America appearances, with 34 games, across the 1941, 1942, 1945, 1947, 1949 and 1953 tournaments. Livingstone, nicknamed "The Frog", was voted player of the tournament in 1941 – becoming the first goalkeeper to win the award – and might have played even more Copa America matches had he not missed out on the 1946 competition. Livingstone, born in Santiago on 26 March 1920, spent almost his entire career in his home country – save for a season with Argentina's Racing Club in 1943–44. Overall, he made 52 appearances for Chile between 1941 and 1954, before retiring and becoming a popular TV journalist and commentator.

OVERALL TOP SCORERS

1	Norberto Mendez (Argentina)	17
=	Zizinho (Brazil)	17
3	Teodoro Fernandez (Peru)	15
=	Severino Varela (Uruguay)	15
5	Ademir (Brazil)	13
=	Jair da Rosa Pinto (Brazil)	13
=	Gabriel Batistuta (Argentina)	13
=	Jose Manuel Moreno (Argentina)	13
=	Hector Scarone (Uruguay)	13

CHILE'S ILL FORTUNE

The first Copa America own goal was scored by Chile's Luis Garcia, giving Argentina a 1-0 win in 1917, in the second edition of the tournament. Even more unfortunately for Chile, Garcia's strike was the only goal by one of their players throughout the tournament – making Chile the first team to fail to score a single goal in a Copa America competition.

LOW–KEY JOSE

The first-ever Copa America goal, in 1916, was scored by Jose Piendibene – setting Uruguay on the way to a 4-0 triumph over Chile. But he is not thought to have marked the moment with any great extravagance – Piendibene, renowned for his sense of fair play, made a point of not celebrating goals, to avoid offending his opponents.

MOST GAMES PLAYED

1	Sergio Livingstone (Chile)	34
2	Zizinho (Brazil)	33
3	Leonel Alvarez (Colombia)	27
4	Carlos Valderrama (Colombia)	27
5	Alex Aguinaga (Ecuador)	25
6	Claudio Taffarel (Brazil)	25
7	Teodoro Fernandez (Peru)	24
8	Angel Romano (Uruguay)	23
9	Djalma Santos (Brazil)	22
10	Claudio Suarez (Mexico)	22

REPEATING THE FEAT

Uruguay's **Pedro Petrone** (in 1923 and 1924) and **Gabriel Batistuta** of Argentina (in 1991 and 1995) are the only players to finish as top scorers in the Copa America on two occasions. Batistuta made his Argentina debut just a few days before the 1991 Copa America, in which his starring performances – including a decisive goal in the final – helped him win a transfer from Boca Juniors to Italy's Fiorentina.

MAGIC ALEX

When Alex Aguinaga lined up for Ecuador against Uruguay in his country's opening game at the 2004 event, he became only the second man to take part in eight different Copa Americas – joining legendary Uruguayan goalscorer Angel Romano. Aguinaga, a midfielder born in Ibarra on 9 July 1969, played a total of 109 times for his country – 25 of them in the Copa America, a competition that yielded four of his 23 international goals. His Copa America career certainly began well: Ecuador went undefeated for his first four appearances, at the 1987 and 1989 events, but his luck had ran out by the time his Ecuador career was coming to an end: he lost his final seven Copa America matches.

START TO FINISH

Colombia playmaker Carlos Valderrama and defensive midfielder **Leonel Alvarez** played in all 27 of their country's Copa America matches between 1987 and 1995, winning ten, drawing ten and losing seven – including third-place finishes in 1987, 1993 and 1995. Valderrama's two Copa America goals came in his first and final appearances in the competition – in a 2-0 victory over Bolivia in 1987 and a 4-1 thrashing of the United States eight years later.

REGULAR GUEST

Of the non-South Americans invited to take part in the Copa America, Mexico's **Claudio Suarez** has appeared the most – 22 games across five tournaments from 1993 to 2004. Suarez, the world's most-capped outfield footballer, was ever-present during Mexico's run to the 1993 final, but missed the 2001 event, when they finished runners-up, to rest before crucial FIFA World Cup qualifiers – only to break his leg just before the 2002 FIFA World Cup itself.

FANTASTIC FIVES

Four players have scored five goals in one Copa America game: Hector Scarone in Uruguay's 6-0 win over Bolivia in 1926; Juan Marvezzi in Argentina's 6-1 win over Ecuador in 1941; Jose Manuel Moreno in Argentina's 12-0 win over Ecuador in 1942; and Evaristo de Macedo in Brazil's 9-0 win over Colombia in 1957.

PELE'S INSPIRATION

Brazilian forward **Zizinho** jointly holds the all-time goalscoring record for the Copa America, along with Argentina's Norberto Mendez. Both men struck 17 goals, Zizinho across six tournaments and Mendez three – including the 1945 and 1946 tournaments, which featured both men. Mendez was top scorer once and runner-up twice and won championship medals on all three occasions, while Zizinho's goals helped Brazil take the title only once, in 1949. Zizinho, Pele's footballing idol, would emerge from the 1950 FIFA World Cup as Brazil's top scorer and was also voted the tournament's best player – but was forever traumatized by the hosts' surprise defeat to Uruguay that cost Brazil the title. On 16 July every year, the anniversary of the match, Zizinho would take his phone off the hook, because people would still call asking him how Brazil lost. He missed out on a place in Brazil's 1958 FIFA World Cup squad, when selectors instead opted for a promising 17-year-old striker – that childhood fan, Pele. The following year, Pele finished as Copa America top scorer for the first and only time, with eight goals.

COPA AMERICA OTHER RECORDS

SUCCESSFUL INVADERS

Only two foreign coaches have led a country to Copa America glory – Brazilian Danilo Alvim, whose Bolivian side won in 1963, and Englishman Jack Greenwell, Peru coach in 1939. Alvim, who won the tournament as a centre-half with Brazil in 1949, not only coached Bolivia to their one and only Copa America triumph – he did it by beating his native land 5-4 in the final match.

HOME COMFORTS

Uruguay have a unique record in remaining unbeaten in 38 Copa America games on home turf, all played in the country's capital Montevideo – comprising 31 wins, seven draws. The last tournament match they hosted was both a draw and a win – 1-1 against Brazil in 1995, with Uruguay emerging as champions, 5-3 on penalties after Fernando Alvez saved Tulio's penalty.

INVITED GUESTS

1993 **Mexico (runners-up), United States**
1995 **Mexico, United States (fourth)**
1997 **Costa Rica, Mexico (third)**
1999 **Japan, Mexico (third)**
2001 **Costa Rica, Honduras (third), Mexico (runners-up)**
2004 **Costa Rica, Mexico**
2007 **Mexico (third), United States**

MULTI–TASKING

Argentina's **Guillermo Stabile** not only holds the record for most Copa America triumphs as coach – he trounces all opposition. He led his country to the title on no fewer than six occasions – in 1941, 1945, 1946, 1947, 1955 and 1957. No other coach has lifted the trophy more than twice. Stabile coached Argentina from 1939 to 1960, having been appointed at the age of just 34. He lasted for 123 games in charge, winning 83 of them – and still managed to coach three clubs on the side at different times throughout his reign. He remained as Red Star Paris manager during his first year in the Argentina role, then led Argentine club Huracan for the next nine years – before leading domestic rivals Racing Club from 1949 to 1960. Stabile's Argentina may have, unusually, missed out on Copa America success in 1949, but that year brought the first of three Argentina league championships in a row for Stabile's Racing Club.

CAPTAIN CONSISTENT

Uruguay's 1930 World Cup-winning captain **Jose Nasazzi** is the only footballer to be voted player of the tournament at two different Copa America tournaments. Even more impressively, he achieved the feat 12 years apart – first taking the prize in 1923, then again in 1935. He was a Cup winner in 1923, 1924, 1926 and 1935. Nasazzi also captained Uruguay to victory in the 1924 and 1928 Olympic Games and in the 1930 World Cup.

ONE–NIL TO THE ANYONE

Perhaps predictably, the most common scoreline in Copa America history is the 1-0 win – the result on no fewer than 106 occasions, most recently when **Javier Mascherano**'s first goal for Argentina saw off Paraguay in the 2007 group stage.

POINTS WIN PRIZES

If every Copa America win were awarded three points, with one for a draw, Argentina would emerge from the tournament's history with the most per game – an average 2.1 points per match, ahead of Brazil's 1.89 and Uruguay's 1.82. The only country to still go without a single Copa America match victory is Japan, who failed to triumph in three matches when invited to take part – for the first and, so far, only time – in the 1999 competition.

FINE HOST

Argentina has hosted more tournaments than any other South American country, followed by Uruguay (seven), Chile (six) and Peru (also six). Despite hosting the final play-off game in 1975, Venezuela remained the last South American country not to host a full tournament until 2007.

WRONG JUAN

It took 21 years, but Uruguay's Juan Emilio Piriz became the first Copa America player sent off, against Chile in 1937 – the first of 170 dismissals so far. Some 127 of those disgraced players have had a red card flourished in their face, since FIFA introduced the card system for referees in 1970.

SEEING RED

Brazil may have the worst FIFA World Cup disciplinary record, but neighbours Uruguay assume that unenviable position in the Copa America. Uruguayan players have been sent off 30 times, followed by Argentina and Peru on 22 dismissals apiece, Brazil (19), Venezuela (18), Chile (15), Bolivia and Paraguay (11 each), Colombia, Ecuador and Mexico (nine each), and Honduras and Japan (one each). Only Costa Rica and the US have, so far, made their way through Copa America participations with eleven men on the field throughout.

TROPHY–WINNING COACHES

6 Guillermo Stabile (Argentina 1941, 1945, 1946, 1947, 1955, 1957)

2 Alfio Basile (Argentina 1991, 1993)
Juan Carlos Corazzo (Uruguay 1959, 1967)
Ernesto Figoli (Uruguay 1920, 1926)

1 Jorge Pacheco and Alfredo Foglino (Uruguay 1916)
Ramon Platero (Uruguay 1917)
Pedro Calomino (Argentina 1921)
Lais (Brazil 1922)
Leonardo De Lucca (Uruguay 1923)
Ernesto Meliante (Uruguay 1924)
Americo Tesoriere (Argentina 1925)
Jose Lago Millon (Argentina 1927)
Francisco Olazar (Argentina 1929)
Raul V Blanco (Uruguay 1935)
Manuel Seoane (Argentina 1937)
Jack Greenwell (Peru 1939)
Pedro Cea (Uruguay 1942)
Flavio Costa (Brazil 1949)
Manuel Fleitas Solich (Paraguay 1953)
Hugo Bagnulo (Uruguay 1956)
Victorio Spinetto (Argentina 1959)
Danilo Alvim (Bolivia 1963)
Marcos Calderon (Peru 1975)
Ranulfo Miranda (Paraguay 1979)
Omar Borras (Uruguay 1983)
Roberto Fleitas (Uruguay 1987)
Sebastiao Lazaroni (Brazil 1989)
Hector Nunez (Uruguay 1995)
Mario Zagallo (Brazil 1997)
Wanderlei Luxemburgo (Brazil 1999)
Francisco Maturana (Colombia 2001)
Carlos Alberto Parreira (Brazil 2004)
Dunga (Brazil 2007)

PART 5:
AFRICA CUP OF NATIONS

THE AFRICAN governing football confederation – Confederation Africaine de Football (or CAF) – is three years younger than UEFA, yet their cross-continental tournament, the Africa Cup of Nations, kicked off before the first European Championship. Formed on 8 February 1957, the CAF announced the first championship just three days later.

Egypt's ultimate triumph in that inaugural tournament set an appropriate pattern – the "Pharaohs" have won a record number of championships overall (seven) – but the competition has changed, and progressed, plenty since then.

Only three teams entered in 1957, but 45 nations will be vying for 14 qualification spots at the next event, in 2012, alongside already qualified co-hosts Equatorial Guinea and Gabon. The global prominence of the Africa Cup of Nations has also grown, especially as the spotlight falls on major African stars taking time off from European club duties every other January. There have been mounting calls for the competition to be moved to the middle of the year, to avoid disrupting European league seasons, but these have been rejected for climatic and seasonal reasons.

Whatever the place in the calendar, the trophy – now in its third physical incarnation – will always be contested with vivacious skills and fierce local pride. There have been more different winners of the ACN than of any other continental championship, with glory being shared among 13 separate nations – including Africa's largest three countries, Sudan, Algeria and Congo DR, as well as mid-sized entrants such as Cameroon, Morocco, the Ivory Coast and early standard-setters Ghana.

And extra significance was achieved when the preliminary rounds for the 2010 event were integrated into Africa's FIFA World Cup 2010™ qualification competition.

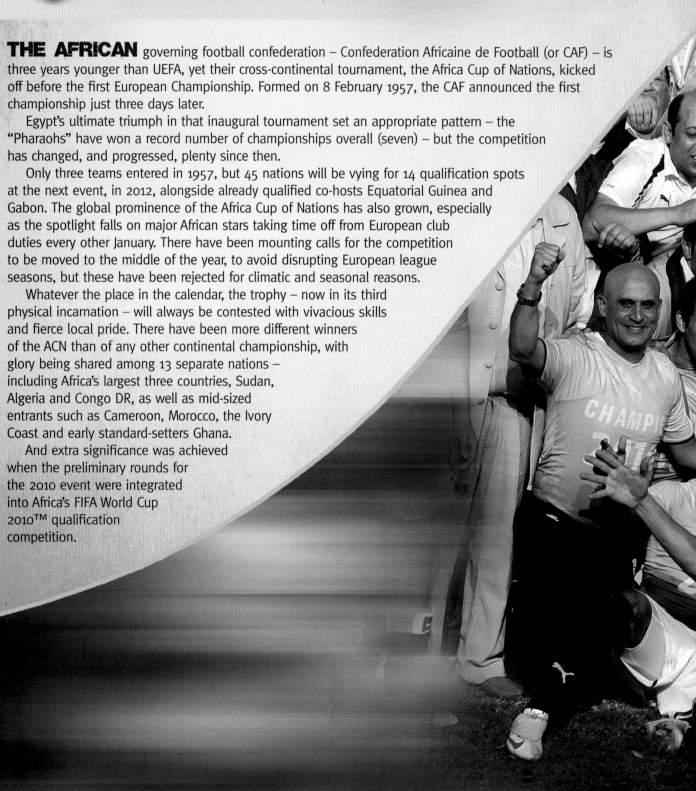

Egypt have not enjoyed the success of other African countries in the FIFA World Cup finals, but they are the pre-eminent team in the Africa Cup of Nations – and 2010 was their seventh triumph.

TEST OF ENDURANCE

The Ivory Coast have won the two highest-scoring penalty shoot-outs in full international history – they beat Ghana 11-10 over 24 penalties in the 1992 Africa Cup of Nations final, and Cameroon 12-11, over the same number of kicks, in the quarter-finals of the 2006 Africa Cup of Nations.

GHANA AGAIN

Ghana's "Black Stars" became the first country to reach the final of four consecutive Africa Cup of Nations, lifting the trophy in 1963 and 1965 and finishing runners-up in 1968 and 1970. They have now reached eight finals in all – a tally matched only by Egypt. The two countries have also staged the tournament four times apiece.

REIGNING PHARAOHS

Egypt dominate the Africa Cup of Nations records. They won the first tournament, in 1957, having been helped by a bye to the final when semi-final opponents South Africa were disqualified, and have emerged as champions another six times since – more than any other country. Their victories in the last three tournaments – 2006, 2008 and 2010 – make them the only country to lift the trophy three times in a row. They have also qualified for a record 22 tournaments, playing 84 matches – 10 more than nearest challenger Nigeria. Egypt have won 45 matches in all, followed by Nigeria on 39, Ghana on 37 and Cameroon on 36.

SIX-YEAR ITCH

Hocine Achiou's (right) 86th-minute goal not only gave Algeria a highly prized 2-1 victory over old rivals Egypt in 2004, his strike also marked the last time Egypt lost an Africa Cup of Nations match, before embarking upon a record-breaking 19-game unbeaten run that included triumphs at the 2006, 2008 and 2010 tournaments. That run included a 4-0 victory over Algeria in a 2010 Africa Cup of Nations semi-final – a match which ended with the Algerians reduced to eight men after three red cards.

BAFANA BAFANA

The Africa Cup of Nations has been won by its hosts on 11 separate occasions – including three times by Egypt and twice by Ghana. But perhaps the most surprising host-country triumph was South Africa's in 1996. The country had returned to international football only four years earlier, post-apartheid, when an 82nd-minute penalty by Theophilus "Doctor" Khumalo gave them a win over Cameroon on 7 July 1992. In February 1996, substitute Mark Williams scored both goals against Tunisia as South Africa won the Africa Cup of Nations trophy – lifted by white captain **Neil Tovey,** and handed over by the country's president Nelson Mandela, in Johannesburg's Soccer City stadium. South Africa were not even meant to be hosts, but stepped in for original choice Kenya who were stripped of staging rights after falling behind on new stadium-building.

UNLUCKY LOSERS

Five countries have qualified for the Africa Cup of Nations, but have yet to win a single match in the finals. Mauritius and Tanzania have played three unsuccessful games apiece, while Namibia have gone six without a win, Benin seven and Mozambique 10. Zaire, or the Democratic Republic of Congo, have lost more Africa Cup of Nations matches than anyone else – suffering defeat 25 times in 56 games. Both Ivory Coast (in 68 games) and Egypt (in 84 fixtures) have lost 24 times.

EQUATORIAL DEBUTANTS

Equatorial Guinea will take part in an Africa Cup of Nations finals for the first time in 2012 – thanks to co-hosting the tournament, along with Gabon. Equatorial Guinea have never managed to qualify before, while Gabon have reached the finals only four times previously. The opening match of the 2012 tournament will be staged in Equatorial Guinea, either in Libreville or Franceville, while the final will be played in one of Gabon's two host cities: Bata or Malabo. The 2012 competition will be only the second to be shared between host nations. Libya has been awarded the right to host the Africa Cup of Nations, for a second time, in 2013 – though Nigeria has been installed as first reserve should any problems arise in 2012 or 2013. Morocco has been picked to host their second Africa Cup of Nations in 2015, then South Africa will stage their second two years later. The 2015 and 2017 hosts were announced in 2011. African football's ruling body had decided in 2006 which countries would stage the 2010, 2012 and 2013 tournaments – the first time three hosting decisions had been made simultaneously.

TOURNAMENT TRIUMPHS

- 7 **Egypt** (1957, 1959, 1986, 1998, 2006, 2008, 2010)
- 4 **Ghana** (1963, 1965, 1978, 1982)
  Cameroon (1984, 1988, 2000, 2002)
- 2 **Zaire/Congo DR** (1968, 1974)
  Nigeria (1980, 1994)
- 1 **Algeria** (1990)
  Congo (1972)
  Ethiopia (1962)
  Ivory Coast (1992)
  Morocco (1976)
  South Africa (1996)
  Sudan (1970)
  Tunisia (2004)

TOURNAMENT APPEARANCES

- 22 **Egypt**
- 19 **Ivory Coast**
- 18 **Ghana**
- 17 **Cameroon, Nigeria**
- 15 **Zaire/Congo DR**
- 14 **Algeria, Tunisia, Zambia**
- 13 **Morocco**
- 10 **Senegal**
- 8 **Ethiopia, Guinea, South Africa**
- 7 **Burkina Faso, Sudan**
- 6 **Angola, Congo, Mali, Togo**
- 5 **Gabon, Kenya, Uganda**
- 4 **Mozambique**
- 3 **Benin, Malawi**
- 2 **Liberia, Libya, Namibia, Sierra Leone, Zimbabwe**
- 1 **Mauritius, Rwanda, Tanzania**

FOUR SHAME

Hosts **Angola** were responsible for perhaps the most dramatic collapse in Africa Cup of Nations history, when they threw away a four-goal lead in the opening match of the 2010 tournament. Even more embarrassingly, they were leading 4-0 against Mali with just 11 minutes left, in the capital Luanda's Estadio 11 de Novembro. Mali's final two goals, by Barcelona's Seydou Keita and Boulogne's Mustapha Yatabare, were scored deep into stoppage-time. Mali failed to make it through the first round, while Angola went out in the quarter-finals.

FASHION POINTS

Cameroon were docked six FIFA World Cup qualifying points by FIFA after wearing a forbidden one-piece kit for the 2004 Africa Cup of Nations. They won the points back on appeal.

STAR STRUCK

Gabon's Chiva Star Nzigou became the Africa Cup of Nations' youngest-ever player when he took the field against South Africa in January 2000, aged 16 years and 91 days. Gabon lost the game 3-1 and finished bottom of Group B without a win from three games.

REVOLUTION #9

No player has scored more goals in one Africa Cup of Nations than Zaire's Mulamba Ndaye's nine during the 1974 tournament. Three months later he was sent off at the FIFA World Cup in West Germany, as his team crashed to a 9-0 defeat against Yugoslavia.

PROLIFIC POKOU

Ivory Coast striker Laurent Pokou scored a record five goals in one Africa Cup of Nations match, as his side trounced Ethiopia 6-1 in the first round of the 1968 tournament. He finished top scorer at that tournament, and the following one – though ended both without a winners' medal. Only modern-day Cameroon star Samuel Eto'o has overtaken his overall Africa Cup of Nations tally of 14 goals.

FAMILIAR FACES

Cameroon's **Rigobert Song** has appeared at more Africa Cup of Nations tournaments than any other player – eight competitions in all, in 1996, 1998, 2000, 2002, 2004, 2006, 2008 and 2010. His 35 consecutive matches in the Africa Cup of Nations is also unsurpassed. He won the trophy in 2000 and 2002 and captained Cameroon to the final in 2008 – though it was his error in that match that helped set up Egypt's winning goal. Ivory Coast goalkeeper Alain Gouamene played at seven tournaments from 1988 to 2000.

TOURNAMENT TOP SCORERS

1957	Mohamed Diab El-Attar (Egypt)	5
1959	Mahmoud Al-Gohari (Egypt)	3
1962	Abdelfatah Badawi (Egypt) Mengistu Worku (Ethiopia)	3
1963	Hassan El-Shazly (Egypt)	6
1965	Ben Acheampong (Ghana) Kofi Osei (Ghana) Eustache Mangle (Ivory Coast)	3
1968	Laurent Pokou (Ivory Coast)	6
1970	Laurent Pokou (Ivory Coast)	8
1972	Salif Keita (Mali)	5
1974	Mulamba Ndaye (Zaire)	9
1976	Keita Aliou Mamadou 'N'Jo Lea' (Guinea)	4
1978	Opoku Afriyie (Ghana) Segun Odegbami (Nigeria) Philip Omondi (Uganda)	3
1980	Khaled Al Abyad Labied (Morocco) Segun Odegbami (Nigeria)	3
1982	George Alhassan (Ghana)	4
1984	Taher Abouzaid (Egypt)	4
1986	Roger Milla (Cameroon)	4
1988	Gamal Abdelhamid (Egypt) Lakhdar Belloumi (Algeria) Roger Milla (Cameroon) Abdoulaye Traore (Ivory Coast)	2
1990	Djamel Menad (Algeria)	4
1992	Rashidi Yekini (Nigeria)	4
1994	Rashidi Yekini (Nigeria)	5
1996	Kalusha Bwalya (Zambia)	5
1998	Hossam Hassan (Egypt) Benni McCarthy (South Africa)	7
2000	Shaun Bartlett (South Africa)	5
2002	Julius Aghahowa (Nigeria) Patrick Mboma (Cameroon) Rene Salomon Olembe (Cameroon)	5
2004	Francileudo Santos (Tunisia) Frederic Kanoute (Mali) Patrick Mboma (Cameroon) Youssef Mokhtari (Morocco) Jay-Jay Okocha (Nigeria)	4
2006	Samuel Eto'o (Cameroon)	5
2008	Samuel Eto'o (Cameroon)	5
2010	Mohamed Nagy 'Gedo' (Egypt)	5

⚽ GOAL RUSH RASHIDI

Rashidi Yekini is Nigeria's all-time leading scorer, with 37 goals in 70 games between 1984 and 1998. Perhaps his most significant strike came against Bulgaria in 1994, Nigeria's first-ever goal at a FIFA World Cup. They won 3-0 and reached the second round. Yet more tangible glory came when Yekini finished top scorer as Nigeria won the 1994 Africa Cup of Nations, 14 years after their only previous triumph in the tournament.

⚽ OPENING GOAL

The first Africa Cup of Nations goal was a penalty scored by Egypt's Raafat Ateya in the 21st minute of their 2-1 semi-final win over Sudan in 1957. But his team-mate Mohamed Diab El-Attar would soon take over – he not only scored Egypt's second goal that day, but all four goals in the final against Ethiopia.

⚽ WRONG KIND OF LUCK

Thomas Nkono, Cameroon's goalkeeper at the 1982 and 1990 FIFA World Cups, was arrested moments before his country's Africa Cup of Nations semi-final against hosts Mali in 2002. Nkono, in his role as goalkeeping coach, was accused of sprinkling "black magic" charms on the pitch. Cameroon won the match 3-0, then beat Senegal 3-2 on penalties in the final after the match had ended in a 0-0 stalemate.

⚽ NO HASSLE FOR HASSAN

Egypt's **Ahmed Hassan** not only became the first footballer to play in the final of four different Africa Cup of Nations in 2010 – he also became the first to collect his fourth winners' medal. Earlier in the same tournament, his appearance in the quarter-final against Cameroon gave him his 170th cap – a new Egyptian record. Hassan marked the game with three goals – one in his own net and two past Cameroon goalkeeper Carlos Kameni – although one appeared not to cross the line.

⚽ AFRICA CUP OF NATIONS ALL-TIME TOP SCORERS

1	Samuel Eto'o (Cameroon)	18
2	Laurent Pokou (Ivory Coast)	14
3	Rashidi Yekini (Nigeria)	13
4	Hassan El-Shazly (Egypt)	12
5	Hossam Hassan (Egypt)	11
=	Patrick Mboma (Cameroon)	11
7	Kalusha Bwalya (Zambia)	10
=	Ahmed Hassan (Egypt)	10
=	Mulamba Ndaye (Zaire)	10
=	Francileudo Santos (Tunisia)	10
=	Joel Tiehi (Ivory Coast)	10
=	Mengistu Worku (Ethiopia)	10

⚽ SAM THE MAN

Cameroon's Samuel Eto'o, who made his full international debut – away to Costa Rica on 9 March 1997 – one day short of his 16th birthday, is the Africa Cup of Nations' all-time leading goalscorer. He was part of Cameroon's victorious teams in 2000 and 2002, but had to wait until 2008 to pass Laurent Pokou's 14-goal Africa Cup of Nations record. That year's competition took his overall tally to 16 goals – only for the former Real Madrid and Barcelona striker, now with Italy's Internazionale, to add another two in 2010. In 2005, Eto'o became the first player to be named African Footballer of the Year three years running. He has also won an Olympic Games gold medal with Cameroon in 2000 and the UEFA Champions League three times, with Barcelona in 2006 and 2009 – scoring in both finals – and Inter in 2010.

AFRICA CUP OF NATIONS: FINALS

1957	(Host country: Sudan) Egypt 4 Ethiopia 0
1959	(Egypt) Egypt 2 Sudan 1
1962	(Ethiopia) Ethiopia 4 Egypt 2 (aet)
1963	(Ghana) Ghana 3 Sudan 0
1965	(Tunisia) Ghana 3 Tunisia 2 (aet)
1968	(Ethiopia) Zaire/Congo DR 1 Ghana 0
1970	(Sudan) Sudan 1 Ghana 0
1972	(Cameroon) Congo 3 Mali 2
1974	(Egypt) Zaire/Congo DR 2 Zambia 2
	Replay: Zaire/Congo DR 2 Zambia 0
1976	(Ethiopia) Morocco 1 Guinea 1 (Morocco win mini-league system)
1978	(Ghana) Ghana 2 Uganda 0
1980	(Nigeria) Nigeria 3 Algeria 0
1982	(Libya) Ghana 1 Libya 1 (aet; Ghana win 7-6 on penalties)
1984	(Ivory Coast) Cameroon 3 Nigeria 1
1986	(Egypt) Egypt 0 Cameroon 0 (aet; Egypt win 5-4 on penalties)
1988	(Morocco) Cameroon 1 Nigeria 0
1990	(Algeria) Algeria 1 Nigeria 0
1992	(Senegal) Ivory Coast 0 Ghana 0 (aet; Ivory Coast win 11-10 on penalties)
1994	(Tunisia) Nigeria 2 Zambia 1
1996	(South Africa) South Africa 2 Tunisia 0
1998	(Burkina Faso) Egypt 2 South Africa 0
2000	(Ghana & Nigeria) Cameroon 2 Nigeria 2 (aet; Cameroon win 4-3 on penalties)
2002	(Mali) Cameroon 0 Senegal 0 (aet; Cameroon win 3-2 on penalties)
2004	(Tunisia) Tunisia 2 Morocco 1
2006	(Egypt) Egypt 0 Ivory Coast 0 (aet; Egypt win 4-2 on penalties)
2008	(Ghana) Egypt 1 Cameroon 0
2010	(Angola) Egypt 1 Ghana 0

TIME TO SAY GOODBYE?

Former Yugoslavia international **Vahid Halilhodzic** was perhaps predictably upset and angry to be fired as Ivory Coast coach after their quarter-final exit to Algeria at the 2010 Africa Cup of Nations. His team had conceded a stoppage-time equalizer and an extra-time winner, though it was his only defeat in 24 matches in charge. Yet he found himself replaced by Sven-Goran Eriksson ahead of the 2010 FIFA World Cup in South Africa. Other coaches who have been sacked in the short period between an Africa Cup of Nations and a FIFA World Cup include Henri Michel, by Tunisia in 2002, and Nigeria's Shaibu Amodu in both 2002 and 2010.

INTERNATIONAL EXILE

South Africa were disqualified from the four-team Africa Cup of Nations in 1957 after refusing to pick a multi-racial squad.

GEDO BLASTER

Egypt's hero in 2010 was Mohamed Nagy, better known by his nickname "Gedo" – Egyptian Arabic for "Grandpa". He scored the only goal of the final, against Ghana, his fifth of the tournament, giving him the Golden Boot. Yet he did all this without starting a single game. He had to settle for coming on as a substitute in all six of Egypt's matches, playing a total of 135 minutes in all. Gedo – born in Damanhur on 3 October 1984 – made his international debut only two months earlier, and had played just two friendlies for Egypt before the tournament proper.

TOGO'S TRAGIC FATE

Togo were the victims of tragedy shortly before the 2010 Africa Cup of Nations kicked off – followed by expulsion from the event. The team's bus was fired on by Angolan militants three days before their first scheduled match, killing three people: the team's assistant coach, press officer and bus driver. The team returned home to Togo for three days of national mourning, and were then thrown out of the competition by the CAF as punishment for missing their opening game against Ghana. Togo were later expelled from the 2012 and 2014 competitions, but this sanction was overturned on appeal in May 2010.

UNFINISHED BUSINESS

Beware – if you go to see Nigeria play Tunisia, you may not get the full 90 minutes. Nigeria were awarded third place at the 1978 Africa Cup of Nations after the Tunisian team walked off after 42 minutes of their play-off, with the score at 1-1. They were protesting about refereeing decisions, but thus granted Nigeria a 2-0 victory by default. Oddly enough, it had been Nigeria walking off when the two teams met in the second leg of a qualifier for the 1962 tournament. Their action came when Tunisia equalized after 65 minutes. The punishment was a 2-0 win in Tunisia's favour – putting them 3-2 ahead on aggregate.

WINNER ON THE PITCH AND IN THE DUGOUT

The only man to win the Africa Cup of Nations as both player and manager is Egypt's **Mahmoud El-Gohary**, top scorer and medal-winner at the 1959 tournament and in charge of the squad lifting the trophy 39 years later. His four separate stints as Egyptian national coach also included taking the team to the 1990 World Cup finals. Egypt's 2010 triumph was a record-equalling third for manager Hassan Shehata – who, as a striker, had finished in third place with Egypt in 1974 and fourth in 1980. Charles Gyamfi, who played for Ghana from 1950 to 1961, coached his national side to success at the 1963, 1965 and 1982 finals.

TUNED IN TO SUDAN

The 1970 Africa Cup of Nations in Sudan marked the first time the tournament was televised. Ghana reached the final for a then unprecedented fourth time in a row, but were beaten 1-0 by the hosts.

RECENT AFRICA CUP OF NATIONS–WINNING COACHES

1988	Claude Le Roy (Cameroon)
1990	Abdelhamid Kermali (Algeria)
1992	Yeo Martial (Ivory Coast)
1994	Clemens Westerhof (Nigeria)
1996	Clive Barker (South Africa)
1998	Mahmoud El-Gohary (Egypt)
2000	Pierre Lechantre (Cameroon)
2002	Winfried Schafer (Cameroon)
2004	Roger Lemerre (Tunisia)
2006	Hassan Shehata (Egypt)
2008	Hassan Shehata (Egypt)
2010	Hassan Shehata (Egypt)

LOCK DEFENCE

Liberia's military leader Samuel Doe threatened to jail the national team if they lost at an Africa Cup of Nations qualifier to Gambia in December 1980 – a game that also doubled up as a FIFA World Cup qualifier. The players escaped punishment by achieving a 0-0 draw, though neither side went on to reach either the Africa Cup of Nations or the 1982 FIFA World Cup.

TREBLE DENIED

Egyptian playmaker Mohamed Aboutrika struck the decisive penalty in the 2006 final shoot-out against the Ivory Coast, then scored the only goal against Cameroon at the climax of the 2008 competition – but missed out through injury in 2010. Aboutrika, a philosophy graduate who was born in Giza on 7 November 1978, has been nicknamed "The Smiling Assassin" for his ruthless goalscoring and cheery appearance.

CUP FOR KEEPS

The 2012 Africa Cup of Nations will feature a new trophy, after **Egypt's third consecutive triumph in 2010** allowed them to keep the cup for good. The new design will actually be the fourth different ACN prize – the first was given to Ghana for keeps in 1978, after they became the first country to win the competition three separate times. The second was retained in 2000 by Cameroon, as they too became three-time winners.

PART 6: OTHER FIFA TOURNAMENTS

FOOTBALL at the highest level is not only about the most high-profile superstars, but also about the working investment of a myriad of enthusiasts at grassroots level across the world. Regional confederations organize international championships for players in a wide range of age groups. In 1977, FIFA extended its own worldwide development programme with the launch of the FIFA World Youth Cup. The first finals were hosted by Tunisia and the Soviet Union beat Mexico in the final. Later, in 1985, came the FIFA U-17 World Cup. Simultaneously, the Olympic Games football tournament was converted into an Under-23 event with, initially, an exception for teams in the finals to field up to three over-age players.

The establishment of such events at the pinnacle of the world game encouraged all the regional confederations to create matching tournaments of their own so that their teams could qualify for a place on the big stage. A flood of outstanding players first made headlines in the age-group system. Most notable among these players was Diego Maradona, who led Argentina to victory in Japan in the FIFA World Youth Cup in 1979. Seven years later, in 1986 in Mexico, he was his country's winning captain and inspiration at the FIFA World Cup. Women's championships were organized in response to the rapid acceleration of interest in the game and, in 2000, FIFA stepped into the senior club sphere too, with the launch of what is now the established, annual FIFA Club World Cup.

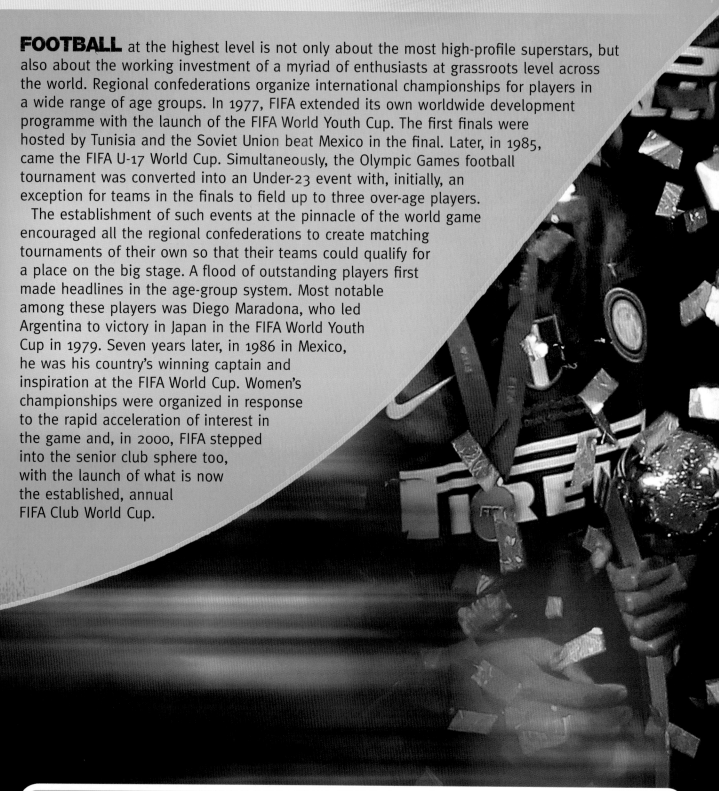

Internazionale Milan ended a fantastic 2010 with victory in the final of the FIFA Club World Cup. The Italian giants, Coppa Italia winners as well, were thus simultaneously domestic, continental and world club champions.

FIFA U-20 WORLD CUP

First staged in 1977 in Tunisia and known as the FIFA Youth World Championship until 2005, the FIFA U-20 World Cup is the world championship of football for players under the age of 20 and has featured some of the game's most notable names. Staged on a bi-annual basis, the tournament's most successful team has been Argentina, who have lifted the trophy on six occasions.

FULL HOUSES

The 2009 tournament saw record crowds – and those crowds saw more goals than in any previous FIFA Under-20 World Cup. Some 1,295,586 fans attended the 52 games, at seven venues across five Egyptian cities, meaning the average attendance was 24,915 per match. The overall tally exceeded the 1,195,299 attending the tournament in Canada two years earlier – but the average crowd of 36,099 for the 32 games in Mexico in 1983 remains a record too. A total of 167 goals were scored during the 2009 competition, two more than in Malaysia 12 years earlier. The Egypt contest had 3.21 goals per game, marginally higher than Malaysia's 3.17. Poor Tahiti helped keep the goal-rate high – they conceded 21 goals in three group games in Egypt, while failing to score themselves.

SUPER SUB

The Soviet Union became the first winners of the FIFA Under-20 World Cup when they beat hosts Mexico 9-8 on penalties after a 2-2 draw in the 1977 final. Their shoot-out hero was substitute goalkeeper Yuri Sivuha, who had replaced Aleksandre Novikov during extra-time. It remains the only time the Soviet Union won the event, though their striker **Oleg Salenko**, a future 1994 FIFA World Cup Golden Boot winner, took the top scorer award in 1989, with five goals. Two years later, fellow Soviet Sergei Sherbakov also finished top scorer, also with five goals, although his full international career was less successful. He played only twice for Ukraine before injuries suffered in a car accident in 1993 left him in a wheelchair.

DOMINANT DOMINIC

Ghana became the first African country to lift the trophy when they upset Brazil in the 2009 final – despite playing 83 of the 120 minutes with just 10 men, following Daniel Addo's red card. The final finished goalless, one of only two games in which **Dominic Adiyiah** failed to score. He ended the tournament as top scorer with eight goals and also won the Golden Ball prize for best player. Immediately afterwards a further reward was a transfer from Norway's Fredrikstad to Italy's AC Milan. The Silver Ball went to Brazil's Alex Teixeira, even though it was his missed penalty, when the final shoot-out went to sudden death, which handed Ghana victory.

LISBON LIONS

In 1991, Portugal became the first hosts to win the tournament with a team that became known as the country's "Golden Generation", featuring Luis Figo, Rui Costa, Joao Pinto, Abel Xavier and Jorge Costa. Portugal's winning squad was coached by **Carlos Queiroz**, who would later manage the full national side twice, with spells in charge at Real Madrid and as assistant at Manchester United in between. Their penalty shoot-out win over Brazil in the final was played at Benfica's iconic Estadio da Luz in the capital Lisbon. In 2001, Argentina became the second team to lift the trophy on home territory.

WAITING GAME

Nigeria were originally scheduled to host the 1995 tournament, but were replaced by Qatar due to concerns about human rights issues – and Nigeria were not even permitted to participate in the competition. The country was finally granted hosting rights for the event four years later. The 2011 edition of the FIFA Under-20 World Cup will be held in Colombia.

SAVIOUR SAVIOLA

Javier Saviola has scored more goals in one FIFA Under-20 World Cup than any other player – he managed 11 in seven games at the 2001 competition, as his side Argentina went on to beat Ghana in the final, with Saviola scoring his team's three unanswered goals. Saviola, born on 11 December 1981 in Buenos Aires, was playing for River Plate at the time but joined Barcelona for £15 million not long afterwards – before later signing for the Spanish side's arch-rivals Real Madrid. When Pele picked his 125 "greatest living footballers" for FIFA in March 2004, 22-year-old Saviola was the youngest player on the list.

CAPTAIN MARVELS

Two men have lifted both the FIFA Under-20 World Cup and the FIFA World Cup as captain: Brazil's Dunga (in 1983 and 1994) and Argentina's Diego Maradona (in 1979 and 1986). Many had expected Maradona to make Argentina's full squad for the 1978 FIFA World Cup but he missed out on selection. He showed his potential by being voted best player at the 1979 youth tournament in Japan.

TOURNAMENT HOSTS AND FINAL RESULTS

1977 (Host: Tunisia) USSR 2 Mexico 2 (aet: USSR win 9-8 on penalties)
1979 (Japan) Argentina 3 USSR 1
1981 (Australia) West Germany 4 Qatar 0
1983 (Mexico) Brazil 1 Argentina 0
1985 (USSR) Brazil 1 Spain 0 (aet)
1987 (Chile) Yugoslavia 1 West Germany 1 (aet: Yugoslavia win 5-4 on penalties)
1989 (Saudi Arabia) Portugal 2 Nigeria 0
1991 (Portugal) Portugal 0 Brazil 0 (aet: Portugal win 4-2 on penalties)
1993 (Australia) Brazil 2 Ghana 1
1995 (Qatar) Argentina 2 Brazil 0
1997 (Malaysia) Argentina 2 Uruguay 1
1999 (Nigeria) Spain 4 Japan 0
2001 (Argentina) Argentina 3 Ghana 0
2003 (United Arab Emirates) Brazil 1 Spain 0
2005 (Holland) Argentina 2 Nigeria 1
2007 (Canada) Argentina 2 Czech Republic 1
2009 (Egypt) Ghana 0 Brazil 0 (aet: Ghana win 4-3 on penalties)

WHAT A MESSI

Lionel Messi was the star of the show for Argentina in 2005, and not just for scoring both his country's goals in the final – both from the penalty spot. He achieved a hat-trick by not only winning the Golden Boot for top scorer and Golden Shoe for best player, but also by captaining his side to the title. This feat was emulated two years later by compatriot Sergio Aguero, who scored once in the final against the Czech Republic, before team-mate Mauro Zarate struck a late winner. Three other men have finished as both top scorer and as the tournament's best player (as voted by journalists) – Brazil's Geovani in 1983, Argentina's Javier Saviola in 2001 and Dominic Adiyiah of Ghana in 2009.

TOURNAMENT TOP SCORERS

Year	Player	Goals
1977	Guina (Brazil)	4
1979	Ramon Diaz (Argentina)	8
1981	Ralf Loose (West Germany), Roland Wohlfarth (West Germany), Taher Amer (Egypt), Mark Koussas (Argentina)	4
1983	Geovani (Brazil)	6
1985	Gerson (Brazil), Balalo (Brazil), Muller (Brazil), Alberto Garcia Aspe (Mexico), Monday Odiaka (Nigeria), Fernando Gomez (Spain), Sebastian Losada (Spain)	3
1987	Marcel Witeczek (West Germany)	7
1989	Oleg Salenko (USSR)	5
1991	Sergei Sherbakov (USSR)	5
1993	Ante Milicic (Australia), Adriano (Brazil), Gian (Brazil), Henry Zambrano (Colombia), Vicente Nieto (Mexico), Chris Faklaris (USA)	3
1995	Joseba Etxeberria (Spain)	7
1997	Adailton Martins Bolzan (Brazil)	10
1999	Mahamadou Dissa (Mali), Pablo (Spain)	5
2001	Javier Saviola (Argentina)	11
2003	Fernando Cavenaghi (Argentina), Dudu (Brazil), Daisuke Sakata (Japan), Eddie Johnson (USA)	4
2005	Lionel Messi (Argentina)	6
2007	Sergio Aguero (Argentina)	7
2009	Dominic Adiyiah (Ghana)	8

SIX APPEAL

Argentina have won the FIFA Under-20 World Cup the most times, winning six times, most recently in 2005 and 2007. Brazil have won four times, Portugal twice, with one success apiece for Germany, Spain, the Soviet Union, Yugoslavia and Ghana. The only final Argentina have contested, but lost, came against arch-rivals Brazil, in 1983, when Geovani struck the only goal.

FIFA U-17 WORLD CUP

First staged in China in 1985, when it was known as the FIFA Under-16 World Championship, the age limit was raised from 16 to 17 in 1991 and the competition became known as the FIFA U-17 World Cup from 2007. Staged on a bi-annual basis, the 2009 edition of the event was staged in Nigeria, the defending champions, who, along with Brazil, are the tournament's most successful countries, with three wins each.

WHOSE SHOE?

Sani Emmanuel can boast of being top scorer while also voted best player, after starring in Nigeria's run to the 2009 final – though that last match was the only one he started. He was awarded the Golden Ball for his performances, but had to settle for the Silver Shoe prize – despite scoring five goals, the same tally as Golden Shoe winner Borja. The Spanish striker took the main award because he managed one more assist. Uruguay's Sebastian Gallegos and Switzerland's Haris Seferovic also finished the tournament with five goals apiece. Yuri Nikiforov scored a joint-best five goals for Russia at the 1987 tournament, including one in the final as his team beat Nigeria on penalties – but FIFA awarded the Golden Shoe to Ivory Coast's Moussa Traore, who also hit five but for a lower-scoring side. The Soviet Union scored 21 overall, to the Ivory Coast's nine.

GOALS FLO

Apart from Cesc Fabregas, the only other man to have won both the Golden Ball and the Golden Shoe is France's **Florent Sinama-Pongolle**, whose nine goals in 2001 set a tournament record for one player. His tally included two hat-tricks in the opening round. Unlike Fabregas, Sinama-Pongolle also ended the final on the winning side. The team goalscoring record is held by Spain, who struck 22 times on their way to third place in 1997.

SEOUL SURVIVOR

The final of the 2007 tournament was the first to be hosted by a former FIFA World Cup venue – the 68,476-capacity Seoul FIFA World Cup Stadium in South Korea's capital, which had been built for the 2002 FIFA World Cup. The game was watched by a crowd of 36,125, a tournament record. The 2007 event was the first to feature 24 teams instead of 16, and was won by Nigeria – after Spain missed all three of their spot-kicks in a penalty shoot-out.

TAKING WING

Nigeria's youth side, the "Golden Eaglets", became the first African nation to win a FIFA tournament when they triumphed at the inaugural Under-16 FIFA World Cup in 1985 (it became an Under-17 event in 1991). Their opening goal in the final against West Germany was scored by striker Jonathan Akpoborie, who would go on to play for German clubs Stuttgart and Wolfsburg.

GOOD AND BAD BOY BOJAN

Barcelona star **Bojan Krkic** quickly went from hero to villain in the final moments of Spain's semi-final victory over Ghana in 2007 – he scored his team's winner with four minutes of extra-time remaining, but was then sent off for a second yellow-card offence just before the final whistle. His expulsion meant he was suspended for the final, which Spain lost on penalties to Nigeria.

GOLDEN HAUL

West Germany's Marcel Witeczek is the only person to finish top scorer at both a FIFA Under-16 World Championship and the Under-20 version of the event. The Polish-born striker hit eight goals at the 1985 Under-16 tournament, followed by seven more at the Under-20 championship two years later. Brazil's Adriano – a different Adriano to the one who later played for the senior side and Serie A club Internazionale – came closest to equalling the feat: he won the Golden Shoe, for top scorer, after scoring four goals at the 1991 FIFA Under-17 World Cup, then the Golden Ball, for best player, at the Under-20 event in 1993.

FAB FABREGAS

Spain's **Cesc Fabregas** joined Florent Sinama-Pongolle as only two players to win both the Golden Shoe, for top scorer, and the Golden Ball, for best player, at a FIFA Under-17 World Cup. He took both prizes after scoring five goals at the 2003 tournament, despite losing the final to Brazil. He and team-mate David Silva would later be part of the senior Spanish team that won the 2008 European Championship and, two years later, the FIFA World Cup in South Africa. Fabregas, born in Arenys de Mar on 4 May 1987, left Barcelona for Arsenal a month after the 2003 tournament, where he later became club captain.

TOURNAMENT TOP SCORERS

1985	Marcel Witeczek (West Germany)	8
1987	Moussa Traore (Ivory Coast)	5
	Yuri Nikiforov (USSR)	5
1989	Khaled Jasem (Bahrain)	3
	Fode Camara (Guinea)	3
	Gil (Portugal)	3
	Tulipa (Portugal)	3
	Khalid Al Roaihi (Saudi Arabia)	3
1991	Adriano (Brazil)	4
1993	Wilson Oruma (Nigeria)	6
1995	Daniel Allsopp (Australia)	5
	Mohamed Al Kathiri (Oman)	5
1997	David (Spain)	7
1999	Ishmael Addo (Ghana)	7
2001	Florent Sinama-Pongolle (France)	9
2003	Carlos Hidalgo (Colombia)	5
	Manuel Curto (Portugal)	5
	Cesc Fabregas (Spain)	5
2005	Carlos Vela (Mexico)	5
2007	Macauley Chrisantus (Nigeria)	7
2009	Borja (Spain)	5
	Sani Emmanuel (Nigeria)	5
	Sebastian Gallegos (Uruguay)	5
	Haris Seferovic (Switzerland)	5

LITTLE ITALY

The 1991 tournament was originally scheduled to take place in Ecuador, but a cholera outbreak in the country meant it was switched to Italy instead – though played in much smaller venues than those that had been used for the previous year's senior FIFA World Cup in the country. The 1991 tournament was the first to be open to Under-17s – the first three had been known as the FIFA U-16 World Cup.

EVER–PRESENT AMERICA

While Brazil and Nigeria have enjoyed the most success in the FIFA U-17 World Cup, with three triumphs each, the only country to take part in all 12 competitions is the United States – their best finish was fourth in 1999.

SWISS SURPRISE

Switzerland were the unexpected winners in 2009, in their first-ever appearance at the tournament. Their 1-0 win over favourites Nigeria in the final, thanks to a Haris Seferovic goal, prevented the Africans from becoming only the second country to retain the trophy. Swiss goalkeeper Benjamin Siegrist, who conceded only four goals in seven games, was given the Golden Glove prize for best goalkeeper. Nigerian preparations for the finals had been disrupted when 15 of their players were found to be over-age and had to be dropped from the squad.

HOSTS AND FINAL RESULTS

(Host country)

1985 (China) Nigeria 2 West Germany 0

1987 (Canada) USSR 1 Nigeria 1
(aet: USSR win 4-2 on penalties)

1989 (Scotland) Saudi Arabia 2 Scotland 2
(aet: Saudi Arabia win 5-4 on penalties)

1991 (Italy) Ghana 1 Spain 0

1993 (Japan) Nigeria 2 Ghana 1

1995 (Ecuador) Ghana 3 Brazil 2

1997 (Egypt) Brazil 2 Ghana 1

1999 (New Zealand) Brazil 0 Australia 0
(aet: Brazil win 8-7 on penalties)

2001 (Trinidad & Tobago) France 3 Nigeria 0

2003 (Finland) Brazil 1 Spain 0

2005 (Peru) Mexico 3 Brazil 0

2007 (South Korea) Nigeria 0 Spain 0
(aet: Nigeria win 3-0 on penalties)

2009 (Nigeria) Switzerland 1 Nigeria 0

FIFA CONFEDERATIONS CUP

The FIFA Confederations Cup has assumed numerous guises over the years. In 1992 and 1995 it was played in Saudi Arabia and featured a collection of continental champions. From 1997 to 2003 FIFA staged a tournament every two years. The tournament was played in its current format for the first time in Germany in 2005. It is now celebrated throughout the football world as the Championship of Champions.

OVERALL TOP SCORERS

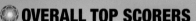

1	Cuauhtemoc Blanco (Mexico)	9
=	Ronaldinho (Brazil)	9
3	Romario (Brazil)	7
=	Adriano (Brazil)	7
5	Marzouq Al-Otaibi	6
6	Alex (Brazil)	5
=	John Aloisi (Australia)	5
=	Luis Fabiano (Brazi)	5
=	Vladimir Smicer (Czech Rep.)	5
=	Robert Pires (France)	5

FAB'S FIVE

Brazil's victory over the United States in the 2009 final made them the first country to complete a hat-trick of FIFA Confederations Cup triumphs, following success in 1997 and 2005. But they did it the hard way, needing to come back from two goals down at half-time before winning 3–2 – thanks to a late goal from captain and centre-back Lucio. Their other two were struck by forward **Luis Fabiano**, who ended as tournament top scorer with five goals overall. His team-mate Kaka was voted best player, with Luis Fabiano second and America's Clint Dempsey third.

TOURNAMENT TOP SCORERS

1992	Gabriel Batistuta (Argentina), Bruce Murray (USA) 2
1995	Luis Garcia (Mexico) 3
1997	Romario (Brazil) 7
1999	Ronaldinho (Brazil), Cuauhtemoc Blanco (Mexico), Marzouq Al-Otaibi (Saudi Arabia) 6
2001	Shaun Murphy (Australia), Eric Carriere (France), Robert Pires (France), Patrick Vieira (France), Sylvain Wiltord (France), Takayuki Suzuki (Japan), Hwang Sun-Hong (South Korea) 2
2003	Thierry Henry (France) 4
2005	Adriano (Brazil) 5
2009	Luis Fabiano (Brazil) 5

FIT FOR A KING

Before being rebranded as the FIFA Confederations Cup, a tournament bringing together the continental champions of the world was known as the King Fahd Cup and was hosted in Saudi Arabia. Copa America holders Argentina reached both finals, beating their hosts in the first in 1992 thanks to goals by Leonardo Rodriguez, Claudio Caniggia and Diego Simeone. Only four teams took part in the 1992 event, with the United States and the Ivory Coast also represented, but world champions Germany and European champions Holland did not participate. In 1995, a six-team version was won by European champions Denmark, when goals from Michael Laudrup and Peter Rasmussen were enough to see off Argentina in the final in Riyadh.

TRIPLE CROWNS

Two countries have held a clean sweep hat-trick of titles at one time. Brazil's FIFA Confederations Cup triumph in December 1997 came six months after they were crowned South American champions, in the Copa America – and while still reigning world champions, after winning the 1994 FIFA World Cup. Patrick Vieira's golden-goal winner for France in the final of the FIFA Confederations Cup 2001 meant they emulated Brazil's feat, having won the FIFA World Cup in 1998 and the European Championship in 2000.

DIFFERENT BALL GAMES

The 2009 hosts South Africa had to amend their plans for staging matches when building work on Port Elizabeth's Nelson Mandela Bay Stadium fell behind schedule – leaving the games shared between Ellis Park Stadium in Johannesburg, Loftus Versfeld Stadium in Pretoria, Free State Stadium in Bloemfontein and Royal Bafokeng Stadium in Rustenburg. The venues also hosted rugby union matches for the British Lions' tour of South Africa in June 2009, though at least nine days separated any rugby and football games in the same stadium.

THREE APIECE

Brazil's Romario holds the record for the most goals scored in a single FIFA Confederations Cup – seven, in five games, as his country took the title for the first time in 1997. His tally included three in the 6-0 final win over Australia – but he had to share the hat-trick glory: the rest of the goals were claimed by his strike-partner Ronaldo.

UNEVEN DISTRIBUTION

Both Saudi Arabia's **Marzouk Al-Otaibi** and Brazil's Ronaldinho were on the scoresheet in their sides' 1999 semi-final, when Brazil won 8-2 – the most goals ever scored in one FIFA Confederations Cup match. Al-Otaibi got two and Ronaldinho hit three, in a match that was even at 2-2 after half an hour.

SCREENS BLANKED

There was controversy over Brazil's dramatic last-gasp win over Egypt in the first round of the 2009 tournament. Their 4-3 win came courtesy of a stoppage-time penalty by Kaka – though English referee Howard Webb had initially signalled for a corner, instead of handball by Egyptian defender Ahmed al-Muhammadi. He then changed his mind, pointing to the spot and sending off al-Muhammadi. The Egyptians later claimed he changed his mind due to information from video replays, and FIFA president Sepp Blatter announced TV monitors would now be banned from the side of the pitch.

CLINT MAKES AMERICA'S DAY

The United States' surprise run to the 2009 final included a shock semi-final win over Spain that ended the European champions' long unbeaten run. Heading into the match, Spain had won a record 15 international matches in a row – and gone 35 successive games unbeaten, a tally shared with Brazil. But their hopes of a record 36th match without defeat were ruined by goals from US striker Jozy Altidore and winger **Clint Dempsey**. The result put the Americans into the final of a FIFA men's senior competition for the first time.

SHARED SADNESS

The 2003 tournament was overshadowed by the tragic death of Cameroon's 28-year-old midfielder **Marc-Vivien Foe**, who collapsed on the Lyon pitch after suffering a heart attack 73 minutes into his country's semi-final win against Colombia. After Thierry Henry scored France's golden-goal winner against Cameroon in the final, he dedicated his goal to Foe, who played much of his club career in the French championship. When the trophy was presented at the Stade de France in Paris, it was jointly lifted by the captains of both teams – Marcel Desailly for France and Rigobert Song for Cameroon.

FIFA CONFEDERATIONS CUP HOSTS AND FINAL RESULTS

1997	(Host country: Saudi Arabia) Brazil 6 Argentina 0
1999	(Mexico) Mexico 4 Brazil 3
2001	(South Korea and Japan) France 1 Japan 0
2003	(France) France 1 Cameroon 0
	(aet: France win on golden goal)
2005	(Germany) Brazil 4 Argentina 1
2009	(South Africa) Brazil 3 United States 2

FIFA CLUB WORLD CUP

As is the case with the FIFA Confederations Cup, the FIFA Club World Cup has been played in many different formats since 1960, when Real Madrid defeated Penarol. In its current guise, the competition pits the champion clubs from all six continents against each other and was staged on an annual basis, in Japan, since 2005. In 2009 and 2010 the tournament was staged in Abu Dhabi.

ONE INTER GO OUT

Many people expected a final between Internazionale and Internacional when the 2010 FIFA Club World Cup was staged in Abu Dhabi, in the United Arab Emirates – but the Brazilian club were eliminated in the semi-finals. No such disappointment for UEFA Champions League holders Internazionale, from Milan in Italy, who beat South Korea's Seongnam Ilhwa Chunma 3–0 in their semi-final. Inter then defeated DR Congo's TP Mazembe 3–0 in the competition's climax – the largest margin of victory of any FIFA Club World Cup final. Inter's scorers against Mazembe were Goran Pandev, **Samuel Eto'o** – who was later named player of the tournament – and Jonathan Biabiany. But clinching Inter's fifth trophy of 2010 was not enough to save the job of coach Rafael Benitez – he left the club five days later, after just six months in charge.

WINNERS BY COUNTRY

9	Argentina
8	Italy
6	Brazil, Uruguay
5	Spain
3	Germany, Holland
2	Portugal
1	England, Paraguay, Yugoslavia

SEVEN UP

Despite Al-Ahly's defeat to Adelaide United in the 2009 fifth-place play-off, the game was a landmark for four of the Egyptian club's players: Mohamed Aboutrika, Wael Gomaa, **Shady Mohamed** and Hossam Ashour were all playing in a FIFA Club World Cup match for a seventh time. They passed the six-match record previously held by Brazilian goalkeeper Dida, who played in the tournament for Corinthians (2000) and AC Milan (2007).

SIX APPEAL

Barcelona's triumph in 2009 made them the first club to lift six different major trophies in one calendar year: the FIFA Club World Cup, the UEFA Champions League, the UEFA European Super Cup, and a Spanish hat-trick of La Liga, Copa del Rey and Super Cup. This made their trophy cabinet one cup heavier than Liverpool's in 2001, when Gerard Houllier's men won the FA Cup, League Cup and Charity Shield in England and the UEFA Cup and Super Cup in Europe.

UAE O.K.

The 2009 tournament was the first of the "new" FIFA Club World Cup events to take place outside Japan – in the United Arab Emirates state of Abu Dhabi, where the tournament was also staged 12 months later. Two stadia shared the workload: the **Al Jazira Mohammed bin Zayed Stadium** and the 60,000-capacity Sheikh Zayed Stadium, the setting for the final each time. The UAE saw off rival bids from Australia and Japan to secure hosting rights for the December 2010 event. But the competition is due to return to Japan in 2011 and 2012.

SWITCHING SYSTEMS

From 1960 until 1968, the Intercontinental Cup was settled, not on aggregate scores, but by using a system of two points for a win and one for a draw. This meant a third, deciding match was needed in 1961, 1963, 1964 and 1967. No team that had not been worse off on aggregate after the first two legs had gone on to win the third match, though before losing their play-off 1-0 to Argentina's Racing Club in 1967, Celtic would have won the two-legged tie if aggregate scores and away goals counted. The Scottish side won their home leg 1-0, before losing 2-1 away. From 1980 onwards, the annual event was a one-off match staged in Japan.

FIGURE OF EIGHT

Manchester United's 5-3 win over Gamba Osaka in the semi-final of the FIFA Club World Cup in 2008 was the highest-scoring single game in the history of the competition in all its forms – bettering the 5-2 victory over Benfica by a Santos team featuring Pele in 1962. Even more amazingly, all but two of the goals in the Manchester United–Gamba game were scored in the final 16 minutes, plus stoppage-time. United were leading 2-0 with 74 minutes gone, before a burst of goals – including two by substitute Wayne Rooney – at both ends. Manchester United became the first team to score five goals in the FIFA Club World Cup's revised format.

LONG-DISTANCE, LONG-RUNNING RIVALRY

The precursor to the modern FIFA Club World Cup was the Intercontinental Cup, also known informally as the World Club Cup and/or the Europe–South America Cup, which pitted the champions of Europe and South America against each other. Representatives of UEFA and CONMEBOL contested the event from 1960 to 2004, but now all continental federations send at least one club to an expanded Club World Cup organized and endorsed by the world federation, FIFA. The original final, in 1960, was between Spain's Real Madrid and Uruguay's Penarol. After a goalless draw in the rain in Montevideo, Real triumphed 5-1 at their own stadium in Madrid – including three goals scored in the first eight minutes, two of them by Ferenc Puskas. The two clubs are among five sharing the record for Intercontinental Cup triumphs, with three victories apiece – the others being Argentina's Boca Juniors, Uruguay's Nacional and AC Milan of Italy. Milan are the only one of these clubs to have added a FIFA Club World Cup to their tally, as the championship was first contested in 2000 (in Brazil) before it was swallowed up by the Intercontinental Cup and was instituted on an annual basis.

SUCCESS IN PHASES

Since FIFA introduced its own, expanded Club World Cup in 2000, with representatives from all the world's continental football federations, Brazilian sides have the best overall record – with Corinthians the first winners. Carlo Ancelotti's AC Milan finally broke the Brazilian stranglehold in 2007, when the trophy was lifted by club captain Paolo Maldini, who had appeared for Milan – alongside Alessandro Costacurta – in five Intercontinental Cup showdowns between 1989 and 2003.

CONGO DANCE

For the first time in unofficial Intercontinental Cup or official FIFA Club World Cup history, an African team contested the 2010 final. TP Mazembe, from the Democratic Republic of Congo, defeated South American champions Internacional, from Brazil, 2–0 in their semi-final. Internacional, winners in 2006, were the first former FIFA Club World Cup champions to compete for a second time. Mazembe achieved the surprise victory despite missing their star striker and captain Tresor Mputu, who was serving a one-year ban for furiously chasing a referee after a match in May 2010. Goalkeeper **Muteba Kidiaba,** sent off during the 2009 FIFA Club World Cup, was man of the match against Internacional a year later. He celebrated the victory by bouncing across the pitch on his bottom.

FIFA CLUB WORLD CUP FINALS (2000–10)

2000	**Corinthians (Brazil)** 0 Vasco da Gama (Brazil) 0 (aet: Corinthians win 4-3 on penalties)
2005	**Sao Paulo (Brazil)** 1 Liverpool (England) 0
2006	**Internacional (Brazil)** 1 Barcelona (Spain) 0
2007	**AC Milan (Italy)** 4 Boca Juniors (Argentina) 2
2008	**Manchester United (England)** 1 LDU Quito (Ecuador) 0
2009	**Barcelona (Spain)** 2 Estudiantes (Argentina) 1 (aet)
2010	**Internazionale (Italy)** 3 TP Mazembe (DR Congo) 0

INTERCONTINENTAL CUP TRIUMPHS (1960–2004)

3 wins: Real Madrid, Spain (1960, 1998, 2002); Penarol, Uruguay (1961, 1966, 1982); AC Milan, Italy (1969, 1989, 1990); Nacional, Uruguay (1971, 1988, 1988); Boca Juniors, Argentina (1977, 2000, 2003).

2 wins: Santos, Brazil (1962, 1963); Internazionale, Italy (1964, 1965); Ajax, Holland (1972, 1995); Independiente, Argentina (1973, 1984); Bayern Munich, West Germany/Germany (1976, 2001); Juventus, Italy (1985, 1996); Porto, Portugal (1987, 2004); Sao Paulo, Brazil (1992, 1993).

1 win: Racing Club, Argentina (1967); Estudiantes, Argentina (1968); Feyenoord, Holland (1970); Atletico Madrid, Spain (1974); Olimpia Asuncion, Paraguay (1979); Flamengo, Brazil (1981); Gremio, Brazil (1983); River Plate, Argentina (1986); Red Star Belgrade, Yugoslavia (1991); Velez Sarsfield, Argentina (1994); Borussia Dortmund, Germany (1997); Manchester United, England (1999).

MEN'S OLYMPIC FOOTBALL TOURNAMENT

First played at the 1900 Olympic Games in Paris, although not recognized by FIFA as an official tournament until the 1908 Games in London, the men's Olympic football tournament was played strictly in accordance with the Games' strong amateur tradition until 1984, when professionals were allowed to play for the first time. Since then, the competition has provided countries with an opportunity to hand their rising young stars an invaluable taste of tournament football under the glare of the world media spotlight.

CZECH OUT

The climax of the 1920 Olympic Games tournament is the only time a major international football final has been abandoned. Czechoslovakia's players walked off the pitch minutes before half-time, in protest at the decisions made by 65-year-old English referee John Lewis – including the dismissal of Czech player Karel Steiner. Belgium, who were 2-0 up at the time, were awarded the victory, before Spain beat Holland 3-1 in a play-off for silver.

MEN'S OLYMPIC FOOTBALL FINALS

1896 Not played
1900 (Paris, France)
Gold: Upton Park FC (GB) Silver: USFSA XI (France) Bronze: Universite Libre de Bruxelles (Belgium) (only two exhibition matches played)
1904 (St Louis, US)
Gold: Galt FC (Canada) Silver: Christian Brothers College (US) Bronze: St Rose Parish (US) (only five exhibition matches played)
1908 (London, England)
Great Britain 2 Denmark 0 (Bronze: Holland)
1912 (Stockholm, Sweden)
Great Britain 4 Denmark 2 (Bronze: Holland)
1916 Not played
1920 (Antwerp, Belgium)
Belgium 2 Czechoslovakia 0 (Silver: Spain, Bronze: Holland)
1924 (Paris, France)
Uruguay 3 Switzerland 0 (Bronze: Sweden)
1928 (Amsterdam, Holland)
Uruguay 1 Argentina 1; Uruguay 2 Argentina 1 (Bronze: Italy)
1932 Not played
1936 (Berlin, Germany) Italy 2 Austria 1 (aet) (Bronze: Norway)
1940 Not played
1944 Not played
1948 (London, England) Sweden 3 Yugoslavia 1 (Bronze: Denmark)
1952 (Helsinki, Finland) Hungary 2 Yugoslavia 0 (Bronze: Sweden)
1956 (Melbourne, Australia) USSR 1 Yugoslavia 0 (Bronze: Bulgaria)
1960 (Rome, Italy) Yugoslavia 3 Denmark 1 (Bronze: Hungary)
1964 (Tokyo, Japan) Hungary 2 Czechoslovakia 1 (Bronze: Germany)
1968 (Mexico City, Mexico) Hungary 4 Bulgaria 1 (Bronze: Japan)
1972 (Munich, West Germany) Poland 2 Hungary 1 (Bronze: USSR/East Germany)
1976 (Montreal, Canada) East Germany 3 Poland 1 (Bronze: USSR)
1980 (Moscow, USSR) Czechoslovakia 1 East Germany 0 (Bronze: USSR)
1984 (Los Angeles, USA) France 2 Brazil 0 (Bronze: Yugoslavia)
1988 (Seoul, South Korea) USSR 2 Brazil 1 (Bronze: West Germany)
1992 (Barcelona, Spain) Spain 3 Poland 2 (Bronze: Ghana)
1996 (Atlanta, USA) Nigeria 3 Argentina 2 (Bronze: Brazil)
2000 (Sydney, Australia) Cameroon 2 Spain 2
(**Cameroon win** 5-3 on penalties) (Bronze: Chile)
2004 (Athens, Greece) Argentina 1 Paraguay 0 (Bronze: Italy)
2008 (Beijing, China) **Argentina 1** Nigeria 0 (Bronze: Brazil)

BARCELONA BOUND

Future Barcelona team-mates Samuel Eto'o and Xavi scored penalties for opposing sides in 2000, when Cameroon and Spain contested the first Olympic final to be settled by a shoot-out. Ivan Amaya was the only player to miss, handing Cameroon gold.

RETROSPECTIVE MEDALS

Football was not played at the very first modern Summer Olympics, in Athens in 1896, and the football tournaments played at the 1900 and 1904 events are not officially recognized by FIFA. Medals were not handed out to the winning teams at the time – with Great Britain represented in 1900 by the Upton Park club from East London – though the International Olympic Committee has since allocated first, second and third place to the countries taking part.

BLOC PARTY

Eastern European countries dominated the Olympic Games football competitions from 1948 to 1980, when professional players were officially banned from taking part. Teams comprising so-called "state amateurs" from the Eastern Bloc took 23 of the 27 medals available during those years. Only Sweden, in 1948, brought gold medals west of the Iron Curtain. Sweden also collected bronze four years later, before Denmark claimed silver in 1960 and Japan bronze in 1968.

LAPPING IT UP

Uruguay have a perfect Olympic football record, winning gold on the two occasions they took part (1924 and 1928). Those Olympics were seen as a quasi-world championship and helped prompt FIFA into organizing the first World Cup in 1930. This was also won by Uruguay, who included 1924 and 1928 gold medallists Jose Nasazzi, Jose Andrade and **Hector Scarone** (right) in their squad. Uruguay's triumphant 1924 team are thought to have pioneered the lap of honour.

AWAY FROM HOME

Olympic football matches often take place outside, even far from, the Games' host cities – some of those staged at the 2012 Summer Olympics in London will be played not only in a different city, but a different country. The Millennium Stadium in Cardiff, Wales, and Hampden Park in Glasgow, Scotland, will host matches, as will Old Trafford in Manchester, St James' Park in Newcastle and the City of Coventry Stadium – but the main focus will inevitably be on London's **Wembley Stadium**, where the final will take place. The furthest afield venues in Olympic football history came at the 1984 Los Angeles Games in the US, when two of the stadia were more than 3,200 km away from LA – the Navy-Marine Corps Memorial Stadium in Annapolis, Maryland, and the Harvard Stadium in Boston, Massachusetts. Not one minute of football that Summer Olympics was played in Atlanta, with the gold medal game coming closest – "just" 75 miles (105 km) away in Athens, Georgia.

AFRICAN AMBITION

Ghana became the first African country to win an Olympic football medal, picking up bronze in 1992, but Nigeria went even better four years later by claiming the continent's first Olympic football gold medal – thanks to Emmanuel Amunike's stoppage-time winner against Argentina. Nigeria's triumph came as a huge surprise to many – especially as their rival teams included such future world stars as Brazil's Ronaldo and Roberto Carlos, Argentina's Hernan Crespo and Roberto Ayala, Italy's Fabio Cannavaro and Gianluigi Buffon, and France's Robert Pires and **Patrick Vieira**. Future FIFA World Cup or UEFA European Championship winners to have played at Summer Olympics include France's Michel Platini and Patrick Battiston (at the Montreal Games in 1976); West Germany's Andreas Brehme and Brazil's Dunga (Los Angeles, 1984); Brazil's Taffarel, Bebeto and Romario and West Germany's Jurgen Klinsmann (Seoul, 1988); France's Vieira, Pires and Sylvain Wiltord, Italy's Cannavaro, Buffon and Alessandro Nesta, and Brazil's Roberto Carlos, Rivaldo and Ronaldo (Atlanta, 1996); Italy's Gianluca Zambrotta and Spain's Xavi, Carles Puyol and Joan Capdevila (Sydney, 2000); and Italy's Daniele De Rossi, Andrea Pirlo and Alberto Gilardino (Athens, 2004).

BLUE STARS FIFA
YOUTH CUP

Staged on an annual basis by Zurich club FC Blue Stars since 1939, and granted FIFA's patronage since 1991, the Blue Stars/FIFA Youth Cup tournament has become football's premier youth event and features many teams from around the globe. Several of the game's greatest names – from Bobby Charlton to David Beckham – gained their first taste of international football competition at the event.

RAISING THE BARÇA

No Spanish side took part until Barcelona's involvement in 1988, with a team featuring midfielder **Josep Guardiola** and right-back Albert Ferrer, both of whom would help the club to their first European Cup triumph in 1992.

HEART OF THE BLATTER

Long before he was elected FIFA president in 1998, Sepp Blatter was a keen amateur footballer who played centre-forward for Swiss club FC Sierre in the Blue Stars tournament in the early 1950s. He is now an honorary member of FC Blue Stars.

BASEL NOT SO FAULTY

FC Basel were the third Swiss winners in four competitions when they took the prize for the first time in 2009, beating Grasshopper Club 1-0 in the final. Basel midfielder Pascal Schurpf was voted the tournament's top outfield player. The only goal of the final was scored by Xherdan Shaqiri.

PORTO SPOT ON

FC Porto became Portugal's first FIFA Blue Stars champions in 2011 – just weeks after the club's senior team clinched a treble of domestic league and cup and the UEFA Europa League. The youngsters beat FC Zurich in the FIFA Blue Stars final, 3-0 on penalties following a goalless draw – the second successive year the final went to spot-kicks. It was double disappointment for FC Zurich: 12 months earlier they lost in the same way to Argentina's Boca Juniors.

BRAZIL FORTUNE

It took until 1999 before the tournament was first won by a club from outside Europe, when Brazil's Sao Paulo beat FC Zurich on penalties, at the Swiss side's Letzigrund stadium. Sao Paulo, having added Kaka to their line-up, retained their title the following year.

BLUE STARS CHAMPIONSHIPS

Manchester United 18
(1954, 1957, 1959, 1960, 1961, 1962, 1965, 1966, 1968, 1969, 1975, 1976, 1978, 1979, 1981, 1982, 2004, 2005)
Grasshoppers 6
(1939, 1956, 1971, 1987, 1998, 2006)
Barcelona 3
(1993, 1994, 1995)
FC Zurich 3
(1946, 1949, 2008)
FC Young Fellows 3
(1941, 1942, 1953)
AC Milan 2
(1958, 1977)
Arsenal 2
(1963, 1964)
AS Roma 2
(1980, 2003)
FK Austria Vienna 2
(1947, 1948)
Sao Paulo 2
(1999, 2000)
Spartak Moscow 2
(1991, 1992)
FC Basel 1
(2009)
Boca Juniors 1
(2010)
FC Porto 1
(2011)

BLUE STARS/
FIFA YOUTH CUP 2011

FIFA FUTSAL WORLD CUP

Developed in South America in the 1930s, Futsal – a variant of five-a-side indoor football – has enjoyed a huge surge in popularity, and participation numbers, in recent years. The first FIFA Futsal World Cup was staged in Holland in 1989 and has been contested on a four-yearly basis since 1992. Two teams have dominated the event: Spain (with two wins) and, above all, Brazil (with four).

FIFA FUTSAL WORLD CUP FINALS (and hosts)

1989 (Hosts: Holland) Brazil 2 Holland 1

1992 (Hong Kong) Brazil 4 United States 1

1996 (Spain) Brazil 6 Spain 4

2000 (Guatemala) Spain 4 Brazil 3

2004 (Chinese Taipei) Spain 2 Italy 1

2008 (Brazil) **Brazil 2 Spain 2**
(aet: Brazil win 4-3 on penalties)

THE FIRST MANOEL

Brazilian Manoel Tobias can claim to be the FIFA Futsal World Cup's most prolific goalscorer, with 43 in 32 appearances. Tobias, born in Salgueiro on 19 April 1971, represented his country in the 1992, 1996, 2000 and 2004 tournaments – only once ending up on the losing side within normal time. He ended both the 1996 and 2000 competitions with the prizes for both best player and top scorer.

CUBAN EMBARGO

Cuba hold the record for the fewest goals scored in a single tournament. They managed only one goal in their three games at the 2000 FIFA Futsal World Cup, while conceding 20 in defeats to Iran, Argentina and eventual champions Spain.

SAMBA SUPREMACY

Predictably for a game relying heavily on swift, deft passing and nimble footwork, Brazilians have excelled at Futsal – an indoor, five-a-side, 40-minute version of the 11-a-side game. Since FIFA inaugurated its Futsal World Cup in 1989, Brazil have won the trophy four times out of a possible six – finishing runners-up to Spain in 2000 and third behind Spain and Italy four years later. Brazil have ended every tournament as the top-scoring team, hitting the back of the net a record 78 times during eight games in 2000 – at a staggering rate of 9.3 goals per match. Their largest FIFA Futsal World Cup win was a 29-2 trouncing of Guatemala in 2000 – though their best-ever scoreline, an overall record for Futsal, came when they beat East Timor 76-0 in October 2006. Strangely enough, though, their first-ever FIFA Futsal World Cup match ended in defeat – 3-2 to Hungary in the first-round group stage in 1989.

SHIFT SWAP

After losing a 2004 semi-final to Spain on penalties, 2008 hosts Brazil redeemed themselves by winning the first-ever final to go to extra-time and then spot-kicks. The penalty-saving hero of the shoot-out was Brazil's substitute goalkeeper Franklin. But the man Franklin replaced at the end of extra-time, Tiago, was nevertheless chosen as the tournament's best goalkeeper.

NINE'S ENOUGH

Russia's **Pula** may have pipped Falcao to the top scorer prize in 2008 (with 16 goals to 15), but the Brazilian, who had already won both the Golden Ball and Golden Shoe awards four years earlier, was voted player of the tournament. Pula's 16 goals across the 2008 event included nine in one game – an all-time FIFA Futsal World Cup record – as the Solomon Islands were thrashed 31-2.

FIFA BEACH SOCCER WORLD CUP

Another variant of the game that can trace its roots to South America, beach soccer is a high-octane, all-action, made-for-TV, goal-crazy version of the game that has enjoyed a rapid surge in popularity in recent years. First contested in 1995 at its spiritual home on Copacabana Beach in Rio de Janeiro, Brazil, the FIFA Beach Soccer World Cup is set to become a biannual event after the 2009 tournament.

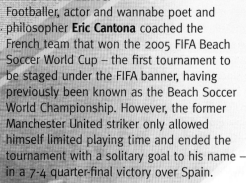

ERIC THE KING

Footballer, actor and wannabe poet and philosopher **Eric Cantona** coached the French team that won the 2005 FIFA Beach Soccer World Cup – the first tournament to be staged under the FIFA banner, having previously been known as the Beach Soccer World Championship. However, the former Manchester United striker only allowed himself limited playing time and ended the tournament with a solitary goal to his name – in a 7-4 quarter-final victory over Spain.

FIFA BEACH SOCCER WORLD CUP FINALS

1995 (Host beach and city/country: Copacabana, Rio de Janeiro/Brazil) **Brazil 8 USA 1**
1996 (Copacabana) **Brazil 3 Uruguay 0**
1997 (Copacabana) **Brazil 5 Uruguay 2**
1998 (Copacabana) **Brazil 9 France 2**
1999 (Copacabana) **Brazil 5 France 2**
2000 (Marina da Gloria, Rio de Janeiro) **Brazil 6 Peru 2**
2001 (Costa do Sauipe, Rio de Janeiro) **Portugal 9 France 3**
2002 (Vitoria/Brazil) **Brazil 6 Portugal 5**
2003 (Copacabana) **Brazil 8 Spain 2**
2004 (Copacabana) **Brazil 6 Spain 4**
2005 (Copacabana) **France 3 Portugal 3 (France win 1-0 on penalties)**
2006 (Copacabana) **Brazil 4 Uruguay 1**
2007 (Copacabana) **Brazil 8 Mexico 2**
2008 (Plage du Pardo, Marseille/France) **Brazil 5 Italy 3**
2009 (Jumeirah, Dubai/United Arab Emirates) **Brazil 10 Switzerland 5**

MADJER FOR IT

In 2006, Angolan-born Portuguese star **Madjer** set a record for goals in one tournament when he put the ball in the net 21 times – one of the five tournaments he has finished as top scorer. His seven goals in one game, against Uruguay in 2009, broke the record he himself set when scoring six against Cameroon in 2006.

GOAL GLUT

The 2003 tournament was the most prolific, with an average of 9.4 goals per game – 150 in total. Two years earlier had brought the lowest average – 7.2 per match, 144 in total.

FRENCH SELECTION

The 2008 tournament, on the beaches of Marseille in the south of France, was the first to take place outside Brazil. In 2009, it was held in Dubai. Future events will take place two years apart, rather than one, with the next tournament scheduled for 2011.

LIFE SAVING

Brazil's Paulo Sergio was voted best goalkeeper for the first four FIFA Beach Soccer World Cups but since then the award has gone to Portugal's Pedro Crespo (1999), Japan's Kato (2000), France's Pascal Olmeta (2001), Thailand's Vilard Normcharoen (2002), Brazil's Robertinho (2003) and Mao (2009), and Spain's Roberto (2004) and Roberto Valeiro (2008). There was no goalkeeper award from 2005 to 2007.

COMPLETELY COMPETING

Brazil and Uruguay are the only two countries to have participated in all 15 tournaments so far, though their fortunes have certainly contrasted: the Brazilians have won the trophy 13 times, while the Uruguayans are still waiting for their first title. They have finished as runners-up three times, in 1996, 1997 and 2006, losing to Brazil in the final each time. Fourteen of the 38 nations to have taken part have come from Europe – though the continent has produced just two champions, Portugal in 2001 and France in 2005. Asia (including Australia) has provided seven competitors, South America six, North and Central America five, Africa also five, and Oceania one.

FIFA INTERACTIVE WORLD CUP

The EA SPORTS FIFA Interactive World Cup, the world's largest football video game tournament, made its debut in 2004 with participants from around the world battling it out on the virtual pitch in FIFA 2005. The inaugural event showcased an eight-player finals tournament in Zurich, Switzerland, and the winner earned a trip to the FIFA World Player Gala in Amsterdam. Since then, the FIWC has expanded its reach into more than 50 countries with 860,000 players competing to qualify for the finals in 2011. The 2011 FIWC grand finals were held in Las Vegas, USA, with 24 contestants battling for the cup on EA Sports™ FIFA 11 on the Sony PlayStation® 3 – and also getting a sneak preview of EA Sports™ FIFA 12 during downtime.

GRAND CHAMPIONS

There have been seven grand champions in FIFA Interactive World Cup history, with the most recent also being the youngest. The first was Brazil's Thiago Carrico de Azevado, winner of the inaugural tournament in 2004. Chris Bullard of England captured the second FIWC title after rolling through the championship field in London. In 2006, Andries Smit, from the Netherlands, captured the championship on his own home soil, besting the field of finalists in Amsterdam. He was succeeded by Spain's Alfonso Ramos in 2008, in Berlin, before France's Bruce Grannec took the 2009 crown and American gamer Nenad Stojkovic emerged triumphant in 2010 – both these latter victories coming in Barcelona. In Los Angeles in June 2011, **Francisco Cruz** not only became the ············· first Portuguese champion, but also the youngest ever – at 16, he was a year younger than Smits had been. Cruz, who had finished third two years earlier, defeated Colombia's Javier Munoz 4-1 in the 2011 final showdown. His prize was $20,000 and two tickets to the 2012 FIFA Ballon d'Or prize gala.

SINGING THE BLUES

Despite being an FC Porto fan, Francisco Cruz played as English club Chelsea at the 2011 FIWC – while the opponent he defeated in the final, Colombia's Javier Munoz, competed as Spanish side Real Madrid.

HOW TO QUALIFY

The 2011 FIWC involved a new qualification process ahead of the grand final, with two places available apiece from six different monthly "seasons" played online by gamers across the world. Defending champion Nenad Stojkovic also qualified automatically and one final, 24th spot was awarded following one last qualification event in Las Vegas on the eve of the tournament.

FIWC FIRST-TIMERS

Thirteen of the 24 FIWC grand finalists were qualifying for the climactic event for the first time – including 15-year-old Egyptian Ramy Dergham, as well as 25-year-old Saudi Arabian Mohammed Almalki, who had only begun playing the game earlier that same year.

MULTI-NATIONAL APPEAL

A total of 14 countries, from every FIFA confederation except Oceania, were represented at the 2011 FIFA Interactive World Cup grand finals: three contenders apiece from Spain and England, two each from Portugal, the USA, Brazil and Colombia, and one from Denmark, France, Germany, Poland, Russia, Australia, Saudi Arabia and Egypt. Twenty-two different nations were represented at the 2010 grand finals.

870K AND COUNTING

Almost 870,000 players took part in the 2011 FIFA Interactive World Cup "online" tournament, a record figure up 95,000 on 2010 and 355,000 on 2009.

PART 7:
WOMEN'S FOOTBALL

UP to 30 million women are playing football around the world and participation has more than doubled over the past ten years. Those simple statistics demonstrate better than perhaps any others how successfully football has managed to break down the old prejudices of bygone eras with greater success than many other sports disciplines. International women's competitions now pull in significant crowds, whose enthusiasm and support has spilled over into national domestic leagues and domestic cup competitions around the world. In fact, women's football is recorded as having been organized in England in the early years of the last century, but it was banned by the Football Association in 1921. That led to the creation of an independent women's association with a cup competition of its own. Women's football developed simultaneously elsewhere and the surge of interest ultimately led, in the early 1980s, to the first formal European Championships and, in 1988, to a FIFA invitational tournament in Chinese Taipei.

FIFA then launched an inaugural world championship in 1991, which was won by the United States to establish their claim to primacy in the game. The Americans duly hosted the next FIFA Women's World Cup, which saw a record crowd of 90,185 celebrate their shoot-out victory over China in the final in Pasadena. They underlined their No. 1 status by winning the first women's football gold medal at the Olympic Games in 1996, taking silver in 2000 and gold again in 2004 and 2008. Meanwhile FIFA set up a world youth championship in 2002, initially for players aged Under-19, later amended to Under-20, and added an Under-17 event to the international calendar in 2008. An initial attempt to create a professional league in the United States to build on the momentum created by the FIFA Women's World Cup and Olympic successes proved unsuccessful, but a second attempt was launched in 2009. Clubs in Women's Professional Soccer signed some of the world's finest players, including Brazil's Marta and England's Kelly Smith. England introduced its own first semi-professional women's league in April 2011 but the main European powerhouse remained Germany, host nation for the FIFA Women's World Cup in June and July that same year.

Striker Svenja Huth (headband) and her German team-mates celebrate with the FIFA Women's U20 World Cup following the host nation's 2-0 defeat of Nigeria in the 2010 final in Bielefeld.

FIFA WOMEN'S WORLD CUP™

The first FIFA Women's World Cup finals were held in China in 1991. Twelve teams, divided into three groups of four, took part, with the top two in each group, plus the two "best losers" going through to the knockout quarter-finals. The tournament was expanded in 1999 to include 16 teams, divided into four groups of four, with the top two in each group progressing to the quarter-finals. That is the current format, although an expansion of the tournament to 24 teams is still under consideration.

FINALS SHOOT–OUT DRAMA

The 1999 clash between the USA and China was the only final in FIFA Women's World Cup history settled by a shoot-out. The losing Chinese had previously been involved in the first shoot-out – in the quarter-finals in 1995, when they beat Sweden 4-3 on penalties after a 0-0 draw. The 1999 third-place game was also settled by a shoot-out, with Brazil pipping Norway 5-4 after a 0-0 draw. These are the only three shoot-outs since the tournament began in 1991.

HAVELANGE'S DREAM COMES TRUE

The FIFA Women's World Cup was the brainchild of former FIFA president **João Havelange**. The tournament began as an experimental competition in 1991 and has expanded in size and importance ever since. The success of the 1999 finals in the United States was a turning point for the tournament, which now attracts big crowds and worldwide TV coverage. The USA and Norway – countries in which football (soccer) is one of the most popular girls' sports – dominated the early competitions. The Americans won the inaugural competition and the 1999 tournament. Norway lifted the trophy in 1995. Germany became the dominant force in the new century, winning the trophy in 2003 and retaining it in 2007. The recent emergence of challengers such as Brazil, China and Sweden underlined the worldwide spread and appeal of the women's game.

US LEAD GAMES TALLY

The USA have played the most games in the finals – 30. They have also recorded the most wins – 24. They have drawn three games and lost three. Germany are the next most successful team. They have played 28, won 20, drawn three and lost five. Norway have also played 28 matches, won 19, drawn two and lost seven.

FIFA WOMEN'S WORLD CUP™ FINALS

Year	Venue	Winners	Runners-up	Score
1991	Ghuangzhou	USA	Norway	2-1
1995	Stockholm	Norway	Germany	2-0
1999	Los Angeles	USA	China	0-0
USA won 5-4 in penalty shoot-out				
2003	Los Angeles	Germany	Sweden	2-1 (aet)
2007	Shanghai	Germany	Brazil	2-0

THIRD–PLACE PLAY–OFF MATCHES

Year	Venue	Winners	Losers	Score
1991	Guangzhou	Sweden	Germany	4-0
1995	Gavle	USA	China	2-0
1999	Los Angeles	Brazil	Norway	0-0
Brazil won 5-4 in penalty shoot-out				
2003	Los Angeles	USA	Canada	3-1
2007	Shanghai	USA	Norway	4-1

US CELEBRATE FIRST ACHIEVEMENT

The USA's victory in the inaugural FIFA Women's World Cup in 1991 made them the first USA team to win a world football title. The USA men's best performance came when they reached the semi-finals in 1930, losing 6-1 to Argentina.

FOUR GAIN DOUBLE MEDALS

Four of the USA's 1991 winners were in the team that beat China on penalties in the 1999 final: **Mia Hamm** (right), Michelle Akers, Kristine Lilly and Julie Foudy.

WINNERS KEEP SQUAD TOGETHER

Six Germany players appeared in their 2003 and 2007 final wins: **Kerstin Stegemann**, Birgit Prinz, Renate Lingor, Ariane Hingst and Kerstin Garefrekes started both games, while Martina Muller came on as a substitute both times.

AUSTRALIA, GHANA LEAD ON REDS

Only two teams have had more than one player sent off in the finals: Australia's Sonia Gegenhuber was red-carded in their 5-0 defeat by Denmark in 1995; and Alicia Ferguson was sent off in 1999, in the second minute of Australia's 3-1 defeat by China. Ghana are the other side to have two players dismissed. Both came at the 1999 finals: Barikisu Tettey-Quao was red-carded in the 1-1 draw against Australia; and Regina Ansah was sent off in the 7-0 defeat by China.

GERMANS SET DEFENSIVE RECORD

In 2007, Germany became the first team to make a successful defence of the FIFA Women's World Cup. They also set another record. They went through the tournament – six games and 540 minutes – without conceding a single goal. As a result, their goalkeeper Nadine Angerer overhauled Italy keeper Walter Zenga's record of 517 minutes unbeaten in the 1990 men's finals. The last player to score against the Germans was Sweden's **Hanna Ljungberg**, who scored in the 41st minute of the 2003 final.

LA FINALE BEATS THEM ALL

The 1999 finals in the USA were the best attended of the five tournaments to date. A total of 3,687,069 spectators watched the matches, at an average of 24,913 per game. The final, between hosts USA and China – at the Rose Bowl, Los Angeles on 10 July – drew 90,185 spectators, a world record for a women's match. The programme that day also included the third-place play-off between Brazil and Norway.

TOP TEAMS

Country	Winners	Runners-up	Third
Germany	2	1	-
US	2	-	3
Norway	1	1	-
Brazil	-	1	1
Sweden	-	1	1
China	-	1	-

TOP TEAM SCORERS

1991:	USA	25
1995:	Norway	23
1999:	China	19
2003:	Germany	25
2007:	Germany	21

TOP ALL-TIME TEAM SCORERS

1	USA	85
2	Germany	84
3	Norway	75
4	China	48
5	Brazil	46

THE FIRST GAME

The first-ever game in the FIFA Women's World Cup finals was hosts China's 4-0 win over Norway at Guangzhou on 16 November 1991. A 65,000 crowd watched the game.

THE REGULAR EIGHT

Eight teams have played in all five finals tournaments – the USA, Germany, Norway, Brazil, China, Japan, Nigeria and Sweden.

NORWAY POST LONGEST WIN RUN

Norway, winners in 1995, hold the record for the most consecutive matchtime wins in the finals – ten. Their run started with an 8-0 win over Nigeria on 6 June 1995 and continued until 30 June 1999 when they beat Sweden 3-1 in the quarter-finals. It ended when they lost 5-0 to China in the semi-finals on 4 July.

UNBEATEN CHINA SENT HOME

In 1999, China became the only team to go through the finals without losing a match, yet go home empty-handed. The Chinese won their group games, 2-1 against Sweden, 7-0 against Ghana and 3-1 against Australia. They beat Russia 2-0 in the quarter-finals and Norway 5-0 in the semi-finals, but they lost on penalties to the USA in the final after a 0-0 draw.

FIFTEEN ON TARGET FOR NORWAY

Norway hold the record for scoring in the most consecutive games – 15. They began their sequence with a 4-0 win over New Zealand on 19 November 1991 and ended it with a 3-1 win over Sweden in the quarter-finals on 30 June 1999.

THE LOWEST CROWD...

The lowest attendance for any match at the finals came on 8 June 1995, when only 250 spectators watched the 3-3 draw between Canada and Nigeria at Helsingborg.

CHAMPIONS RUN UP 11

The biggest victory margin in the finals was **Germany**'s 11-0 win over Argentina in Shanghai on 10 September 2007. Argentina keeper Vanina Correa punched a Melanie Behringer corner into her own net after 12 minutes. Birgit Prinz and Sandra Smisek scored hat-tricks, with Germany's other goals coming from Renate Lingor (2), Behringer and Kerstin Garefrekes.

LILLY KEEPS SETTING RECORDS

Kristine Lilly is the only player to have appeared in five finals tournaments. She has played a record 340 games for the USA and scored 129 goals. She is also the oldest scorer in finals history – she was 36 years, 62 days when she netted the third in the USA's 3-0 quarter-final win over England at Tianjin on 22 September 2007.

QUICKEST RED AND YELLOW

The record for the fastest red card is held by Australia's Alicia Ferguson, who was sent off in the second minute of their 3-1 defeat by China in New York on 26 June 1999. North Korea's Ri Hyang Ok received the quickest yellow card, in the first minute of their 2-1 defeat by Nigeria in Los Angeles on 20 June 1999.

THE FASTEST GOAL

Lena Videkull of Sweden netted the fastest goal in finals history when she scored after 30 seconds in their 8-0 win over Japan at Foshan on 19 November 1991. Canada's **Melissa Tancredi** struck the second-fastest goal – after 37 seconds – in their 2-2 draw with Australia in Chengdu on 20 September 2007.

NORDBY THE LONG–DISTANCE KEEPER

Norway goalkeeper Bente Nordby is the only other player to have gone to five FIFA Women's World Cup tournaments. She was a squad member in 1991, but did not play any games. Four years later, she conceded only one goal in six matches as Norway won the trophy. She retired from the national team in January 2008, after making 172 appearances.

DANILOVA THE YOUNGEST SCORER

The youngest scorer at the finals was Russia's Elena Danilova. She was 16 years 96 days when she scored her country's only goal in the 2003 quarter-final against Germany at Portland on 2 October. The Germans scored seven in reply.

MORACE HITS FIRST HAT–TRICK

Carolina Morace of Italy scored the first hat-trick in finals history when she netted the last three goals in Italy's 5-0 win over Taiwan at Jiangmen on 17 November 1991.

HOT SHOT AKERS SETS THE STANDARD

US forward Michelle Akers (born in Santa Clara on 1 February 1966) hold the record for the most goals scored in a single finals tournament – ten in 1991. She also set a record for the most goals scored in one match, with five in the USA's 7-0 quarter-final win over Taiwan at Foshan on 24 November 1991. Akers grabbed both goals in the USA's 2-1 victory in the final, including their 78th-minute winner. Judges voted her as FIFA's Women's Player of the 20th Century.

THE FASTEST SUBSTITUTIONS

The fastest substitutions in finals history were both timed at six minutes. Taiwan's defender Liu Hsiu Mei was subbed by reserve goalkeeper Li Chyn Hong in their 2-0 win over Nigeria in Jiangmen on 21 November 1991. Li replaced No. 1 keeper Lin Hui Fang, who had been sent off. Therese Lundin subbed for the injured Hanna Ljungberg, also after six minutes, in Sweden's 2-0 win over Ghana at Chicago on 26 June 1999.

NEW STARS DOMINATE THE FINALS

The FIFA Women's World Cup has been dominated by a series of great players. American attackers Michelle Akers and Carin Jennings starred in the opening tournament in 1991. Playmaker **Hege Riise** and top scorer Ann-Kristin led Norway to victory four years later. Another American great, Mia Hamm, was at the top of her form when the USA triumphed for a second time in 1999. That tournament marked the emergence of the best-ever Chinese player, Sun Wen, who finished joint top scorer and won the Player of the Tournament award. Birgit Prinz of Germany was Player of the Tournament and top scorer when Germany won for the first time in 2003. The Brazilian forward, Marta, matched that feat in 2007, though, unlike Prinz, she found herself on the losing side in the final. Hamm, Prinz and Marta are the only winners of FIFA Women's Player of the Year award, introduced in 2001. Hamm took the prize in 2001 and 2002. Prinz won it in 2003, 2004 and 2005. Marta came top of the voting list in 2006, 2007, 2008 and 2009.

MOST FINALS APPEARANCES (BY TOURNAMENTS)

5 Kristine Lilly (US – 1991, 1995, 1999, 2003, 2007)
4 Bente Nordby (Norway – 1995, 1999, 2003, 2007)
  Joy Fawcett (US – 1991, 1995, 1999, 2003)
  Julie Foudy (US – 1991, 1995, 1999, 2003)
  Mia Hamm (US – 1991, 1995, 1999, 2003)
  Hege Riise (Norway – 1991, 1995, 1999, 2003)
  Sun Wen (China – 1991, 1995, 1999, 2003)
  Bettina Wiegmann (Germany – 1991, 1995, 1999, 2003)
  Formiga (Brazil – 1995, 1999, 2003, 2007)
  Katia (Brazil – 1995, 1999, 2003, 2007)
  Tania (Brazil – 1995, 1999, 2003, 2007)
  Sandra Minnert (Germany – 1995, 1999, 2003, 2007)
  Birgit Prinz (Germany – 1995, 1999, 2003, 2007)
  Sandra Smisek (Germany – 1995, 1999, 2003, 2007)
  Maureen Mmadu (Nigeria – 1995, 1999, 2003, 2007)
  Andrea Neil (Canada – 1995, 1999, 2003, 2007)
  Cheryl Salisbury (Australia – 1995, 1999, 2003, 2007)
  Homare Sawa (Japan – 1995, 1999, 2003, 2007)
  Briana Scurry (US – 1995, 1999, 2003, 2007)

SUN RATTLES THE MEN

In 1999, Shanghai-born **Sun Wen** became the first woman player ever to be nominated for the Asian Footballer of the Year award, following her performances in China's run to the 1999 FIFA Women's World Cup final. Three years later, she won the Internet poll for FIFA's Women's Player of the 20th Century.

PRINZ SEIZES FINALS CHANCE

In 2007, Birgit Prinz became the first player to appear in three FIFA Women's World Cup finals. She was also the youngest player to appear in a FIFA Women's World Cup final. The Germany forward was 17 years 336 days when she started in the 2-0 defeat by Norway in 1995. Team-mate Sandra Smisek was just 14 days older. The oldest finalist was Sweden's Kristin Bengtsson, who was 33 years 273 days when her side lost to Germany in the 2003 final.

MARTA'S FINAL AGONY

Brazil's **Marta** may have been the star of the 2007 tournament, but she was heartbroken in the final after Germany goalkeeper Nadine Angerer saved her penalty that would have put Brazil level. Germany won the match 2-0.

FIFA WOMEN'S WORLD CUP™ PLAYER OF THE TOURNAMENT

Year	Venue	Winner
1991	China	Carin Jennings (USA)
1995	Sweden	Hege Riise (Norway)
1999	USA	Sun Wen (China)
2003	USA	Birgit Prinz (Germany)
2007	China	Marta (Brazil)

FIFA WOMEN'S WORLD CUP™ FINALS TOP SCORER

1991	Michelle Akers (USA)	10
1995	Ann-Kristin Aarones (Norway)	6
1999	Sissi (Brazil)	7
2003	Birgit Prinz (Germany)	7
2007	Marta (Brazil)	7

ALL–TIME TOP SCORERS

1	Birgit Prinz (Germany)	14
2	Michelle Akers (USA)	12
3	Sun Wen (China)	11
=	Bettina Wiegmann (Germany)	
5	Ann-Kristin Aarones (Norway)	10
=	Marta (Brazil)	
=	Heidi Mohr (Germany)	
8	Linda Medalen (Norway)	9
=	Hege Riise (Norway)	
=	Abby Wambach (USA)	

FIFA WOMEN'S WORLD CUP™ WINNING CAPTAINS

1991	April Heinrichs (USA)	
1995	Heidi Store (Norway)	
1999	Carla Overbeck (USA)	
2003	Bettina Wiegmann (Germany)	
2007	Birgit Prinz (Germany)	

MOST FINALS APPEARANCES (BY GAMES)

30	Kristine Lilly (USA)
24	Julie Foudy (USA)
23	Mia Hamm (USA)
22	Bente Nordby (Norway)
	Birgit Prinz (Germany)
	Hege Riise (Norway)
	Bettina Wiegmann (Germany)

THE FIRST SENDING OFF

Taiwan goalkeeper Lin Hui Fang was the first player to be sent off in finals history. She was red-carded after six minutes of Taiwan's 2-0 win over Nigeria in Jiangmen on 21 November 1991.

OTHER WOMEN'S TOURNAMENTS

PRINZ ALWAYS ON TARGET

Germany forward **Birgit Prinz** is the only player to have scored in all four Olympic finals tournaments. Prinz is the joint overall leading scorer, along with Brazil's Cristiane. Both have ten goals. Next in the scoring list are two Brazilians, Pretinha (8) and Marta (6).

WOMEN'S OLYMPIC FINALS

Year	Venue	Winners	Runners-up	Score
1996	Atlanta	USA	China	2-1
2000	Sydney	Norway	USA	3-2
	Norway won with a golden goal			
2004	Athens	USA	Brazil	2-1 (aet)
2008	Beijing	USA	Brazil	1-0 (aet)

THIRD-PLACE PLAY-OFFS

Year	Venue	Winners	Losers	Score
1996	Atlanta	Norway	Brazil	2-0
2000	Sydney	Germany	Brazil	2-0
2004	Athens	Germany	Sweden	1-0
2008	Beijing	Germany	Japan	2-0

MEDALLISTS

Country	Gold	Silver	Bronze
US	3	1	-
Norway	1	-	1
Brazil	-	2	-
China	-	1	-
Germany	-	-	3

WOMEN'S OLYMPIC TEAM TOP SCORERS

1996:	Norway	12
2000:	USA	9
2004:	Brazil	15
2008:	USA	12

WOMEN'S OLYMPIC INDIVIDUAL TOP SCORERS

1996:	Ann-Kristin Aarones (Norway)	
	Linda Medalen (Norway)	
	Pretinha (Brazil)	4
2000:	Sun Wen (China)	4
2004:	Cristiane (Brazil)	
	Birgit Prinz (Germany)	5
2008:	Cristiane (Brazil)	5

CRISTIANE'S TREBLE DOUBLE

Brazil striker **Cristiane** is the only player to score two hat-tricks in FIFA Olympic history. She netted three in a 7-0 win over hosts Greece in 2004 and added another treble in a 3-1 win over Nigeria in Beijing four years later. Birgit Prinz is the only other hat-trick scorer, with four goals against China in 2004.

HAPPY HOSTS AND UNCERTAIN GUESTS

Germany became the first hosts to win the FIFA U-20 Women's World Cup when they beat Nigeria 2–0 in the 2010 final, in the city of Bielefeld. The triumph also meant Germany joined the United States in having won the tournament twice. As host country, Germany were guaranteed qualification – but their final opponents Nigeria went into the tournament with doubts over whether they would even take part. The country had been barred from competitive international football in June 2010, after state president Goodluck Jonathan banned the men's senior side from all matches for two years in anger at their failure in the men's FIFA World Cup in South Africa. He quickly relented and the FIFA suspension was lifted on 5 July, nine days before the U-20 women's team's opening match.

GERMANS CHALK UP BIGGEST WIN

Germany hold the record for the biggest win in the Olympic finals. They beat China 8-0 at Patras on 11 August 2004, with Birgit Prinz scoring four times. The Germans' other goals came from Pia Wunderlich, Renate Lingor, Conny Pohlers and Martina Muller.

OLDEST, YOUNGEST PLAYERS

The oldest player in Olympic women's finals history was the Brazil goalkeeper Meg, when she appeared in the third-place play-off against Norway on 1 August 1996, aged 40 years 212 days. The youngest was also a Brazilian, Daniela, who made her finals debut against Sweden on 13 September 2000, aged 16 years 244 days.

GOLDEN TREBLE

South Korea's **Yeo Min-Ji** not only collected a winner's medal, but was also awarded both the Golden Ball for best player and Golden Shoe for top scorer at the 2010 FIFA Under-17 Women's World Cup. Both individual prizes two years earlier went to players who did not even reach the final – Golden Ball winner Mana Iwabuchi played for quarter-finalists Japan, while six-goal top scorer Dzsenifer Marozsan starred for third-placed Germany.

KOREA CHANGE

Two years after North Korea won the inaugural FIFA Under-17 Women's World Cup, neighbours South Korea lifted the trophy the second time around, this time in Trinidad and Tobago. The final on 25 September was the first to go to penalties, with South Korea beating Japan 5–4 in the shoot-out after a thrilling 3–3 draw. South Korea had recovered to reach the final despite a 3–0 first-round defeat to Germany, who scored 22 goals in three games before losing a quarter-final 1–0 to North Korea.

US DOMINATE OLYMPIC GOLDS

The USA have dominated the Olympic football tournament since it was introduced at the 1996 Games in Atlanta. They have won three gold medals and finished runners-up in the other final. Norway and China were the Americans' early challengers, with Brazil and FIFA Women's World Cup holders Germany proving their toughest rivals in the past two Olympics (2004 and 2008). The tournament has rapidly grown in popularity, attracting record crowds at the 2008 Olympic Games in Beijing. FIFA have added two worldwide competitions for younger teams, too. The FIFA U-20 Women's World Cup was staged for the first time in 2000 and the first edition of the Under-17 event followed in 2008. Once more, the USA have been prominent, though they have faced a strong challenge from North Korea in recent years.

FIFA U-20 WOMEN'S WORLD CUP

FINALS

Year	Venue	Winner	Runners-up	Score
2002	Edmonton	USA	Canada	1-0 (aet)
2004	Bangkok	Germany	Chile	2-0
2006	Moscow	North Korea	China	5-0
2008	Santiago	USA	North Korea	2-1
2010	Bielefeld	Germany	Nigeria	2–0

TOP SCORERS

2002	Christine Sinclair (Canada)	10
2004	Brittany Timko (Canada)	7
2006	Ma Xiaoxu (China), Kim Song Hui (North Korea)	5
2008	Sydney Leroux (USA)	5
2010	Alexandra Popp (Germany)	10

FIFA U-17 WOMEN'S WORLD CUP

FINALS

Year	Venue	Winner	Runners-up	Score
2008	Auckland	North Korea	USA	2-1 (aet)
2010	Port of Spain	South Korea	Japan	3–3 (aet)

(South Korea won 5–4 on penalties)

TOP SCORERS

2008	Dzsenifer Marozsan (Germany)	6
2010	Yeo Min-Ji (South Korea)	8

SYDNEY TRANSPLANT

Sydney Leroux competed in her second FIFA Under-20 Women's World Cup for the USA in 2010 – but her third overall. As a 14-year-old, she played two games without scoring for Canada in the 2004 tournament, when it was for Under-19s, before switching nationality. She finished as competition top scorer in 2008 with five goals – including the USA's opener in their 2–1 victory over South Korea in the final. She netted another five two years later, though this was not enough to retain the Golden Shoe.

SINCLAIR HITS FIVE

Christine Sinclair of Canada and Alexandra Popp of Germany share the record for most goals scored in a single FIFA Under-20 Women's World Cup. Each struck 10, Sinclair in 2002 and Popp eight years later. Sinclair also holds the record for the most goals in one game. She netted five in Canada's 6–2 quarter-final win over England at Edmonton on 25 August 2002. But Popp is the only player to score in all of her country's six games at a tournament. Only Sinclair and Popp have won both the Golden Ball for best player and Golden Shoe for top scorer.

KIM GRABS ONLY HAT-TRICK

North Korea's **Kim Song-Hi** netted the only hat-trick in any final of the FIFA Under-20 Women's World Cup. It came in their 5–0 win over China on 3 September 2006.

APPENDIX 1: FIFA AWARDS

ONE OF FOOTBALL'S biggest social events is the FIFA Gala at which the world federation rewards a range of achievements in the international game over the previous 12 months.

The January 2011 event marked a new departure for the event after the announcement in Johannesburg, during the 2010 World Cup, of a merger between the FIFA World Player award and the Ballon d'Or prize organized since 1956 by the Paris magazine *France Football*; originally this had been known as the European Footballer of the Year award. The two voting systems were merged, meaning that to the system used formerly by FIFA (three votes for the national coach and captains of all the world's national associations) were added the votes of one journalist per country (as preferred by *France Football*).

The Gala too was restyled as the FIFA Ballon d'Or Gala. But one aspect had not changed: the first winner of the award in the new era was the same as the previous year: Barcelona and Argentina's Lionel Messi, who received his accolade at the Zurich Kongresshaus. No change either in the identity of the top women's player, Marta of Brazil, for the fifth successive year.

Best coach awards were handed out for the first time – rewarding Jose Mourinho, who won the UEFA Champions League as well as an Italian league and cup double with Internazionale, and Silvia Neid, in charge of the Germany women's team. Turkish international Hamit Altintop won the second Ferenc Puskas award for outstanding goal, for his long-range volley in a UEFA European Championship qualifier against Kazakhstan. His award was presented by the goalkeeper he beat: Andrei Sidelnikov.

Haiti's under-17 women's team received the FIFA Fair Play prize for persevering after the country's January 2010 earthquake and competing in the 2010 CONCACAF championship two months later. Appropriately, after a year which saw the first World Cup in Africa, the Presidential Award from Sepp Blatter went to the Nobel Prize-winner, Archbishop Desmond Tutu.

FIFA BALLON D'OR
WINNER 2010

LIONEL MESSI

Few would dispute that **Lionel Messi** is the finest footballer in the world today – a status even more emphatically confirmed by his second consecutive FIFA Player of the Year prize, for his performances in 2010.

Argentina international Messi became the first player since former Barcelona team-mate Ronaldinho, five years earlier, to receive the prize two years running. Messi was also the first man since Johan Cruyff, in 1974, to be hailed the world's best despite not having finished up on the winning side in a year when a European country won the FIFA World Cup.

Some observers thought Messi had under-performed a little for Argentina in the 2010 tournament in South Africa – and yet, despite his failure to score, he was by far his country's most exciting, and unlucky, performer. But it was his extraordinary – and extraordinarily consistent – displays for Spanish giants Barcelona that secured him the FIFA prize, ahead of shortlisted clubmates Andres Iniesta (who finished second) and Xavi (third).

That golden trio won a second consecutive La Liga title with Barcelona, who finished the league season with an all-time Spanish record tally of 99 points. Messi won the European Golden Boot for top scorer, ending the year with 60 goals in 59 games, and also scored more than any other player in the 2009–10 UEFA Champions League – though holders Barcelona were narrowly knocked out in the semi-finals by Internazionale of Italy.

Perhaps most memorable was the quarter-final night when Messi virtually single-handedly destroyed English club Arsenal, scoring all his side's four spectacular goals. Messi's 2010 Player of the Year triumph was the 11th success for someone from Spain's La Liga, and Barcelona's eighth.

In 2009 the votes had been cast in Messi's favour to an unprecedented degree, meaning he topped the ballot on 1,073 points, with Cristiano Ronaldo a distant second on 352. In 2010, however, the count was much closer: Messi finished first with 22.65 per cent of the vote, followed by Iniesta on 17.47 per cent and Xavi with 16.46 per cent.

At that point Messi's club honours at Barcelona had added up to four league titles, five domestic cup trophies, two UEFA Champions League triumphs plus UEFA European Super Cup and FIFA Club World Cup success for good measure.

He also won Olympic gold for Argentina in 2008, having been winning captain, top scorer and player of the tournament at the FIFA Under-20 World Cup three years earlier. Not bad for someone still aged only 23.

PREVIOUS WINNERS

1991 **Lothar Matthaus (Germany)**
1992 **Marco van Basten (Netherlands)**
1993 **Roberto Baggio (Italy)**
1994 **Romario (Brazil)**
1995 **George Weah (Liberia)**
1996 **Ronaldo (Brazil)**
1997 **Ronaldo (Brazil)**
1998 **Zinedine Zidane (France)**
1999 **Rivaldo (Brazil)**
2000 **Zinedine Zidane (France)**
2001 **Luis Figo (Portugal)**
2002 **Ronaldo (Brazil)**
2003 **Zinedine Zidane (France)**
2004 **Ronaldinho (Brazil)**
2005 **Ronaldinho (Brazil)**
2006 **Fabio Cannavaro (Italy)**
2007 **Kaka (Brazil)**
2008 **Cristiano Ronaldo (Portugal)**
2009 **Lionel Messi (Argentina)**

FIFA WOMEN'S PLAYER OF THE YEAR 2010

MARTA

Brazilian sensation **Marta** made it five in a row when she won
the FIFA Women's Player of the Year award yet again in 2010
– having previously been placed third and second. She now
surely stands as one of the greatest – if not the best – female
footballer of all time.

Born on 19 February 1986, Marta Vieira da Silva has
won a string of team awards and personal prizes.
She won the Golden Ball as best player
and the Golden Boot as seven-goal top
scorer at the 2007 FIFA Women's World
Cup and was a silver medallist with Brazil
at both the 2004 and 2008 Olympic Games, in
Athens and Beijing respectively. Marta has twice
been a winner at the Pan-American Games and
was voted the best player at the 2004 FIFA
Under-19 Women's World Championships in
which she scored six goals.

At the age of 14, Marta's teenaged
footballing talents took her 1,200 miles
south from Dois Riachos, Alagoas,
where she was born and brought up,
to Rio de Janeiro, where she startled
coaches and other players with her
attacking skill for Vasco da Gama and
Sao Martins. In 2004, she transferred
to Swedish club Umea, with whom
she won four league titles and one
domestic cup before moving on to
Los Angeles Sol in the new Women's
Professional Soccer championship in the
United States in early 2009. Later the same
year, she went on loan to Brazil's Santos and
spearheaded them to glory in both the Copa
Libertadores and the Copa do Brasil.

The glory kept on rolling in 2010. Marta
returned to the US to win the league with
FC Gold Pride, taking the top scorer and best
player individual prizes at the same time. She
also scored nine goals in seven games, all won
by Brazil, at the 2010 South American Women's
Championship, in Ecuador in November. This
saw Brazil qualify in some style for the 2011 FIFA
Women's World Cup.

PREVIOUS WINNERS

2001 Mia Hamm (United States)
2002 Mia Hamm (United States)
2003 Birgit Prinz (Germany)
2004 Birgit Prinz (Germany)
2005 Birgit Prinz (Germany)
2006 Marta (Brazil)
2007 Marta (Brazil)
2008 Marta (Brazil)
2009 Marta (Brazil)

OTHER FIFA AWARDS

In conjunction with the FIFA World Player of the Year awards (for both men and women), and tournament-specific prizes for best player, top scorer and top goalkeeper, in recent years the game's governing body has handed out other prizes at its end-of-year gala: the presidential award, the fair play award, a development prize, and recognition to the best rankings mover of the year and the team of the year.

1991
Fair Play award: Real Federacion Espanola de Futbol (Spanish FA), Jorginho (Brazil)

1992
Fair Play award: Union Royale Belge des Societes de Football Association

1993
Fair Play award: Nandor Hidgekuti (Hungary)*, Football Association of Zambia
Top Team of the Year: Germany
Best Mover of the Year: Colombia
award presented posthumously

1994
Top Team of the Year: Brazil
Best Mover of the Year: Croatia

1995
Fair Play award: Jacques Glassmann (France)
Top Team of the Year: Brazil
Best Mover of the Year: Jamaica

1996
Fair Play award: George Weah (Liberia)
Top Team of the Year: Brazil
Best Mover of the Year: South Africa

1997
Fair Play award: Irish spectators at the FIFA World Cup preliminary match versus Belgium, Jozef Zovinec (Slovak amateur player), Julie Foudy (United States)
Top Team of the Year: Brazil
Best Mover of the Year: Yugoslavia

1998
Fair Play award: National associations of Iran, the United States and Northern Ireland
Top Team of the Year: Brazil
Best Mover of the Year: Croatia

1999
Fair Play award: New Zealand football community
Top Team of the Year: Brazil
Best Mover of the Year: Slovenia

2000
Fair Play award: Lucas Radebe (South Africa)
Top Team of the Year: Holland
Best Mover of the Year: Nigeria

2001
Presidential award Marvin Lee (Trinidad)*
Fair Play award: Paolo Di Canio (Italy)
Top Team of the Year: Honduras
Best Mover of the Year: Costa Rica
award presented posthumously

2002
Presidential award: Parminder Nagra (England)
Fair Play award: Football communities of Japan and Korea Republic
Top Team of the Year: Brazil
Best Mover of the Year: Senegal

2003
Presidential award: Iraqi football community
Fair Play award: Fans of Celtic FC (Scotland)
Top Team of the Year: Brazil
Best Mover of the Year: Bahrain

2004
Presidential award: Haiti
Fair Play award: Confederacao Brasileira de Futebol
Top Team of the Year: Brazil
Best Mover of the Year: China PR
Interactive World Player: Thiago Carrico de Azevedo (Brazil)

2005
Presidential award: Anders Frisk (Sweden)
Fair Play award: Football community of Iquitos (Peru)
Top Team of the Year: Brazil
Best Mover of the Year: Ghana
Interactive World Player: Chris Bullard (England)

2006
Presidential award: Giacinto Facchetti (Italy)*
Fair Play award: Fans of the 2006 FIFA World Cup
Top Team of the Year: Brazil
Best Mover of the Year: Italy
Interactive World Player: Andries Smit (Holland)
award presented posthumously

2007
Presidential award: Pele (Brazil)
Fair Play award: FC Barcelona (Spain)
Top Team of the Year: Argentina
Best Mover of the Year: Mozambique

2008
Presidential award: Women's football (presented to the United States women's team)
Fair Play award: Armenia, Turkey
Development award: Palestine
Interactive World Player: Alfonso Ramos (Spain)
Top Team of the Year: Spain
Best Mover of the Year: Spain

2009
Presidential award: Queen Rania Al Abdullah of Jordan [co-chair of 1Goal: Education for All]
Fair Play Award: Sir Bobby Robson (England)*
Development prize: Chinese Football Association
Interactive World Player: Bruce Grannec (France)
Top Team of the Year: Spain
FIFA Ferenc Puskas Award (outstanding goal): Cristiano Ronaldo (Manchester United v Porto)
award presented posthumously

2010
Coach of the year (men): Jose Mourinho (Internazionale, then Real Madrid)
Coach of the year (women): Silvia Neid (Germany women)
FIFA Ferenc Puskas Award (outstanding goal): Hamit Altintop, Turkey v Kazakhstan
Presidential award: Archbishop Desmond Tutu, South Africa
Fair Play Award: Haiti under-17 women's team

FIFA/FIFpro World XI:
Iker Casillas (Spain)
Maicon (Brazil)
Lucio (Brazil)
Gerard Pique (Spain)
Carles Puyol (Spain)
Wesley Sneijder (Netherlands)
Xavi (Spain)
Andres Iniesta (Spain)
Lionel Messi (Argentina)
David Villa (Spain)
Cristiano Ronaldo (Portugal)

Note: The FIFA Fair Play award was instituted in 1987 and, before its inauguration into the annual gala, was made as follows:
1987: Fans of Dundee United (Scotland)
1988: Frank Ordenewitz (Germany) and spectators at the Olympic football tournament in Seoul
1989: Spectators of Trinidad & Tobago
1990: Gary Lineker (England)

APPENDIX 2: FIFA/COCA-COLA WORLD RANKINGS 2011

Germany were No.1 when FIFA's world rankings system was first calculated and published in December 1992. The system, simplified after FIFA World Cup 2006™, provides a monthly statistical insight into the rise and fall in fortunes of traditional football giants and aspiring minnows alike and are based on results from all A international matches, but weighted to take account multiple factors, – final score, confederations and strength of the opposition. The rankings come out every month.

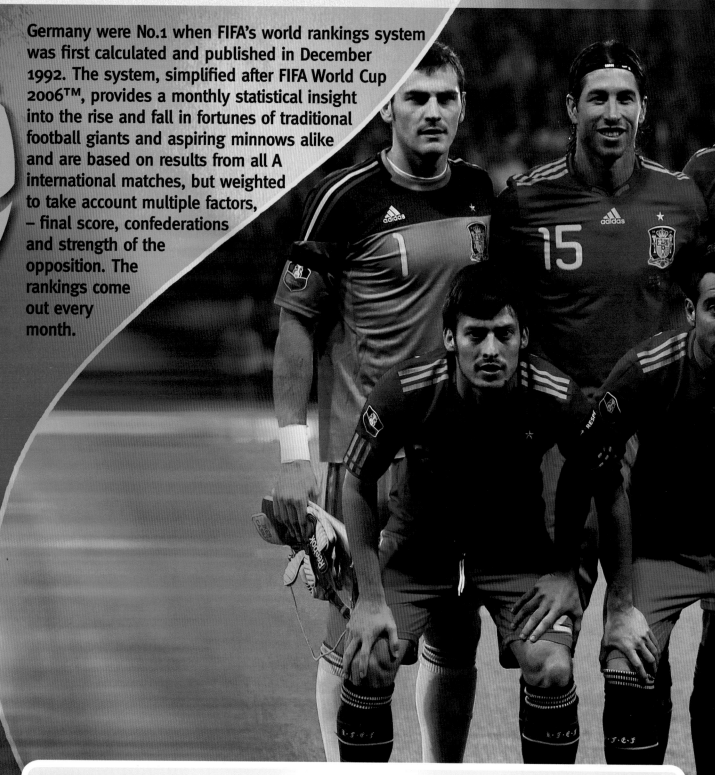

Spain took over as the world's top team after the country won the 2010 FIFA World Cup. Europe's champions became the first country to lose their opening game of a FIFA World Cup finals and still win the tournament.

FIFA/COCA-COLA WORLD RANKINGS 2011

Spain have gone top of the FIFA/Coca-Cola World Rankings on three separate occasions – the latest when they beat the Netherlands 1-0 in the final of the 2010 FIFA World Cup, and they have retained their place since then despite some eyebrow-raising friendly defeats to Argentina and Portugal. Their first rise to the peak came after they won the 2008 UEFA European Championship, only to be toppled a year later when Brazil lifted the FIFA Confederations Cup in South Africa. The rankings take into account a decline in the value of past results, over the course of the previous four years being judged. Some strange quirks can still be seen sometimes – Israel reached a national best 15th place in November 2008, despite never having qualified for a FIFA World Cup or a UEFA European Championship.

RANKINGS (May 2011)

Pos.	Country	Points
1	Spain	1857
2	Netherlands	1702
3	Brazil	1425
4	Germany	1413
5	Argentina	1276
6	England	1163
7	Uruguay	1094
8	Portugal	1052
9	Italy	1019
10	Croatia	991
11	Norway	987
12	Greece	985
13	Chile	967
14	Japan	961
15	Ghana	918
16	Serbia	907
17	Slovenia	903
18	Russia	896
19	France	883
20	Australia	876
21	Cote d'Ivoire	867
22	USA	855
23	Paraguay	847
24	Montenegro	820
25	Switzerland	819
26	Slovakia	809
27	Denmark	808
28	Mexico	802
=	Sweden	802
30	Turkey	795
31	Korea Republic	754
32	Czech Republic	722
33	Israel	709
34	Republic of Ireland	681
35	Ukraine	678

Pos.	Country	Points
36	Egypt	676
37	Belgium	654
38	South Africa	653
39	Nigeria	637
40	Senegal	613
41	Algeria	609
42	Romania	607
43	Honduras	503
44	Burkina Faso	600
45	Bosnia-Herzegovina	594
46	Bulgaria	592
47	Lithuania	577
48	Iran	575
49	Cameroon	572
50	Colombia	564
=	Albania	564
52	Hungary	559
53	Belarus	557
54	Peru	548
55	Jamaica	546
56	Costa Rica	541
57	Georgia	536
58	Libya	534
59	Gabon	529
60	New Zealand	528
61	Tunisia	527
62	Armenia	524
=	Guinea	524
64	Ecuador	523
65	Northern Ireland	520
66	Scotland	517
67	Panama	493
68	Venezuela	489
69	Botswana	479
70	Mali	451

Pos.	Country	Points
71	Poland	449
72	Malawi	446
73	Morocco	445
74	Austria	443
75	Estonia	440
76	Canada	439
77	China	438
=	Latvia	438
79	Cape Verde Islands	421
80	Benin	418
81	Cuba	416
=	Finland	416
83	Uzbekistan	403
84	Uganda	402
85	Macedonia	398
86	Moldova	394
87	El Salvador	391
88	Saudi Arabia	386
89	Cyprus	383
=	Iraq	383
=	Zambia	383
92	Qatar	380
93	Jordan	378
94	Mozambique	358
95	Trinidad and Tobago	353
96	Haiti	348
97	Bahrain	338
98	Grenada	337
99	Niger	335
100	Antigua and Barbuda	322
101	Kuwait	320
102	Bolivia	312
103	Gambia	308
104	Angola	295
=	Sudan	295
=	Syria	295

LEFT: Italy goalkeeper **Gianluigi Buffon** was a mainstay of the national side, not only winning the FIFA World Cup in 2006 but also topping the world rankings for much of the following year – even if they did subsequently once slip as low as 11th.

RIGHT: Wins over Austria and Azerbaijan for **Marouane Fellaini** and Belgium saw the country rise 25 places to 37th between March and April 2011. By a strange coincidence, over the 19 years of the FIFA World Rankings, Belgium's average place is 37th.

Pos.	Country	Points
107	Oman	294
108	Azerbaijan	288
109	Togo	285
110	Guyana	284
111	United Arab Emirates	273
112	Suriname	267
113	Central African Republic	263
114	Wales	258
115	North Korea	255
116	Iceland	254
117	Tanzania	252
118	Sierra Leone	246
119	St Kitts and Nevis	245
120	Thailand	242
121	Congo	232
122	Rwanda	228
123	Kenya	227
124	Guatemala	222
125	Luxembourg	221
126	Congo DR	219
=	Zimbabwe	219
128	Ethiopia	218
129	Yemen	203
130	Indonesia	200
131	Dominica	193
132	Barbados	180
=	Puerto Rico	180
134	Vietnam	172
135	Tajikstan	171
136	Faroe Islands	168
=	Guinea-Bissau	168
138	Madagascar	164
139	Kazakhstan	151
140	Namibia	150
141	Turkmenistan	149

Pos.	Country	Points
142	Equatorial Guinea	146
143	Malaysia	144
144	Singapore	140
145	India	139
146	Hong Kong	138
147	Nepal	135
148	Maldives	133
149	Chad	127
=	Burundi	127
151	New Caledona	123
152	Curacao	121
153	Liechtenstein	116
=	St Vincent and the Grenadines	116
155	Fiji	103
156	Philippines	96
157	Liberia	93
158	Cayman Islands	90
159	Swaziland	89
160	Chinese Taipei	86
161	Malta	84
162	Bermuda	80
163	Bangladesh	79
164	Afghanistan	77
165	Vanuatu	76
166	Nicaragua	75
167	Myanmar	74
168	Pakistan	72
169	Sri Lanka	70
=	Kyrgyzstan	70
171	Palestine	67
172	Belize	66
=	Dominican Republic	66
174	Laos	57
=	Tahiti	57

Pos.	Country	Points
176	Cambodia	56
=	Lesotho	56
178	Lebanon	51
179	Mongolia	48
180	Mauritania	45
181	Eritrea	42
182	Solomon Islands	40
183	British Virgin Islands	38
184	Macau	32
185	St Lucia	31
186	Samoa	26
187	Somalia	23
188	Comoros	19
189	Mauritius	18
190	Cook Islands	17
=	Tonga	17
192	Djibouti	15
193	Turks and Caicos Islands	13
194	Seychelles	11
195	Guam	10
196	Bahamas	9
=	Bhutan	9
=	Brunei Darussalam	9
199	Aruba	7
200	Timor-Leste	3
=	US Virgin Islands	3
202	American Samoa	0
=	Andorra	0
=	Anguilla	0
=	Montserrat	0
=	Papua New Guinea	0
=	San Marino	0

PICTURE CREDITS

The publishers would like to thank the following sources for their kind permission to reproduce the pictures in this book. The page numbers for each of the photographs are listed below, giving the page on which they appear in the book and any location indicator (C-centre, T-top, B-bottom, L-left, R-right).

Action Images: /Matthew Childs: 230BL; /Paul Childs: 233; /Lee Smith: 185R

Getty Images: 48BL, 157T, 197BR; /2010 FIFA World Cup Organising Committee: 183L; /2010 Qatar 2022: 182R; /AFP: 53C, 83C, 93BR, 115TL, 115BL, 159BR, 167L, 178BR, 194BR, 199R, 206BL, 208L; /Odd Andersen/AFP: 33R; /Mladen Antonov/AFP: 96BR, 200TR; /Rodrigo Arangua/AFP: 110R; /Brian Bahr: 146TR; /Dennis Barnard/Fox Photos: 105TL; /Lars Baron: 36L, 59R, 105B, 169B; /Juan Barreto/AFP: 112C; /Robyn Beck/AFP: 66BR, 177TR; /Sandra Behne/Bongarts: 132BL; /Fethi Belaid/AFP: 119BR, 121C, 121BL; /Bentley Archive/Popperfoto: 76C, 77BL, 165BR; /Jefferson Bernardes/AP: 116-117; /Gunnar Berning/Bongarts: 173BL; /Monirul Bhuiyan/AFP: 150-151, 185B; /Bongarts: 36BL, 163BL, 247R; /Shaun Botterill: 10-11, 65BL, 72C, 76TR, 81T, 115TR, 124TR, 132L, 158L, 173TR, 185TR, 196BR, 215TL, 247TR; /Shaun Botterill/FIFA: 13BR, 56R, 166L, 176BR; /Cris Bouroncle/AFP: 220T; /Gabriel Bouys/AFP: 42B, 172C; /Clive Brunskill: 109R; /Simon Bruty: 78B; /Martin Bureau/AFP: 23TR; /Eric Cabanis/AFP: 154R; /Jose Cabezas/AFP: 152TR; /David Cannon: 18BL, 31TL, 72BR, 104BL, 141TR; /Nico Casamassima/AFP: 178BL; /Ron Case/Keystone: 125B; /Mario Castillo/Jam Media/LatinContent: 144BR; /Massimo Cebrelli: 82TR; /Central Press: 75BL; /Central Press/Hulton Archive: 60BR; /Andre Chaco/FotoArena/LatinContent: 181BL; /Graham Chadwick: 92BR; /Robert Cianflone: 28TL, 79T, 81L, 129TR; /Thomas Coex/AFP: 57BL, 161R; /Fabrice Coffrini/AFP: 152BR, 188-189; /Chris Cole: 174TR; /Phil Cole: 55BR, 63TL, 84C, 118B, 131R; /Yuri Cortez/AFP: 148BR; /Stephane de Sakutin/AFP: 136BL, 185L; /Carl de Souza/AFP: 13TR, 41T, 169TR; /Adrian Dennis/AFP: 196TR; /Sebastian Derungs/AFP: 8-9; /Philippe Desmazes/AFP: 184TR; /Khaled Desouki/AFP: 118TR, 215BL, 217TL; /Kevork Djansezian: 142-143, 147TL, 147C; /Nikolay Doychinov/AFP: 50C; /Denis Doyle: 43BR, 45BL, 46L; /Stephen Dunn: 122BR; /Paul Ellis/AFP: 27C; /Darren England: 154BL, 154BR; /Francisco Estrada/LatinContent: 134BR; /Evening Standard: 130; /Franck Fife/AFP: 18BR, 19TR, 21BR, 105TR, 121TR, 212C, 215R, 217C, 247BR; /Julian Finney: 60C, 97TR; /Stu Forster: 39R, 54C, 64BL, 71BL, 90BL, 91L, 103TL, 246BL; /FotoArena/LatinContent: 245C; /Stuart Franklin: 59T, 193B; /Stuart Franklin/Bongarts: 72TR; /Stuart Franklin/FIFA: 242-243; /Romeo Gacad/AFP: 56L; /Gallo Images: 190BL; /Lluis Gene/AFP: 244L; /Paul Gilham: 124C, 167B, 176TR; /Paul Gilham/FIFA: 29TR, 47TL; /Georges Gobet/AFP: 57BR, 86L; /Laurence Griffiths: 52BL, 54BL, 16oT; /Alex Grimm/Bongarts: 5L; /Gianluigi Guercia/AFP: 4R, 31R, 120R, 186BL, 210-211, 214BC; /Jorge Guerrero/AFP: 7; /Jack Guez/AFP: 79R, 94R, 192TR; /Pascal Guyot/AFP: 133TR; /Valery Hache/AFP: 39BR, 118C, 137R, 173C, 198BL; /Ronny Hartmann/AFP: 52TR, 86TR, 192B; /Alexander Hassenstein/Bongarts: 22TR; /Haynes Archive/Popperfoto: 156TR, 157B, 205BL; /Richard Heathcote: 38BR, 103B; /Richard Heathcote/FIFA: 149BL; /Patrick Hertzog/AFP: 19BR, 41BR, 88TR, 156BL; /Mike Hewitt: 4B, 63BR, 229L; /Mike Hewitt/FIFA: 25TR; /Antonia Hille: 96C; /Stan Honda/AFP: 129C; /Boris Horvat/AFP: 38BL, 197T; /Hulton Archive: 14TC, 14BL, 61TR, 156BR, 164BL; /Karim Jaafar/AFP: 100TR, 125L, 134L, 175BL; /Liu Jin/AFP: 164TL; /Hannah Johnston: 152L; /Jasper Juinen: 14TL, 14C, 42R, 44C, 45TL, 85C, 226L, 227TR; /Yuri Kadobnov/AFP: 74TR; /Atta Kenare/AFP: 138TL; /Keystone: 18TR, 60BL, 75BR; /Keystone/Hulton Archive: 31BL; /Saeed Khan/AFP: 152BL; /Ian Kington/AFP: 16TR, 55TR; /Ross Kinnaird: 70BR, 168TR; /Toshifumi Kitamura/AFP: 155C; /Joe Klamar/AFP: 32BR, 55L, 65TR, 217BR; /Christof Koepsel/Bongarts: 23BR, 109TL, 225C; /Christof Koepsel/FIFA: 226BL; /Mark Kolbe: 129TL, 131BL; /Jean-Philippe Ksiazek/AFP: 112BR; /Jimin Lai/AFP: 132TR; /David Leah: 171TL; /David Leah/Mexsport: 144TR; /Streeter Lecka: 108C; /Christopher Lee: 91TR; /Bryn Lennon: 63TR, 70TR, 90BR; /Matthew Lewis: 66TR; /Alex Livesey: 20R, 57T, 75C, 83TR, 90C, 123C, 165R, 178TL, 179L, 191BR, 201TR, 224L, 247BL; /Alex Livesey/FIFA: 44BL, 111TR, 174BL; /Juan Mabromata/AFP: 178TR; /John MacDougall/AFP: 73BR; /Gabriele Maltinti: 30C; /Pierre-Philippe Marcou/AFP: 44TL, 87BR, 122TL, 153TC, 166TR; /Francois-Xavier Marit/AFP: 177TL; /Clive Mason: 26L, 46BR, 66L, 87BL, 113BR, 123TL, 161BL, 170TL, 179TR; /Jamie McDonald: 38T, 54BR, 70C, 123BR, 145C; /Chris McGrath: 101TR, 176TL; /Buda Mendes/LatinContent: 182L; /Luiz Fernando Menezes/FotoArena/LatinContent: 245BR; /Philippe Merle/AFP: 115R; /Aris Messinis/AFP: 58BL; /Douglas Miller/Keystone: 12BL; /Jeff Mitchell/FIFA: 103C; /Filippo Monteferto/AFP: 92C, 181C; /John Mottern/AFP: 144BL; /Dean Mouhtaropoulos: 190TR; /Beate Mueller/Bongarts: 50BL; /Peter Muhly/AFP: 94BL, 193L; /Marwan Naamani/AFP: 218-219; /Hoang Dinh Nam/AFP: 146C; /Kazuhiro Nogi/AFP: 48TR; /Mark Nolan: 129BR; /Mustafa Ozer/AFP: 251; /Doug Pensinger: 68TR, 102TL, 180BL; /Ryan Pierse: 92L, 140TR, 170B; /Ryan Pierse/FIFA: 14BL, 201BL; /Vincenzo Pinto/AFP: 172BL; /Jan Pitman/Bongarts: 180TR; /Hrvoje Polan/AFP: 52C, 67L, 67TR; /Joern Pollex: 26TR, 28R; /Joern Pollex/Bongarts: 29TL; /Joern Pollex/FIFA: 222C, 223R; /Popperfoto: 21TL, 26BR, 28BL, 29B, 51BR, 53BR, 62BL, 107BR, 109BL, 133L, 136R, 137T, 138BR, 139BR, 147BL, 155BR, 163BR, 165L, 194BL, 195C, 198TR, 200B, 207BL, 208BR, 228BL; /Savo Prelevic/AFP: 97B; /Craig Prentis: 145TR; /Gary M Prior: 170C; /Ben Radford: 45R, 131T, 171BR, 246R; /Roslan Rahman/AFP: 139TR; /Aizar Raldes/AFP: 113L, 114TL; /Michael Regan: 12TR, 17TR, 88B; /Michael Regan/FIFA: 232BL; /Miguel Riopa/AFP: 43TR, 69BR; /Rolls Press/Popperfoto: 15B, 33B, 106TR; /Quinn Rooney/FIFA: 13C; /Clive Rose: 77C, 79BL, 89BL, 248-249; /Martin Rose: 234-235, 240BR; /Martin Rose/Bonagrts: 74C, 87TR, 126-127; /Karim Sahib/AFP: 135TR; /Jewel Samad/AFP: 37TR, 40TL, 59BL, 69TR, 172BL; /Mark Sandten/Bongarts: 120BL, 179BR; /Issouf Sanogo/AFP: 213BR, 216; /Genia Savilov/AFP: 89BR; /Roberto Schmidt/AFP: 111BL, 160BL, 174C, 181TR, 187L; /Antonio Scorza/AFP: 20BL; /Lefty Shivambu/Gallo Images: 124L, 212TR, 213TR, 214BL, 215C; /Raul Sifuentes/STR/LatinContent: 104TR; /Torsten Silz/AFP: 167TR; /Christophe Simon/AFP: 100BR, 107L, 163TR; /Javier Soriano/AFP: 159L, 183B, 244B; /Cameron Spencer: 164TR; /Jamie Squire: 2, 119TL, 168BL; /Michael Steele: 51T, 80TR, 82BL, 159TR, 186TR; /Patrik Stollarz/AFP: 24TR, 95BL, 187BR; /Boris Streubel: 191BL; /Henri Szwarc/Bongarts: 32TL, 112L, 195B; /Bob Thomas: 15TL, 25L, 32BL, 34B, 37L, 40B, 47BR, 49L, 62TR, 63BL, 67BR, 70BL, 76L, 81BR, 90TR, 91B, 95R, 102BR, 106BL, 108BL, 111BR, 114B, 119TR, 133BR, 153TR, 164BR, 180C, 184B, 186BR, 193TR, 194T, 195TL, 196L, 199BL, 205BC; /Mark Thompson: 64TR, 95C, 212BR; /John Thys/AFP: 48C; /Omar Torres/AFP: 134TR, 145BR, 162TR; /Pedro Ugarte/AFP: 158R; /Robert van den Brugge/AFP: 49BR; /Jean-Christophe Verhaegen/AFP: 93TR; /Claudio Villa: 33TL, 35T, 250; /Claudio Villa/Grazia Neri: 34TR; /Ian Walton: 61BR; /Koji Watanabe: 98-99, 101BL, 228TR; /Jung Yeon-Je/AFP: 166BR

Press Association Images: 16BL, 24B, 60TR, 78TR, 102R, 229TR; /ABACA Press: 161TL; /AP: 5C, 35BL, 135B, 157TR, 162BL; /Matthew Ashton: 71C, 107C, 128BL, 140BL, 149TR, 225BL, 238BR; /Greg Baker/AP: 237BL; /Jon Buckle: 239BL; /Adam Butler: 16L; /Felice Calabro/AP: 176BL; /Roberto Candia/AP: 237TL; /Niall Carson: 5B; /Barry Coombs: 49TR, 58TR, 229BR; /Malcolm Croft: 155TL; /Claudio Cruz/AP: 224C; /DPA: 22L, 27TL, 37B, 128TR, 158BL; /Adam Davy: 236BR; /Sean Dempsey: 25BR; /Paulo Duarte/AP: 68L, 68C, 220BL; /Mike Egerton: 148TR; /Paul Ellis/AP: 74BL; /Fred Ernst/AP: 221BR; /Denis Farrell/AP: 239BC; /Gouhier-Hahn-Orban/ABACA: 84TR; /Michel Gouverneur/Reporter: 222BL; /Zhang Guojun/Landov: 236BC; /Tim Hales/AP: 82C; /Anthony Harris/AP: 241TL; /Jae C Hong/AP: 141B; /Nam Y Huh/AP: 207R; /Intime Sports/AP: 58C; /Silvia Izquierdo/AP: 209BR, 232L, 232R; /Julie Jacobson/AP: 238TL, 241BR; /Lee Jin-Man/AP: 238TR; /Alik Keplicz/AP: 191TR; /Ross Kinnaird: 207C; /Junji Kurokawa/AP: 226TR; /Tony Marshall: 4T, 5BL, 34L, 39TL, 86B, 106TL, 128C, 146BR, 154TL, 163TL, 204T, 205TR, 221BL, 224TR, 225TR, 230TR; /John McConnico/AP: 84BL; /Cathal McNaughton: 12C; /Martin Meissner/AP: 27BR; /Ricardo Moraes/AP: 231TR; /Francois Mori/AP: 22R; /Jussi Nukari/Lehtikuva: 223BL; /Phil O'Brien: 30BL; /Panoramic: 222R; /Eraldo Peres/AP: 231BL, 231BR; /Natacha Pisarenko/AP: 202-203, 208C; /Nick Potts: 19BR; /Duncan Raban: 104BR; /Peter Robinson: 35BR, 36TR, 62C, 76BR, 78L, 80BL, 89TR, 100L, 110BL, 120TL, 175TR, 220BR; /S&G and Barratts: 15TR, 17B, 68BR, 71BR, 172TR; /SMG: 77TR; /Murad Sezer/AP: 23C; /Sven Simon: 106BR; /Neal Simpson: 51BL, 73TR, 75TR, 85BR, 125TR, 206BR; /Michael Sohn/AP: 149BR, 240TR; /Jon Super/AP: 227BR, 237TR; /Topham Picturepoint: 69BL, 83BL, 94TL; /Fernando Vergara/AP: 204BR, 205BR; /John Walton: 5T, 103TR, 209L; /Aubrey Washington: 65C; /Witters: 177B; /Ren Yong/Landov: 240TC; /Vincent Yu/AP: 241BC

Every effort has been made to acknowledge correctly and contact the source and/or copyright holder of each picture and Carlton Books Limited apologises for any unintentional errors or omissions that will be corrected in future editions of this book.

ABOUT THE AUTHOR

Keir Radnedge has been covering football for more than 40 years. He has written countless books on the subject, from tournament guides to comprehensive encyclopedias, aimed at all ages. His journalism career included the *Daily Mail* for 20 years, as well as the *Guardian* and other national newspapers and magazines in the UK and abroad. He is a former editor of *World Soccer*, generally recognized as the premier English-language magazine on global football. In addition to his writing, Keir has been a regular analyst for BBC radio and television, Sky Sports and the American cable news channel CNN. He also edited a tournament newspaper at the FIFA World Cup tournaments of 1982, 1986 and 1990. He has also scripted video reviews of numerous international football tournaments. He is also the London-based editor of SportsFeatures.com, the football and Olympic news website.